PENGUIN BOOKS

MODERN TIMES

The founder of French existentialism, Jean-Paul Sartre (1905–1980) has had a great influence on many areas of modern thought. A writer of prodigious brilliance and originality, Sartre worked in many different genres. As a philosopher, a novelist, a dramatist, a biographer, a cultural critic and a political journalist, Sartre explored the meaning of human freedom in a century overshadowed by total war.

Born in Paris, Sartre studied philosophy and psychology at the Ecole Normale Superieure, where he established a life-long intellectual partnership with Simone de Beauvoir. He subsequently taught philosophy in Le Havre and in Paris. His early masterpiece, *La Nausee* (1938), explored the themes of solitude and absurdity. A remarkable collection of short stories, *Le Mur* (1939), further established his literary reputation. Conscripted into the French Army in 1939, Sartre was captured in June 1940 and imprisoned in Stalag XIID in Trier. He soon escaped to Paris where he played an active role in the Resistance. This experience of defeat and imprisonment, escape and revolt served to push Sartre beyond the flamboyant anarchist individualism of his early writings. *L'Etre et le neant* (1943) is an elaborate meditation on the possibility of freedom. *Les Chemins de la liberte* (1945–9) is a trilogy of novels about the collective experience of war. In 1944 Sartre abandoned his career as a philosophy teacher. He was soon installed at the centre of Parisian intellectual life: editing *Les Temps modernes*, a literary–political review, travelling the world, quarrelling with Albert Camus, his erstwhile friend, and vigorously defending the idea of the Soviet Union against its cold-war enemies. From 1944 until 1970, when his eyesight began to fail, Sartre enjoyed an immense international reputation as the most gifted, the most versatile and the most outspoken literary intellectual of the age. In a gesture that perfectly symbolized his audacity, he refused the Nobel Prize for Literature in 1964. Fired by a passion for freedom and justice, loved and hated in his own day, Sartre stands as the authentic modern successor to Voltaire, Victor Hugo and Emile Zola.

Robin Buss is a writer and translator who works for the *Independent on Sunday* and as television critic for *The Times Educational Supplement*. He studied at the University of Paris, where he took a degree and a doctorate in French literature. He is part-author of the article 'French Literature' in *Encyclopaedia Britannica* and has published critical studies of works by Vigny and Cocteau, and three books on European cinema, *The French Through Their Films* (1988), *Italian Films* (1989) and *French Film Noir* (1994). He has also translated a number of volumes for Penguin Classics.

Geoffrey Wall was born in Cheshire in 1950 and educated at the universities of Sussex, Paris and Oxford. He now teaches at the University of York and works, by night, as a translator, a literary biographer, a travel writer and a journalist.

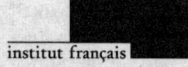

institut français

This book is supported by the French Ministry for Foreign Affairs, as part of the Burgess Programme headed for the French Embassy in London by the Institut Français du Royaume-Uni.

JEAN-PAUL SARTRE

Modern Times
Selected Non-Fiction

translated by Robin Buss
edited by Geoffrey Wall

PENGUIN BOOKS

PENGUIN BOOKS

Published by the Penguin Group
Penguin Books Ltd, 27 Wrights Lane, London w8 5TZ, England
Penguin Putnam Inc., 375 Hudson Street, New York, New York 10014, USA
Penguin Books Australia Ltd, Ringwood, Victoria, Australia
Penguin Books Canada Ltd, 10 Alcorn Avenue, Toronto, Ontario, Canada M4V 3B2
Penguin Books (NZ) Ltd, Private Bag 102902, NSMC, Auckland, New Zealand

Penguin Books Ltd, Registered Offices: Harmondsworth, Middlesex, England

This collection first published in Penguin Classics 2000
2

Original text copyright © Éditions Gallimard as follows:
'New York: Colonial City', 1946; 'Naples: Food and Sex', 1938; 'Rome: A Ghoulish Hobby', 1952; 'Venice from My Window', 1953; 'Havana', 1960; 'Photos of China', 1955; 'What is Desire', 1943; 'Maternal Love', 1971; 'Masturbation', 1947; 'Homosexuality', 1947; 'The Liberation of Paris', 1945; 'Is This a Democracy?', 1952; 'The Genesis of Stalinism', 1957; 'Czechoslovakia 1968', 1970; 'After Colonialism', 1961; 'On Surrealism', 1947; 'Theatre and Cinema', 1973; 'Brecht and the Classics', 1957; 'Seriality', 1960; 'The Man with the Tape-recorder', 1969; 'Baudelaire', 1946; 'Gide', 1951; 'Reply to Albert Camus', 1952; 'Albert Camus', 1960; 'Genet', 1952; 'Tintoretto', 1957.
'Portrait of Sartre', 'Havana' translation and editorial matter
copyright © Geoffrey Wall, 2000
All other translations copyright © Robin Buss, 2000

All rights reserved

The moral right of the translators and editor has been asserted

Set in 10/12.5pt PostScript Monotype Sabon
Typeset by Rowland Phototypesetting Ltd,
Bury St Edmunds, Suffolk
Printed in England by Clays Ltd, St Ives plc

Except in the United States of America, this book is sold subject
to the condition that it shall not, by way of trade or otherwise, be lent,
re-sold, hired out, or otherwise circulated without the publisher's
prior consent in any form of binding or cover other than that in
which it is published and without a similar condition including this
condition being imposed on the subsequent purchaser

Contents

Portrait of Sartre	vii
Suggestions for Further Reading	xlii
Acknowledgements	xliv
Chronology	xlv

Cities — 1
New York: Colonial City — 3
Naples: Food and Sex — 10
Rome: A Ghoulish Hobby — 14
Venice from My Window — 21
Havana — 33
Photos of China — 42

Sexualities — 55
What Is Desire? — 57
Maternal Love — 90
Masturbation — 115
Homosexuality — 125

Revolutions — 139
The Liberation of Paris — 141
Is This a Democracy? — 146
The Genesis of Stalinism — 152
Czechoslovakia 1968 — 166
After Colonialism — 172

Modern Times — 185
- On Surrealism — 187
- Theatre and Cinema — 199
- Brecht and the Classics — 204
- Seriality: The Bus Queue and the Radio Broadcast — 208
- The Man with the Tape-recorder: A Psychoanalytic Dialogue — 233

Portraits — 261
- Baudelaire — 263
- Gide — 285
- Reply to Albert Camus — 289
- Albert Camus — 301
- Genet — 304
- Tintoretto: The Prisoner of Venice — 323

Portrait of Sartre

BY GEOFFREY WALL

I

Sartre is our last humanist. His great argument is liberty. His writings tell us what it was like to be born in the first decade of the twentieth century, to wear the crisp sailor-suit of boyhood and then the shabby conscript's uniform of 1939, to escape in disguise from Stalag XIID, to know the fiery delight of Liberation and the everlasting grey anguish of Cold War, and through it all to hold to an idea of liberty, damaged but undiminished.

In my favourite black and white photograph of him, there is just a man writing. A robust, bespectacled and devilishly ugly man in a fifties suit. Just Sartre. He's sitting alone at a café table, gripping a large black fountain pen, perfectly engrossed in his thoughts. He pauses now and again to sample the rich chaotic hum of café conversation or to peer out, with all the sudden intensity of the short-sighted, at the miscellaneous street-life of a city that might be Paris, Rome or Berlin. Wrapped in a soft blue-grey cloud of pipe-smoke, he conjures up that magical, dishevelled abundance of novels, plays, prefaces, letters, essays, editorials, biographies, pamphlets and philosophies to which we refer, so casually, as Sartre. This anthology is a disentangling of that abundance. Its immodest ambition is to reinvent Sartre for a new generation of readers, to pass on to them his sense of the century that he anatomized with such imperious and compassionate lucidity.

2

Sartre always scorned the pathos of origins. His fictional characters, so vividly present, are surprisingly ill-equipped with memories. Sartre believed that most of our attachments to the past are a form of bad faith, just a stubborn and timid refusal to become what we are. Accordingly, in his favourite version of his own life, Sartre was a self-generating man of genius. He was just Sartre, a man from nowhere, equally at home everywhere, possessing nothing more than one might carry to the nearest railway station in a battered suitcase. Distinctively, Sartre acknowledged no begetter, no precursor. He spurned all encumbering treasures of the sentimental or the ancestral kind. Nothing was to be allowed to befuddle the sovereign intelligence as it pursued the fierce and solitary task of creation. How are we to put such an imaginary being back into his real history? Where did Sartre begin? Where did he come from?

Sartre was only fifteen months old when his father died of a lingering tropical fever contracted while on patrol in the South China Sea. The surviving portrait photograph of Jean-Baptiste Sartre shows a steadfast and splendidly mustachioed naval officer in his early twenties. For many years this photograph of Jean-Baptiste hung on the wall above his infant son's bed. It was virtually all he left him. There were no little memories, no affectionate legend, nothing that a son might learn to cherish. Even that emblematic photograph 'disappeared' in 1917 when his mother married again.

Only once did the adult Sartre ever go looking for his father. At the age of fifty-five, on an impulse, without telling anyone where he was going, he took a train from Paris to the town of Périgueux, the scene of his father's boyhood. When the quester knocked on the door of the silent old house opposite the cathedral there was no reply. He was three months too late. Hélène Lannes, his father's sister, the last surviving relative, had died earlier that year. Thwarted, Sartre abandoned the search. In his brief autobiography, *Words*, he dispatched this insubstantial father with triumphant comic alacrity. Scattering a handful of jokes about avoiding the Oedipus complex,

Sartre gave thanks for all the years in which he had his mother to himself.

Sartre had much more in common with his father than he could ever acknowledge. They shared the same physical stature, the same precocious intelligence, the same marginality. At a deeper level both father and son were loyal, in their odd way, to the bourgeois radicalism of their nineteenth-century provincial ancestors. The man from nowhere turns out to be rather well-connected.

Jean-Baptiste, mustachioed naval officer, father of Jean-Paul Sartre, boasted an impeccable bourgeois lineage. Behind him, metaphorically, he had four generations of energetically self-improving Sartres. They had risen from farmer to village pharmacist, from prosperous country doctor to prize polytechnic graduate. All of them were vociferously anti-clerical freemasons.

In the last years of the nineteenth century, which is where this twentieth-century story begins, the Sartre family occupied a spacious three-storey house of smooth white stone, set on the main square, between the church and the pharmacy, in the village of Thiviers, on the main road from Périgueux to Limoges. But all that solid tranquillity had a sour edge to it. Family meals were eaten in silence. Jean-Baptiste's parents were profoundly estranged. With twenty rooms to choose from they could avoid each other's company almost entirely.

Their youngest son, who was exceptionally good at maths, resolved to escape. Breaking with cautious family tradition, Jean-Baptiste was educated in Paris at the École Polytechnique, the school created by Napoleon for the training of military engineers. Like his more famous son, Jean-Baptiste was a brilliant student. When he graduated in 1895 he chose the career that would take him as far away as possible from the poisonous atmosphere of the house on the picturesque square in Thiviers. Within a year he was to be found somewhere off the coast of Manila, on board the *Descartes*, a fourteen-gun five-thousand-horse-power naval cruiser. His superiors were already saying that Jean-Baptiste Sartre had the makings of a future admiral.

His job was to aim the big guns. In a scene from the pages of a novel by Joseph Conrad, the *Descartes* was bombarding coastal villages which were resisting French annexation. Finding himself stationed up at the sharp end of French colonial enterprise, Jean-Baptiste did not much like what he saw. Between the lines of his letters home there were intimations of bitter disappointment. Within a year he fell seriously ill and was repatriated back to France. During the seven remaining years of his life Jean-Baptiste's naval career stagnated. Promotion came very slowly and he decided, in the end, to leave the navy. On leave in Cherbourg he met up with one of his former classmates, Georges Schweitzer. Georges introduced him to his sister, an elegant, deferential, taciturn girl of twenty-one. She was just what he was looking for. Three weeks later Jean-Baptiste requested Professor Charles Schweitzer's permission to marry his daughter.

3

Anne-Marie Schweitzer, the bride, was head and shoulders taller than the man standing at her side in the church at Passy in May 1904. She was of excellent stock and brought with her a generous dowry of 40,000 francs. Seven generations of Schweitzer forefathers had taught in the village schools of Alsace. Liberal Protestants, left-wing republicans, passionately pedagogical, the Schweitzers took great pride in their mission to educate the people. The men of the family were also exceedingly difficult to live with. Early in her marriage Anne-Marie's mother, Louise, the one that Sartre would call *Mami*, had taken refuge from her husband's domineering personality by immersing herself in one of those mysterious, chronic, late nineteenth-century female ailments that so intrigued Sigmund Freud. Her condition obliged her to stay lying down in a quiet room for most of the day, reading Diderot and Voltaire, and assembling a whole arsenal of pungently cynical jokes, her best weapons in the never-to-be-declared war that she fought with her husband.

In the spring of 1906, when his son Jean-Paul was eleven months old, Jean-Baptiste Sartre inherited a large rural property from his grandmother. With his wife and son he left Paris and moved back into the family house in Thiviers. His troublesome cough was becoming more and more painful. He took to his bed. It was the room where he had slept as a boy, and there, on a September evening, with an odd farewell smile, he died, to the sound of fifteen-month-old Jean-Paul weeping from the pain of his new baby teeth. The coffin, decorated with a naval officer's sword and insignia, was carried from the church by Jean-Baptiste's polytechnic classmates.

4

Anne-Marie Schweitzer was rapidly and irrevocably ostracized by her husband's family. They resented her claim on *their* property. Faced with such tight-lipped, tight-fisted hostility she decided to pack her bags and take the train back to her parents' house in Paris. Thus began the ten happy years: Sartre was left in undisputed possession of his youthful widowed mother. Though he was too young for the fact to become conscious knowledge, he may already have observed with a certain desolate childish lucidity that his grandparents, both the Schweitzers and the Sartres, could scarcely bear to be in the same room together.

Education was a hereditary Schweitzer passion; this pleasingly receptive young boy was a splendid challenge. Sartre's grandfather, Charles Schweitzer, immediately set to work, and soon he was commending the child's ability. The boy had 'prodigious natural intelligence . . . an eloquence and a facility that could be the making of a lawyer or a politician'.[1]

The infant Sartre received intact from Charles Schweitzer's hands the moral and political substance of a distinctly nineteenth-century bourgeois radicalism. It was a powerful mix: one part individualism, archaic and flamboyant, one part critical intelligence, autonomous and dissenting, all held in focus by a practical passion for liberty. It was also an awkwardly miscellaneous package, but it would see him through many trials. Sartre was no ordinary petit-bourgeois

---

1. Cohen-Solal, 56.

anarchist. At his back, invisible to the world, there always stood a great host of opulently-bearded republican ancestors, men of principle endowed with powerful voices and large libraries.

Charles Schweitzer's study held several thousand books. There Sartre could explore the spacious landscape of good literature. There he acquired an effortless lifelong intimacy with the great writers of past. As the imaginative companions of his childhood they imposed no burden of reverence. Interestingly, Charles Schweitzer did not encourage Sartre to write. Perhaps he regarded it as a distraction. It was Sartre's mother and his uncle who enthused over his early literary efforts, copying out his stories and passing them round the family circle. Risking her father's disapproval, his mother also encouraged in her son a mildly subversive taste for illustrated American comics. Sartre soon assembled an extravagantly comprehensive only-child's collection of the adventures of Nick Carter, Buffalo Bill and Texas Jack. His mother also took him to the cinema, an initiation into an art-form that he always cherished.

Around the year 1912, *annus mirabilis* of modernism, Sartre was evidently being fed a wonderfully nutritious chance combination of cultural ingredients: grandfather's leather-bound volumes, plus disreputable garish American comics, plus the ghostly melodrama and the wild comedy of early silent cinema. It was solid high-bourgeois classical literary culture, weighty texts, with an effervescent addition of demotic populist narrative imagery.

Because there were so few other children to play with, Sartre played with his mother, the sombre girl-widow who had for the moment retreated back into her original maiden condition. Through the unremembered early years of his childhood she pampered and adored her little son. He was constantly being photographed, and the images were then neatly retouched by his mother, using her special coloured crayons. It was a wise precaution. The boy might be as fragile as his father.

When he told the story of his early years, Sartre exaggerated the contrast between the princely infant he had once been and the ridiculously ugly toad-child suddenly revealed to the world when his baby-curls were cut off at the age of five. It was the first, the most ignoble of his transformations. Survive *that*, survive anything. Life as Sartre was a hectic, jolting series of shocks and reversals. Existence was profoundly and instructively uncomfortable. Sartre never knew the smooth upward curve of the emerging personality, the slow orderly accumulation of personal merit. Hence Sartre's stoical motto *loser wins*. Little wonder that the adult Sartre wrote such idiosyncratic biographies of Baudelaire, Genet and Flaubert. He knew about damaged lives.

At the age of four a mysterious fever damaged Sartre's right eye, leaving him with only ten per cent residual vision and a divergent squint. For this child the visible world was skewed from the start. Even his own face in the mirror looked odd. Squinting at the world, he was endlessly denied all the tender reciprocities of the answering gaze. Even as a child he knew he was ugly, and as a man he couldn't imagine that anyone would enjoy touching him. Perhaps Sartre's melancholy acuity in the realm of the gaze, the body and the object is rooted in the fact that even for the young boy things would be forever just out of true.

There were certain consolations to be had. Sartre's grandfather, a handsome old philanderer, always encouraged his young protégé to regard the little girls of his acquaintance as a collection of *fiancées*. The polygamous family that Sartre later assembled around himself is a comically precise realization of his grandfather's little joke. Sartre's first love was a younger cousin, Annie, from Thiviers. They spent holidays together, and they wooed each other with a rich sentimental traffic of letters and presents, books and toys.

A photograph taken in the summer of 1913 when Sartre was eight catches the mood and the setting of his early years. The picture shows a well-dressed family group sitting together on a grassy slope with a range of pine-trees in the background. With their parasols and bonnets, Panama hats and walking-sticks, they are visibly well-equipped for a genteel early twentieth-century walk in the country. Anne-Marie, Sartre's mother, now in her early thirties, is sitting close beside her strikingly benign and vigorous seventy-year-old father, Charles. In his white linen suit, sitting nearer to the camera than anyone else, he is slightly larger than life.

5

In 1917, when Sartre was eleven, his mother remarried. The cherished photograph of Jean-Baptiste was removed from the bedroom wall. Her new husband was a friend of her brother's. His name was Joseph Mancy. Mancy became Sartre's joint guardian, inevitably an unhappy arrangement. Mancy was the hateful fairy-tale stepfather: conventional, authoritarian and heavy-handed. (In the name of propriety, Mancy always refused to meet Simone de Beauvoir.) The family now moved from Paris to the windswept dockyard town of La Rochelle. There began the unhappiest chapter of Sartre's life. In his writings he never mentioned these grim adolescent years in La Rochelle.

At school Sartre was bullied for being small. In the streets, which were buzzing with the violence of the war, he was beaten up by rival gangs of boys. At home in the evenings Mancy tried to teach his reluctant stepson geometry and algebra. These lessons often ended in blows. In despair Sartre began to take money from his mother's purse. He planned to bribe his persecutors with expensive cakes. The discovery of this petty theft added to the burden of his humiliations. This was the moment when Sartre first told himself that he was a genius. Writing was a great consolation, for it raised him up in his own eyes. And his stepfather disapproved, which was perversely encouraging. Having such an enemy was an inspiration. The adult Sartre observed with some satisfaction, 'He was the kind of man I was writing against. All my life.'[2]

The family returned to Paris when Sartre was fifteen. There at last, among the boys of the Lycée Henri IV, Sartre found friends of his own age. Self-consciously sophisticated in their tastes, they were reading the new writers of the day, Proust and Valéry. In this more congenial setting Sartre could shrug off the tribulations of La Rochelle and begin a new and more rewarding chapter of his life.

He grew especially close to one of his classmates, Paul Nizan.

2. *La Cérémonie des adieux*, 186.

The two boys had much in common: literary ambitions, memories of a morbidly lonely childhood and the fact that they both had a squint. Indeed they looked so alike that they were often mistaken for one another, both at school and in later years. At Nizan's suggestion they agreed upon a secret pact of brotherhood. Walking the streets of Paris together, 'moved to tears when the very first electric advertising signs lit up', they were Nietzschean supermen.[3]

With Nizan Sartre first discovered all the advantages of being one of a couple. In alliance with Nizan, he constructed a powerful new social personality. The whole process took only a few months. Recognizing a genius in their midst, Sartre's *lycée* classmates chose him as their *satyre officiel*. This untranslatably tribal phrase suggests a real talent for disruption. The schoolboy Sartre soon stepped into the joyful role of chief hell-raiser, hoaxer, provocateur and master of the dirty joke. The squinting victimized loner from La Rochelle was suddenly a great success. Down in the schoolyard he was popular among his own age-group. Up in the less strenuous arena of the classroom he won prizes for academic excellence. Legend has it that Nizan and Sartre brought their *lycée* career to a glorious drunken close by vomiting, simultaneously, over their headmaster's shoes. Simultaneously? Perhaps that was how it should have been.

6

Sartre combined his duties as *satyre officiel* with some serious intellectual work. At the *lycée* he read Bergson and discovered his vocation. Written in a powerfully metaphorical style, Bergson's *Essay on the Immediate Data of Consciousness* (1889) offered an eclectic blend of philosophy, psychology and aesthetics, with a congenial emphasis on the spontaneity and the creativity of consciousness. The book also appealed to Sartre as a description of his own psychic life.

3. *Situations IV*, 144.

In the summer of 1924 Sartre and Nizan passed the ferociously competitive exams that would admit them to the École Normale Supérieure, the austere and lofty summit of the republican educational system. When Sartre stepped through the prestigious gates of the rue d'Ulm he discovered dust, dirt and poor food as well as an intense literary-intellectual life. While pursuing his philosophical vocation, Sartre did not neglect his unofficial career as actor, singer, pianist and mimic. His contemporaries remembered the skill and the enthusiasm which Sartre brought to the task of baiting Gustave Lanson, the ageing conservative director of the school.

Sartre's ambition was 'to be the man who knows the most'. His appetite and his capacity for intellectual work were both legendary. He read 300 books every year. His conversation overflowed with lyrical enthusiasm. His thinking was audacious and inventive. His style was peremptory and magisterial. His field was psychology, philosophy, ethics and sociology. Nobody's disciple, he was already sketching the outline of a philosophy of freedom.

When the libraries closed, so the cinemas opened and Sartre could indulge his passion for the moving image. He immersed himself in the films of the twenties and the thirties: Charlie Chaplin, D. W. Griffith and Friedrich Murnau. Sartre was fascinated by the new art form, drawn especially to its disreputable energy and its vividly casual revelation of the contingency of everyday actions. Populist and democratic, the cinema also seemed to stand for a culture that was free of class values. This was, after all, the distinctive aesthetic invention of the twentieth century.

It is an odd fact that Sartre never pursued this enthusiasm creatively. He never wrote about cinema at any real length, and the experience of watching a film scarcely figures in his fiction. He judged cinema by traditional literary standards. He tried once or twice to write for the new medium, but without great success. A man of the written word, his love of images was forever unconsummated.

Politically, Sartre was a natural anarchist. By the late 1920s, his symbiotic friendship with Nizan was dissolving. Nizan was moving towards the Communist Party and he now scorned many of the things that Sartre still cherished. 'I remained the friend of his adolescence, the petit-bourgeois he was fond of . . .'[4] Though Sartre was moving away from Nizan, it was not clear what direction he might take. Through the crisis years of the 1930s he took no interest in organized politics, read no newspapers and didn't vote in elections.

During Sartre's first year at the École Normale the last link with his father's family was broken when Annie, his favourite cousin, died in 1925 at the age of nineteen. With her insolently superior intelligence and her seductive self-assurance, Annie is commemorated in many of Sartre's female characters. The death of Annie also led by chance to Sartre's first serious liaison. At his cousin's funeral he met the voluptuous, capricious, scandalous Simone Jollivet. She was tall and blonde with cold blue eyes and a sophisticated taste for sexual intrigue, amateur prostitution and fancy-dress orgies. According to de Beauvoir, who was abjectly jealous of her, Simone Jollivet possessed 'all the glamour of the heroine of some novel'.[5] For three years Sartre pursued her avidly. To whet his appetite she gave him her purple lace-trimmed culottes to use as a lampshade. Then she kept him waiting outside all night, sitting on a wooden bench. And when they met she told him in great detail of her exploits with her rich admirers. He in turn sent her long passionate autobiographical letters. Simone Jollivet also inspired Sartre's first novel. Woven into the story of a perverse love-triangle is the theme of masculine creative force. The physical activity of writing is imagined in muscular terms. The hero 'gripped his pen so tight he almost broke it'.[6] Writing was powerful. The word could change the world.

During his final year as a student Sartre met Simone de Beauvoir. He was the double she had been dreaming of ever since the age of fifteen. He told her, 'I'm going to take you in hand.' He laid down various conditions for their relationship. There would be lots of travelling together. There would be other lovers, and they were to pledge themselves to 'transparency', an exemplary intimacy without

4. ibid., 146.
5. *The Prime of Life*, 66.
6. Cohen-Solal, 114.

secrets. They graduated together in the summer of 1929. Impressing his examiners by the extraordinary confidence with which he spoke in the oral, Sartre was given first place and de Beauvoir, notoriously, was allowed second place. The great intellectual partnership was established, on a basis that was never perfectly equal.

7

When he left the École Normale Supérieure in the summer of 1929, the pattern of Sartre's life was clear. He would teach philosophy in a *lycée*, and in the long summer vacations he would travel. In 1930, at the age of twenty-five, Sartre inherited 100,000 francs from his grandmother. Over the next few years he and de Beauvoir spent this money travelling around Europe. They visited Spain, Morocco, Italy, Germany, Austria, Czechoslovakia and Greece. Though they climbed the mountains and they visited the churches and castles, it was not the poetry of the past that they were after. It was the quest for human here-and-now of the cities that drew them down the rough back-streets, towards the docks and the factory yards, to the places where they could inhale the unmistakably authentic collective odour of the 1930s. Between teaching and travelling Sartre would also toil over the manuscript of his 'pamphlet' about contingency, the first major work of his maturity. Published in 1938 as *Nausea*, it took seven years of writing and rewriting, seven years of learning how to fuse fiction and philosophy, a remarkably tormented apprenticeship for a writer who seemed so certain of himself intellectually.

At the *lycée* in Le Havre Sartre's unconventional style soon made a great impression on his students. Fifty years on they still remembered how he used to arrive in the classroom wearing a black shirt (to economize on laundry costs), no hat, no tie, hands in his pockets, smoking a pipe. 'Nous n'avions jamais vu ça.'[7] Sartre would sit on a desk and begin to speak, without notes, rapidly, lucidly and confidently, with an intellectual honesty and an egalitarian directness

7. ibid., 126.

that won the hearts of his adolescent audience. His students also passed their exams, to the dismay of Sartre's more punctilious colleagues.

Sartre the *lycée*-teacher had to renounce his long-cherished vision of early literary fame. It was painful. 'I imagine fame,' he told Simone Jollivet, 'as a crowded ball-room where gentlemen in evening dress and ladies in low-cut gowns are raising their glasses in my honour. It's utterly clichéd, but I've had that image ever since my childhood.'[8] All through the early thirties his writings were repeatedly turned down by Gallimard, the most influential literary publisher of the day. For all his robust self-assurance, Sartre lived with a growing sense of failure. He would spend many more years as a teacher than he had ever envisaged. Not until he was forty could he live on the money he earned from his writing. Yet it was precisely those 'wasted years' of *lycée*-teaching that nourished Sartre's enduring moral sympathy for the aspirations of adolescence. 'Youth,' he said, 'was the metaphysical age par excellence.' In the classroom he found the ideal audience for a philosophy of freedom.

Yet the contrast between Sartre's faltering début and the brilliant career of Paul Nizan was inescapably depressing. Since joining the Communist Party in 1929 Nizan had been assigned high political and cultural responsibilities. He had become the very type of the politicized literary intellectual of the 1930s. He was an aggressively militant intelligence at the service of the party, organizing anti-fascist congresses, producing journalism, pamphlets, lectures and essays on the topics of the hour, as well as publishing distinctively sceptical novels.

Sartre meanwhile was stuck in Le Havre, where his schoolmasterly existence displayed all the worst features of that familiar, lamentable type: the petit-bourgeois anarchist. At the end of his first school year Sartre scandalized the assembled parents with a prize-day speech in praise of the cinema, that disreputable invention. The following year, on the same occasion, he staggered from the official platform before the ceremony was over, evidently drunk. To add

---

8. *Lettres au Castor*, I, 9.

to the scandal, Sartre had been seen the night before with his students, celebrating in a local brothel. They said he was carried upstairs on the back of a sturdy whore, and, to his credit, he never denied it.

In these years, like his unheroic hero Roquentin, Sartre travelled to the edge of the bourgeois world. He was living in a shabby hotel, the Printania, a disreputable dump in a rough bit of Le Havre, between the railway station and the harbour. The Printania was no place to cultivate the inner life. All the after-dark noises of the city washed through the thin walls of his room. Sartre's everyday life was nomadic, transparent. He inhabited the raw uneasy world of the cheap hotel, the café, the seafront, the cinema, the brothel, the railway station, the public park and the municipal library. There was no comfortable little retreat where you could 'be yourself'. The noisy, threadbare, anonymous impermanence of the Hôtel Printania was far from the ancestral places of his boyhood. Sartre had turned his back on that joyless, spacious family house on the village square, its cupboards stacked with clean linen and home-made jam.

8

He was travelling light, reading avidly, obliviously, serving out the long years of his apprenticeship. Prompted by Raymond Aron, one of his old sparring partners from the École Normale, who told him, teasingly, that a phenomenologist would be able to make philosophy from an apricot cocktail, Sartre now immersed himself in the work of the German philosopher Husserl. To master Husserl's austere meditations on the nature of Being demanded four years of exhausting intellectual effort. Sartre was simultaneously reading his way through modern fiction, absorbing the discoveries of James Joyce and Virginia Woolf, Hemingway, Faulkner and Dos Passos. In Le Havre, in the early thirties, he gave a series of lectures in the municipal library, tracing the emergence of an 'absolute realism'.

Husserl and Hemingway? Sartre was assembling his apparatus. It was a piece of highly idiosyncratic intellectual improvisation. Using this combination of German philosophy and Anglo-American fiction, Sartre hoisted himself up above the meditative refinements of Proust, Gide and Valéry, his neo-classical literary precursors, a generation with its roots in the old century. Not the good old things, but the bad new ones were to be his chosen domain.

In the autumn of 1933, the year that Hitler came to power, Sartre won a nine-month scholarship to the French Institute in Berlin. He was going to read Husserl in the orginal. The French Institute was an opulent suburban villa, the former residence of a Prussian general. Here Sartre was well insulated from the violent political drama that was unfolding on the streets of Berlin. He was also isolated by his imperfect command of the language. Though he could read the philosophers, Sartre soon realized that his German was not adequate for the more mundane purposes of seduction.

In the nicely improbable setting of a large high-panelled first-floor room with a balcony (it had been the old general's smoking-room), we may picture Sartre at work. He spent the mornings reading Husserl and in the afternoon he worked on the drafts of *Nausea*. It was a characteristically parallel enterprise. The investigation of Being accompanied and guided the writing of fiction.

These ten months in Berlin are one of the minor mysteries of Sartre's biography. According to de Beauvoir, none of his letters from Berlin have survived. But stranger still is the fact that neither the panelled room, nor the suburban villa nor the politically comatose city has left any trace in Sartre's writings. This whole period, between September 1933 and June 1934, is like the page that has been torn from the diary.

9

It was also a welcome holiday from the dreary responsibilities of life in Le Havre. He left Berlin in June 1934, on the eve of his thirtieth birthday, and spent the summer travelling. Once back in Le Havre, Sartre entered the darkest phase of his life. His troubles began in a little narcissistic crisis. Looking in the mirror he realized he was overweight and going bald. It was a symbolic disaster, a reminder of the dreadful day they had cut off his angelic curls. The ugly man of genius was growing inescapably uglier. Perhaps he was not the genius he had always taken himself for. Feeling 'old, fallen, finished', he was visited by thoughts of death.[9]

In this dark mood, in February 1935, Sartre had himself injected with the hallucinogenic drug mescaline. In March his maternal grandfather, Charles Schweitzer, died at the age of ninety-one. The mescaline and the bereavement, coming so close together, pitched Sartre's life into chaos.

Taking mescaline was meant to be a dispassionate intellectual experiment. Sartre was interested in hallucinations. What could be more enlightening than to experience them for himself? There was some slight risk, but the effects of mescaline usually lasted no more than eight hours.

That was what they had told him. But something went wrong. The effects of the mescaline were terrifying. It was like being trapped inside one of the surrealist texts he had so enjoyed back in the 1920s. An umbrella turned into a vulture. Huge devil-fish swarmed over his body. De Beauvoir's shoes turned into beetles. Giant lobsters followed him along the streets. Sartre felt he was drifting into insanity. 'I'm on the edge of a chronic hallucinatory psychosis.'[10] His hallucinations lasted for months, and then dwindled to a depression that lasted for several years.

In his mescaline visions Sartre was attacked from all directions. But he held his ground and he began to explore the zone of darkness that lay revealed. Without this season in hell he would have been a lesser writer, for Sartre had never acknowledged that consciousness held hidden depths. He liked to imagine his own mind as an operating theatre, the brightly lit scene of an unflinching analysis. He also regarded the fertile abundance of the natural world as less-than-human. Claiming he was 'allergic to chlorophyll', he had always shunned that world, imaginatively and intellectually. Now he was being pursued by a vengeful crew of birds and fishes, beetles, apes

9. *War Diaries*, 78.
10. *The Prime of Life*, 210.

and lobsters. The omnipotent intellectual personality, devised in adolescence, was coming apart. The comic-aggressive pessimism that had always served him so well was breaking up into its primitive components. Sartre felt powerless, terrified at being dragged to the very edge of madness.

The short stories that Sartre began writing in 1936 explore various shades of black. With their sober and fastidious realism they coax us towards the wild dangerous zone of the mind where the Surrealists officially congregated. In five stories, published as *Le Mur* (*Intimacy* in English), Sartre offers an unguided tour of the psychopathology of the age. Here are the night-thoughts of an imprisoned Spanish anarchist who is to be shot in the morning. The moral anguish of the woman who steps inside her husband's madness. The fantasy life of the proto-fascist who humiliates a prostitute and then fires down randomly at a crowd from his balcony. The clichéd erotic intrigues of two shop-girls. The psychosexual humiliations of a boy from a rich family who turns to fascism.

Bringing together Dostoevsky and Dos Passos, Proust and Hemingway and Virginia Woolf, Sartre's stories map a world which is historically recognizable as that of Europe between the wars. But Sartre's implied politics were outrageously idiosyncratic. Both his pessimism and his individualism went against the progressive tide of the thirties. His interest in the psychological roots of fascism was some years ahead of its time. I imagine that anyone reading *Le Mur* when it was first published in February 1939, the month of the final fascist victory in Spain, would have drawn no clear political lesson from its pages.

To escape the distress of being alone with the lobsters, Sartre sought out the company of a young student of de Beauvoir's called Olga Kosakiewicz. Olga walked the streets with Sartre, talking him through the hours of anguish. Olga was another Annie, another Simone Jollivet. She was eighteen, elegant, disdainful and capricious, the daughter of white Russian émigrés. Sartre fell for her. The heroically lucid consciousness was thrown into erotic turmoil. Olga Kosakiewicz was the philosopher's *amour fou*. 'My passion for her burned away my workaday impurities . . . I grew thin as a rake and distraught.' For two years Sartre and de Beauvoir were rivals for Olga's unpredictable affections. Now in their early thirties, Sartre and de Beauvoir were abjectly in pursuit of a woman who embodied all the recklessness of their fading youth. 'We fell,' said Sartre, 'beneath the intoxicating spell of that naked, instant consciousness which seemed only to feel with violence and purity...'[11] It was 'a kind of desolate greed to see myself feel and suffer, not in order to know myself, but in order to know all natures, suffering, pleasure, being-in-the-world.'[12]

10

We catch sight of Sartre once again as he returns to the surface in 1937. It was the year that things changed for the better. In April, after seven discouraging years of rewriting and several devastating publisher's rejections, *Nausea* was accepted for publication. In October Sartre said a last farewell to French provincial towns and took up a new teaching post in a Paris *lycée*. His literary début, so long delayed, was now carried off to loud applause from the critics of the day. Sartre had made his name. But his brief interlude of fame was cut short by the beginning of the war.

Sartre was mobilized in September 1939. It was a blessing in disguise. All through the first nine months of the war, the uneventful period known as the phoney war, Sartre wrote for twelve hours a days. Serenely prolific, he managed about a million words. Contemplating the great stack of hand-written pages, he declared with some pleasure: 'I have always considered abundance to be a virtue.'[13] Already well accustomed to working on the move, Sartre could now be found sitting writing in the corner of a requisitioned school classroom, ignoring all the clamour of military life. Or he would be somewhere outside, on guard duty, sitting out of sight, writing on

11. *War Diaries*, 77.
12. ibid., 62.
13. *Lettres au Castor*, II, 147.

his knee. It was the perfect creative refuge from the realities of war. He wrote dozens of letters, filled fifteen large notebooks and wrote the novel that would be published in 1945 as *The Age of Reason*.

Sartre's notebooks soon took on a magical life of their own. They protected him from 'the melancholies, the morosities and the sadnesses of war'. He had never written with such fluency before. 'The notebook form is very important . . . this free, broken form does not enslave me to former ideas, you write everything on the spur of the moment and sum up only when you feel like it.'[14] The notebooks allowed Sartre to draw to the surface the energy that had flowed underground for so long. Suspended, forced into living somewhere outside his real life, Sartre rapidly sketched out most of the themes of his subsequent work. It was another of his recurrent feats of self-transformation, another example of his triumphant ability to survive disaster.

This ability was soon to be tested again. On 21 June 1940, the day of his thirty-fifth birthday, without having ever fired a shot, Sartre and his fellow-soldiers surrendered to advancing German troops. He was lucky to be uninjured, but he was unlucky to be taken prisoner only a few hours before the armistice was declared. He was kept with a large group of French prisoners, locked up in an attic and sleeping on the floor. There was so little to eat that he became delirious.

Still thinking that everyone would soon be released, he found himself being put on board a train heading for northern Germany. He was unloaded at Stalag XIID, a prison camp set on a hill above the city of Trier. He was fortunate. The view from the hill was excellent. The prisoner's gaze could encompass the historic city, the bright curves of the river Moselle, and the red roads that climbed up through the vineyards. As an ardent reader of Stendhal, Sartre would have grasped the pleasant paradox of a prison with a wonderful view.

While many men were damaged by the experience of captivity, Sartre thrived on it. Stalag XIID was uncannily like being back at boarding-school. The iron routine, the malodorous dormitory, the

14. ibid., 21.

close comradeship of other men, the austere moral and material simplicity of their enforced collective life, all of this was deeply congenial to a man who had spent his happiest years in the Lycée Henri IV and the École Normale.

During the eight months of his captivity, Sartre was gloriously busy. He read avidly, indiscriminately, timelessly, like a child, held in an imagined world by the power of the word. He filled the hours with Sophocles and Somerset Maugham, Nerval and Rilke and detective novels. He also threw himself energetically into the collective life. He wrote his first play, *Bariona*. He sang in the choir, played piano concerts, composed songs, gave lectures and even organized a discussion group on Heidegger, having somehow obtained a clandestine copy of *Sein und Zeit* from the library of the local monastery. He also took part in a bantam-weight boxing match over two rounds and was delighted when he managed to achieve a draw against a younger opponent. Prison friendships were unexpectedly rewarding. Sartre soon fell in with a professional poacher from the Ardennes, a man called Braco. Though illiterate, Braco was highly intelligent. In the camp he was King Rat, the fixer, amassing a fortune from his astute dealings on the black market. Between Sartre and Braco there was a warm mutual admiration rooted in a keen sense of each other's special talents. Sartre was always fascinated by tough guys, gangsters, desperadoes and deviants. They were the great *lumpen* alternative to respectability. Braco, Camus and Jean Genet, who became his close friends, Baudelaire and Flaubert, who drew from him the ambivalent tribute of a biography, they are all exotic individualists.

Sartre found himself once again playing the part of comic bard. In the evenings the inmates of Stalag XIID were locked up inside their big wooden huts for the night, forty to a room. When the lights went out at eight thirty the men lay down on their bunks. Then they lit candles stuck inside little tins. To cheer them all up Sartre would sit at the table in the middle of the hut and improvise a string of tall stories spiced with lots of coarse jokes. His talents as Official Satyr were undiminished. But he soon found, to his great delight, that he could move an audience as well as make it laugh. Sartre always remembered this story-telling scene in fond detail. For the man who had written *Nausea*, an austere parable of masculine solitude, this prison-hut story-telling was a revelation. It confirmed a fluent narrative gift, an easy popular touch, and it encouraged him to write for a wide audience – the French nation which had just lived through a singular historical experience. The second and the third volumes of Sartre's wartime trilogy of novels, *The Reprieve* and *Iron in the Soul*, were written with the sustaining memory of that appreciative bedtime audience.

11

In March 1941 Sartre escaped from Stalag XIID and made his way back to Paris, an episode which is still wrapped in mystery. Three published accounts of Sartre's escape each tell a different story. In the authorized version, as told by Sartre to de Beauvoir, it is said that he was officially repatriated to France as a civilian, after having convinced the camp doctor that he would be unfit for military service. In a more dramatic version of the escape, as told by a fellow-prisoner, Sartre walked through the prison gates disguised as a local farmer. According to the version of events put about by the communists, Sartre's escape was staged by the Germans. They released Sartre in return for his promise to work for them once he was back in Paris. More intriguing, more plausible and quite unverifiable is the authentically Kafkaesque possibility that the Germans, unknown to Sartre, acquiesced in his escape. They could have stopped him at the prison gate. Or they could have recaptured him at any time over the next few years, when he was living openly in Paris. But they decided, at some unknown point, that it would be to their advantage to leave him alone, at liberty, writing and publishing and organizing. Sartre in Paris, a fully functioning literary intellectual, was evidence that a Nazified France was less oppressive than its critics liked to think. Whatever the content of his writings, the mere fact of their publication announced to the world that France had already returned to 'Business as Usual'.

Prison life had been simple. Back in Paris everything was more complicated. He felt an odd nostalgia for 'the unanimous life' he had left behind. His fellow-writers, those who still remained in France, were confused and isolated, waiting to see what would happen next. Censorship was complicated, ubiquitous and unpredictable. To the surprise of his friends, Sartre returned from Trier full of political optimism. After long months of imprisonment, he was eager to begin organizing a resistance group. He declared to those who would listen that the new France, if it were to be worth anything, would be socialist.

By June 1941, three months after Sartre's return to Paris, he had organized a small resistance network. Down in the cellars of the École Normale, hidden away behind piles of dusty old furniture, they had an arthritic duplicator and a purloined supply of paper. With this clandestine printing press at their disposal, Socialism and Liberty was launched.

A quarrelsome mix of anarchists, Marxists and Trotskyists, embracing every known species of the non-communist left, the group aimed to occupy the narrow political ground that existed somewhere between the nationalists and the communists. The distant goal was an independent socialist Europe, a third force, in between Moscow and Washington. This was Sartre's favourite territory. It was, in a phrase from the 1960s, the revolution within the revolution. Over the next three decades, through all the twists and turns of the Resistance, the Liberation and the Cold War, Sartre's political thinking was guided by two principles: a rejection of anti-communism and a belief in the possibility of the third way.

In the summer of 1941, to explain his vision of the future, Sartre composed a 100-page draft constitution for a post-war socialist France. A formidably comprehensive document, ten copies were produced on the basement duplicator. None survived. They were all hastily flushed down the toilet in a railway train when the agent carrying them into the southern zone thought she was about to be searched. However ignominious its fate, this document suggests two key features of Sartre's politics: virtuoso individualism allied to visionary impatience. Sartre was not and would never be a Party man. Not for him the grubby tedious practicalities of collective political organization. He preferred to do it all himself, sitting alone with his pen, drafting constitutions, a prophetic voice.

In that same summer of 1941 Sartre and de Beauvoir crossed over into the 'free' southern zone of France, with their bicycles. They planned to contact Gide and Malraux, the most prestigious writers of the pre-war generation, and talk them both into supporting Socialism and Liberty. For two pleasantly adventurous months Sartre and de Beauvoir cycled around the region between Lyon, Marseille and Grenoble. Deeply preoccupied, Sartre would pedal along so indolently that he sometimes fell off his bike into the ditch. 'My mind was elsewhere . . .' he told de Beauvoir.[15] The meeting with Gide, in a village café, was symbolically pleasing but politically inconclusive. Malraux, the audacious adventurer of the 1930s, was now comfortably installed in a splendid villa on the Côte d'Azur. He was biding his time because it was obvious, he said, that the war would eventually be won by Russian tanks and American aircraft.

Discouraged by the grandiose torpor of Gide and Malraux, Sartre reluctantly decided to disband Socialism and Liberty. The group was too small and too isolated to achieve anything significant. As the Nazi persecution of dissidents grew ever more lethal and efficient, they were all in great danger. To add to the group's difficulties the Communists were treating Sartre with intense sectarian malice. As an alleged collaborator and as the loyal defender of the dead renegade Nizan, Sartre was to be shunned by all members of the party. After months of intense but unrewarding political activity Sartre decided to cut his losses. He would concentrate on writing.

Sartre's initiative was clearly premature. Thwarted by circumstances, he turned away from political action, intent on keeping his fragile vision of liberty intact. In this he was true to the larger pattern of his life in which periods of intense collective activity were followed by a withdrawal into writing. It is the energetic alternation of these two phases which imparts an exceptional creative tension to the best of his work.

15. *The Prime of Life*, 492.

12

All through the harsh winter of 1941–2 Sartre worked long hours on *Being and Nothingness* and on his play *The Flies*. Occupied Paris was a ghost city. There were curfews and arrests, deportations and executions. No cars on the streets, no food in the shops, no pictures in the Louvre and no statues in the public parks. Sartre lay low, working in the warm back room of his favourite café, filling his pipe with dog-ends and endeavouring to write on an empty stomach.

His formidable powers of concentration served him well. He could write anywhere, with a single-minded intensity of purpose that amused and perplexed those around him. In her memoirs, de Beauvoir recalls leaving Sartre sitting on a rock in the middle of a field, one August afternoon in 1942, while she went off to climb a mountain. When she returned, several hours later, Sartre was to be found sitting obliviously on the same rock, still writing, while the breeze attacked the precious accumulation of pages.

We need to remember these peculiar circumstances when reading *Being and Nothingness*. Sartre's passionate but tactically oblique declaration of liberty was written in the shadow of the immense unmentionable fact of a recent fascist victory. The book combines a wonderful defamiliarizing intensity of abstraction with an everyday human vividness in the examples that illustrate the larger argument. Holding hands, giving up smoking, romantic friendship, sadness, sadism, fascination, relics of the dead, gambling, skiing: *Being and Nothingness* achieves a uniquely generous and playful miscellaneousness.

The fact that Sartre's work was being published and performed during the Occupation was held against him by some. Questions were asked. Why did Sartre, as a teacher, stay silent when all the Jewish teachers in France were sacked? How did he manage to keep his job at the *lycée* when others were being dismissed for their anti-Nazi views? Why did he write an article for a collaborationist journal, *Comoedia*?

The evidence, such as it is, proves very little. Amplified by political malice, professional envy or simply by the general paranoia of dangerous times, it suggests only that Sartre was waiting to see what would happen.

We touch here upon difficult moral and political issues. Sartre's plays and novels often explore the dizzying ambiguities of political action. In the 1930s you were either an anti-fascist or you were not. But in August 1939 the Hitler–Stalin pact threw millions into desperate political confusion. History seemed to teach only that our most deeply considered deeds will have unforeseen consequences. Whatever his mistakes, hesitations or inconsistencies, Sartre taught a perplexed generation to think about political morality in a way that is different from either the Leninist or the liberal traditions. From 'Le Mur' (1937) to *Dirty Hands* (1948), in stories, plays and novels, Sartre offers a intricately sceptical critique of 'the political'.

Sartre began to emerge, tentatively, from his productive seclusion in the latter months of 1942. The communists had relaxed their former sectarian line and were prepared to work with him. He finished the writing of *Being and Nothingness* and then in the early months of 1943 he was drawn into writing for a clandestine resistance journal.

For all the audacity of its purpose, *Les Lettres françaises* was a modest artefact. The few surviving copies testify to the glorious and slightly mad eloquence of the classic twentieth-century illegal publication. Four pages of thin grey mimeographed paper, clumsily laid out on an old typewriter with hand-written headings, *Les Lettres françaises* was produced in an impressive edition of 12,000 copies, to be dropped by night, from an aeroplane, into fields all across France. Between April 1943 and July 1944 Sartre wrote four unsigned articles for *Les Lettres françaises*. They address the ethics of literature. As well as denouncing collaborationist writers, Sartre looked into the post-war political future and sketched out the new human values that a liberated literature might help to create.

With great fluency and confidence Sartre was now writing and publishing in many forms, for many audiences. As well as the clandestine writings he had a new play, *The Flies*, being performed, officially, in Paris. *Being and Nothingness* was published. Extracts from *The Age of Reason* appeared in Switzerland. And now he was offered a lucrative contract to write screenplays for Pathé. There were essays on Camus, Blanchot and Bataille. *In Camera* was written in two weeks in the autumn of 1943. *The Reprieve*, second volume of the *Roads to Freedom* trilogy, was almost completed. *La gloire*, with all of its pleasures, responsibilities and vexations, was not far away.

In June 1944, the week after his thirty-ninth birthday, Sartre decided to end his career as a *lycée* teacher of philosophy. He would henceforth earn his living as a professional writer. Everything was now within his grasp, and he sensed that he would be among the architects of France's future. The Liberation of Paris was imminent. When it came, in the last week of August 1944, Sartre was there, on the streets, witnessing the great event, day by day, hour by hour. He wrote an account of it for *Combat*, the newspaper edited by his friend Camus. 'It begins like a festival,' he wrote on 28 August. 'The street has once again become – as it did in 1789 and in 1848 – the theatre of great collective actions . . . In this time of drunkenness and joy everybody feels the need to plunge back into the collective life.' This was Liberation: a glorious confusion of festival and tragedy, epic and farce. Sartre's moment had arrived.

13

The new chapter of Sartre's life as a professional writer began auspiciously. In January 1945, through his work for *Combat*, he was invited to America as one of a party of French journalists. America was the El Dorado of his boyhood, the land of the perpetual superlative. It was the home of Nick Carter and Buffalo Bill, Faulkner and Hemingway and Dos Passos. It was the land of skyscrapers and jazz and cinema. It looked irresistible.

The reality of America was of course more complicated. As a guest of the US State Department Sartre was expected to write something flattering about the American war effort. After a two-day flight across the Atlantic in a military DC8, Sartre was installed in a suite at the Plaza Hotel overlooking Central Park. In the month of January 1945, when everything in Europe was still tightly rationed, the New York Plaza was probably the most opulent place on the planet. Sartre and his fellow-journalists were treated as heroes. They were interviewed and photographed and given new clothes and plied with food and drink and secretly trailed by FBI men. Their neatly archived reports cover every hour of Sartre's first months in America.

Sartre was front-page news. America gave him what it had once given Charles Dickens, his first taste of real celebrity. Sartre drank his fill but he also kept a clear head, using his New York press-conferences to remind the world how deviously the USA had tried to hinder de Gaulle from assuming the leadership of post-war France.

The little group of journalists were flown all over America in their own military B29. There were all too many organized visits to armaments factories, though Sartre also got to see a Hollywood film studio in action. When he visited the American South Sartre befriended the black writer Richard Wright, and his eyes were opened to the realities of racism. Tactlessly, he reported what he saw.

Sartre spent nearly five months in America, returning to France in May 1945. His belated transformation from provincial philosophy teacher to famous author was now complete. The next stage, in which he became a public figure addressing a world audience, was just beginning.

14

In September 1945 there appeared the first two volumes of his great trilogy of novels, *The Roads to Freedom*. 'My intention,' said Sartre, 'is to write a novel about liberty. I have tried to trace the path of several characters ... between 1938 and 1944. This path will lead them to the Liberation of Paris, though perhaps not to their own.'[16]

In October 1945 there appeared the first issue of Sartre's new

16. *Œuvres romanesques*, 1911.

monthly journal devoted to literature and politics, *Les Temps modernes*. Named after the film by Charlie Chaplin, sponsored by the prestigious publishing house of Gallimard, with an editorial committee that included Simone de Beauvoir, Michel Leiris and Merleau-Ponty, *Les Temps modernes* held its position at the centre of Parisian and European intellectual debate for over twenty years. It also placed Sartre in a position of great personal influence. He now presided over a whole team of writers, directing an ambitious collective programme of research and creation.

The first issue of *Les Temps modernes* opened with Sartre's manifesto-essay 'What is Literature?' After a exuberantly polemical, marvellously aphoristic survey of French literary history since 1789, Sartre mapped out a whole programme of leftist cultural endeavour. Sartre seized his moment with great tactical skill. The streets of Europe were littered with the rubble of war. Across many continents, soldiers were making their way home, full of awkward, angry questions. The old values, the old names were discredited. Sartre offered a sober, compassionate, imperious lucidity. It was perfectly attuned to the needs of the hour.

Not everyone was carried away. In October 1945 he gave a public lecture in Paris entitled 'Is Existentialism a Humanism?' His first deliberately self-popularizing venture in philosophy, the lecture attracted an enormous crowd and intense publicity. The event itself has subsequently entered French cultural mythology as the Birth of Existentialism. It provoked a storm of disdainful polemics. There were sermons and editorials denouncing Sartre as a corrupter of youth, the saboteur of the classical literary tradition. There were caricatures and cartoons insinuating that Sartre and de Beauvoir were glamorously debauched anarchists. Journalists, keen to exploit a novelty, announced that Existentialism was a way of dressing, a hair-cut, a dance or just an area of Paris.

Over the next few years, between 1946 and 1949, Sartre was at his most prodigiously creative. There were forty publications in three years. They included lectures and essays, plays and articles, prefaces and radio broadcasts, biographies, novels, journalism, songs and screenplays. Like Dickens and Victor Hugo, Sartre now began to earn large amounts of money from his writing. Like them he also had a growing entourage of dependants. He was a rich man and he began to carry big wads of banknotes in his pockets, like a gangster. Everything he owned had to be immediately available. The classic rewards – money, fame and the love of women, according to Freud – were now all showering down upon him. But mingled with the fame there was also hatred and mockery and misunderstanding and all the subtle corruption of self-importance. 'It is not at all pleasant,' said Sartre, 'to be treated as a public monument while you are still alive.'[17]

15

By 1950 Sartre's books were being published in a dozen languages. He was in danger of becoming a national asset. 'It was a great shock for a writer reared in the old tradition . . . success seemed almost a sign of mediocrity. Compared to Baudelaire's obscurity the inane glory that had burst upon Sartre had something annoying about it.'[18]

In the great glare of publicity we lose track of Sartre. Most of the fine detail, the living nuance of the personality, is obscured. What are we to make of these headlines? these public appearances? this slide-show? Sartre in Havana. Sartre in Moscow. Sartre in Rio. Sartre in Peking. Sartre in Prague. The biographers become impatient with Sartre. The portrait, classic image of achieved individuality, fades and breaks up. Sartre vanishes in a fifteen-year whirl of activity, with ominous pauses for a week in hospital, here and there.

Outwardly he played on. He had a world audience. Populist cultural forms now complemented his socialist politics. He was an indefatigable giver of interviews, a great signer of petitions, a writer of prefaces, a professional traveller, an international lecturer, a presider at conferences. The champion pamphleteer also began to

17. *Situations II*, 43.
18. *Force of Circumstance*, 48.

destroy himself with a relentless amphetamine-accelerated routine of writing. Corydrane, swallowed ten at a time, peeled the skin from his tongue. Alexei Stakhanov, the model Soviet worker of the 1930s, the man who could dig coal twice as fast as anyone else, would surely have applauded Sartre's prodigious output.

To survive his own success, Sartre withdrew into a self-preserving creative secrecy. He had officially given up literature. There would be no more novels, no sequel to *The Roads to Freedom*. After Auschwitz and Hiroshima, in a decade marked by neo-colonial warfare in Korea, Algeria and Vietnam, perhaps literature alone could not illuminate the darker corners of our modernity. Perhaps literature was part of the problem, a superior narcotic, dulling the senses and diverting the mind from the imperatives of the age. Ever since his precocious reading of *Madame Bovary* (at the age of seven), Sartre had never resolved his quarrel with the imaginary. His scandalous and self-disparaging post-war pronouncements about literature did not endear him to the disappointed admirers of his early work.

Below the surface, meanwhile, Sartre worked on two new projects which lingeringly demolish the very idea of literature. His autobiography, *Words*, is a scornful, throwaway account of his early childhood. Like Proust *à rebours*. Its companion piece is a voluminous extravaganza-biography of Gustave Flaubert, *The Family Idiot*, which explores the exemplary neurotic instance of the bourgeois literary vocation. These two books, the huge biography and the laconic autobiography, both spent a decade or more in manuscript. So long deferred, they were Sartre's subterranean life, impregnably sheltered somewhere beneath the surface.

How does a portrait end? Unlike a biography, a portrait has no ending. Conventionally it shows the subject looking out, beyond the present moment and into the future which is – rather nicely – where we are. A Sartrean portrait of Sartre must catch precisely this futurity, showing the subject as he might wish to be remembered, in motion, with many years ahead of him, his creative powers undepleted. In this broadly sympathetic spirit I want to look briefly at the infamous, intemperate, pamphleteering, political Sartre of the 1950s and 60s. I want to see what happens when a writer so extravagantly gifted throws himself so wholeheartedly into politics. *I want to see what happens*: the phrase describes Sartre's own happy sense of this his final metamorphosis. He expected it of himself. It was what French writers did, towards the end. Some time around the age of fifty they became involved in the great political arguments of their day. Victor Hugo had taken up arms against Napoleon III. Émile Zola had campaigned on behalf of Dreyfus. André Gide had visited the Congo and Soviet Russia. 'That was how I saw my life,' said Sartre in 1974. 'I would end up in politics.'[19]

16

In the Sartrean annals of liberty, Cuba is the miraculous link between the liberated Paris of August 1944 and the re-liberated Paris of May 1968. The Cuban revolution was in its thirteenth month when Sartre arrived to visit the island in February 1960. 'It's the honeymoon of the Revolution,' he told de Beauvoir. 'Direct contact between leaders and people, and a mass of seething and slightly confused hopes.'[20] The Cuba of the early sixties, known across the world through the romantic photo-iconography of Castro and Che Guevara, was exactly what Europe's dejected ex-Stalinists had been longing for. The embarrassingly vicious military dictatorship of Fulgencio Batista had been overturned by a boatload of audacious idealists, most of them around the age of thirty. This revolution, situated a mere ninety miles away from the coast of Florida, looked quite unlike most twentieth-century communist revolutions. Unencumbered by all the weighty rhetorical trappings of orthodox Marxism, this was a revolution that had been supported by peasants and brought about by a war of liberation. Without any invigorating images of Lenin or Stalin, without even using the word socialism, the Cubans all seemed to be gloriously making it up as they went along. In February 1960 most of the world still wished them well.

19. *La Cérémonie des adieux*, 475.
20. *Force of Circumstance*, 503.

Sartre, weary from his recent work on the *Critique of Dialectical Reason*, confounded by the sudden death of Camus, dismayed by the rancorous violence of France's Algerian crisis, found Cuba irresistibly delightful. There would be time, in later years, for more critical second thoughts, as Cuba was dragged into the machinery of Soviet power. But this was the moment of popular victory, the perfect romantic moment of unanimity. Aware of his immense cultural influence and skilled in deploying it to best effect, Sartre did all he could to convey his approval to the world. He was photographed standing beside Castro: striking front-page images of a bearded young giant in battledress shaking hands with a smiling, bespectacled, slightly plump man of fifty-something dressed in a suit. Each of them was the perfect embodiment of an idea. This was Youth and Energy fraternizing with Philosophy. This was the Spirit of Revolution, consecrated by the benign presence of Literature.

Sartre spent a month in Cuba. He appeared on Cuban TV, introduced to the people by Castro as 'your friend'. Sitting in the back of the presidential Buick, Sartre toured the island, observing Castro at work. He saw a benevolent and still-hesitant leader, encouraging, advising and cajoling his infinitely expectant people. Castro took Sartre to spend the night in the presidential retreat. The Cuban equivalent of the palace at Rambouillet, this turned out to be a reassuringly egalitarian shed with a corrugated iron roof and grey concrete walls, set in the middle of a swamp. Sartre applauded such simplicity. It was a world away from the decadent splendours of the French Republic. Castro and his entourage all slept in bunk beds arranged along the walls of a single large room. It was a familiar feeling for a man who had passed through the dormitories of the École Normale and of Stalag XIID. There were memorable late-night political conversations, with Castro and with Che Guevara, conversations that have subsequently entered the mythology of the New Left. Sartre would often quote Guevara's artfully modest joke, 'Can I help it if reality is Marxist?'

The nonchalant youthful splendour of the leaders of the Cuban revolution made a deep impression on Sartre. These men were all young enough to be his students, and he was correspondingly old enough to be their father. 'Touring the island,' Sartre joked appreciatively, 'I met my sons . . . in all the positions of authority.' In an astute premonition of the sixties, Sartre dwelt on the fact that the victorious rebels still wore the beards and the long hair that had been the original badge of the insurrection. 'The beards,' Sartre explained to his readers, 'are the consequence of a vow – no shaving before the end of the war . . . the disorder of their hair testified that these brigands conspired against order.' Batista's clean-shaven soldiers had very soon learnt to live in fear of the Beard. 'It meant ambush, the law of the jungle, extermination. Toward the end, when they saw a beard behind a shining rifle in a narrow mountain pass, they broke ranks.'[21] Soon after Sartre left Cuba, in July 1960, there came an order that long hair was to be cut. The party was over. In a slightly forlorn footnote Sartre observed that this 'marked the transition from revolution to administration'.[22] It turns out that this was a remarkably astute observation. The sky over Cuba was already darkening. The week before Sartre's visit, Anastas Ivanovich Mikoyan flew into Cuba from Moscow to sign an initial agreement on economic cooperation. On 17 March 1960, the week of Sartre's departure, President Eisenhower privately instructed the CIA to begin training Cuban exiles for a future invasion of the island.[23]

While he was in Cuba Sartre worked away, ambidextrous as ever, at an essay on Paul Nizan. After breakfasting with de Beauvoir on black coffee and fresh pineapples, Sartre spent the mornings writing, in the anonymous air-conditioned hotel room, looking out over the Caribbean and the old quarter of Havana. The essay was intended as a preface to a reissue of one of Nizan's novels, but the subject soon ran away with its author. The Nizan essay stands as one of Sartre's most obliquely inventive and most deeply felt political texts. Revisiting the difficult years of his late boyhood, Sartre draws many strands together. He incorporates an evocation of his high-minded adolescent friendship with Nizan, a celebration of Nizan's militant

21. *Sartre on Cuba*, 109.
22. ibid., 110.
23. Bethell (ed.), 461, 462.

political and moral integrity, a ferocious attack on the French Communist Party for their efforts to slander Nizan as a traitor to the cause. Sartre's Nizan is the hero in an improvised parable of the century's revolutionary politics. He represents 'a violent purity'[24] and he brings a powerful prophetic message for the young. Using Nizan as his mouthpiece, Sartre spells it out: 'You are dying of modesty. Dare to desire. Be insatiable. Release those fearful powers which clash and whirl around beneath your skin. Don't be ashamed to ask for the moon. You ought to have it.'[25] Memories of Nizan, impressions of Che Guevara, conversations with Castro, here they all come together in Sartre's mind. The exuberance of the young romantic anarchist is allowed to prevail, briefly, over the scrupulous melancholia of the old dialectician. 'Let us try,' suggests Sartre, 'to go back to the time of hatred, of unquenched desire, of destruction, that time when André Breton ... expected to see the Cossacks watering their horses in the fountain of the Place de la Concorde.'[26] Sartre's wish encompasses everything: Surrealism, Bolshevism, and distant echoes of 1793. Conjuring up three revolutionary traditions in one sentence, Sartre seems to be passing on the recipe for some magically effervescent compound. Like one of Baudelaire's imaginary alchemists, tinkering with the hopes and memories prompted by Cuba and Nizan, Sartre had inconspicuously invented the 1960s.

On his return to Paris, working at top speed, Sartre composed a great eulogy for the Cuba he had seen. Entitled *Storm Over Sugar*, it was a vividly populist history of the revolution combined with his first-hand impressions of everyday life on the island. *Storm Over Sugar* was then edited down into a series of sixteen articles which were published in *France-Soir*, the biggest-selling French daily newspaper of the time. In this form Sartre's account of Cuba reached 1.5 million French readers, though nobody knows how many of them groaned at the very sight of the author's name and threw his latest contribution to the national culture straight into the bin. In later years, as Castro

24. *Situations IV*, 134.
25. ibid., 140.
26. ibid., 141.

found himself increasingly under the thumb of his Soviet sponsors, Sartre began to have second thoughts about Cuba. *Storm Over Sugar*, never reprinted, was excluded from the ten volumes of Sartre's collected essays. Castro and Cuba were banished. Perhaps the hopes which they excited were too unsettling to be acknowledged.

WORKS CONSULTED

Bethell, L. (ed.), *The Cambridge History of Latin America*, Vol. VII, Cambridge, Cambridge University Press, 1990.

Cohen-Solal, Annie, *Sartre*, Paris, Gallimard, 1985.

Contat, Michel, and Rybalka, Michel, *The Writings of Jean-Paul Sartre*, translated by Richard McCleary, Evanston, Northwestern University Press, 1974.

De Beauvoir, Simone, *The Prime of Life*, translated by Peter Green, Harmondsworth, Penguin Books, 1965.

—— *Force of Circumstance*, translated by Richard Howard, Harmondsworth, Penguin Books, 1968.

—— *La Cérémonie des adieux*, Paris, Gallimard, 1981.

Hayman, Ronald, *Writing Against: A Biography of Sartre*, London, Weidenfeld & Nicolson, 1986.

Sartre, Jean-Paul, *Situations II: Qu'est-ce que la littérature?* Paris, Gallimard, 1948.

—— *Sartre on Cuba*, Connecticut, Greenwood Press, 1961.

—— *Situations IV: Portraits*, Paris, Gallimard, 1964.

—— *Œuvres romanesques*, edited by Michel Contat and Michel Rybalka, Paris, Gallimard, 1981.

—— *Lettres au Castor et à quelques autres*, Paris, Gallimard, 1983.

—— *War Diaries: Notebooks from a Phoney War*, translated by Quintin Hoare, London, Verso, 1984.

Suggestions for Further Reading

WORKS BY DE BEAUVOIR

De Beauvoir, Simone, *The Mandarins*, translated by Leonard Friedman, London, Collins, 1957.

—— *Memoirs of a Dutiful Daughter*, translated by James Kirkup, Harmondsworth, Penguin, 1963.

—— *The Prime of Life*, translated by Peter Green, Harmondsworth, Penguin, 1965.

—— *Force of Circumstance*, translated by Richard Howard, Harmondsworth, Penguin, 1968.

—— *All Said and Done*, translated by Patrick O'Brian, Harmondsworth, Penguin, 1977.

—— *Adieux: A Farewell to Sartre*, translated by Patrick O'Brian, London, Deutsch, 1984.

—— *Letters to Sartre*, translated by Quintin Hoare, London, Radius, 1991.

WORKS ABOUT SARTRE

Barnes, Hazel E., *Sartre and Flaubert*, London, University of Chicago Press, 1981.
Caws, Peter, *Sartre*, London, Routledge & Kegan Paul, 1979.
Cohen-Solal, Annie, *Sartre*, Paris, Gallimard, 1985.
Contat, Michel, and Rybalka, Michel, *The Writings of Jean-Paul Sartre*, translated by Richard McCleary, Evanston, Northwestern University Press, 1974.

Hayman, Ronald, *Writing Against: A Biography of Sartre*, London, Weidenfeld & Nicolson, 1986.

LaCapra, Dominick, *A Preface to Sartre*, London, Methuen, 1978.

Laing, R. D., and Cooper, D., *Reason and Violence: A Decade of Sartre's Philosophy 1950–1960*, London, Tavistock Publications, 1964.

Palmer, Donald D., *Sartre for Beginners*, London, Writers and Readers, 1995.

Poster, Mark, *Existential Marxism in Postwar France: Sartre to Althusser*, Princeton NJ, Princeton University Press, 1975.

POSTHUMOUS WORKS BY SARTRE

Sartre, Jean-Paul, *War Diaries: Notebooks from a Phoney War*, translated by Quintin Hoare, London, Verso, 1984.

—— *The Freud Scenario*, edited by J.-B. Pontalis, translated by Quintin Hoare, London, Verso, 1985.

—— *Witness to My Life: The Letters of Jean-Paul Sartre to Simone de Beauvoir 1926–1939*, edited by Simone de Beauvoir, translated by L. Fahnestock and N. MacAfee, London, Hamish Hamilton, 1992.

Acknowledgements

This anthology has its shadowy existential origin in the carnivalesque events of 1968 and in the many gloriously speculative political conversations that followed. My belated thanks to all who may still recognize themselves here, between the lines, in the magically bright Sartrean mirror. Especially to Hamid, the infinitely benevolent Maoist who quoted Rimbaud, to Edouard Goldstucker, the Prague exile who spoke of Europe and the historical imagination, to Gillian Perry, who talked me round the Louvre, and to Christine Nugent who embodied the alluring fiery spirit of the age, as well as having a superb record collection.

More recently, for simply keeping me at it, with a sustaining mix of shrewd advice, lavish encouragement, inspiring conversation and delicious cooking, I am variously indebted to Julian Atterton, Jean-Pierre Boulé, Malcolm Bowie, Robin Buss, Alex Callinicos, Mark Crowe, Elizabeth Fallaize, Angela Hurworth, Paul Keegan, Annie Lee, Hermione Lee, Stephen Minta, Guy Mitchell, Sara Perren, Adam Phillips, Graham Robb, Anna South, Catherine Weinzaepflen, Nick Wetton and Ian Kennedy White.

Geoffrey Wall, September 1999

NOTES

Footnotes using the asterisk system are those of the original Sartre text; numbered footnotes are by the editor and translator of this volume.

Chronology

1904 May: marriage of Jean-Baptiste Sartre, naval officer, and Anne-Marie Schweitzer.

1905 June: birth of Jean-Paul Sartre.

1906 September: death of Sartre's father, Jean-Baptiste. Sartre and his mother go to live with maternal grandparents in a suburb of Paris.

1912 Sartre reads *Madame Bovary* and the novels of Jules Verne. He receives no regular education until the age of ten.

1915 October: Sartre enters the Lycée Henri IV in Paris. Beginning of the friendship with Paul Nizan.

1917 Sartre's mother remarries. Sartre remains with his grandparents. Thus begins 'the four worst years of my life'.
Joins his mother and stepfather in La Rochelle.

1920 Sent back to school in Paris.

1922 Passes *baccalauréat*. Prepares for the École Normale Supérieure. Reads Bergson.

1924 Begins four years at ENS, studying psychology and philosophy. Discovers Rilke and the Surrealists.

1925 Liaison with Simone Jollivet.

1926 Thesis on the nature of mental images.

1929 Meets Simone de Beauvoir.
November: begins eighteen months of deferred military service.

1931 April: teaching philosophy at a *lycée* in Le Havre. Begins writing a 'pamphlet on contingency' which will become *Nausea*. Gives public lectures on contemporary literature.

1932 Discovers Céline and Dos Passos.

1933 Discovers Hemingway and Husserl.

September: scholarship to study phenomenology in Berlin. Reads Faulkner and Kafka. Finishes second version of *Nausea*.

1934 October: returns to Le Havre. First meeting with Olga Kosakiewicz.

1935 February: experiments with mescaline. Depression and hallucinations ensue.

March: death of maternal grandfather, Charles Schweitzer, at the age of ninety-one.

1936 Publishes *The Imagination*. Living in a trio with Simone de Beauvoir and Olga Kosakiewicz. Gallimard refuse to publish his novel *Nausea*. Writing short stories. Moves to teach at a *lycée* in Laon.

1937 *Nausea* accepted for publication.

Autumn: appointed to Lycée Pasteur in Paris.

1938 *Nausea* published. Essays on Faulkner and Dos Passos. Begins writing *The Age of Reason*.

1939 February: publishes *The Wall*, a volume of short stories.

December: publishes *Sketch for a Theory of the Emotions*. Essays on Mauriac, Husserl and Faulkner. Reading Heidegger.

September: Sartre is conscripted and stationed in Alsace.

1940 May: death of Nizan.

June: the Fall of France. Sartre is captured without being under fire. Transported to Nazi prison-camp near Trier.

1941 March: freed from prison. Founds short-lived Resistance group 'Socialism and Liberty'. Finishes writing *The Age of Reason*. Teaching at Lycée Condorcet, Paris. Writing *The Flies*. Begins work on *Being and Nothingness*.

1942 Begins writing *The Reprieve*.

1943 Publication of *Being and Nothingness*. First meeting with Camus. Writes *In Camera*.

1944 First meeting with Genet.

August: Liberation of Paris. Writing for *Combat*.

September: Establishes *Les Temps modernes*, a literary and political review.

November: finishes *The Reprieve*.

1945 January–May: visits USA as special correspondent for *Com-

bat. Liaison with Dolores Vanetti. Refuses Légion d'Honneur. September: publication of *The Age of Reason* and *The Reprieve*.

October: first issue of *Les Temps modernes*. Existentialism becomes fashionable. French Communist Party attacks Sartre as 'a false prophet'.

December: lecture tour of American universities.

1946 June: lecturing in Switzerland and Italy. Spends first of many summers in Rome. Publishes 'Matérialisme et révolution', a series of objections to Stalinism.

October: first meeting with Koestler. Moves into a flat with his recently widowed mother. Writing *What is Literature?* Begins to use amphetamines to 'accelerate' his output.

1947 Publishes *Situations I*, the first of ten volumes of collected essays. Publishes *What is Literature?* Essay on *Baudelaire*.

October–November: series of weekly radio discussions sponsored by *Les Temps modernes*. Suppressed after first six broadcasts.

1948 Publishes *Dirty Hands* and *Situations II*. Works as founder member of new socialist party, the Rassemblement Démocratique Révolutionnaire. Vatican places Sartre's work on the Index of Forbidden Books. Publishes *Iron in the Soul*.

August: officially denounced by Soviet Union as 'a hyena with a fountain-pen'.

December: quarrel with Malraux. Begins writing study of Mallarmé.

1949 Publishes *Situations III*. Polemic with Lukács. First meeting with Charlie Parker.

June: dissolution of RDR. Renounces political activity. Travels in Central America with Dolores Vanetti. Meets Hemingway in Havana. Begins work on a study of Genet.

1950 Begins *Queen Albemarle and the Last Tourist*, a book about Italy.

June: breaks with Dolores Vanetti. Enters period of isolation.

1951 Film version of *Dirty Hands*. New collaborators join editorial board of *Les Temps modernes*.

CHRONOLOGY

1952 Publication of *Saint Genet*. Rapprochement with Communist Party. Final quarrel with Camus. Begins 'four years almost entirely dominated by politics'. Working on fourth volume of war novel.

December: attends Peace Congress in Vienna.

1953 Begins work on *Words*, a polemical autobiography. Merleau-Ponty resigns from the editorial board of *Les Temps modernes*. Writes *Kean*.

1954 June: first visit to USSR.

November: beginning of Algerian War.

1955 *Les Temps modernes* supports the Algerian radicals of the FLN.

September–November: first visit to China.

1956 Publishes *Nekrassov*. Working on a study of Flaubert. Condemns Soviet invasion of Hungary. Publishes *The Ghost of Stalin*. First meeting with Arlette El Kaim.

1957 Publishes *The Question of Method*. Publishes *The Prisoner of Venice* (a study of Tintoretto). Begins writing *The Critique of Dialectical Reason*.

1958 Writes Freud film-script. Friendly contacts with Italian Communist Party.

October: heart attack precipitated by over-work.

1959 Finishes *The Critique of Dialectical Reason*.

September: *The Condemned of Altona*.

1960 Publication of *The Critique of Dialectical Reason*.

January: death of Camus.

February–March: visit to Cuba. Conversations with Castro and Che Guevara.

May: visit to Yugoslavia.

November: visit to Brazil. Confiscation of *Les Temps modernes*.

1961 July: Sartre's flat is bombed by the OAS. Conversations with Fanon.

1962 January: Sartre's flat bombed again.

June–July: visit to Poland and Soviet Union. Makes contact with Soviet liberals.

1963 January: visit to Moscow. Revises *Words*.
August–September: visit to Leningrad.
1964 Publishes *Words*. Publishes *Situations IV, V* and *VI*.
March: legally adopts Arlette El Kaim as his daughter.
June–July: visit to Soviet Union.
October: refuses Nobel Prize for Literature.
1965 Publishes *Situations VII*.
March: cancels American lecture-series.
July: visit to USSR.
October: TV version of *In Camera*.
1966 Publication of extracts from study of Flaubert.
May: visit to USSR. Agrees to take part in Bertrand Russell's Vietnam War Crimes Tribunal in Stockholm.
September–October: visit to Japan.
1967 February–March: visits to Egypt and Israel.
May: presides at first session of Russell Tribunal in Stockholm.
1968 May: supports student insurrection in Paris.
July: visits Yugoslavia and Czechoslovakia.
1969 Rewriting study of Flaubert. Death of mother.
1970 Becomes figurehead editor of banned French Maoist weekly newspaper, *La Cause du peuple*. First meeting with Maoist Pierre Victor, who becomes his close collaborator.
1971 May: publishes study of Flaubert, *The Family Idiot*. Charged with libel for articles in *La Cause du peuple*.
April: breaks with Castro.
June: founds left-wing press agency, *Libération*.
1972 Publishes *Situations VIII* and *IX*. Postpones work on final volume of *The Family Idiot* in order to concentrate on launch of daily newspaper, *Libération*.
1973 May: first issue of *Libération*.
June: eyesight deteriorating.
1980 April: dies aged seventy-five.

Cities

Sartre was a solitary, bookish, indoor sort of child, feeding his imagination on exotic fast-action adventure stories set in darkest Africa or the wilds of America. When he played at being one of his fantasy heroes he sensed that the whole world was waiting for him to come and take possession of it. He would be a great traveller. In 1930, at the age of twenty-five, Sartre inherited 100,000 francs from his grandmother. Over the next few years he and Simone de Beauvoir spent this money travelling around Europe during their summer vacations. They visited Spain, Morocco, Italy, Germany, Austria, Czechoslovakia and Greece. Sartre's description of Naples belongs to this phase of his life as a traveller.

In 1945 Sartre got on a plane to America and so began a new chapter of political travelling. Over the next twenty years he travelled the world, visiting Algeria, Cuba, China, Poland, Egypt and Russia. He was a cultural celebrity, meeting other celebrities, giving lectures and interviews. But he was also a political observer and commentator, relaying his impressions and opinions in published essays and articles. His descriptions of Havana and China belong to this official mode.

From 1953, to escape the relentless demands of his new political identity, Sartre always spent the summer months in Italy. Rome and Venice were his favourite cities. There he could walk the streets or sit outside, unmolested, contemplatively smoking his pipe. The two essays on Rome and Venice are a richly idiosyncratic tribute to the country that became Sartre's second home.

New York: Colonial City

> This began life as a magazine-piece, first published in *Town and Country* (London) and *Time* (New York) in May 1946. The French version appeared in *Situations III* (1949), where it figured in a sequence of linked pieces about America.

I was quite certain that I would like New York, but I never thought I would fall in love with it immediately, as I fell in love with the red bricks of Venice and the massive, sombre houses of London. I didn't realize that, for the European fresh off the boat, there is a 'New York sickness', no different from seasickness, air sickness or mountain sickness.

An official car drove me at midnight from LaGuardia airport to the Plaza Hotel. I pressed my forehead against the window, but all I could see were red and green lights, and dark buildings. The next day, there I was, without any period of adjustment, on the corner of Fifty-Eighth Street and Fifth Avenue. I walked for a long time under an icy sky. It was a Sunday in January 1945, a deserted Sunday. I looked for New York and couldn't find it. It seemed to be retreating in front of me, like a ghost city, as I walked down an avenue that struck me as coldly featureless and unoriginal. What I was looking for, no doubt, was a European city.

We Europeans subsist on that myth of the great city which we created during the nineteenth century. American myths are not ours, and American cities are not our cities: they have neither the same nature, nor the same functions. In Spain, Italy, Germany and France we find round cities, originally encircled by ramparts which were designed not only to protect the inhabitants from enemy attack,

3

but also to disguise from them the inexorable presence of nature. Moreover, these towns are subdivided into districts, and these are also round and enclosed. The houses, piled up on each other, tangled together, weigh heavily on the earth. They seem to have a natural tendency to cluster together, to such an extent that one is forced, from time to time, to take an axe to it and hack away new paths, as in the virgin forest. Streets break into other streets: closed at both ends, they do not seem to lead towards the outskirts of the town; one just goes round in circles. These are more than simple paths of communication: each of them constitutes a whole social environment. One can stop, meet people, drink, eat and linger there. On Sundays, people dress up and go for a walk, for the simple pleasure of greeting one's friends, seeing and being seen. It is such streets that inspired Jules Romains' 'unanimism':[1] they are alive with a collective spirit that varies from day to day.

So my short-sighted, European eyes, advancing slowly, watching everything, tried in vain to discover something in New York to catch their attention; something, anything: a row of houses suddenly barring the way, a street corner or an old house showing the patina of time. In vain: New York is a city for the longsighted: one can only focus on infinity. My gaze met nothing but empty space; sliding across blocks of houses, each exactly like the next, with nothing to arrest it, it eventually lost itself in the blue yonder, in the horizon.

Céline[2] said of New York that it was 'a vertical city'. This is true, but to me it seems above all a lengthways one. The traffic, which comes to a halt in the cross streets, always has priority and flows ceaselessly along the avenues. How many times have taxi drivers, who are happy to accept passengers going north or south, refused point blank to take them east or west! The cross streets serve hardly any purpose except to define the limits of the housing blocks between the avenues. The latter cut through them, push them aside and hurry northwards. This is why, being a naïve tourist, I looked long and

---

1. *Jules Romains 'unanimism'*: influential early twentieth-century formulation of collective experience
2. *Céline*: L. F. Céline, French novelist (1894–1961). He visited America in the 1920s.

fruitlessly for 'districts'. In France, the urban mass surrounds and protects us: the rich quarter protects the rich from the poor; the poor quarter guards us against the contempt of the rich; and in the same way, the whole city protects us against nature.

In New York, where the main thoroughfares are the parallel avenues, only in lower Broadway did I manage to discover any districts; otherwise there are just atmospheres, gaseous masses extending lengthwise, with nothing to mark where they begin or end. Gradually, I learned to recognize the atmosphere of Third Avenue, where people meet, smile and chat, in the shadow of the noisy overhead train, without even knowing one another; and the Irish bar where a German, passing beside my table, paused for a moment to say: 'Are you French? I'm a Boche.' There is the reassuring comfort of the shops on Lexington, the melancholy elegance of Park Avenue, the cold luxury and stuccoed impassibility of Fifth Avenue, the merry frivolity of the Sixth and Seventh, the food markets of the Ninth, the no man's land of the Tenth. Each avenue enfolds the surrounding streets in its own atmosphere; but, a block further on, you are suddenly plunged into another world. Not far from the quivering silence of Park Avenue, where the bosses' cars glide by, I find myself in First Avenue, where the ground shudders perpetually as the lorries drive over it. How can I feel safe on one of these endless 'north–south' trajectories when, a few steps away, to the east or the West, other longitudinal worlds are lying in wait? Behind the Waldorf Astoria and the white and blue awnings outside the 'high-class' blocks of flats, I can see the El which carries with it a little of the poverty of the Bowery.

All of New York is striped in this way with parallel, non-communicating meanings. These long, perfectly regular lines suddenly gave me a feeling of space. This is what our European cities are built to protect us against: the houses cluster together like sheep. But space crosses through New York, enlivens it and expands it. Space, the great empty space of the steppes and the pampas, flows through its veins like a current of fresh air, separating those on the right bank from those on the left. In Boston, an American friend, showing me round the fashionable part of town, pointed to the left-hand side of a boulevard and said: 'That's where the high-class folks live.' And, pointing to the right-hand side, he added ironically: 'No one's ever found out who lives over there.' It's the same in New York: there is an infinite distance between the two sides of a street.

New York is half-way between a city for pedestrians and a city for cars. One doesn't walk in New York, one goes by: it's a city in motion. When I'm walking quickly along, I feel at ease; if I should stop, I start to feel anxious and wonder: 'Why am I in this street, rather than in one of the hundreds of others just like it? Why in front of this drugstore, this branch of Schrafft's or Woolworth's, rather than any other branch, any other among the thousands of drugstores, each just like the others?'

Then suddenly pure space appears. I imagine that a triangle, if it were possible for it to become conscious of its position in space, would be terrified to learn the strictness of the coordinates that define it, and at the same time to discover that it is simply any old triangle, anywhere. In New York, you can never lose your way: a simple glance is enough to set you right: you are on the East Side, on the corner of 52nd Street and Lexington. But this spatial precision does not correspond to any feeling of emotional precision. In the numerical anonymity of streets and avenues, I am merely anyone, anywhere. In longitude and latitude. But there is no valid reason why I should be in one place rather than another, since this place and any other are so nearly identical. Never astray, always lost.

Am I lost in a city or in nature itself? New York offers no protection against the violence of nature. It is a city open to the sky. Storms flood its streets, which are so wide and take so long to cross when it rains. Hurricanes shake the brick-built houses and make the skyscrapers sway. The radio announces their arrival with as much solemnity as a declaration of war. In summer, the air vibrates against the houses; in winter, the city is drowned, so much so that one might believe oneself in a Parisian suburb when the Seine is in flood: but there it is not a question of melting snow.

Nature weighs so heavily upon New York that this most modern of cities is also the dirtiest. From my window, I can see the wind tossing around thick, muddy pieces of paper that flutter across the paving stones. When I go out, I walk through blackish snow, a sort

NEW YORK: COLONIAL CITY

of puffy crust, the same shade as the pavement, so that you might think the pavement itself was buckling. As soon as May ends, the heat crashes down on the city like an atomic bomb. It is Evil itself. People stop one another and say: 'It's murder.' Trains carry away millions of the inhabitants escaping from it who, when they get out, leave a damp trace behind them on the carriage seat, like snails. It is not the city that they are fleeing, but Nature. In the furthest depths of my apartment, I suffer the assaults of this hostile, indifferent, mysterious Nature. I feel as though I am camping in the midst of a jungle swarming with insects. There is the moaning of the wind; there are the static electricity shocks that I get every time I touch a door handle or shake hands with a friend; there are the cockroaches running around my kitchen, the lifts that make me feel sick and the inextinguishable thirst burning in my throat from morning to night. New York is a colonial city, a camp site. All the hostility and all the cruelty of Nature are present here, the most prodigious monument that mankind has ever erected to itself. It is a light city, and this apparent lack of weight surprises most Europeans. In this vast, malevolent space, in this rocky desert that will tolerate no vegetation, they have built thousands of houses out of brick, wood or reinforced cement that all seem about to take flight.

I love New York. I have learned to love it. I have grown accustomed to its massive blocks and its grand vistas. My eye no longer rests on a façade looking for a house that will achieve the impossible feat of being unlike all the others. It immediately makes for the horizon, looking for mansions lost in the mist which are nothing more there than pure volume, nothing more than a frame for the sky. Once you have learned how to look at the two rows of apartment blocks which, like cliffs, line one of these great avenues, then you are rewarded: their mission is accomplished down there, at the far end of the avenue, in simple harmonious lines, and a scrap of sky hovers between them.

New York only reveals itself at a certain height, a certain distance, a certain speed: they are not the height, distance or speed of a pedestrian. This city is astonishingly similar to the great plains of Andalucía: monotonous when you cross them on foot, magnificent and ever-changing when you do so in a car.

7

I have learned to love its sky. In the towns of Europe, where the roofs are low, the sky crawls along at ground level and seems tamed. The New York sky is beautiful because the skyscrapers thrust it far, far up above our heads. Solitary and pure as a wild beast, it mounts guard and watches over the city. And this is not only local protection: one feels that it spreads across the whole of America; it is the sky of the whole world.

I have learned to love the avenues of Manhattan. These are not serious little walkways shut in between the houses: they are major highways. As soon as you set foot on one of them, you realize that it has to travel on to Boston or Chicago. It fades away outside the town and your eye can almost follow it into the countryside. A wild sky above great parallel rails: that is New York, chiefly. In the heart of the city, you are at the heart of nature.

I had to get used to it, but now that I have there is nowhere that I feel so free as in the middle of a New York crowd. This light, ephemeral city that seems every morning and every evening, beneath the curious rays of the sun, to be a simple assemblage of rectangular parallelepipeds side by side, is never oppressive or depressing. Here, one may know the anguish of solitude, but not that of being overpowered.

In Europe, we become attached to a district, to a bunch of houses, to a street corner, and we are not free. But hardly have you immersed yourself in New York than you start to live completely on the scale of New York. You can admire it in the evening from the top of Queensborough Bridge, in the morning from New Jersey, at noon from the 77th floor of the Rockefeller Center; but you will never be captivated by any of its streets, because none of them is distinguished by a beauty peculiar to itself. Beauty is present in all of them, just as all Nature and the sky of all America are present. Nowhere can you have a better sense of the simultaneity of human lives.

Despite its austerity, New York is a moving experience for Europeans. Of course, we have learned to love our old cities, but what we find touching in them is a Roman wall built into the front of an inn, or a house once inhabited by Cervantes, or the Place des Vosges, or the town hall in Rouen. We like museum-towns – and all our towns are a little like museums where we stroll among the homes of our ancestors. New York is not a museum-town; yet for French people of my generation, it already has some of the melancholy of the past. When we were twenty, around 1925, we heard about skyscrapers. For us they symbolized all the fabulous prosperity of America. We were amazed when we discovered them in films. They were the architecture of the future, just as the cinema was the art of the future and jazz the music of the future. Today, we know all about jazz: we know that it has more of the past in it than of the future. It is black popular music, capable of limited development, in slow decline. Jazz is outliving itself. Talking pictures have not fulfilled the promise of silent cinema. Hollywood is stuck in a rut.

The war doubtless revealed to the Americans that America was the greatest power in the world. But the days of easy living are over; many economists fear the coming of a new crisis. So no more skyscrapers are being built. It appears they are too difficult to rent out.

A man walking in New York before 1930 would have seen in the great blocks which dominated the city the forerunners of a type of architecture that was destined to spread out across the whole land. In those days, the skyscrapers were alive. Now, to a Frenchman arriving from Europe, they are no more than historical monuments, relics of a vanished era. They still rise into the sky, but my spirit no longer goes with them, and the New Yorkers walk by their feet without even looking up. I cannot help feeling a kind of sadness as I look at them: they speak of a time when we believed that the war to end wars had just ended, when we believed in peace. Already, they are being slightly neglected: perhaps tomorrow they will be pulled down. In any event, building them required a faith that we no longer possess.

I am walking between some little brick-built houses, the colour of dried blood. They are younger than houses in Europe, but their fragility makes them seem older. In the distance I can see the Empire State Building, and the Chrysler Building, pointing vainly towards the heavens, and suddenly it occurs to me that New York is about to acquire a History, and that it already has its ruins.

This is enough to soften the edges a little on the harshest city in the world.

Naples: Food and Sex

> Salvaged from an unpublished short story set in Naples, this piece was originally published in the journal *Verve* in November 1938 under the title 'Nourritures'.

It was in Naples that I discovered the repulsive kinship of food and sex. It didn't happen at once: Naples doesn't give up its secrets at first, being a city that is ashamed of itself. It tries to make foreigners believe that it is populated by casinos, villas and palaces. I arrived by sea one September morning and it greeted me from afar with chalky flashes of light. All day I walked in broad, wide streets, the Via Umberto, the Via Garibaldi, failing to perceive, beneath the greasepaint, the suspicious scars in their sides.

Around evening, I pitched up on the terrace of the Café Gambrinus, in front of a granita which I watched melancholically as it dissolved in its enamel beaker. I was slightly depressed, having taken in nothing as I went by except little multicoloured facts, confetti. I asked myself: 'Am I really in Naples? Is there such a place as Naples?' I have known some cities like that – for example, Milan – false cities which crumble away as soon as you enter them. Perhaps Naples was only a name given to thousands of shimmerings along the ground, thousands of lights behind thousands of window panes, thousands of lonely passers-by and hummings in the air. I turned round and saw, on my left, the Via Roma leading away, as dark as the hollow of an armpit. I got up and began to walk between its high walls. This was another disappointment: that warm, vaguely obscene shadow had been only a curtain of mist, from which one emerged after a dozen steps. On the far side, I came across a long, antiseptic

NAPLES: FOOD AND SEX

corridor which bathed me in its milky light, displaying the magnificence of its grocers' shops with their raw ham, mortadella and every variety of dried blood, their luminous advertisements and the fine garlands of lemons that the lemonade-sellers hang on the canopies of their stalls. A current carried me forward, leading me up that dazzling boulevard; I brushed shoulders with men clothed in white linen, with brushed teeth and eyes shining and weary. I looked at them, and on the left at their food which was sparkling in the shop windows. I thought: 'That's what they eat!' It suited them so well: clean food – no, more than clean, chaste. That prosciutto was muslin, that scarlet tongue looked like sumptuous velvet; these people, who hid their bodies beneath light-coloured clothing, were feeding themselves on fabrics and wallpapers. And on trinkets: I stopped by the Caflish pastry shop and it looked like a jeweller's. On the whole, cakes are human, they resemble faces. Spanish cakes are ascetic, with a swaggering look; they fall to dust between your teeth. Greek cakes are fatty like little oil lamps: when you squeeze them, the oil runs out. German cakes have the ample smoothness of shaving cream: they are made so that soft, fat men can eat them with abandonment, not bothering about the taste, but merely filling their mouths with sweetness. But these Italian cakes had a cruel perfection, small, neat: barely larger than *petits fours*, they gleamed. Their hard, garish colours deprived one of any desire to eat them; one rather considered putting them on the sideboard, like coloured porcelain. I thought: 'Enough! Now all I have to do is go to the cinema!'

This is when I discovered, twenty yards away from the Caflish patisserie, one of the numberless scars on this poxed city, a fistula, a tiny street. I went over to it and the first thing I saw, in the midst of a little stream, was another piece of food – or, at least, something edible: a slice of watermelon (I still remembered the half-opened watermelons in Rome, looking like strawberry and pistachio ice-creams studded with coffee berries), a mud-spattered slice of watermelon, buzzing with flies like a corpse and bleeding in the last rays of the sun. A child in rags went up to this rotten fruit, picked it up and began to eat it, in the most natural way in the world. At that moment, I seemed to detect what the shopkeepers of the Via Roma were hiding behind their alimentary jewels: the *truth* of food.

I turned left, then right, then right again: all the sidestreets were the same. No one paid any attention to me and only once or twice did my eyes cross the empty look in another's. The men did not speak, the women exchanged a few words between long silences, standing in groups of five or six, pressed against one another, their rags making bright spots against the ash-grey walls. I had been struck, as soon as I arrived, by the pallor in the faces of the Neapolitans, and now it no longer surprised me: they were blanched in the darkness of a steaming dish. The women's flesh, in particular, looked as if it had been boiled under the dirt; the back-street had digested their cheeks: they were still in place, but one could have torn strips off them with one's fingers. I was relieved to see a young girl with thick lips and a moustache: at least they looked raw. All these people seemed turned in on themselves, not even dreaming: they too were surrounded by their foodstuffs, living scraps, stems, obscene meats, and tainted, open fruit; they revelled in their organic life, in sensual indolence. Children were climbing over the furniture, exposing naked bottoms beside the innards of fish; or else they pulled themselves up the steps leading to the inner rooms, flat on their bellies, waving their arms as though swimming and scraping their trembling little penises against the stone. I too felt digested: it began with a feeling of nausea, though very soft and sweet, then spread through my whole body like a strange kind of tickling. I looked at these meats, all of them, the bloody ones, the pale ones, the naked arm of an old blind woman, the reddish cloth stuck to a white bone; and I felt that *something* was to be done with them. But what? Should one eat? Stroke? Vomit? At the corner of one street, a bank of lightbulbs lit up, shining on a Virgin in her niche, a black Mary holding Jesus in her arms. 'Is it night-time?' I looked up. Above the houses, above the washing hanging like dead skins, a long way away, up there, I saw that the sky was still blue.

At the bottom of a hole was a shape on a bed. It was a young woman, sick. She was in pain, her head turned towards the street, her breasts making a soft patch under the sheets. I stopped and

NAPLES: FOOD AND SEX

looked at her for a long time; I should like to have run my hands across her thin neck . . . I shook myself and strode away; but it was too late, I had been caught. I could see nothing except flesh, paltry flowers of flesh hovering in a blue darkness, flesh for squeezing, sucking, eating, damp flesh, bathed in sweat, urine, milk. Suddenly a man knelt near a little girl and looked at her, laughing. She laughed back and said: 'Papa, my papa.' Then, lifting the edge of the child's dress, the man bit into her grey buttocks as if they were bread. I smiled: no gesture had ever seemed so natural, so *necessary*. At the same moment, in the Via Roma, my white-clothed brothers were buying varnished knick-knacks for dinner . . . 'That's it!' I thought. 'That's it!' I felt as though I had been plunged into a vast, carnivorous existence, a dirt-stained, pink existence that was coagulating around me: 'That's it, I *am* in Naples!'

Rome: A Ghoulish Hobby

First published in July 1952 in the weekly journal *France-Observateur*, under the title 'Une parterre des capuchines', this is a fragment from an abandoned book about Italy called *Queen Albemarle and the Last Tourist*. According to Simone de Beauvoir, *Queen Albemarle* was to have been both a capricious description of Italy and a meditation on what it means to be a tourist. It was reprinted in *Situations IV* (1964), along with 'Venice from My Window'.

Three o'clock. The shower caught me on the Nomentana, north-west of the city. It was a flight of angry birds: a whirl of feathers, twittering, black feathers flying around the sky. When calm was restored, I felt my jacket: it was dry and already a straw sun was breaking through the blue-grey cottonwool of the clouds. To the west, a street, broad and empty, leads up between the houses and ends against the sky. I can never resist the temptation to climb these short dunes to look over the far side. The finest in Europe is rue Rochechouart when you look at it from the boulevard Barbès; beyond the crest, you feel as though you can sense the sea. The rain starts to fall again, spraying me as I walk up. A smear of bitumen slides from the top of the hill and settles against the unhealthy whiteness of a wall. This wall brings the imposture of Rome to an end: beyond it, there is a patch of cabbages, a beach of acid light, a last vestige of humanity; then the desert. A desert in the rain. Far, far away, the Alban hills run like blue-black ink into the sky. This land city is more alone in the midst of these lands than a boat on the sea.

Taxi to the Via Veneto, autumnal, bourgeois, a street of rich

ROME: A GHOULISH HOBBY

foreigners. But the rich foreigners are hiding in their hotels. Shaken by the storm, the plane trees have shed their leaves, the colour of Roman walls, on the pavement and on the steps of Santa Maria della Concezione: it is as though the *palazzi* are moulting. Ochre, bright red, chrome yellow in the puddles: a marinade of dead skins. Santa Maria della Concezione is the Capuchin church. I go inside. The nave is empty. Silence, nothing. St Michael noiselessly crushes the Devil's head; gilded chandeliers circle the altar. At the far end, on the right, near the sacristy, warding off questions, a sullen friar puts his left index finger to his lips and points me to a stairway leading underground. The left hand, suspended for a moment in the air, is cupped, hollowed and pressed against my stomach. I give him twenty lire and go past, down some stairs, to find myself in a gallery of catacombs: the crypt. No: the left-hand wall is perforated by meshed windows and through the mesh, if I go up on tiptoe, I can see a little garden. I am in a hospital corridor. The ambiguity is very Italian: here I am on a ground floor lit by the cold clear light of autumn and in a basement beneath the clear yellow of the electric lights. On the right, the corridor goes past four small rooms, unequal in size: mortuary chapels, like cells protected by a low balustrade which simultaneously reminds me of a communion rail and the ropes which cordon off the drawing-rooms in French châteaux. Because of that, as I approach them, the chapels become drawing-rooms: four little rococo boudoirs, their walls, white under the grime, are flanked by the dark niches with alcoves or divans in their lower part and decorated above with agreeable, rather uncomplicated arabesques, roses, ellipses and stars, quite crudely designed. The only unusual thing about the decoration and the furnishings is the material of which they are made: bone. What ingenuity! All you need for a cherub is a skull and two shoulder-blades, using the latter as the wings. By tastefully piling up skulls and femurs, you can have niches decorated in rocaille. Even the old chandeliers, their light made paler by the daylight, are bundles of tibias suspended from the ceiling on chains. Each *salotto* has its inhabitants: standing by its bed, a skeleton in a monk's habit salutes me; a mummy rises on its couch; it is as though the dead here were for sale: they have tickets on their clothes, but with no price on them, only their name and status. Now Death is above my head, floating, with his hourglass and scythe: I am not sure if he is swimming or flying, but the air around him coagulates disturbingly into a gelatinous mass. Between the three walls of each *salotto*, under a blackish compost, its grains shining and tightly packed (is it anthracite or caviar?), some more favoured monks are resting. The soil comes from the Holy Land, as we learn from the inscriptions on the crossbars of crosses set right in the middle of the sacred bed, like those markers which tell you the genera of the plants in the Jardin des Plantes. *Terra Sancta*: a species of tufa, not native to these parts: found principally in Palestine, with other varieties in Lhasa, Mecca and elsewhere. I study the baroque incrustations on the walls and wonder why the Capuchins decided to break the nitrogen cycle and preserve these organic products from dissolution. Did they wish to show that everything sings to the glory of God, even those unusual flutes of which we are composed? I should like to think so. But why these exceptions? Why set up that skeleton on this heap of sticks that once were men? Why so arrange this bed of bones for this carefully reconstituted friar? To these dead, who are dust and grimaces, the living have subjected others of the dead. I am reminded of a postcard that I used to look at in the window of a newsagents' on the Boulevard Saint-Michel, when I was a child: from a distance, you could see the head of Bonaparte as the Petit Caporal. As you approached, the head began to swarm: it became a heap of maggots. Nearer still, and the maggots turned out to be naked women. So we delight in humiliating great men: the eye of the victor of Austerlitz is nothing more than a buttock; and we delight in humiliating women: the most beautiful woman in the world, squeezed tight against many others of the same kind, only deserves to serve as conjunctive tissue for the male. It is not God that we find in these chapels, but the image of one of the circles of hell: the exploitation of one dead person by another. Bones make a wheel around other bones, all the same, in the figure of that other rose: a skeleton. I start. Someone has spoken next to me. Heavens above! With femurs, tibias and skulls, you can also make human beings. A fat Italian man with fierce eyes drops on one knee, crosses himself, gets up quickly and makes his escape. Two French women are poised between admiration and terror.

'My sister-in-law found it upsetting, but I don't. Does it bother you?'

'No, I'm not bothered by it.'

'No, I agree. It's so . . .'

'So well-ordered. So well-designed.'

That's it: well-designed. And, most of all, it's made out of nothing. I imagine Picasso would be delighted. 'A box of matches!' he said once. 'A box of matches that is *at the same time* a box of matches and a frog!' He would like these bones that are, at the same time, the bones of a forearm and the spokes of a wheel. In actual fact, this masterpiece owes its value more to the material than to the form. The material is poor, but sufficient to inspire horror. It is not really brittle or likely to crumble, yet how fragile it is, having the drab life of hairs that carry on growing after death. If I tried to smash it, it would split lengthways against my palm, a bundle of splinters that would bend without breaking. Faced with this squalid panelling, dead and alive, rough and smooth, I draw back, slipping my hands into my pockets: I don't want to touch or even brush against anything. My mouth is hermetically sealed, but there are always the damned nostrils: in all such suspect places, they dilate and the surroundings are swallowed up in the form of a smell. Yes, I have a hint of a bone smell, a mixture, one-quarter old plaster, three-quarters bedbug. Try as I may to tell myself that I am inventing it, there is nothing to be done: I have 4,000 Capuchins up my nose. Because there were 4,000 of them, who had to be disinterred one by one. I would estimate that around the year 1810 the seeds of collective madness liberated this burst of sadistic poetry among decent monks and drove them to dash around on all fours sniffing the ground until they had unearthed these outsized truffles. There are, apparently, other cases – in Palermo, so I'm told. Towards the end of the French occupation, the order of Capuchins must have caught a heavy dose of pre-Romanticism.

'They have no right!'

Angry and disturbed, a very beautiful woman stops on the bottom stair and turns to her old husband, coming down behind her.

'They have no right!'

Her voice was too loud: the Frenchwomen are staring at her. The old husband is smiling, in apologetic embarrassment.

'They're monks, you know . . .'

She looks up at the cherubs, her lovely eyes full of fury:

'They have no right,' she says, emphatically.

I give her a smile; I quite agree: they shouldn't be allowed. But who forbids it? Christianity, perhaps; but not the Church, which profits by this capuchinade. But surely it shows a lack of reverence, playing jigsaws with an ossuary; grave-robbing, sadism, necrophilia: blatant sacrilege. My fellow-countrywomen cross themselves. These ladies are the victims of a misapprehension: they came to pay their respects to the dead only to find themselves in a place where the dead are made a mockery. I forgive them: perhaps, under their dresses, they have stockings worn away at the knees on the steps of the Scala Santa; perhaps, this very morning, they saw the telegrams piling up at Santa Maria di Aracoeli around a doll swaddled in gold cloth; you need a strong head in Rome to distinguish religion from witchcraft. If these good women, without knowing it, had not been changed into witches, they would not confuse the frisson that they feel with the pious disgust that preachers excite when they describe the decomposition of the flesh. The sovereign condemnation of the body that we find in some Spanish paintings: that is good Catholicism. Shall we show kings eaten by worms? Fine! The maggots make a shimmering, silky vestment above their torn purple robes, bunches of macaroni are coming out of their eye sockets and despite this, because of this, these bodies remain the ghastly images of ourselves: they are men decomposing, death is a human adventure. In short, one is allowed to laugh at a corpse, but only as far as the bones. The flesh flows aside and frees the trinkets that have been hiding in this pudding; after which, a soul in heaven and mineral on earth, you have earned your rest. See the calm face of death, the tidy little demise exhibited in the Protestant Cemetery: those old ladies are pure mineral. But here, the Capuchin gangrene attacks

ROME: A GHOULISH HOBBY

the bones themselves. What heresy! To persecute these rotten relics, one must believe that there is some soul remaining in them. And what hatred! These Capuchins are the great-uncles of the Milanese crowd that slapped the face of the dead Mussolini when he was hanging up by his feet. Death is a disgrace, as far as hatred is concerned: deprived of its prey, it is left dumbfounded in front of the hated corpse, like a man who has just got rid of his hiccups. These monks preserve human remains in order to extend the pleasure, they refuse to allow man to become nothing in order to be able to treat him like a thing; they snatch the bones away from their mineral destiny so that they can subject them to the caricature of some human order; they are exhumed with great pomp and ceremony so that they can be turned into building materials. Monks used to consider beauty diabolical when it belonged to time and the world, but they become aesthetes when it is a question of putting everything, even beauty, before their neighbour. They deck their chapels out with pieces of men just as the guards at Buchenwald made lampshades out of human skin. I go up to a notice and read: 'Do not write on the skulls.' Really? Why not? Armchairs, sofas, grottoes, chandeliers, repositories ... so why should these bones not also serve as paper, paperweights, blotting paper? It would only complete the degradation if one were to read on one of these bald heads: 'Here Peter and Mary made love.' But no: the best trick the Capuchins have played is to force their victims on the living as objects of adoration. The two ladies have left, the beautiful Italian woman is starting down the corridor with a handkerchief pressed to her nose; and I am off, leaving these remnants bewitched by a hatred stronger than death. The Capuchin is still there, sullen and bearded, in front of the sacristy. I go by without looking at him, slightly embarrassed, like the patron of a brothel going past the under-Madam: he knows what I have just seen; my skeleton passes next to his. I go out. It is raining. All large cities are the same in the rain. Paris is no longer in Paris, or London in London; but Rome remains in Rome. A black sky has settled above the houses, the air has changed to water and one can no longer clearly make out shapes. But thirty centuries have impregnated the walls with a sort of phosphorus: I am walking along in the rain surrounded by soft solar lighting. The Romans run in the midst of these drowned suns, laughing and waving some antique utensils which they seem uncertain how to use: umbrellas. I emerge into a sub-marine square between drowned carcasses. The rain stops, the earth emerges: the carcasses are ruins: a temple, an obelisk, in short – skeletons. I walk round the devastated Pantheon; the emballed obelisk is carried on the back of an elephant who does not look at all happy; this whole African ensemble serves to glorify Christianity. That's Rome: it emerges from the water, already dry, a whole accursed ossuary. The Church fell upon the monuments of Antiquity like the Capuchins on their colleagues: when the Popes stole the bronze of the Pantheon to ensure Christ's triumph over the pagans, it was the same violation of sepulchres. Antiquity *is alive* in Rome, with a magic life imbued with hatred, because it has been prevented from dying entirely so that it can be maintained in slavery. The result has been to give it this insidious eternity and to enslave us in turn: if we are tempted to sacrifice ourselves to these stones, it is because they are bewitched; the order of ruins fascinates us because it is both human and inhuman: human because it was established by men, inhuman because it rises alone, preserved in the alcohol of Christian hatred, self-sufficient, sinister, gratuitous, like the bed of Capuchins that I have just been to visit.

Venice from My Window

> First published in January 1953 in the review *Verve*, this is another fragment from *Queen Albemarle and the Last Tourist*. It was reprinted in *Situations IV* (1964), along with 'Rome: A Ghoulish Hobby'.

The water is too well-behaved: you can't hear it. In a moment of uncertainty, I lean out: the sky has fallen into it. The surface hardly dares to budge and its millions of pleats are vaguely rocking the sullen Relic which flashes intermittently. Further away, eastwards, the canal ends and gives way to the vast milky pool which extends as far as Chioggia: but over there, it is the water that has gone missing: my gaze skids over a glazed surface, slides and peters out within sight of the Lido, in a cheerless incandescence. It is cold; we can expect the chalkiness of a hopeless day; once again, Venice imagines herself to be Amsterdam; those grey pallors over there are palaces. That's how it is, here: air, water, fire and stone continually mix or encroach upon one another, exchanging natural attributes or normal locations, playing tag or king-of-the-castle: old-fashioned games, with nothing innocent about them; what we see here is an illusionist in training. For the inexpert tourist, this unstable compound holds many surprises: while you are sticking your nose in the air to see what the weather will be like, the entire celestial system with its meteors and clouds may perhaps be summarized at your feet in a silver coil. Today, for example, there is nothing to prove that an early-morning Assumption has not spirited away the lagoon and put it in place of the sky. I look up: no, there is nothing there except a hole, dizzying, without light or darkness, rent solely by the colourless beams of cosmic rays. Foam puffs around the surface of this inverted chasm, all in vain, to disguise the undeniable non-appearance of the sun. As soon as it can, that Celestial Body slips away, being fully aware that it is unwanted and that Venice insists on seeing it as a hated image of dictatorial rule. The city, in fact, consumes more light than Palermo or Tunis, especially if one takes into consideration the amount absorbed by the deep, dark alleyways; but she would not like to have it said that she owes the daylight that illuminates her to the generosity of a single source. Let us examine the legend: at the beginning, the lagoon was plunged into perpetual, radiant night. The patricians were happy to contemplate the constellations, whose equilibrium, founded on mutual mistrust, reminded them of the advantages of an aristocratic regime. All was for the best: the Doges, kept under close watch, were resigned to being no more than the puppets of commercial capitalism. One, Fallero, a cuckold and subject to public ridicule, did make a brief show of resistance, but he was instantly clapped into jail. His judges had no difficulty in persuading him of his culpability: he had committed a capital offence by trying to impede the forward march of History, but if he acknowledged his guilt, posterity would duly honour his unfortunate bravery. So he did indeed go to his end asking the people to forgive him and praising the justice of the sentence that was about to be carried out. After that, nothing disturbed the peace; Venice was peaceful under her stars.

Then the Grande Concilio decided to have a high frieze painted as a decoration in its Council Chamber with the portraits of dead Doges, and when they came to Fallero, these vindictive merchants ordered that his picture should be covered by a veil with these insulting words: *Hic est locus Marini Falleri decapitati pro criminibus*. Now the poor lamb really lost his temper: was this what he had been promised? Not only was posterity not rehabilitating him, but it was actually consecrating his memory to future abhorrence. In no time, his severed head had risen above the horizon and started to revolve around the town; the sky and the lagoon turned purple and the proud patricians on the Piazza San Marco hid their eyes behind horrified fingers, crying: *Ecco Marino*. Since then he has come back every twelve hours, the town has been haunted and, as ancient custom decrees that the Doge elect should appear on his balcony to throw jewels and florins to the crowd, so the murdered Potentate ironically casts floods of gold tainted by his blood across the squares.

Nowadays, this myth has been shown to be without foundation; beneath the vestibule of the chapel of the Madonna della Pace, in SS. Giovanni e Paolo, a sarcophagus was discovered containing a human skeleton with its head on its knees; so everything returned to normal, except that the Venetians, relentless in their resentment, immediately converted the sarcophagus into a water trough. No matter. By means of this story, when the gondoliers tell it, one may judge the people's state of mind and their animosity against the day star. No doubt, the city does like to find in the golden sky what it has recovered from the sea, but only provided that it remains stitched above it like the outspread emblem of its greatness, or that summer embroiders it in shafts of heraldic lightning across the heavy green hangings that it drapes down into the Canal. In this way, in Rome, that overgrown inland village, I am always happy to witness the birth of a peasant king. But when I have spent some time drifting around the canals of Venice, and seen copper fumes rising above the Rio and fickle lights take flight above my head, I can only admire this system of indirect lighting: I have a feeling of discomfort as I step out again on to the Riva degli Schiavoni and see Marino Fallero's great uncouth head floating above the subtle shimmerings of the town.

So there is no sun today; it is playing at being Louis XVI in Paris or Charles I in London. The orb has vanished, creating an imbalance; what remains are patches of light, with no top or bottom; the landscape revolves, and I with it, now hanging by my feet above an emptiness and under the frescoes of the Canal, now standing on a promontory above the ruination of a sky. I, the ceiling and the floor are the Ixion on this wheel, revolving in the most absolute immobility. In the end, I feel seasick: the void is unbearable. But, then, that's the thing: in Venice, nothing is simple, because it's not a city; it's an archipelago. How could one forget it? From your little island you look enviously across at the one opposite: over there is

. . . what? A solitude, a purity and a silence which, you would swear, are not to be found on this side. Wherever you happen to be, the real Venice is always to be found elsewhere. At least, that's how it is for me. Normally, I'm pretty much content with what I have, but in Venice, I fall prey to a sort of jealous madness. If I did not restrain myself, I should be constantly on this bridge, or that gondola, insanely searching for the secret Venice on the far side. Needless to say, as soon as I step down, everything withers. I turn around: the quiet mystery has reappeared on the other side. I have long been resigned to this fact: Venice is wherever I am not. Those princely houses over there, opposite me: they really are rising from the water, aren't they? One cannot imagine them to be floating, because houses don't float. And they cannot be resting on the lagoon: it would sink under their weight. And they must have some weight, because you can see that they are built of bricks, stone and wood. So what, then? You have to *feel* them emerge. You survey the palaces on the Grand Canal from bottom to top, enough to discover that they are caught in a sort of frozen flight, which is, if you like, their density reversed, the inversion of their mass. A surge of petrified water: it is as though they had just appeared and there was nothing there before these stubborn little outcrops. In short, they always have something of the *apparition* about them. You can guess what an apparition would be like; it would happen instantaneously and underline the paradox of the moment: pure nothingness would still persist, yet the being would already be there. When I look at the Palazzo Dario, leaning to one side, it seems to leap out aslant; I always have the feeling that it is there, very much so, but that at the same time there is nothing. All the more so, since it sometimes happens that the whole city vanishes. One evening when I was coming back from Murano, my boat was the only object as far as the eye could see: no more Venice; where the disaster had occurred, the water was vaporizing beneath the gold of the sky. For the time being, everything is clearly defined. All those fine plumes of silence are present and correct, but they do not fulfil you in the way that a great wench of a mountain landscape does, as it tumbles away beneath your window, in utter abandon. Is it a matter of expectation or challenge? There is something provocative about this maidenly reserve. And this, what is this opposite me? Is it the *Other* pavement in a residential street or the *Other* bank of a river? In any event, it is always the *Other*. If the truth be told, the left and right of the Canal are not so very dissimilar. Of course, the Fondaco dei Turchi is on one side, the Ca' d'Oro on the other. But broadly speaking you have the same little boxes, decorated with the same marquetry, and separated here and there by the roar of those great white marble city halls, eaten away by tears of dirt. Sometimes, as my gondola has slid along between these two funfairs, I wondered which was the reflection of the other. In short, it is not their differences that divide them, far from it. Imagine going up to a mirror; an image appears in it: your nose, your eyes, your mouth, your suit. It's you; or, rather, it *should* be you. Yet there is something in the reflection – something that is not exactly the green of the eyes, or the shape of the lips, or the cut of the suit – something that makes you exclaim: there is *another* person in the mirror, in place of my reflection. That gives you some idea of the impression that one has, at any time of day, from the 'Venices opposite'. Nothing would prevent me, today, from considering our funfair to be the real one and the other merely its image, very slightly shifted towards the East by the wind from the Adriatic. Just now, as I opened my window, I caused a similar window to open on the third floor of the Palazzo Loredan which corresponds to this one. Logically, I should even have appeared in it myself, but instead it was a woman who, in my place, put her head out and leant towards the water, as she unfurled a carpet like a roll of parchment and pensively began to beat it. In the event, this morning carpet-beating, the only movement to be seen, quickly subsided, the darkness of the room devoured it and the window closed behind. Desolate, these miniatures are swept away in a motionless glide. But that is not what bothers me: we are sliding together. Something else, too, an underlying strangeness, very slight, which vanishes whenever I try to pin it down and returns as soon as I start to think of something different. In Paris, when I look out of my window, I often find it impossible to understand the merry-go-round of sparkling little people, gesticulating on the terrace of the Deux Magots; and I shall never know why, one Sunday, they leapt out of their chairs and ran over to a Cadillac parked alongside the pavement, and why they laughed and berated it. No matter: what they did, I did with them; I shook the Cadillac from my vantage point, because they are my natural crowd. I need only a minute, at the very most, to join them; and when I lean out and look at them, I am already in their midst, looking out of my window, with their crazy ideas flowing through my head. It is not even true to say that I *look* at them, because when it comes down to it, I have never seen them. I *touch* them. Why? Because there is a land route between us, the reassuring crust of the planet. The *Others* are overseas.

The *Other* Venice is overseas. Two women in black are coming down the steps of Santa Maria della Salute; they scurry across the piazza, accompanied by their pale shadows, and set off across the bridge leading to San Gregorio. They are suspect and wonderful. Of course, they are women, but as distant as those Arab women whom I saw from Spain bowing down upon the soil of Africa. *Bizarre*: they inhabit those untouchable houses, Holy Women from Across the Sea. And there is another untouchable, that man who has taken up position in front of the church they have just left, so that he can look at it, as it is no doubt customary to do in this unknown island. How awful, he is *mon semblable, mon frère*, holding the Blue Guide in his left hand and with a Rolleiflex slung over his shoulder. What can be less shrouded in mystery than a tourist? Well, this one, let me tell you, frozen in suspect immobility, is as disquieting as the savages in horror films who hold apart the rushes, then disappear, after looking, with shining eyes, at the heroine walking through the swamp. He is a tourist from the Other Venice and I shall never see what he does. Opposite me, the brick and marble walls have the fleeting oddness of those small towns, perched all alone, that you see from a train window.

It is all because of the Canal. If that was an inlet of the sea, plain and simple, honestly admitting that its function was to keep human beings apart, or else a raging torrent, tamed, but still reluctant to carry boats, there would be no problem: we should just say that there was such-and-such a town over there, different from our own and, by that very fact, quite similar. A town like every other. But this Canal claims to *unite*; it makes out that it is a water highway, specifically designed for walking on foot. The stone steps leading to street level, like the white front steps of pink villas in Baltimore, the gates which should open to let a horse and carriage into the yard of a house, the little brick walls protecting a garden from the curiosity of passers-by and the long braids of honeysuckle hanging down the walls and trailing along the ground: all this invites me to run across the roadway and make sure whether the tourist on the far side is really one of my own kind and can see nothing that I cannot. But the temptation vanishes before it has altogether taken shape and has no effect except to inflame my imagination: I can already feel the ground opening up; the Canal is merely an old branch, which has rotted away beneath the moss, beneath the dry black hulls covering it, which would crack if you were to set foot on them; I am going under, I am sinking, with my arms upraised, and the last thing I see will be the indecipherable face of the Unknown Man on the Far Bank, who has now turned round to look at me and is either tormented by his inability to do anything or else enjoying the sight of me falling into the trap. In short, this false link only pretends to bring things together, the better to keep them apart; it circumvents me easily and gives me to believe that communication with my fellow men is impossible; the very proximity of that tourist is an optical illusion like the striped creatures that the Brides of the Eiffel Tower mistook for bees when in fact they were desert tigers. The waters of Venice give the whole city a nightmarish tint: it is in nightmares that tools let us down and a revolver pointed at a homicidal maniac fails to go off; it is in nightmares that we find ourselves fleeing a deadly enemy and suddenly the road starts to melt away when we try to cross it.

The tourist goes off with his mystery. He steps on to the little bridge and vanishes, leaving me alone above the motionless Canal. Today, the far bank seems still more inaccessible. The sky has torn the water, which is in tatters; who would believe that the Canal has a bottom? I can see the sky shining, beneath the water, across the great grey lagoons that divide it up. Between the two quays there is *nothing*: a scarf hastily thrown across a void. Those cottages are separated from ours by a crevice that runs through the whole earth. Two halves of Europe are moving apart, slipping away from each other, slowly at first, then faster and faster: as in *Hector Servaduc*,[1] now is the time to wave one's handkerchief. But the far quay is deserted, all the windows are shut. Already there are *two* human races, their destinies are already dividing irrevocably, but no one yet realizes it. In an hour's time, a maid will step out on to one of the balconies to beat the carpets and be aghast to see a void beneath her and a large yellow and grey mass revolving, ten thousand miles away. Venice is constantly in process of breaking up. If I am on the Riva degli Schiavoni, looking at San Giorgio, or on the Nuova Fondamenta looking at Burano, what I find opposite me is always a Land's End, emerging from a chaotic sterility, a vain interstellar agitation. This morning, the precious architecture opposite, which I never before took entirely seriously, seems to possess an impressive austerity: I see the smooth walls of a retreating human world; a little world, so limited, so enclosed, rising up conclusively like a thought in the midst of a desert. *I am not in it*. The floating island is the whole earth, round and overburdened with humanity; it is drifting away while I am left behind on the quayside. In Venice, as in a few other places, one has time to study the destiny of man from outside, with the eyes of an angel or an ape. We have missed Noah's Ark. Of course, last summer off the North Cape, that impression was even stronger: it was undeniable, or almost. The sea was a little rough; southwards the last claws of Europe scratched the sea, northwards, millions of grey waves and the solitude of a dead star. In the end, I felt we were in interstellar space, the revolving satellite of an unattainable earth. In Venice, the feeling is not so disturbing, and yet Mankind drifts away across a calm lake. The human race – or, who knows, the historical process – retracts, to become a little seething ferment, limited in space and time. I can see it in its entirety,

1. *Hector Servaduc*: a novel by Jules Verne.

from some point situated outside time and space, and experience a gentle, treacherous feeling of abandonment.

The present is what I am touching, it is the tool that I can handle, it is whatever is acting on me and whatever I can change. These delicate little chimeras are not my present; there is no simultaneity between me and them. All it takes is a little sun to change them into promises; perhaps they are reaching me from the depths of the future. On some spring mornings, I have seen them coming towards me, a floating garden, still *Other*, but like a premonition, like what I shall be tomorrow. But the gloomy brightness of this morning has killed their colours and locked them into their finiteness. They are flat, inert, carried away from me by the drift. Surely, they do not belong to my experience, but rise up from the furthest depths of a memory that is in process of forgetting them, a strange, anonymous memory, the memory of sky and water. In Venice, the slightest thing can turn light into a look. Light has only to enfold this imperceptible insular distance, this constant shifting apart, for the light to seem like a thought; it rouses or deletes the meanings scattered round the floating clusters of houses. This morning, I am reading Venice in another's eyes, a glassy stare has settled on the fake corpse, wilting the sugar candy roses and the lilies made of bread dipped in milk; everything is under a glass dome; I am watching the awakening of a dismal memory. From the depths of some ancient gaze my eyes try to fish out sunken palaces, but only bring up generalities. Am I observing or recalling? I see what I know. Or, rather, what another person knows already. Some *Other* memory is haunting mine, the remembrances of Another rise up before me, an immobile flight of dead budgerigars; everything has the weary air of what is already past, already seen. The garden of the Abbey of San Gregorio is just a patch of greenery, the simplified rose windows are architect's drawings; the façades, beyond a glacial lake, sad and rigid water-colour sketches, appear with perfect clarity, almost too perfect, crystalline, but I cannot make out any details. Small houses, small palaces, fine follies, bankers' and shipowners' whims, the Cappriccio Loredano, the Folie Barbaro: all have been more or less digested and dissolved into generalities. The Gothic Idea is applied to the Moorish Idea; the Idea of marble is united with the Idea of rosy pink; the garnet-coloured blinds and the shutters of rotten wood are now only some watercolour painter's brushstrokes: a little green, a patch of burnt topaz. What will remain in this memory, as bit by bit it forgets? A long pink and white wall, then nothing. The palaces, that which is being forgotten, are beyond my reach, no longer on the far side of the water, but in a near past, yesterday perhaps, or just now; they are becoming remoter without moving, having already lost the simple brutality of a presence, that silly, peremptory self-importance of a thing that is there and *cannot be denied*, everything that one can love, when one does love: accidental blemishes, scars, cuts, the malignant softness of moss, water and old age; all is compressed, cancelled out by this urgent and superficial light; there is no space left in them, but a sort of extent without parts: they are things known, matter worn down to transparency, and the joyful vulgarity of being is attenuated to the point of disappearing altogether. They are not there. Not entirely there. I see the plans and sketches of their architects. Death has frozen these pretty little sirens with its dull, counterfeit eyes, fixing them in a climactic contortion. Wherever I go today, I am sure to arrive on the spot five minutes too late and find only the impersonal memory of the disaster, the sky and the water meeting again, but still momentarily recalling a drowned city, before breaking up and dispersing in a spray of pure space. How superfluous I shall feel, myself, the only one present in the midst of this universal obsolescence, running a serious risk of bursting apart like one of those deep-water fishes when they are brought to the surface, because we are used to living under infinite pressure and such rarefaction is no good for us. There are days like this, here: Venice is content merely with the memory of itself and the tourist wanders in bewilderment through this hall of mirrors where water is the chief illusion.

A glimmer of hope: born out of some absence, a simple refraction of the void, a false ray of sunshine lights up the brass figure of Fortune on the terrestrial globe above the Customs House, whips up the soapy whiteness of Santa Maria, repaints some naïve and minutely tufted foliage through the iron grilles of the Abbey, changes the idea of green into wooden shutters and the idea of topaz into old blinds gnawed away by salt and sky; it draws a languid finger across the dried-out façades and causes the entire bed of roses to open; this whole expectant little world awakens. At the same time, a heavy black vessel appears in the west: a barge. In its excitement, the water comes alive beneath its burden of sky, shakes its white feathers and turns over; the sky is disturbed, it cracks and, pulverized, it scatters shining maggots upon the waves. The barge turns and vanishes into the shadows of a *rio*; it was a false alarm; the water reluctantly settles down and pulls its disordered mass into heavy, trembling heaps; already large patches of blue are re-emerging ... A sudden flight of pigeons: the sky, crazed with fear, is flying away, the landing-stage beneath my window creaks and tries to climb the wall: the *vaporetto* goes past, its passage announced by the mooing of a conch shell. This long, beige cigar is a throwback to Jules Verne and the Exhibition of 1875. There is no one on deck, but its wide wooden benches are still haunted by the gentlemen with *Cronstadt* beards who opened the Exhibition. On a little tin roof over the rear deck, painted beige, wreaths are piled in threes: perhaps they are thrown into the water as floating monuments to commemorate those who died by drowning. On the bow, a figurehead in a fur coat is open to the winds. Around her blonde hair, she has tied a muslin shawl which flaps against her neck: a dreaming passenger from 1900. There is no one to be seen, except this dead woman who knew Wagner and Verdi. A model of a ghost ship is carrying an Italian countess who died in the sinking of the *Titanic*, from one ancient festival to another. Nothing surprising: every day the Grand Canal is covered with anachronisms. It's a floating museum: the management sends items from the collection in front of the balconies of the great mansions – Gritti, Luna, Bauer-Grunewald. The water laughs with joy and plays: under the keel it's everyone for himself, wavelets are jostling and flapping away, cluck-clucking, their panic breaking beneath my feet. Boats and gondolas are gambolling around some huge barbarous, gilded posts, striped like the poles outside barbers' shops in America. The *vaporetto* is already far away, but I am the spectator to a whole nautical cavalcade, with foam, wreathed naiads, sea horses. On the quay, the ray of sunshine has vanished, once more depriving the buildings of their individuality. The silence proudly rises in red bricks above this impotent chattering. In the distance, a trumpet sounds, then stops. Here is a painting for the tourists: Eternity enclosed in Time to Come, or the intelligible World floating above matter. There is still some squawking under my windows, but never mind: silence has severed the noises with its icy scythe. In Venice, silence is visible: the challenging taciturnity of the Other Bank. Suddenly, the whole marine cortège sinks; the water is like a dream, without any sequence to its thoughts: now it has gone flat and I am leaning out over a great torpid clump; you might imagine that it envied the corpse-like rigidity of the palaces on either side. The defiant sky has not come back from aloft; the fake corpse is going green between the quays and already, appearing on the right, I can see the pale reflection of the Palazzo Dario. I look up: everything is the same again. I need heavy, weighty presences; I feel empty when I am confronted with these fine feathers painted on glass. I'm going out.

Havana

First published in the newspaper *France-Soir* in June 1960, this was the first in a series of sixteen articles by Sartre on Cuba and the recent Cuban revolution. These articles were published under the title *Storm Over Sugar: A Major Report from Cuba about Fidel Castro*. Sartre's report was also published in various forms in Buenos Aires, Havana, New York, Berlin and Moscow.

A great flood of electric light was streaming over Havana, lighting up the boulevards, the restaurants and the night-clubs. 'That's the glitter of foreign gold,' I said to myself. Because these riches are not Cuba's and the true owners of the island are the big American companies. This city, so simple in 1949, had me really confused. This time round I understood almost nothing at all.

We're staying in the rich part of town. The Hotel Nacional is a bastion of luxury, guarded by two square towers with crenellations.

The guests, who come from the mainland, are supposed to be people of wealth and taste. But those qualities so seldom coexist that if you have the first you will be granted the second without a murmur.

In the lobby I often come across big energetic well-dressed 'Yankees' (that's what they still call them in Cuba, unless they use the word 'Americano') and I'm slightly puzzled when I look at their blank faces. What can it be that's weighing them down? Is it their millions or is it their sensitivity?

Anyway, their troubles are no concern of mine.

The whole of my Paris apartment would fit inside this millionaire's bedroom of mine. How shall I describe it? There are silk hangings and little screens, flowers real and embroidered, and two double beds with every refinement, all of it just for me.

I turn the air-conditioning right up. I want to feel the cool air that's kept for the rich. With the temperature at thirty in the shade I go over over to the window with a voluptuous shiver and I watch the people sweating as they walk past.

It didn't take me long to discover why the Nacional is still incontestably the best in town. I only had to lift the blinds when I walked in. I could see the long slender ghostly shapes stretching up into the sky.

The Nacional looks out over the sea, like one of those colonial citadels which have been keeping watch over the harbour for the last three hundred years. Behind it, there is nothing, just the Vedado.

The Vedado was an exclusive hunting-ground. Men were kept out, but not the plants. These forbidden acres were being nibbled away by demented vegetation. The ground was parcelled out and all the grass suddenly disappeared in 1952. What remains is an empty lot, wracked by the great convulsions, the horrible swellings that they call skyscrapers.

Personally, I like skyscrapers. The ones on the Vedado, taken individually, look very nice. But there are dozens of them, a riot of shapes and colours. When you try to grasp them as a whole they defeat the eye. No unity at all, it's every man for himself. Many of them are hotels, the Habana, the Hilton, the Capri, and twenty others.

It's a competition to see who can have the most floors. 'Forty-five. Any advance on forty-five?' At fifty floors you are still just a pocket skyscraper. They are all craning their necks to get a glimpse of the sea over each other's shoulders. Mighty in its disdain, the Nacional has turned its back on this hubbub. Six floors, and no more. They are its patent of nobility.

Consider the issue further. The revolution is devising its own architecture which will be a thing of beauty. It is conjuring its own cities out of the earth. Meanwhile it is fighting Americanization by recourse to the colonial past.

Against the greedy motherland that was Spain, Cuba used to

HAVANA

invoke the independence and the liberty of the United States. These days, up against the United States, Cuba is looking for its national roots and bringing its deceased old colonials back to life.

The skyscrapers of the Vedado are the emblems of Cuba's degradation. They were born in the days of the dictator. The Nacional is certainly not ancient, but it came out of the ground before the rot set in, before the years of hopelessness.

The revolutionaries only feel sympathetic towards the buildings put up by their grandfathers in the early days of democracy.

The fact remains that they are merely opposing one form of luxury against another. That, I said to myself, was certainly not the real substance of Cuban national aspirations. The revolution, of course, they mentioned it to me every day. But I had to see it in action, working out its policies.

Meanwhile I went out looking for it on the streets of the capital. We walked around for hours, Simone de Beauvoir and I; we went everywhere; I felt that nothing had changed. Or rather, yes it had. In the poor quarters conditions were neither worse nor better than before. Elsewhere the visible signs of wealth had increased.

The number of cars had doubled and tripled. Chevrolet, Chrysler, Buick and De Soto, they were all there. You waved down a cab, it stopped, it was a Cadillac. These spacious sumptuous carriages paraded past at walking pace or waited in line behind a handcart.

Every evening a flood of electric light pours over the city. They're painting the sky pink and purple; neon signs everywhere are babbling about splendid things *Made in the USA*.

We knew that the government was taxing luxury imports. We also knew or thought we knew that they had imposed currency controls, that they were trying to discourage foreign holidays while taking steps to encourage domestic tourism. It didn't stop an airline company from offering, on the main sea-front, in letters of fire, to transport Cuban citizens to Miami.

There are dozens of high-class restaurants. The food is decent but the prices are high, never less than three thousand francs a head, often over five thousand.

One of these places was once a 'folly' belonging to a corrupt government minister. His Excellency had a rock garden built for himself, all pebbles and weirdly elaborate grottoes. He had the boulders carved into living shapes, decorated the cement pathways with petrified plants and animals, conscientiously reinvented the mineral world, carved stones into the shape of stones.

To bring this miniature universe to life he added a few real lions, kept in cages. The cages have remained empty.

Instead of the lions and the Minister you see a swirl of light-coloured dresses; conspicuously international gentlemen gaze absent-mindedly at the bewitched stonework. The evening I was there, they were speaking English on every table. They were dining by candlelight, which is the summit of luxury for a free citizen of the United States. Electricity will come streaming out at the flick of a switch but you prefer to abstain. You despise such ignoble abundance. Little tears of wax convey to the world at large an austere nuance in the costly ritual of nourishment.

The night-clubs are more numerous than ever. There is a whole swarm around the Prado. Above their doors electricity comes back into its own. Seductive names flash on and off, dazzling your eyes as you walk by.

At the Tropicana, the biggest dance-hall in the world, there was a crowd around the green baize tables. Were they gambling, even in Cuba? Was there still gambling? One of our companions replied curtly: 'There is gambling.'

Slot-machines have all been banned. But the National Lottery is still allowed. There are casinos and in all the big hotels there are gaming-rooms.

As for prostitution, they closed down a few brothels, in the beginning, but since then they have been allowed to carry on. Thinking over this rather negative impression, I often said to myself, during the first few days: 'Revolutions in their early stages are all, or almost all, characterized by their austerity. So where is the austerity in Cuba?'

Today, on a cloudless morning, I am sitting at my table and through the windows I can see the congealed confusion of rectangular parallelepipeds and I feel cured of that dreadful ailment which had

HAVANA

all but concealed from me the truth about Cuba: *retinitis pigmentosa*.

That is not a phrase in my vocabulary. Until this morning I had no idea of the malady to which it refers. To tell you the truth I have just come across it whilst reading a speech by a Cuban government minister, Oscar Pinos Santos, given on 1 July 1959: 'After just a few days or a few hours in Havana,' he said, 'I do not believe that a foreign tourist can grasp that Cuba is one of the nations most afflicted by that international tragedy we call underdevelopment . . .

'All that he will have seen of the island is a city with splendid boulevards selling high-quality goods in the most modern shops. How is he to believe in our poverty when he counts the number of TV aerials? Won't all the signs lead him to think that we are rich, equipped with modern machinery and thus capable of high levels of productivity?'

There. The uninformed visitor has every excuse. Reassured, I told myself I would be found not guilty. I was wrong. They get you suddenly. If he lets himself be duped and leaves the island feeling pleased with himself, then the tourist has had it.

There is a disease of the eyes, says Pinos Santos, which is called *retinitis pigmentosa*. It brings a loss of peripheral vision. Anyone who takes home an optimistic image of Cuba is suffering from just such a disease. They see what's right in front of them, but they see nothing else.

Retinitis: a very useful word. But I realized my great mistake several days ago. I felt my prejudices crumbling. All of a sudden it occurred to me that I would only get at the truth about this city if I approached it from the opposite angle.

It was night. I was flying back from a trip to the interior of the island. The pilot called me into the cockpit; we were about to land. We were already plunging down towards a sparkling carpet of diamonds, rubies and turquoises.

The memory of a recent conversation flashed into my mind and spoilt my enjoyment of that peninsula of fire set against the dark expanse of the sea. These treasures did not belong to Cuba at all. A Yankee company was in charge of generating and distributing electricity for the whole island.

They had invested Yankee dollars in Cuba but their headquarters was back in the USA and that was where the profits went.

The lights got brighter, the precious stones grew in size until they turned into ripening fruit, the dark fabric of the night was torn apart. Down at ground level I could see lights, but I said to myself, 'That's the glitter of foreign gold.'

Thereafter, in the evening, when I pressed the light-switch, I knew that my room was rescued from darkness thanks to a foreign company, the same one, so they told me, which has the electricity monopoly in all or nearly all the countries of Latin America. Now I understood the real meaning of the torch brandished aloft by that huge, hollow Statue of Liberty in New York harbour. North America brings light to the peoples of the New World by selling them, at a nice profit, their own electricity.

The Cuban telephone system also belongs to an American company which has invested its surplus capital in the venture. When the Cubans pick up the telephone they are in fact communicating with the benign permission of the United States.

I had got it all the wrong way round. What I had thought were signs of wealth were in fact signs of poverty and dependence.

Whenever a telephone rang, whenever a neon light flashed, a tiny bit of a dollar left the island and headed for the United States where all the other little bits were waiting to come together again in one big dollar.

What can you say about a country whose public services are farmed out to foreigners? There is a clash of interests. What can they do, the Cubans, against the giant monopoly trust that sells electricity all across Latin America? That company must have a foreign policy and Cuba is just a pawn in the game.

Now a nation forges its unity in so far as its members are able to communicate with each other. If a foreigner, whoever he be, imposes himself, whenever he likes, as a permanent intermediary on that nation's citizens, if they all have to go through him to comprehend their work, their education or even their private lives, if the electrification of the countryside is approved or delayed in another capital city, by the inhabitants of another country, in the interests of another country, then the nation is fractured, afflicted in its very being. In the act of communication its citizens are separated. The US monopolies in Cuba have set up a State within the State. They rule over an island rendered anaemic by the haemorrhaging of its currency.

Every time the big cranes lowered a brand new American car down on to the quayside, the blood flowed out faster and faster. They said to me, 'Those cars cost us millions every year.'

I looked at them more closely and eventually I realized that they bore the faint stamp of the revolution. They were being polished, true enough. Their badges and their chrome bits were gleaming. But they were slightly out of date. The newest vehicles were at least a year or even eighteen months old. In Chicago and Milwaukee their twin sisters were already on the scrap-heap.

In short, Cuba was behind the times. The government knew what it was doing when it put such heavy taxes on luxury imports. The owners of the big cars would no longer be able to keep up the pace.

Gazing at the endless parade of cars which had so surprised me the day before, I said to myself that they were corpses. It was the revolution that had brought them back to life, decreed that they be driven carefully and made to last a long time.

These adoptive sons of Cuba would serve their country for many years to come. After being patched up ten or twenty times they would have saved the island ten or twenty times the millions they had originally cost. In this sector at least the bleeding had been stopped.

I then understood more clearly the system that was clogging the streets of Havana with these great big machines. I noticed that they were packed in six or seven to a car and that the drivers wore casual or even shabby clothes.

In Europe, cars go with being well-dressed, with being well-off. They are bought by the middle classes, by and large.

But Cuba has been under American influence for many years. In America the petit-bourgeois and even the best-paid workers have enough cash to buy cars.

The Cubans imitate the Yankees but without having their income.

The most expensive cars were within reach of people on small incomes if they were happy to starve to death. So they starved gently, without complaining, behind the scenes, so as to appear in public at the wheel of a Chrysler.

I also learnt to see the Vedado and its skyscrapers in a different light. One evening I was asking Franqui, the editor of the newspaper *Revolución*, about the fever that gripped the Vedado in 1952.

– Who did the building?
– They were Cubans.
– Where did they get the capital?
– From Cuba.
– Are they that rich?
– Not at all. There were some large investments but mainly it was modest private savings. Imagine a shopkeeper about to retire with a lifetime's savings of five or even ten thousand dollars. Where are they going to invest it when Cuban industries don't exist?
– Did nobody propose to set them up?
– Speculators did, now and again. Malcontents who wanted to build up a business. It never came to any good. The big landowners didn't like it at all. They spoke out and the foolhardy manufacturer got the message eventually. Anyway they never could have sold a single share. That's how we are. It all goes into buildings. For the middle classes that's the best investment.

Now I think I can look beyond the buildings, and see just how these modern palaces spring from the bad habits of an underdeveloped country.

Wealth, in Cuba, takes the form of land. It turns a few families into millionaires, almost into aristocrats. The bourgeoisie, impressed by the apparent fixity of land, imagine that it guarantees the stability of ground-rents.

They can't afford fields, so they buy a little plot. They can't grow anything on it, so they build all over it instead. Rather than risky industrial ventures they prefer the bogus stability of rents. Machines go round, things change, they need replacing, everything moves on, where does it all end?

Think of *real* estate though. Even the phrase is reassuring. Bricks and mortar are inert, stable. And you stay where you are because you never have to move.

At the instigation of Batista and speculators all around him, these modestly rich citizens of a poor country threw themselves blindly into the mad enterprise of competing with Miami. Now they find they're left with these splendid monoliths to look after. The Vedado skyscraper is a copy which just doesn't match the original. In the United States they installed the machinery first and that determined the style of residence.

In Cuba this sudden crop of skyscrapers means one thing only: the stubborn refusal of the bourgeois investor to industrialize the country.

Translated by Geoffrey Wall

Photos of China

> Written in Moscow, the year before Sartre's first visit to China in the autumn of 1955, this was the preface to a book of photographs by Henri Cartier-Bresson entitled *China in Transition* (1955). Cartier-Bresson's photographs were taken in 1948–9, during the climactic months of the Chinese revolution. Sartre's preface was republished in *Situations V* in 1964.

The picturesque originates in war and a refusal to understand the enemy: in reality, our first knowledge of Asia came from soldiers and overwrought missionaries. Later, travellers arrived – merchants and tourists – who are soldiers cooled down: their pillage is called 'shopping' and their rapes are carried out at considerable expense in specialized outlets. But the underlying attitude has not changed: the natives are less often killed, but they are despised wholesale, which is a civilized form of massacre; one indulges in the aristocratic pleasure of enumerating *separations*. 'I cut my hair, he plaits his; I use a fork, he uses chopsticks; I write with a goosequill, he paints his characters with a brush; I think straight, he thinks crooked; have you noticed that he detests travelling in straight lines and is only happy when everything is bent and twisted?' This is called the game of anomalies: if you can find a new one to add, if you can discover a fresh reason for not understanding, you will be awarded points for sensitivity in your own country. When there are those who in this way reconstruct their fellow men as a mosaic of insurmountable differences, one must not afterwards be surprised when they wonder how it is possible to be Chinese.

As a child, I was a victim of the picturesque: everything was done

PHOTOS OF CHINA

to make the Chinese intimidating. I was told about rotten eggs – they were very fond of them; about men sawn between two planks; about reedy and discordant music. In the world around me, there were some things in particular which were called Chinese: they were tiny and terrible, they slipped between one's fingers, attacked from behind and suddenly burst into some weird racket, shadows gliding as fish do along the wall of an aquarium, hooded lanterns, incredible and pointless refinements, ingenious tortures, chiming hats. Then there was the Chinese soul, which was simply described as impenetrable. 'Orientals, you know . . .' Negroes didn't bother me: I had been told that they were harmless, good-natured creatures; mammals, like ourselves. But Orientals scared me: like crabs scurrying between two furrows in a rice paddy or locusts descending on a vast plain and destroying everything. We are the lords of fishes, lions, rats and monkeys; the Chinese is a superior arthropod, who reigns over the arthropoda.

Then along came Michaux, the first to show the Chinese with no soul or shell, China without lotus or Loti.

A quarter of a century later, Cartier-Bresson's album completes the task of demystification.

There are photographers who incite war, because they indulge in literature. They hunt out a Chinese man who looks more Chinese than the rest, and eventually they find one. Then they make him adopt a typically Chinese pose and surround him with chinoiseries. What do they photograph? *A* Chinaman? No, the Idea of China.

Cartier-Bresson's photographs never gossip. They are not ideas, but they give one ideas. Unintentionally. His Chinese are disconcerting: most of them never look quite Chinese enough. If the tourist is a wit, he will wonder how they manage to tell one another apart. But, for myself, after looking through this album of photographs, I wonder rather how we ever managed to confuse them and put them all in the same drawer. The Idea of China is starting to fade into the distance: it is just a convenient designation. What remains are humans who look alike *as human beings*. These are living, physical presences, not yet stamped and classified. We should be grateful to Cartier-Bresson for his nominalism.

CITIES

The picturesque retreats into language. If I were to describe this old eunuch for you in words, how exotic he would sound! He lives in a monastery, with other eunuchs. He has a jar in which he lovingly preserves his 'jewels'; in the days when the Empress Tseu-hi, the Oriental Agrippina, was still only a concubine, some evenings he would undress her, wrap her in a purple shawl and carry her in his arms to the imperial bed: Agrippina concubine, empress undress – it rhymes – purple shawl: each of these terms casts its light on the others. What is missing is everything that can be offered to the sight: reality. Now, open the album. What do you see first and foremost? A life unravelling, an old man. What gives him this lined, waxen face is not a result of castration, it is the universal effect of old age – old age has tanned his skin, not China. Does he look like a woman? Maybe, but that is because the difference between the sexes is gradually effaced by age. He has lowered his eyes, slyly, sanctimoniously, holding out a hand for the note which is being casually waved in front of him by a laughing interpreter. Where are the lights of the imperial court? Where are the empresses of yesteryear? For all I know, he may be a eunuch; but what difference would it make, at his age, if he were not? The picturesque vanishes, goodbye to our *European* poetry; what remains is the material truth, the poverty and greed of an old parasite from a bygone regime.

Here is a peasant eating his lunch. He has come into town to sell the produce of his land. Now, he is eating rice soup, in the open, with the voracity of a countryman, surrounded by townsfolk who take no notice of him: alone, starving, tired, he has at this very moment a brother in every major agricultural city of the world, from the Greek driving his sheep along the avenues of Athens to the Chleuh, down from the mountains, wandering through the streets of Marrakesh. Here we have other peasants, who were driven by hunger to Peking, and stayed there. What can one do in a capital city with no industry, when any kind of craftwork requires a long apprenticeship? They drive bicycle rickshaws. We hardly glanced at them: there was something familiar about this means of transport; we had our own *vélo-taxis* during the Occupation. True, they seemed cleaner. We put our dirt elsewhere. And poverty is the best distributed thing in the world: we have no shortage of poor. Admittedly, we have abandoned the custom of hitching them to sedan chairs for them to carry the rich; but are they any the less our beasts of burden for that? We harness them to machines.

And who gets carried? Respectable gents, in trilby hats and long robes, the very same who are now leafing through the pages of some books, on a bookseller's stall, and who congratulate themselves on being able to read. Do you laugh at their robes? Well, then, you'd better laugh at our priests. At their hats? Then laugh at yourself. The uniform of the élite, over there, is a trilby and a long robe; for us, it's a three-piece suit. In any case, what's ludicrous, with them and with us, is the existence of élites, of gentlemen who are alone in being able to read or do sums, and who wear the mark of their superiority on their backs.

Pictures bring human beings closer together when they are materialist, in other words when they begin at the beginning, with bodies, needs, work. To hell with rotten eggs and sharks' fins; do you think these foods are exotic because nearly 40 million French people don't know how they taste? Then they are still more exotic in China since 400 million Chinese, or thereabouts, have never eaten them. Four hundred million Chinese who, like Italian day-labourers, are hungry; who, like French peasants, are exhausted by their work; and who are exploited by the family of Chiang Kai-shek, just as three-quarters of Westerners are by the great feudal dynasties of capitalism. Having said that, of course, we don't speak their language or share their customs; but there will be plenty of time to talk about differences. We have to learn what divides us; what brings us together can be seen at a glance. This man approaching us: you have to decide straight away if you want to see him *first* as a German, a Chinaman, a Jew . . . or firstly as a man. And by deciding what he is, you will determine what you are. Turn that coolie into a Chinese grasshopper and you will immediately become a French frog. Pose your models and you will give them time to become something else, something different from you, different from mankind, different from oneself. A 'pose' gives us the élite and the pariahs, generals and Papuans, native Bretons, wily Orientals and charitable old ladies: the ideals. Cartier-Bresson's snaps catch mankind on the hop, leaving it no time to be superficial. At a hundredth of a second we are all *the same*, all at the heart of our human condition.

Out of this vast agricultural empire, they only show us the towns: the Communists are in control of the countryside. But every photo uncovers the evils of a backward economy: small craftwork, overpopulation, poverty. 'The Chinese,' Michaux says, 'are a people of born craftsmen . . . Anything you can find by tinkering and making do, the Chinese have found.' This is true: look at the merchants, with their mischievous, patient faces; look at the hands, nimble, never idle, rolling two walnuts between them, just as Greek hands tell the amber beads of a rosary; they were made to fix things and to spirit them away: 'In China, cunning is not at all associated with Evil, but with everything; virtue is whatever is most cleverly devised.' All of them, of course, are schemers, all craftsmen, artists, conmen. But if you believe that they owe their craftiness to the pigmentation of their skins, the shape of their skulls or their diet, I would simply ask you: which is more ingenious, the more wily and more resourceful: a Chinese or a Neapolitan? Naples v. Peking: more Chinese than China? It would probably be a draw. Naples would lead with counterfeit anoraks allegedly stolen; with watches, really stolen, not really for sale; cars with doctored meters. If you buy your tobacco from a retailer in the street, God knows what you'll be smoking. But what about the street-seller whose stall is watched over by one Chiang Kai-shek and two Sun Yat-sens? His eyes are heavy, his lip is drooping; he seems too stupid to be dishonest, yet he has opened every packet he has for sale, unpacked the cigarettes and filled them with rubbish which he disguises at both ends with a pinch of tobacco. Made industrious by the absence of industry, these and those spend their time repairing, supporting, containing, tying up; they fill holes, stop walls and roofs from collapsing, then, in the space between two disasters, they sit on the edge of the pavement and wait for the rich to come along, devising complicated schemes for relieving them of a few pence. Their ingenuity and their good-natured dishonesty are explained by poverty and the absence of machines.

PHOTOS OF CHINA

The Asian crowds. We must be grateful to Cartier-Bresson for not having had the idea of conveying how they seethe and mill about; because they don't seethe, or very little; they organize themselves. Of course, they invade everything and destroy everything: these old women walking along with little steps, little bows, little smiles – these are old servants, the Mother Goddesses of the crowd. One of them has only to go, shyly, into a rich person's house, to visit a servant, who may be her niece or her cousin, and immediately they are all there, heaven knows how, and the place is swarming. The house is too small to hold them, the walls collapse. Americans in particular dread these numberless female visitors.

But no one has the right to compare this swarming with an invasion of locusts. The Chinese crowds are organized: they occupy the pavements and spill out over the roadway; but each, as soon as this happens, occupies his own space while *recognizing* his neighbour's. Look at those hairdressers: each has his own living space and no one tries to dispute it with him. That is because this crowd, with its wide, loose meshes, bleeds when you squeeze it; in Shanghai, the government puts gold on the market and buyers queue for it: the multitude is suddenly condensed. Result: seven deaths and several broken legs. In China, the face in the crowd has to keep a respectful distance: the famous politeness of the Chinese is first and foremost an emergency measure to avoid suffocation. Everywhere, Cartier-Bresson allows us to sense this phantom proliferation, broken down into minute constellations; this unobtrusive, but ever-present threat of death. I love the crowd as I love the sea and for me these Chinese multitudes seem neither fearsome nor even alien; they do kill, but they bury their dead in their midst and absorb the blood as a sheet of blotting-paper absorbs ink: out of sight, out of mind. Our mob is crueller and more excitable. When it withdraws, it leaves its dead behind and the abandoned pavements are spattered with red. That's the only difference.

In the early years of the century, tourists had a great fondness for poverty. Captain Carpeaux, son of the sculptor Carpeaux, wrote in 1911 regretting the fact that some Chinese Haussmann had built boulevards through the imperial city: 'Alas, what has happened to the Peking high street which was so picturesquely full of life, so deliciously dirty and dilapidated? Where are all those extraordinary pedlars with their tiny displays of nameless objects? . . . Everything has been driven out, removed, knocked down, levelled, and the great, broken, centuries-old paving stones have vanished, together with the grimy little pedlars, who were so curious to see . . .'

'Grimy', 'deliciously dirty', 'extraordinary': after all, this is what happens to people when they are ground under the heel of poverty; and they complain?

Blessed be cold and hunger for inspiring so many comical novelties and peculiar notions. Added to which, the poor are conservative: they keep their old furniture, old clothes, old tools, because they can't afford to replace them. You could find the traditions of ancient China in their hovels. What pomp and ceremony there was in these royal rags, not to mention the delightful tracery of grime on a young breast. Have we changed so much? We no longer go and visit the poor in their homes; one might even think that we try to avoid them. That's because they've been overdoing it. For some time now, they have been an embarrassment to the rich.

Imagine Barrès[1] in Peking. Why not? It might be in 1908, and he would be walking slowly back from some hospitable occasion, considering that he might write a 'Chinese *Bérénice*'. Suddenly he stops and looks down at a heap of fabric lying at his feet. In China, just think, when a child dies, they tie it up in a red cloth and leave it at night-time in the corner of a building; in the morning the refuse collection trucks will take it away to the common grave. Now Barrès is getting emotional: how could one not be touched by this pretty custom; and what a pure artistic pleasure he takes in looking at these little scarlet heaps, adding a touch of bright, lively colour to the greyness of dawn. Near this one, someone has left a dead cat. Dead cat, dead child: two vaguish little souls. Barrès unites them in a single funeral prayer and then moves on to make some more elevated comparisons: at this very moment, perhaps, they are carry-

---

1. *Barrès*: Maurice Barrès (1862–1923), novelist, pamphleteer, patriot and authoritarian traditionalist.

ing the lovely warm body of a concubine, wrapped in purple silk, towards the imperial bed. One little warm body, one little cold body; and the same bloodstain on each of them. Now we have it: blood, eroticism, death. Lucky Barrès: he in turn is dead now, carrying with him to the grave the secret of a clear conscience. While we who remain, we saw children die like rats in the blitz or in the Nazi camps: when they show us an impressive scene of red earth and palm trees, and in it flies clustering round the eyes of new-born children, we turn away, and our conscience feels uneasy. How can you explain that? In a small street in Naples, one day, a stable door opened on a dark cavern. On a huge double bed, a six-month-old baby was lying, tiny, lost, his face wrinkled like cloth, looked as though he was wearing make-up: he was the spitting image of the ninety-year-old cardinal who said mass at St Peter's the Sunday before. The child was dead. For me, it was enough just once to see that death in Naples, indiscreetly displayed: I am unable to appreciate fully the poetic value of the shroud that covers these poor little Chinese: I look right through it and perceive a wrinkled face, too young to be childish. One must conclude that we have become insensitive: we no longer think to conjure up the silken shawl and the silky skin of lovely Tseu-hi. It merely occurs to us that we must prevent children from dying. And, confronted with this murdered child, waste from the Kuomintang, we make a wish for the victory of the Eighth Army. This album is an obituary: it announces the end of tourism. It gently informs us, without any unnecessary pathos, that poverty has lost its picturesque charm and will never regain it.

Yet it is there, unbearable but unobtrusive. On every page, it makes itself known, by three actions: carrying, rummaging, pilfering.

In every capital of poverty, the poor carry parcels, which they never let out of sight: when they sit down, they put their packets down beside them and keep an eye on them. What do they have in there? Everything: wood gathered in a park, surreptitiously, crusts of bread, wire pulled off a fence, scraps of cloth. If the load is too heavy, they pull it or push it, in wheelbarrows or handcarts. Poverty always looks as though it's doing a midnight flit. In Peking, in Shanghai, in Nankin, everyone is pushing and pulling: these men are trying to move a cart; they are on a bridge, the road is uphill, they have to try even harder. Some boys are hanging around nearby, always ready to lend a hand for a few coppers. Like the unemployed man in *Due soldi di speranza*[2] who positions himself in the middle of a hill and leads cab horses by the reins. The building in the background is a lighthouse. On top of this lighthouse is the eye of the West; it turns constantly, sweeping across China: the three upper stories have been reserved for foreign correspondents. How high up they are! Far too high to see what is happening at ground level. They are dancing in the midst of the sky with their wives and mistresses. Meanwhile, down below, the porters are pushing their carts and Chiang Kai-shek is being beaten by the Communist armies. The Americans cannot see the low-roofed shacks of China, or the peasants up in arms, or the porters. But the porters have only to look up to see the lighthouse of America.

In every capital of poverty, people rummage. They rummage around the ground and underground. They gather around dustbins and slip into the midst of rubbish tips: 'Whatever others throw away is mine; whatever is no use to them is good enough for me.' On a piece of waste ground near Peking, the garbage piles up. This is the detritus of poor people: they have already sieved everything and rummaged through their own cast-offs, and left, reluctantly, only what is uneatable, unusable, indescribable, unmentionable. Yet the herd is there, on all fours. Every day, all day, it rummages.

In every capital of poverty, people pilfer. Is it theft? No, gleaning. These packages have just been unloaded. If they stay another hour on the quayside, they will vanish. No sooner have they been put down, than the crowd hurries forward and surrounds them. Everybody tries to tear off a handful of cotton: a lot of handfuls make a garment. I recognize the look in the eyes of these women; I have seen it in Marseille, in Algiers, in London, in the streets of Berlin: it is serious, swift and harassed, a mixture of anxiety and avidity. One must take before one is taken. When the packages have been loaded on to a truck, the children run after it, holding out their

---

2. *Due soldi de speranza*: film (1952) by Renato Castellani.

hands. Meanwhile, in Nankin, they are shooting at random in the streets. Alone in the midst of a boulevard, a man is leaning over an armchair with the stuffing coming out: he wants that stuffing. If he doesn't stop one of the bullets whistling around his ears, he will have garnered enough fuel for one hour on one winter's day.

Every day, the poor carry, rummage, pilfer. Every day, the craftsmen repeat their traditional gestures; every morning, at dawn, the officers exercise in the gardens of the Forbidden City, while aged ghosts slide through the corridors of the palaces. Every morning, Peking resumes the face it wore the night before, the week before, the millennium before. Here, in our countries, industry breaks the boundaries of everything; but why should anything change over there? Cartier-Bresson has photographed eternity.

A fragile eternity: it is a constantly repeated melody, and to stop it one must break the record. And that indeed is what is about to happen. History is at the city gates: it is being made from day to day, in the ricefields, the mountains and the plains. One more day, and one more after that, and it will be over; the old record will break into pieces. These timeless photos are precisely fixed in time: they record, for ever, the last moments of Eternity.

Between the circular time of old China and the irreversible time of the new China, there is an intermediary stage, a gelatinous space equally distanced from History and from repetition: this is the period of waiting. The city has unravelled the skein of its thousand daily gestures; no one files, or trims, or scrapes, or pares, or fixes, or polishes any more. Giving up their little living spaces, their ceremonials, their neighbours, people gather in great, formless masses, in front of the stations or on the platforms. The houses empty; so do the workshops; so do the markets. The crowds gather in unaccustomed places, press together, coagulate. Their delicate structures are crushed. Heavy, dense images replace the airy ones of old Peking. Waiting. When they are not taking responsibility for History, the masses experience great events as endless periods of waiting. The masses of Peking and Shanghai are not making History; they are undergoing it. So, too, for that matter, are the policemen guarding them, the soldiers walking around among them, returning from the front, constantly returning from the front but never going there, the mandarins taking flight, the generals escaping. Those who are making History have never seen the great imperial cities, they know only mountains and fields: the fate of China was decided in the fields and in the mountains. For the first time, a capital is waiting on the wishes of the countryside: History will appear in the form of a procession of peasants. Townspeople think of the country as a neutral space which serves to join cities together, and which armies march over and ravage until they decide, in the cities, to make peace. But now, suddenly, it is finding itself: it is living flesh and muscle; in the muscle, the cities are embedded like grains of urate. But the crowds are not afraid. Up there, the eye of America takes fright and turns round and round. At ground level, however, they had known for a long time that the Communists had won. The rich curse Chiang Kai-shek as much as they curse Mao Tse-tung. The peasants want to go home: since everything is in the hands of the Communists, one might as well find them in the villages as in the towns. The workers and the poor start to hope: the thousand individual expectations from the time of Repetition have come together and melted into a single hope. The rest of the population goes on marches and prays for peace – for any peace whatever. It's a way of killing time: before joining the priesthood and burning paper sticks, you take the opportunity to settle your personal affairs. You go, on your own account, to rub the nose of an idol, infertile women press their bellies against those of the statues, and after the ceremony, in the large chemist's shop near the temple, they will buy pellets of dried herbs which will restore their ardour to flagging husbands and warm the feet of wives.

While the authorities stay in place, the crowd stays under pressure. The police surround and contain it; but, unlike our police, they seldom hit out. We have one here who is getting impatient because the people are pressing in on him. He raises his leg: is he about to kick out? No, he stamps in a puddle, spattering the people, who draw back. But the gentlemen of the Kuomintang don't stay where they are: they start to drift away. Now there are a thousand left, now a hundred. Soon, there will be none. Those gentlemen who are unable to leave, whether yellow skinned or white, are all green with fear. During the interregnum, the baser instincts of the people are unleashed: there will be pillage, rape, murder. Suddenly, the bourgeois of Shanghai long for the Communists: better any order than the fury of the mob.

This time, it really is the end. The leading citizens have gone, the last cop has vanished; only the middle classes and the people are left in town. Pillage, not pillage? What an admirable mob: as soon as it felt the lifting of the burden from its shoulders, it hesitated for a moment then, little by little, was decompressed: these vast masses return to their former gaseous state. Look at the photos: everyone has started to run. Where are they going? To loot? Not even that: they went into the fine abandoned houses and rummaged around, as only yesterday they used to rummage in the garbage tips. What did they take? Almost nothing: the floorboards, to light their fires. Everything is calm; so now let them come, the peasants from the North: they will find a well-ordered city.

Do you remember June 1940, and those funereal giants driving in their lorries and tanks through an empty Paris? That was certainly picturesque: not much pleasure, but lots of pomp, blood and death. The Germans wanted a ceremonial victory. They had one, and the handsome SS men, standing in their armoured cars, were like priests, executioners, martyrs, Martians – everything except men. Now, open the photo album. Children and young people have gathered in crowds on the victors' route; they are amused, curious and calm, they cross their arms and look. Where is the victory? Where is the terror? This is the first Communist soldier anyone has seen in Shanghai since the start of the civil war; he is a little man with a good-looking dark face, carrying his equipment on the end of a stick, as our soldiers used to do when they came back from the wars. This exhausted little man, these young spectators: you might think it was the finish line of a marathon. Now turn the page and look at them from behind, these soldiers of the Eighth Army, under their parasols, dwarfed by a wide avenue in Shanghai. Did these peasants take the city, or has the city taken them? They sit down.

CITIES

On the road, on the pavement, at the very spot where, only a day ago, the crowd was sitting, waiting for them. The crowd has now got up and is pressing itself right up against them, towering over them and watching. Normally, conquerors hide when they want to rest, but with these, you would think that they are not worried about intimidating anybody. And yet, they it was who routed the troops of the Kuomintang (who had been armed by the Americans), and it was they who held back the Japanese Army. They seem crushed by the high buildings around them. The war is over; now they must win the peace. The photos brilliantly convey the solitude and the anxiety of these peasants in the heart of the magnificent and rotten city. Behind their drawn blinds, the gentlemen recover their confidence: 'We'll do what we want with them.'

It did not take long for the gentlemen to change their tune. But that is another story and Cartier-Bresson doesn't tell it. But we must thank him for having succeeded in showing us the most human of victories, the only one which one can unreservedly love.

Sexualities

'Beneath the words of love, a hairy mass...' This cool dismayed curiosity is the key to Sartre's sexual world. It makes for a memorably detailed and disenchanted experience of the Other as a realm of enticingly warm but seldom fragrant flesh. Sartre always loathed what he called *letting go*. 'Even as a little boy I thought it horrible ... I really disliked my mother's self-abandon ... it pulls you down into the past.'[1] Physically ugly, he had to be tough, powerful and eloquent. Swimming, boxing, body-building and sexual seduction were all part of a pattern of ferocious activity.

He was well versed in the darker arts of love. In addition to a prosaic French schoolboy expertise on the subject of brothels, Sartre knew all the lofty fetishistic ecstasies of Baudelaire's sex-poems and the melancholy-ludicrous neurasthenia of Proust's Baron Charlus. From the Surrealists, with their mock-evangelical cult of Eros, he took a vision of the pedantically bizarre shadow-world of human desire. When he read Freud he immediately began a long and fruitful quarrel with the very notion of the unconscious.

In Sartre's fiction the characters are always strongly embodied, insistently aware of themselves and of each other as physical sexual creatures. In the philosophy too, Self – whatever its aspirations and ideas – must abide the disconcerting imperatives of human physiology. The emphasis is familiar. We find it in Zola. We find it in Joyce. But Sartre gives it a special tragi-comic twist. In a marvellous throwaway phrase from *Being and Nothingness*, our sexuality is always *cette immense affaire*.

---

1. *Entretiens*, 402.

What Is Desire?

This is a section from *Being and Nothingness* (1943). Its four-headed subject is *Indifference, Desire, Hate, Sadism*. It corresponds to pages 382–407 of the 1958 translation by Hazel Barues.

My original attempt to grasp the free subjectivity of the Other, through his objectivity-for-myself, is *sexual desire*. One may be surprised at finding a phenomenon which is usually classed among 'psycho-physiological reactions' cited at the level of primary attitudes which simply exhibit our original manner of Being-for-Others. Indeed, for most psychologists, desire, as a fact of our consciousness, is closely linked to the nature of our sexual organs and can only be understood in conjunction with an extensive study of these organs. But since the differentiated structure of the body (mammalian, viviparous, etc.) and consequently the particular structure of the sexual organs (uterus, fallopian tubes, ovaries, etc.) belong to the realm of absolute contingency and in no way derive from the ontology of consciousness or of the *Dasein*, it would appear to be the same for sexual desire. Just as the sexual organs are a contingent and particular formation of our bodies, in the same way the desire which corresponds to them should be a contingent function of our psychic life; in other words, one that can only be described through an empirical psychology based on biology. This is evident in the term *sexual instinct*, which is reserved for desire and all the psychic structures associated with it. The word 'instinct' is always, in fact, applied to contingent formations in the psyche which have the double character of being coextensive with the whole duration of that life – or, at any rate, of not deriving from our 'history' – and, nonetheless, that of not being able to be deduced from the very essence of the psyche. This is why existential philosophies have not considered it necessary to take account of sexuality. Heidegger, in particular, makes not the slightest allusion to it in his existential analysis, so that we are left with the impression that his *Dasein* is asexual. And, indeed, one can doubtless consider that, for 'human reality', it is a contingency whether one defines oneself as 'masculine' or 'feminine'; one can certainly argue that the problem of sexual differentiation has nothing to do with that of *Existence* (*Existenz*), since man exists neither more nor less than woman.

This argument is not entirely convincing. We are prepared, at a pinch, to accept that sexual difference belongs to the realm of facticity; but should this mean that the For-itself is sexual 'by accident' through the pure contingency of having this or that kind of body? Can we accept that the immensely important question of sexual life is a mere appendage of the human condition – when it seems at first sight that desire, and its converse, sexual repulsion, are fundamental structures of being-for-others? Obviously, if sexuality originates in the *sexual organ*, as a contingent, physiological determinant of mankind, then it cannot be indispensable to the being of the For-Others. Then, perhaps, one would be entitled to ask if the problem is not by chance of the same order as the one we encountered in relation to feelings and sense organs. Man, they say, is a sexual being because he possesses a sexual organ. And suppose the opposite were the case? Suppose the sexual organ was only the instrument and, as it were, the *image* of some underlying sexuality? Suppose man were only to possess a sexual organ because he is originally and fundamentally a sexual being, since he is a being who exists in the world in relation to other humans? Infantile sexuality precedes the physiological maturation of the sexual organs; eunuchs do not, by virtue of their being such, cease to feel desire. Nor do many old men. The fact of having at one's disposal a sexual organ capable of fertilizing and procuring an orgasm only represents one phase and one aspect of our sexual life. There is a mode of sexuality 'with the possibility of satisfaction', and the developed sexual organ represents and concretizes this possibility. But there are other modes of sexuality, deriving from non-satisfaction; and, if one takes these into account, one must accept that sexuality appears at birth and does not disappear until death. In any case, neither the tumescence of the penis, nor any other physiological phenomenon, can explain or incite sexual desire – any more than the vaso-constriction or dilation of the pupil (or mere awareness of these physiological changes) can explain or incite fear. In both cases, if we are to understand them, though the body has an important role to play, we must turn to the being-in-the-world and being-for-others: I desire a human being, not an insect or a mollusc, and I desire this human to the extent that he or she is and I am situated in the world, and that he or she is an Other for me, and I am an *Other* for him or her. So the basic problem of sexuality can be formulated as follows: is sexuality a contingent accident linked to our physiological nature, or is it a necessary structure of the being-for-itself-for-others? The very fact that the question can be formulated in these terms means that it is an ontological one; and, indeed, ontology can only decide it if it is concerned with determining and fixing the meaning of sexual existence for the Other. To be sexed actually means – in terms of the description of the body that we tried to formulate in the previous chapter – to exist sexually for an Other who exists sexually for me – with the proviso naturally that this Other is not necessarily or primarily *for me* – or I for him or her – a *heterosexual* existent, but merely a sexed being in general. Seen from the viewpoint of the For-itself, this apprehension of the Other's sexuality cannot be a purely disinterested contemplation of his primary or secondary sexual characteristics. The Other is not *first and foremost* sexed for me because I deduce from the distribution of hair, roughness of hands, sound of voice and degree of strength that he belongs to the male sex. These are deductions which refer to a primary state. The first apprehension of the Other's sexuality, in so far as it is lived and experienced, can only be *desire*: it is through desiring the Other (or in realizing that I am incapable of desiring him), or by an awareness of his desire for me, that I discovered his sexual being; and desire reveals to me, *at the same time*, my own sexual being and his sexual being; *my* body as sexed and *his* body. And so, in trying to determine the nature and ontological status of sex, we are brought back to a study of desire. So what is desire?

And, first of all, desire *for what*?

We must straight away give up the notion that this desire is a desire for sensual pleasure or the desire to quench a pain. It is impossible to see how, from this state of immanence, the subject could emerge and 'attach' his desire to an object. Any subjective and immanentist theory must fail to explain how it is that we desire *a woman*, and not merely our own satisfaction. It is therefore proper to define desire by its transcendent object. However, it would also be quite wrong to say that desire is the desire for 'physical possession' of the desired object, if here one takes 'possession' to mean: making love with. Of course, the sexual act does relieve us for a short time from desire and it may be that in certain cases it is explicitly stated as the wished-for end of desire – for example, when the desire is painful and tiring. But this would mean that the desire itself was the object which one posited as 'to be overcome', and this could only be achieved by means of a reflective consciousness. Yet desire is in itself irreflective: it could not posit itself as an object to be suppressed. Only a rake offers himself an image of his desire, treats it as an object, excites it, 'suspends' it temporarily, or delays satisfying it, and so on. But in that case, we must point out that it is desire that becomes the thing desired. The mistake here comes from having learned that the sexual act suppresses desire. Hence we have added an element of knowledge to desire itself and, for reasons external to its essence (procreation, the sacred character of motherhood, the exceptional intensity of the pleasure procured by ejaculation, the symbolic value of the sexual act), we have linked it from outside to pleasure, as its normal satisfaction. So the average man, from mental idleness and conformism, cannot conceive any other end to his desire than ejaculation. This is what has allowed desire to be thought of as an instinct with strictly physiological origins and goals since, in a man, for example, it has its cause in erection and its final end in ejaculation. But desire in no way by itself implies the sexual act; it does not posit it thematically, it doesn't even hint at it, as we can see when it is a matter of desire in very young children or in adults who know nothing about the 'techniques' of lovemaking. Similarly, desire is not the desire for any specific erotic act: this is clear enough if we think of the diversity of such acts, which vary according to social group. Broadly speaking, desire is not the desire to *do something*. 'Doing' only comes later, attaches itself to desire from outside and requires training: there is a practice of lovemaking that possesses its own ends and means. So, since desire cannot posit its own suppression as its ultimate end, or choose a particular act as its final goal, it is purely and simply the desire for a transcendent object. Here we come back to the affective intentionality that we mentioned in earlier chapters, which has been described by Scheler and Husserl. But what is the object desired? Can one say that desire is the desire of a *body*? In one sense, this cannot be denied. But we must know what we mean by it. Certainly, it is the body that disturbs us: a glimpse of an arm or a breast, perhaps a foot. But first of all we must observe that we never desire the arm or the breast that we glimpse, except in terms of the presence of the entire body as an organic whole. The body itself, as a whole, may be masked; I can only see a naked arm. But the body is there, it is that which allows me to appreciate the arm as an arm. It is as much present and as much connected to the arm that I see, as the arabesques of the carpet which are hidden by the table legs are connected to and present in the arabesques that I can see. And my desire is not taken in: it does not address itself to a sum of physiological elements, but to a total form; better still: to a form *in a situation*. Attitude, as we shall see later, does much to arouse desire. But implied in attitude are the surroundings, and ultimately the world. And here, suddenly, we are at the furthest extreme from a simple physiological itch: desire posits the world, it desires the body in terms of the world and the beautiful hand in terms of the body. It follows exactly the procedure that we described in the previous chapter, through which we apprehend the Other's body in terms of its situation in the world. Moreover, there is nothing astonishing in this, since desire is only one of the main forms that can be assumed by the uncovering of the other's body. But precisely for that reason, we do not desire the body as a pure material object: a pure material object is *in a situation*. So that organic whole which is immediately present to desire is only desirable to the extent that it reveals not only life, but also an appropriate consciousness. However, as we shall see, this being-in-situation of the Other that is uncovered by desire is of an entirely original nature. Furthermore, the consciousness that is envisaged is still only a *property* of the desired object, that is to say that it is nothing more than a sense of the passing flow of objects in the world, precisely to the extent that this flow is limited, localized and made part of *my* world. It is true, admittedly, that one can desire a sleeping woman, but only to the extent that her sleep is apparent against a background of consciousness. In this way, consciousness always remains at the horizon of the desired body, giving it its *meaning* and its unity. A living body, as an organic whole in a situation, with consciousness at the horizon: this is the object to which desire addresses itself. And what does desire want from this object? We cannot determine this before answering a preliminary question: *who* is doing the desiring?

Without any doubt, *I* am the one who desires and desire is a specific mode of my subjectivity. Desire is consciousness, since it can only exist as a non-positional consciousness of itself. However, one should not believe that desiring consciousness differs, for example, from cognitive consciousness, except in the nature of its object. For the For-itself, to choose oneself as desire does not mean producing a desire, while remaining indifferent and unchanged, in the way that a Stoic cause produces its effect: it is to place oneself on a certain plane of being that is not the same as that, for example, of a For-itself that chooses itself as a metaphysical being. As we have seen, every consciousness has a certain relationship with its own facticity, but this relationship can vary from one state of consciousness to another. For example, the facticity of a painful consciousness is a facticity revealed to be in perpetual flight. The same is not true of the facticity of desire. The man who desires *exists* his body in a particular way and hence situates himself on a particular level of being. In reality, each of us will accept that desire is not only a longing, a clear and translucid *longing* which, through our body, attaches itself to a particular object. Desire is defined as being *stirred up*. And the phrase can help us to determine its nature: waters that are stirred up are the opposite of transparent, just as a 'confused' picture is the opposite of a clear one. Water that has been stirred up remains water, with the fluidity and the other essential characteristics of water, but its transparency has been clouded by an intangible presence which is inherent in it, everywhere and nowhere, and which we apprehend as the water somehow 'clogging' itself. Of course, it can be explained by the presence of fine solid particles in suspension in the liquid; but that is the *scientist's* explanation. Our first perception of troubled waters suggests that they have been altered by the presence of *something* invisible, which cannot be distinguished in itself and is manifested as pure actual resistance. The desiring consciousness is stirred up, because it bears an analogy with troubled waters; and to make this analogy more precise, we can compare sexual desire with another form of desire, for example hunger. Hunger, like sexual desire, assumes a particular state of the body, which may be defined as thinning of the blood, copious salivary secretions, contractions of the tunica, etc. These different phenomena are described and classified from the point of view of the Other. For the For-itself, they appear as pure facticity. But this facticity does not compromise the basic nature of the For-itself, because the For-itself immediately drives it towards its potential, which is to say towards a certain state of 'hunger-satisfied', which we have described in Part Two as the 'In-itself-for-itself' of hunger. Hunger is thus pure transcendence of physical facticity and, to the extent that the For-itself becomes aware of this facticity in a non-thetic form, what it immediately becomes conscious of is a facticity surpassed: here the body is indeed the *past*, the *sur-passed*. Of course, one can find in sexual desire that structure which is common to all appetites: a physical state. The Other may observe various physiological changes (erection of the penis, turgescence of the nipples, changes to the heart rate, a rise in temperature and so on). And the desiring consciousness exists in this facticity; it is *on the basis of* this facticity – one might even say, *through* it – that the desired body appears desirable. However, if we were to confine ourselves to this description of it, sexual desire would appear as a *clear, dry* desire, similar to the desire for eating and drinking: it would be a pure flight from facticity towards other possibilities. Yet each of us knows that there is a huge gulf between sexual desire and other appetites. We all know the notorious saying: 'Make love with a pretty woman when you need to, just as you would drink a glass of cold water when you are thirsty'; and we know how unsatisfactory, or even shocking, the mind finds this notion; because one does not desire a woman while remaining oneself entirely outside the desire: the desire *compromises* me, I am the accomplice of my desire; or, rather, the desire is a total lapse into complicity with the body. Each of us has only to examine his own experience: we know that in a state of sexual desire, consciousness is, as it were, clogged: it seems as though we allow ourselves to be invaded by facticity, that we cease to flee it and slip towards a *passive* acceptance of desire. At other times, it seems that facticity invades the consciousness in its very flight and renders it opaque to itself; it is like a yeasty raising of the fact. Hence the expressions that we use with reference to desire are a clear enough indication of its specificity. We say that it *takes hold* of one, that it *overwhelms* us, that it *transports* us. Can one imagine these same expressions being used about hunger? Is there any notion of a hunger that might 'overwhelm' you? It would only make any sense, conceivably, to give the impression of a person who is starving, while on the contrary, the weakest desire is already overwhelming. One cannot hold it at bay, as one can hunger, and 'think of something else', while merely retaining – as a sign of the body as background – an undifferentiated tonality of non-thetic consciousness which desire would then be. But *desire is consent to desire*. Consciousness, weighed down, swooning, slips towards a languor comparable to sleep. Moreover, everyone can perceive the appearance of desire in others: suddenly, a man who desires acquires a heavy tranquillity which is frightening; his eyes become fixed and seem half-closed, his gestures take on a heavy, languid softness; many appear to be on the point of sleep. And when one 'struggles against' desire, this languor is precisely what one has to resist. If one did succeed in resisting, before it vanished desire would become quite dry and quite clear, like hunger; and then there would be an 'awakening'; one would feel lucid, but with heavy head and beating heart. Of course, all these descriptions are inexact: they show more or less the way in which we interpret desire. Yet at the same time they do point to the primary fact about desire: in desire, consciousness chooses to exist its facticity on another plane. It no longer tries to escape it, it tries to subordinate itself to its own contingency, to the extent that it apprehends another body – that is, another contingency – as desirable. In that sense, desire is not only the uncovering of the other's body, but also the revelation of my own – and that, not to the extent that my own body is an *instrument* or a *point of view*, but to the extent that it is pure facticity, that is to say a simple contingent form of the necessity of my contingency. I *feel* my skin and my muscles and my breath, and I feel them not in order to transcend them *towards* something, as in the case of emotion or appetite, but as a living and inert datum; not simply as the supple and discrete instrument of my action on the world, but as a *passion* through which I am engaged in the world and in danger in the world. The For-itself is not this contingency, it continues to exist, but it experiences the dizziness of its own body; or, if one prefers, this dizziness is precisely its manner of existing its body. Non-thetic consciousness abandons itself to the body, *wants to be* body and to be only body. In desire, the body, instead of being solely the contingency from which the For-itself flees towards potentials that are proper to it, becomes at the same time the most immediate potential of the For-itself. Desire is not only desire for the body of the other; it is, united in a single act, the project, not thetically experienced, of being drawn into the body; so the last degree of desire might be fainting – as the last degree of consent to the body. It is in this sense that desire can be called desire for another body: in fact, it is an appetite *towards* the other's body, which is experienced as a dizziness of the For-itself confronted with its own body, and the being that desires is consciousness *being made body*.

However, while it is true that desire is a consciousness made body in order to appropriate the body of the other, apprehended as an organic totality in a situation with consciousness at the horizon, what is the meaning of desire; that is to say, why does consciousness become, or try in vain to become body, and what does it expect from the object of its desire? It will be easy to answer this if one considers that, in desiring, I make myself body *in the presence of another in order to appropriate the flesh of that other*. This means that it is not only a question of grasping shoulders or hips or of drawing a body against me; I have to grasp it with that particular instrument that is the body, in the sense that it 'clogs' consciousness. Hence, when I grasp these shoulders, one might say not only that my body is a means to touch them, but that the other's shoulders are a means for me to discover my body as a fascinating revelation of my facticity, that is to say, as flesh. So desire is the desire to appropriate a body to the extent that this appropriation reveals my own body to me, as flesh. But the body which I wish to appropriate, I wish to appropriate *as flesh*. Yet that is just what it is not, at the start, for me: the Other's body appears as a synthetic form in action; as we have seen, one cannot perceive the Other's body as pure flesh, that is to say as an isolated object having relationships of exteriority with other *thises*. The Other's body is originally a body in situation, while flesh, on the contrary, appears as *pure contingency of presence*. It is commonly disguised with make-up, clothes and so on; above all, it is masked by *movement*: nothing is less 'in the flesh' than a dancer, even if she is naked. Desire is an attempt to divest the body of its movements, as of its clothes, and to make it exist as pure flesh; it is an attempt at *incarnation* of the Other's body. It is in this sense that caresses are an appropriation of the Other's body: it is clear that, if caresses were to be only lightly stroking or brushing, there could be no relation between them and the powerful desire that they are supposed to satisfy; they would remain on the surface, like looks, and could not *appropriate* the Other to me. We know how unsatisfactory is the phrase: 'skin in contact with skin'. A caress is not meant to be mere contact; it seems that only man can reduce it to contact and that in this case it has missed its true meaning. This is because a caress is not just a light stroking; it is a *fashioning*. In caressing the Other, I bring her flesh alive by my caress, beneath my fingers. A caress is the totality of the ceremonies that make the Other *incarnate*. But, you may ask, was he or she not incarnate already? No, precisely not. The flesh of another did not explicitly exist for me, because I apprehended the Other's body in a situation; nor did it exist for her, since she transcended it towards her possibilities and towards the object. The caress brings the Other to birth as flesh for me and for him or herself. And, by 'flesh', we do not mean a *part* of the body, e.g, dermis, conjunctive tissue or, in fact, skin. Nor is it necessarily a question of the body 'in repose' or languidly drowsing, even though this is often when its flesh is best revealed. But the caress reveals the flesh by divesting the body of its action and dividing it from the possibilities that surround it: it is performed in order to reveal the web of inertia beneath the act – that is to say, the pure 'being-there' that supports it. For example, in *taking* and *caressing* the Other's hand, I discover, under the *clasping* which this hand is at first, an extent of flesh and bone which can be taken; and, in the same way, my look caresses when it discovers, beneath what starts as a leaping of the dancer's legs, the curvature of the thighs. So the caress is in no way distinct from desire: caressing with one's eyes and desiring are the same thing; *desire expresses itself in caress as thought in language*. Indeed, the caress reveals the Other's flesh as flesh to me *and to the Other*. But it reveals this flesh in a very special way: to grasp another reveals her own inertia and her passivity as a transcendence-transcended; but that is not what we mean by caressing her. In the caress, it is not my body as a synthetic form in action that caresses the Other, but it is my body of flesh that endows the flesh of the Other with life. The caress is designed to give life through pleasure to the Other's body, to the Other and to myself as passivity touched, to the extent that my body becomes flesh to touch her with its own passivity, that is to say by caressing itself against the Other, rather than caressing her. This is why amorous gestures have a languor that might almost be called studied: it is not so much a matter of *taking* part of the Other's body, as of *placing* one's own body against the Other's, not so much pushing or touching, in an active sense, as of *putting against*. It is as though I were to *carry* my own arm, like an inanimate object, and *place* it against the side of the desired woman; as though the fingers that *I run* across her arm were inert on the end of my hand. Hence the revelation of the Other's flesh is achieved through my own flesh: I make my self incarnate in desire and in the caress which expresses it, in order to realize the incarnation of the Other; and the caress, by *realizing* the incarnation of the Other, reveals my own incarnation to me. In other words, I make myself flesh in order to lead the Other to realize – for-herself and *for me* – her own flesh; and my caresses give birth for me to my flesh to the extent that it is, for the Other, *flesh causing her to be made flesh*. I make her taste my flesh through her flesh in order to feel herself flesh. In this way *possession* truly appears as *a reciprocal double incarnation*. Hence, in desire, there is an attempt to make consciousness incarnate (what we described earlier as the clogging of the consciousness, a murky consciousness, etc.) in order to bring about the incarnation of the Other.

It remains to determine what is the *motive* of desire; or, if one prefers, its meaning. Because anyone who has followed the descriptions that we have attempted here will have understood long ago that, for the For-itself, being is choosing its manner of being against the background of an absolute contingency of its being-there; so desire does not *arrive* in the consciousness as heat arrives to a piece of iron that I put near a flame. Consciousness chooses itself as desire. Of course, to do this it must have a motive: I do not desire anyone whomever at any time whatever. But in the first half of this book we have shown that a motive is something that is created out of the past and that consciousness confers weight and value on it by *returning* to it. Thus there is no difference between the choice of desire as a motive and the meaning of the creation – in the three ecstatic dimensions of duration – of a consciousness that makes itself a desiring one. This desire, like the emotions, or the imagining attitude, or in general any of the attitudes of the For-itself, has a significance that both constitutes it and exceeds it. The description that we have just tried to make would have no interest if it were not to lead us to the question: *why* does consciousness nihilate itself in the form of desire?

One or two preliminary remarks will help us to answer the question. First of all, we must note that the desiring consciousness does not desire its object against the background of an unchanged world. In other words, it is not a matter of making the desirable appear as a certain 'this' against the background of a world that maintains its instrumental relationships with us and its organization into complexes of utensils. The same is true of desire as of emotion: we have noted elsewhere* that emotion is not apprehension of an emotive

---

* See my *Esquisse d'une théorie phénoménologique des Emotions*.

WHAT IS DESIRE?

object in an unchanged world; but, as it corresponds to global modification of consciousness and its relationships with the world, it is translated by a radical alteration of the world. Similarly, desire is a radical modification of the For-itself, since the For-itself makes itself be on another level of being, it determines to live its body differently, to be 'clogged' by its facticity; and the world must come into being for it in a correspondingly new way: there is a world of desire. In actuality, if my body is no longer felt as the instrument that can be used by no instrument, that is to say as the synthetic organization of my actions in the world, and if it is experienced as flesh, then I shall apprehend the objects in the world as references to my flesh. This means that I shall make myself passive with regard to them, and that it is from the point of view of this passivity, in and through it, that they are revealed to me (since passivity is the body and the body does not cease to be a point of view). So now the objects are the transcendent whole that reveals my incarnation to me. A contact is *caress*; that is to say, my perception is not a utilization of the object and transcending the present towards a goal: to perceive an object, in the attitude of desiring, is to caress myself on it. Hence the fact that I am aware, more than of the form of the object and its instrumentality, of its matter (lumpy, smooth, warm, greasy, rough and so on) and in my desiring perception I discover something resembling a *flesh* of objects. My shirt rubs against my skin and I feel it: something that is normally for me the most indistinct object becomes the most immediately sensible, the warmth of the air, the breath of the wind, the rays of the sun, etc. – everything is present to me in a certain way, as if settling directly on me and revealing my skin through its skin. From this point of view, desire is not only the 'clogging' of a consciousness by its facticity, it is correlatively the entrapment of a body by the world; and the body makes itself *tacky*, *adhesive*: the consciousness is sucked into a body that is being sucked into the world.* Hence the ideal proposed

---

* Of course, we must here, as everywhere, allow for the coefficient of adversity of things. These objects are not only 'caressing'. But in the general perspective of the caress, they may also appear as 'anti-caressing', that is to say of a roughness or a cacophony or a hardness that, precisely because we are in a state of desire, clashes with us in an unbearable manner.

here is being-in-the-midst-of-the-world. The For-itself tries to achieve a being-in-the-midst-of-the-world, as the final project of its being-in-the-world, which is why sensual pleasure is often linked to death – which is also a metamorphosis or 'being-in-the-midst-of-the-world'; for example, we know the theme of the 'pseudo-death', of which there are many examples in every literature.

However, desire is not firstly nor chiefly a relationship to the world. The world appears here only as a grounding for explicit relations with the *Other*. Ordinarily, it is in the event of the presence of the Other that the world is revealed as a world of desire. Additionally, it may be revealed as such in the event of a particular Other's *absence*, or even in the event of the absence of *all* Others. But we have already noted that absence is a concrete existential relationship of the Other to myself which appears on the primitive grounding of the Being-for-Others. Admittedly, I can, on becoming aware of my body in solitude, feel myself suddenly as flesh, 'choke' with desire and perceive the world as 'suffocating'. But this solitary desire is an appeal to *an* Other or for the presence of the undifferentiated Other. I desire to reveal myself as flesh through and for another flesh. I try to bewitch the Other and to make this Other appear; and the world of desire gives back a negative image of the Other for whom I am calling. So desire is not at all a psychological accident, an itch of the flesh that might fortuitously attach us to the flesh of another; but, on the contrary, so that my flesh and the flesh of the Other *can be*, consciousness must first of all flow into the mould of desire. This desire is a primitive mode of relations with the Other, which constitutes the Other as desirable flesh on the grounding of a world of desire.

Now we can tease out the deep meaning of desire. In my primary reaction to the Other's look, I constitute myself as look. But if I look at the look, in order to defend myself against the Other's freedom and to transcend it, as freedom, the Other's freedom and look collapse: I see *eyes*, I see a being-in-the-midst-of-the-world. From then on, the Other escapes me: I would like to act on his freedom and appropriate it; or, at least, to have myself recognized as freedom by it. But this freedom is dead, it is absolutely no longer

WHAT IS DESIRE?

in the world in which I encounter the Other-object, because its characteristic is to be transcendent over the world. Admittedly, I can *grasp* the Other, grip him, push him around; if I have the power, I can force him to perform such or such an act and to say such or such words: but all this is as though I were trying to grasp hold of a man who had fled, leaving his overcoat in my hands. What I possess is the overcoat, the cast-off skin. I shall never seize anything more than a body, a psychic object in the midst of the world; and, although all the actions of that body may be able to be interpreted in terms of freedom, I have altogether lost the key to the interpretation: I can only act on a facticity. If I have retained the knowledge of a transcendent freedom of the Other, this knowledge irritates me in vain, by referring to a reality that is in principle beyond my reach and by revealing to me at every moment that I do not have it, that everything that I do is done 'blind' and takes its meaning elsewhere, in a sphere of existence from which I am *a priori* excluded. I can make someone plead for mercy or beg forgiveness, but I shall always remain ignorant of what this submission means for and in the freedom of the Other. Moreover, at the same time, my *knowing* is modified: I lose the precise understanding of the *being looked at* which, as we know, is the only way for me to test the Other's freedom. Hence I am engaged in an enterprise the very meaning of which I have forgotten. I have lost my way in front of this Other whom I see and touch, without knowing what to do with it. I have barely retained the vague memory of a certain *Beyond* what I can see and touch, a Beyond which I know to be the very thing I am trying to appropriate. This is when I become desire. Desire is a conduit of enchantment. Since I cannot grasp the Other except in his or her objective facticity, it is a matter of fixing his or her freedom in this facticity: one must ensure that it 'sets', as one says of a blancmange that it is set, so that the Other's For-itself can appear on the surface of his or her body, and extend through the whole body, so that in touching the body, I finally touch the Other's free subjectivity. This is the true sense of the word 'possession'. It is certain that I want to *possess* the Other's body, but I want to possess it to the extent that it is itself a thing 'possessed', that is to say to the extent that the Other's consciousness has identified with it. This is the impossible ideal of desire: to possess the transcendency of the Other as pure transcendency and yet as *body*; to reduce the Other to simple facticity, because he or she is then in the midst of my world, but to ensure that this facticity is a perpetual apprehension of its nihilating transcendence.

But in reality the Other's facticity (her pure being-there) cannot be given to my intuition without a profound change to my own being. To the extent that I surpass my personal facticity towards my own potential, and to the extent that I exist my facticity in a leap of flight, I also go beyond the Other's facticity – and, for that matter, the simple *existence of things*. In the act of leaping itself, I bring them into instrumental existence and their pure and simple being is concealed beneath the complexity of the indicative references that constitute their *malleability* and their *implementicity*. To pick up a pen holder already means surpassing my being-there towards the possibility of writing, but it also implies surpassing the pen holder as a simple extant towards its potential and, thence, again, towards certain future extants which are the 'words-to-be-written' and, finally, the 'book-to-be-written'. This is why the being of extants is commonly concealed by their function. The same is true of the Other's being: if the Other appears to me as a servant, an employee, a clerk or just as the passer-by whom I have to avoid or as the voice talking in the next room which I am trying to *understand* (or, on the contrary, to forget because it is 'stopping me sleeping'), it is not only its extramundane transcendence that escapes me, but also its 'being-there' as a pure contingent existence in the midst of the world. This is precisely because, in so far as I treat him as a servant or an office worker, I surpass him towards his potentialities (transcendence-transcended, dead-possibilities) by the very project by which I surpass him and nihilate my own facticity. If I wish to return to his simple presence and enjoy it *as presence*, I must try to reduce myself to my own presence. Every transcending of my being-there is in reality a transcending of the being-there of the Other. And if the world is around me as the situation that I surpass towards myself, then I grasp the Other on the basis of *his situation*,

WHAT IS DESIRE?

that is to say already as a centre of reference. And indeed, the desired Other must also be grasped in a situation; it is a woman *in the world*, standing *near a table*, naked *on a bed* or sitting *at my side* that I desire. But if desire flows from the situation of the being which is in that situation, it is in order to dissolve the situation and erode the relationships of the Other in the world: the desiring movement which goes from the 'surroundings' to the desired person is an isolating movement, which destroys the surroundings and cuts off the person being considered to bring out her pure facticity. But as it happens this is only possible if every object that brings me back to the person is frozen in its pure contingency at the same time as it refers me to her; and if, subsequently, this movement of return to the being of the Other is a movement of return to myself, as pure being-there. I destroy my possibilities in order to destroy those of the world and to constitute the world as a 'world of desire', that is to say as a destructured world, which has lost its meaning and where things jut out like fragments of pure matter, like qualities in their primitive state. And, since the For-itself is choice, this is only possible if I project myself towards a new possibility: that of being 'absorbed into my body like ink into blotting-paper', that of summarizing myself in my pure being-there. This project to the extent that it is not simply conceived and stated thematically, but lived, that is to say in so far as its realization is not distinguished from its conception, means disturbance. Indeed, one should not understand the preceding descriptions as meaning that I deliberately put myself into a state of turmoil with the aim of discovering the pure 'being-there' of the Other. Desire is a lived project which does not imply any preliminary consideration, but which contains in itself its own meaning and interpretation. As soon as I cast myself towards the facticity of the Other, as soon as I want to set aside her acts and her functions in order to reach her in the flesh, I make myself incarnate, because I cannot either wish for or even conceive of the incarnation of the Other unless in and through my own incarnation; and even the first draft of a desire (as when we 'idly undress a woman with a look') is a first draft of turmoil, because I only desire with my own turmoil, I only undress another by undressing myself, I only make a first

SEXUALITIES

outline draft of the Other's flesh by making the outline of my own.

But my incarnation is not only the precondition for the appearance of the Other *in my eyes* as flesh. My aim is to make her incarnate as flesh *in her own eyes*. I have to take her with me into the realm of pure facticity, she has to be reduced for herself to become only flesh. In this way I shall be reassured as to the permanent possibilities of a transcendence which can at any moment transcend me from all sides: it *will be no more than this*; it will remain confined within the limits of an object; and moreover, for that very reason, I shall be able to touch it, feel it, possess it. So the other meaning of my incarnation – that is to say of my turmoil – is that it is an enchanting language. I make myself flesh in order to fascinate the Other with my nudity and to arouse a desire for my flesh in her, precisely because this desire, in the Other, will be nothing except an incarnation similar to my own. Hence, desire is an invitation to desire. It is my flesh alone that can find the way to the flesh of the Other, and I bring my flesh into contact with hers to arouse her to a sense of flesh. In a caress, in fact, when I slowly slide my inert hand against the Other's thigh, I make her feel my flesh and that is something that she can only do, herself, by making herself inert; the shudder of pleasure that then travels through her is very exactly the awakening of her awareness of flesh. Reaching out my hand, taking it away, clasping it, I once more become a body in action; but by the same token I make my hand vanish as flesh. Allowing it to run casually along her body, or reducing it to a soft brushing movement, almost devoid of sense – to a pure existence, pure matter, slightly silky, slightly satiny, slightly rough – means giving up being in oneself the one who sets the markers and establishes distances; it is to make oneself pure mucous membrane. At that moment, the communion of desire is achieved: each consciousness, by incarnating itself, has achieved the incarnation of the other, each turmoil has produced turmoil in the other, and each has grown accordingly. In each caress, I feel my own flesh, and that of the Other through my own flesh, and I am aware that this flesh which I feel and appropriate to myself through my flesh is flesh-felt-by-the-other. It is no accident that desire, while aiming at the whole body, reaches it chiefly through the least differentiated, most crudely nerveless masses of flesh, those least capable of spontaneous movement: through the breasts, the buttocks, the thighs, the belly; these are like the image of pure facticity. This is why the true caress is the contact of two bodies in their most fleshy parts: the contact of bellies and chests. The caressing hand is really too finely-tuned, too close to a perfected tool. But the fulfilment of fleshes one against the other, and one by the other, is the true end of desire.

However, desire is itself condemned to failure. We have seen that coitus, which is its usual termination, is not its proper end. Admittedly, several elements in our sexual make-up are a necessary translation of the nature of desire, in particular the erection of the penis and the clitoris. This is nothing more, in reality, than the affirmation of flesh by flesh, so it is absolutely necessary that it should not occur *voluntarily*, that is to say that we should not be able to employ it as an instrument but, on the contrary, that it should be an autonomous biological phenomenon, the autonomous and involuntary occurrence of which accompanies and signifies the submerging of consciousness in the body. What we must understand, is that not any slender and prehensile organ, linked to striated muscles, might be a sexual organ, a *sex*; if sex were to appear as an organ, it could only be a manifestation of vegetable life. But contingency reappears if we consider that, precisely, *there are sexes and sexes of this particular kind*. The penetration of the female by the male, especially, remains a perfectly contingent aspect of our sexual life, although it conforms to this radical incarnation which desire strives to be: note, indeed, the organic passivity of the sexual organ in coitus: it is the whole body that goes backwards and forwards, which *carries* the organ forward or brings it back; and the hands help in the insertion of the penis, the penis itself appearing as an instrument which is manipulated, thrust in, pulled out and used – just as the opening up and lubrication of the vagina cannot be achieved voluntarily. But sexual pleasure, properly so called, is also pure contingency. In truth, it is normal for the swallowing up of the consciousness in the body to have its conclusion, that is to say a particular kind of ecstasy in which consciousness is no longer anything except consciousness of (the) body and, hence, a reflective consciousness of corporeality. Pleasure, like excessive pain, causes the appearance of a reflective consciousness that is an '*attention to pleasure*'; except that pleasure is the death and failure of desire. It is the death of desire because it is not only its completion, but its end and its goal. Moreover, this is only an organic contingency: it *happens* that incarnation is manifested in erection and that erection ceases with ejaculation. But in addition pleasure is the sluice-gate of desire because it motivates the appearance of a reflective consciousness *of* pleasure, the object of which becomes orgasm, i.e. which is *attention to the incarnation of the reflected For-itself* and, at the same time, neglect of the incarnation of the Other. This no longer belongs to the field of contingency. No doubt it remains contingent that the passage to fascinated reflection should be made on the occasion of that particular mode of incarnation which is pleasure – though there are many cases of a transition to the reflective without intervention of pleasure – but desire, in so far as it represents an attempt at incarnation, involves this permanent danger: that the consciousness, in becoming incarnate, loses sight of the incarnation of the Other and that its own incarnation absorbs it to the extent of becoming its ultimate goal. In that case, the pleasure of caressing is transformed into the pleasure of being caressed: what the For-itself demands is to feel its body expand inside it to the point of nausea. There is consequently a break in contact, and desire fails to achieve its aim. It even frequently happens that this failure of desire causes a passage to masochism, that is to say that the consciousness, grasping itself in its facticity, demands to be grasped and transcended as a body-for-an-Other by the conciousness of the Other: in that case the object-Other collapses and the look-Other appears, and my consciousness is a consciousness that swoons in its flesh beneath the Other's eyes.

But, conversely, desire is at the origin of its own failure to the extent that it is desire to *take* and to *appropriate* for itself. It is not enough for turmoil to bring the incarnation of the Other into being: desire is the desire to appropriate this incarnate consciousness. So naturally it no longer prolongs itself in *caresses*, but in acts of seizure and penetration. The only aim of the caress was to impregnate the body of the Other with consciousness and freedom. Now that this body has been saturated, it must be taken and grasped, one must enter it. But by the mere fact of my now trying to seize, drag, grasp and bite, my body ceases to be flesh and reverts to being the synthetic instrument *that I am*; and at the same moment the *Other* ceases to be an incarnation and reverts to being an instrument in the midst of the world that I apprehend in terms of its situation. Her consciousness, which hovered on the surface of her flesh and which I tried to *taste** with mine, vanishes beneath my eyes: nothing remains but an *object* with object-images contained within it. At the same time my turmoil goes away: this does not mean that I have ceased to desire, but that desire has lost its matter, it has become *abstract*; it is the desire to handle and to take, but my very insistence makes my incarnation disappear: now I am once more surpassing my body towards my own possibilities (here, the possibility of taking) and similarly the Other's body, surpassed towards its potential, descends from the status of *flesh* to that of pure object. Its situation implies a breach in the reciprocity of incarnation which was precisely the proper end of desire. The Other can remain in turmoil, she can remain flesh *for herself*, and I can understand it: but this is a flesh that I no longer grasp through my flesh, a flesh that is now only the *property* of an object-Other and not the incarnation of a consciousness-Other. So I am a *body* (a synthetic totality in a situation) confronted with a *flesh*. I have reverted, very nearly, to the very situation from which I was trying to escape by desire, that is to say that I am trying to use the Other-object to account for its transcendency and that, precisely because she is *all* object, she escapes me with *all* her transcendency. I have even once again lost a precise understanding of what I was looking for, yet I am still involved in looking. I take and I discover myself taking, but what I grasp in my hands is something *different* from the thing that I wanted to grasp; I feel it and suffer, but without being able to say what

---

* Doña Prouhèze (in Paul Claudel, *Le Soulier de satin*, 2e journée): 'He will not know the taste of me.'

I wanted to grasp because, together with my turmoil, the very understanding of my desire escapes me. I am like a sleeper who wakes up and finds that he is clutching at the headboard of his bed without being able to recall the nightmare that made him do so. This situation is the primary cause of *sadism*.

Sadism is passion, dryness and perseverance. It is relentless determination because it is the state of a For-itself that realizes it is engaged without understanding *what* it is engaged in, and which persists in its engagement without having a clear awareness of the goal which it has set itself nor a precise memory of the value which it attached to this engagement. It is dryness because it appears when desire has been emptied of its turmoil. The sadist has once more come into possession of his body as a synthetic totality and centre of action; he has re-placed himself in a perpetual flight from his own facticity and he experiences himself vis-à-vis the Other as pure transcendency; he has a horror of turmoil *for himself*, considering it as a humiliating state; it is also possible that he is simply unable to *achieve* it in himself. To the extent that he is coldly obsessed, that he is at the same time perseverence and dryness, the sadist experiences passion. His goal, like that of desire, is to grasp the Other, and obtain the Other's submission not only as an object-Other, but as pure incarnate transcendency. But, in sadism, the stress is on the instrumental appropriation of the incarnate-Other. In sexuality, this 'moment' of sadism is the one when the incarnate For-itself surpasses its incarnation to appropriate the incarnation of the Other. Sadism is thus at the same time a refusal to incarnate oneself and a flight from all facticity, and simultaneously an effort to grasp hold of the Other's facticity. But since it cannot or will not achieve the incarnation of the Other through its own incarnation – as, by this very fact, it has no alternative but to treat the Other as a tool-object – it tries to use the Other's body as an implement to make the Other realize its incarnate existence. Sadism is an attempt to incarnate the Other through violence and this 'forced' incarnation must already be an appropriation and utilization of the Other. The sadist tries to denude the other (as desire does) of the acts that hide him or her. It seeks to discover the flesh beneath the action. But instead of the

For-itself of desire being lost in its own flesh to reveal to the Other that it too is flesh, the sadist rejects his own flesh at the same time as he employs instruments to reveal the Other's flesh to the Other by force. The object of sadism is immediate appropriation. But sadism is out of kilter because it takes pleasure not only in the Other's flesh but, directly linked to that flesh, in its own non-incarnation. It *wants* non-reciprocity in sexual relations, it takes pleasure in being the free, appropriating power, vis-à-vis a freedom made captive by the flesh. This is why sadism wants to make the flesh *differently* present to the Other's consciousness: it wants to make it present by treating the Other as an instrument, it makes it present through pain; because in pain, facticity invades consciousness and, in the end, the reflective consciousness is fascinated by the facticity of the unreflected consciousness. So there is such a thing as incarnation through pain. But, at the same time, the pain is procured *through instruments*, and the body of the For-itself that applies the torture is nothing more than an instrument for giving pain. Hence the For-itself can from the start harbour the illusion that it is instrumentally taking possession of the Other's freedom, that is to say, pouring that freedom into flesh, without ceasing to be the one that *causes*, grasps, seizes and so on.

As for the type of incarnation that sadism would like to achieve, it is precisely of the kind that is designated *the Obscene*. The obscene is a *species* of Being-for-Other, which belongs to the *genus* of the 'disgraceful'. But everything that is disgraceful is not obscene. In *grace*, the body appears as a psychic being in situation. Above all, it reveals its transcendency, as transcended transcendency; it is in action and is understood from the situation and the goal being pursued. Hence every movement is appreciated in a perceptual process that travels from the future to the present. For this reason, a gracious action has on the one hand the precision of a well-designed machine and, on the other, the perfect unpredictability of the psychic, since as we have seen the psychic is, for another, the *unpredictable object*. So at every moment a gracious action is perfectly comprehensible, to the extent that one considers that in it which has *already happened*. Even more, this already accomplished part of the action is implied in a sort of aesthetic necessity which derives from its perfect suitability. At the same time, the goal-to-be illuminates the totality of the action, but all the future part of the action remains unpredictable, even though one may feel about the body itself in action that it will appear necessary and well-suited as soon as it has happened. It is this moving image of necessity and freedom (as a property of the object-Other) which properly speaking constitutes grace. Bergson gave a good description of it. In grace, the body is the instrument that makes freedom manifest. A gracious action, in so far as it reveals the body as a precision instrument, supplies it constantly with a justification for its existence: the hand *is for* taking and demonstrates first of all its being-for-taking. To the extent that it is appreciated in a situation that demands grasping, it seems as though *demanded* in its being, it has a *calling*. And, in so far as it makes its freedom manifest by the unpredictability of its gesture, then it seems to be at the origin of its being: it appears to be producing itself in response to the justifying appeal of the situation. So grace represents the objective image of a being that is *the founding of itself in order to* . . . Hence facticity is covered and masked by grace: the nakedness of the flesh is entirely present, but it cannot be *seen*. This means that the ultimate coquetry and the ultimate challenge of grace is to exhibit the uncovered body, with no other clothing or veil than grace itself. The most gracious body is the naked body which is wrapped by its actions in an invisible garment that altogether deprives it of flesh, even though the flesh is entirely present in the eyes of the spectators. The disgraceful, on the other hand, occurs when the one of the elements of grace is thwarted in its realization. Movement can become *mechanical*. In that case, the body is still part of a whole that justifies it, but with the status of a pure instrument; its transcended-trancendency disappears and, with it, the *situation* vanishes as a lateral super-determination of the tool-object of *my* universe. It may also be that the actions are abrupt and violent; in that case, what collapses is one's adaptation to the situation; the situation remains, but between it and the Other in the situation there enters as it were a void, a hiatus. In that case, the Other remains free, but this freedom is only apprehended as pure

WHAT IS DESIRE?

unpredictability and it resembles the *clinamen* of Epicurus' atoms, in short an indeterminate. At the same time, the goal remains stated and the Other's gesture is still perceived by us in terms of the future. But the failure of adaptation brings a consequence, which is that the perceptive interpretation by the future is always too broad or too narrow: it is an interpretation through *more or less*. As a result, the justification of the Other's gesture and the Other's being is imperfectly realized; at the worst, clumsiness is an unjustifiable; all its facticity, which was engaged in the situation, is absorbed by it and flows back into it. The clumsy inopportunely liberates its facticity and suddenly places it where we can see it: just when we expected to grasp a key to the situation, arising spontaneously from the situation itself, we suddenly come up against the unjustifiable contingency of an unadapted presence; we are brought face to face with the existence of an extant. However, if the body is entirely in the act, facticity is not yet flesh. The *obscene* appears when the body adopts postures which entirely divest it of its actions and reveal the inertia of its flesh. The sight of a naked body, from behind, is not obscene; but some involuntary waddling movements of the rump are obscene. This is because at such moments only the legs of the walking person are in action and the rump appears as an isolated cushion, carried on them, swaying purely in obedience to the laws of gravity. It cannot be justified by its situation; on the contrary, it is entirely destructive of any situation, since it has the passivity of a 'thing' and has itself carried along like a thing by the legs. Hence it reveals itself as injustifiable facticity: it is 'superfluous', as any contingent being is. It is isolated in this body, the present meaning of which is walking; it is naked, even if covered in clothing, because it no longer participates in the transcended-transcendency of the body in action; its swaying movement, instead of being interpreted from the future, is interpreted and understood from the past, as a physical fact. These same remarks can naturally be applied to cases where it is the whole body which becomes flesh, either because of some softness or other in its gestures, which cannot be interpreted by the situation, or by a deformity in its structure (proliferation of fatty cells, for example) which displays an overabundant facticity to us relative to the effective presence demanded by the situation. And this flesh revealed is specifically obscene when it is exposed to someone not in a state of desire and *without exciting his desire*. A particular disadaptation which destroys the situation at the very time when I am apprehending it and which displays to me the inert expansion of the flesh as a sudden apparition under the slender garment of the gestures which clothe it, when I am not in a state of desire with regard to that flesh: this is what I shall describe as obscene.

We can now see the sense of the sadistic imperative: grace reveals freedom as a property of the object-Other and refers us obscurely – as do the contradictions of the perceptible world in the case of Platonic reminiscence – to a transcendent Beyond of which we have only a confused memory and which we cannot reach except by a radical modification in our being, that is to say by resolutely taking on our being-for-Others. At the same time, it uncovers and covers the flesh of the Other, or if one prefers, it uncovers it to recover it immediately: in grace, flesh is the inaccessible Other. The sadist aims to destroy grace in order *really* to constitute another synthesis of the Other: he wants to make the flesh of the Other appear; in the very act of appearing, the flesh will destroy grace and facticity will reduce the object-freedom of the Other. This reduction is not an annihilation: for the sadist, it is the *free-Other* that appears as flesh; the identity of the *object-Other* is not destroyed by these metamorphoses, but the relationship between freedom and flesh is inverted: in grace, freedom is contained and concealed facticity; in the new synthesis that is to be brought about, it is facticity that contains and masks freedom. Hence, the sadist aims to make the flesh appear suddenly and under constraint, that is to say not with the assistance of his own flesh, but of his body as instrument. He aims to make the Other adopt attitudes and positions such that his or her body should appear in the guise of the *obscene*. Hence he remains on the level of instrumental appropriation since he brings the flesh into being through acting forcibly on the Other – and the Other becomes an instrument in his hands; the sadist manipulates the Other's body, presses down on the shoulders so as to bend it towards the ground and raise the hips, and so on; and, moreover, the aim of this instrumental use is inherent in itself: the sadist treats the other as an instrument to make the Other's flesh appear; the sadist is the one who apprehends the Other as a tool, the function of which is his own incarnation. The sadist's ideal is thus to reach the moment when the Other is already flesh without having ceased to be an instrument, flesh to bring flesh into being; the moment when the thighs, for example, are already offered in a state of obscene and ripe passivity, while still being instruments that he manipulates, puts aside and bends, in order to emphasize the buttocks even more and make them incarnate in their turn. But make no mistake: what the sadist seeks with such determination, what he wants to knead with his hands and bend beneath his fist, is the Other's freedom: it is there, in that flesh, it *is* that flesh, since there is a facticity of the Other; so this is what the sadist tries to appropriate. Hence the sadist's effort is directed to embedding an Other in his or her flesh by violence and pain, appropriating the body of the Other through the fact of treating it as flesh to bring other flesh into being; but this appropriation surpasses the body that it appropriates, because it only wants to possess it to the extent that it has embedded in it the Other's freedom. This is why the sadist wants manifest proof of this subjection of the Other's freedom by the flesh: he will try to make the Other beg forgiveness, he will force the Other to humiliate himself or herself, and to deny what he or she holds most dear, through torture and threats. This is said to be due to a taste for domination or a will to power. But this explanation is either vague or absurd. The first thing that one would have to explain is the taste for domination – and obviously this taste cannot predate sadism as its basis, because it comes into being, as sadism does, and on the same plane as sadism, out of unease vis-à-vis the Other. In reality, if the sadist enjoys forcing out a recantation through torture, it is for reasons similar to those that allow us to interpret the meaning of *Love*. We have seen that love does not demand the abolition of the Other's freedom, but its subjection as freedom, that is to say its subjection by itself. In the same way, sadism does not seek to supress the freedom of the victim, but to force this freedom to identify itself freely with the flesh that is being tortured. This is why the moment of pleasure, for the torturer, is that in which the victim recants or humiliates himself. In truth, whatever the pressure exerted on the victim, the act of recanting remains *free*: it is a spontaneous outburst, a response to the situation, it shows human-reality; whatever the degree of resistance shown by the victim, however long he may have waited before begging for mercy, he might in spite of all that have waited ten minutes, one minute, one second longer. He was the one who decided the moment when the pain became unbearable. And the proof of this is that he will subsequently suffer feelings of remorse and shame at having recanted – making it entirely his responsibility. On the other hand, the sadist meanwhile considers himself to have caused him to recant. If the victim resists and refuses to beg for mercy, the game is all the more enjoyable: one more turn of the screw, one additional twist and resistance will eventually crumble. The sadist adopts the attitude of one who 'has all the time in the world'. He is calm and unhurried, setting out his implements like a technician, trying them one after another, like a locksmith trying various keys in a door. He takes pleasure in this ambiguous and contradictory situation: because, on the one hand, he plays the one who, at the hub of a universal determinism, patiently directs certain means towards an end that will *automatically* be reached – just as the lock will automatically open when the locksmith has found the 'right' key – while, at the same time, this predetermined end can only be attained through the free and total cooperation of the Other; so it remains up to the very end simultaneously predictable and unpredictable. And the goal achieved is, for the sadist, ambiguous, contradictory and unbalanced, since it represents at the same time the rigorous effect of a technical use of determinism and the manifestation of an unconditional freedom. The spectacle that is offered to the sadist is that of a freedom struggling against the 'ripening' or 'flowering' of flesh, which ultimately makes a free choice of allowing itself to be submerged by the flesh. At the moment of the recantation, the desired result is obtained: the body is entirely flesh, gasping and obscene; it retains the position that the torturers have given it, not the one that it would have adopted on its own; the ropes binding it support it like an inert object and, by that very token, it ceases to be an object that moves spontaneously. And it is with just this body that a freedom chooses to identify itself through recanting: this disfigured, gasping body is the very image of freedom broken and enslaved.

These few remarks are not meant to exhaust the problem of sadism. We simply wanted to show that it exists in embryo in desire itself, as the failure of desire: indeed, as soon as I try to *take* an Other's body, which I have brought to incarnation through my incarnation, I break this reciprocity of incarnation, I surpass my body towards its own possibilities and I turn in the direction of sadism. Thus sadism and masochism are the two reefs on which desire can founder, either because I surpass turmoil towards an appropriation of the Other's flesh, or because, drunk with my own turmoil, I no longer pay attention to anything except my own flesh and ask nothing of the Other, except to be the look that helps me to realize my flesh. It is because of this inconsistency of desire, and its perpetual oscillation between these two 'reefs', that 'normal' sexuality continues to be called by the name 'sado-masochistic'.

However, sadism itself, like blind indifference and desire, contains within it the principle of its own failure. First of all, there is a profound incompatibility between an apprehension of the body as flesh and its use as an instrument. If I make an instrument of flesh, it refers me to other instruments and to potentialities, in short to a future; it is particularly justified in *being there* by the situation I create around me, just as the presence of the nails and the tapestry to be hung on the wall justifies the existence of the hammer. Immediately, its nature as flesh — that is to say as unusable facticity — gives way to that of a tool-thing. The 'tool-flesh' complex that the sadist has tried to create falls apart. This deep collapse in the complex can be hidden as long as flesh is an instrument to reveal flesh, because in this way I have constituted a tool with an immanent end. But when the incarnation is complete, when I do indeed have a panting body in front of me, I no longer know how to *use* this flesh: no further end can be assigned to it for the very reason that I have made manifest its absolute contingency. It *is there* and it is there *for nothing*. In that sense I cannot seize hold of it in so far as it is flesh, I cannot integrate it into a complex system of instrumentality without its materiality as flesh, its 'carnation', immediately escaping me. I can only remain speechless before it, in a state of contemplative astonishment, or else become incarnate in my turn, allow myself to be seized with turmoil, in order at least to resituate myself on the ground where flesh reveals itself to flesh in its most total carnation. Thus sadism, at the very moment when its aim is about to be accomplished, gives way to desire. Sadism is the failure of desire and desire of sadism. One cannot escape this vicious circle except by satisfaction and what is supposed to be 'physical possession' – and in that, a new synthesis of sadism and desire becomes a given. The tumescence of the sexual organ shows incarnation, while the fact of 'entering into . . .' or of being 'penetrated' symbolically carries out the sadistic and masochistic attempt at appropriation. But if pleasure offers an escape from the circle, it is because it at once kills desire and sadistic passion without satisfying them.

At the same time and on a quite different plane, sadism contains another cause of failure. What it tries to appropriate is indeed the transcendent freedom of the victim; but this freedom remains in principle unattainable. And the more the sadist persists in treating the Other as an instrument, the more this freedom escapes him. He can only act upon freedom as an objective property of the object-Other: that is to say, on freedom in the midst of the world with its dead-possibilities. But since his goal was precisely to recover his being-for-others, he misses it in principle, because the only Other with whom he has any dealings is the Other in the world who has only 'mental images' of the sadist attacking him.

The sadist discovers his error when his victim *looks* at him; that is to say when he experiences the absolute alienation of his being in the freedom of the Other. Then, not only does he realize that he has not recovered his 'being-outside', but also that the activity through which he is trying to recuperate it is in itself transcended and frozen into 'sadism' as *habitus* and property, with its train of dead-possibilities; and that this transformation takes place by and for the Other whom he wishes to enslave. Whereupon he discovers that he cannot act on the freedom of the Other, even by forcing the Other to humiliate himself and beg for mercy, because it is precisely in and through the absolute freedom of the Other that a world comes into being, in which there is a sadist and instruments of torture, and a hundred pretexts for humiliating oneself and recanting. No one has better conveyed the power of a victim's look on his tormentors than Faulkner in the final pages of *Light in August*. The 'respectable' citizens have just hunted down the black man, Christmas, and castrated him. He is dying:

'But the man on the floor had not moved. He just lay there, with his eyes open and empty of everything save consciousness, and with something, a shadow, about his mouth. For a long moment he looked up at them with peaceful and unfathomable and unbearable eyes. Then his face, body, all, seemed to collapse, to fall in upon itself and from out the slashed garments about his hips and loins the pent black blood seemed to rush like a released breath. It seemed to rush out of his pale body like the rush of sparks from a rising rocket; upon that black blast the man seemed to rise soaring into their memories forever and ever. They are not to lose it, in whatever peaceful valleys, beside whatever placid and reassuring streams of old age, in the mirroring face of whatever children they will contemplate old disasters and newer hopes. *It will be there, musing, quiet, steadfast, not fading and not particularly threatful, but of itself alone serene, or itself alone triumphant.* Again from the town, deadened a little by the walls, the scream of the siren mounted toward its unbelievable crescendo, passing out of the realm of hearing.'[1]

Thus the explosion of the Other's look in the world of the sadist makes the sense and the goal of sadism collapse. And, at the same time, sadism discovers that it was *that freedom* that he wanted to enslave and, simultaneously, he discovers the futility of his efforts. Once again we come back to the *looking-being* and the *looked-at*; we cannot escape from this circle.

*

* Emphasis added.

SEXUALITIES

We did not intend in these few remarks to exhaust the matter of sexuality, and even less so that of attitudes towards the Other. All we wished was simply to point out that the sexual attitude is a primitive form of behaviour towards Others. It goes without saying that this behaviour necessarily includes in itself the original contingency of the being-for-others and that of our own facticity. What we cannot accept is that it should be subjected from the start to a physiological and empirical constitution. As soon as 'there is' the body and 'there is' the Other, we react with *desire*, with *Love* and with the attitudes which we have mentioned deriving from these. Our physiological structure merely expresses the permanent possibility in us of adopting one or other of these attitudes, and does so symbolically and in the field of absolute contingency. So we might say that the For-itself is sexual in the very fact that it looms up when confronted with Others and that, through it, sexuality comes into the world.

Obviously we do not pretend that attitudes towards Others can be reduced to these sexual attitudes that we have just described. If we have considered them at some length, it is for two reasons: first of all because they are fundamental; and, secondly, because all complex conduct of human beings towards one another is only the elaboration of these two basic attitudes (and of a third, hatred, that we shall describe shortly). No doubt concrete types of conduct (collaboration, struggle, rivalry, emulation, engagement, obedience*, etc.) are infinitely more subtle to describe, because they depend on the historical situation and on the concrete peculiarities of each relationship of a For-itself with an Other; but all of them include within them, like a skeleton, sexual relations. And this is not because of the existence of something called '*libido*', which manages to insinuate itself everywhere, but simply because the attitudes that we described are the fundamental projects by which the For-itself *realizes* its being-for-others, and tries to transcend this given situation. This is not the place to show how much love and desire may be contained in pity, admiration, disgust, envy, gratitude

---

* See also maternal love, pity, kindness, etc.

and so on – though each individual can ascertain this by referring to his own experience, and also to an eidetic intuition of these various essences. Of course, this does not mean that these different attitudes are simple disguises assumed by sexuality. But we must understand that sexuality is integral to them as their foundation, and that they enfold it and transcend it just as the idea of a circle enfolds and transcends that of a segment turning around one of its extremities which remains fixed. These foundation-attitudes may remain hidden, as a skeleton is hidden by the flesh surrounding it. This is in fact what usually happens: the contingency of the body, the structure of the original product that I am and the history that I historialize can determine that the sexual attitude normally remains implicit, within more complex behaviours; in particular, it does not frequently happen that one explicitly desires Others 'of the same sex'. But, behind the interdictions of morality and the taboos of society, the original structure of desire remains, at least in that particular form of turmoil that is named sexual disgust. And one must not understand this permanence of the sexual project as if it remained 'in us' in some unconscious state. A project of the For-itself can only exist in conscious form. Simply it exists as integrated in a particular structure and dissolves into it. This is what psychoanalysts sensed when they made sexual affectivity a '*tabula rasa*' which derived all its determinations from the history of the individual. However, one must not believe that sexuality is, at the outset, *indeterminate*. In reality it contains all its determinants as soon as it arises from the For-itself in a world in which 'there are' Others. What is indeterminate and what has to be decided by the history of each individual is the type of relationships with the Other, in the event of which the sexual attitude (desire-love, masochism-sadism) will manifest itself in its explicit purity.

Maternal Love

This is an early chapter, entitled 'La Mère', from Sartre's biography of Flaubert. It half describes and half imagines the inner world of Caroline Flaubert, the novelist's mother. Here, in the last years of his writing life, Sartre explores a subject he had always avoided. Sartre's veteran translator Hazel Barnes has praised this chapter as containing some of his finest writing. She adds, 'Critics have complained that it reads like a novel.'

It corresponds to *L'Idiot de la famille* (1971), I: 82–102.

Caroline Flaubert, daughter of Doctor Fleuriot and Anne-Charlotte-Justine, *née* Cambremer de Croixmare, had the saddest childhood. Her parents married on 27 November 1792. They say it was a great romance and there was even talk of elopement; in any case, they were passionately in love. On 7 September 1793, the young woman died giving birth. The infant had to be given to a wet nurse. It is not at all uncommon for a widower to harbour resentment against a child who has caused the death of his wife; and the criminal offspring is imbued with an early sense of its guilt. We cannot say definitely that this was what happened to poor Caroline, but in any event the doctor did not love her enough to want to go on living: *he suffered a bodily grief*, duly sickened and died, in 1803. His daughter was ten years old, years which she seems to have spent mainly in an empty house, in Pont-Audemer, in the company of an inconsolable father who was as dismal a companion as all widowers. Then the double frustration: being without a mother, she adored her father. Even though he might be wrapped up in himself and often gloomy, at least he was there, living beside her. But after this flickering flame was extinguished, the girl was left alone. She lost the love of Doctor Fleuriot – which was already in short supply – and, above all, the happiness of loving.

Orphans experience bereavement in some way as a form of repudiation: their parents, sick of them, have rejected and abandoned them. Did Caroline, who was already persuaded of her guilt, see this hurried departure as a condemnation? We cannot tell. What we do know, however, is that from this moment her future requirements were engraved on her heart: she would marry no one but her father. Two ladies from Saint-Cyr ran a boarding-school in Honfleur. They promised to keep her there until she reached her majority, but then died in their turn. Maître Thouret, a cousin and a notary, decided to send the poor unwanted child to Doctor Laumonier, head surgeon at the Hospice de l'Humanité: Mme Laumonier had been born a Thouret. Caroline was sixteen or seventeen, and a remark by C. Commanville throws some light on her character: it appears that life with the Laumoniers was fun, their morals were lax. But the girl's 'extremely serious nature . . . protected her from the dangers of such an environment'.[1] Here was a child who belonged to no one, she was passed from hand to hand, people would rather die than look after her: the dominant feeling was one of guilt. And lack of self-confidence. A rather rich sensibility, capable of violence, but blocked. An insurmountable gap separated her from others, who were indifferent or mercenary, and only too quick to depart this life. She had no future outside marriage; in the present, no home; in the past, no roots. She was adrift; hence her reserve, her extreme shyness; and hence, too, her coldness. She has no use for what Commanville calls 'light morals': Caroline Fleuriot, thrown off course at birth, is already all too light; if they lighten her any further, she will fly away. What she needs is ballast, so she tries to halt her indefinite slide by taking on the heaviest cargo, virtue: she will be *weighty* and sometimes unbending; having no anchor to put down, she tries to find a bearing: it will be unwavering uprightness. She is

---

[1]. Caroline Commanville, Flaubert's niece, published a brief memoir of her uncle in 1895. It was entitled *Souvenirs sur Gustave Flaubert*.

a girl who knows very little: the ladies from Saint-Cyr taught her nothing, and she hardly feels any more than she knows: her years in the ice have frozen her. Soon she will love, and utterly, but for the moment her heart is silent – not that it is dead, on the contrary; but its early frustrations have so well conditioned it and it has such rigorous and demanding standards that they will not reveal themselves until the man who can satisfy them has appeared. Meanwhile, there is virtue: good conduct and pious habits are the benchmarks. And Pride, which arises in the guilty, the oppressed and the humiliated, sniffs around and seeks to compensate with rhetorical triumphs for the degradation from which it arises. In her own eyes, Caroline was not degraded, but *empty*. Her pride was innocent: it was not so much a matter of enhancing an individual's singularity, as of halting at any cost the slipping of a life that was imprecise, hovering between one extreme and the other. She needed something to cling to. Caroline dreamed of an aristocratic lineage on her mother's side and a Chouan connection on her father's. In reality, her father died too soon to take part in the Chouan revolt in the West, while the Cambremers de Croixmare, who were lawyers and priests, never did belong to the old nobility. No matter. Caroline Commanville writes: 'Through her grandmother, her mother had ties to the oldest families in Normandy.' And Gustave, in his correspondence, often refers to his noble ancestry. This was one of the chief Flaubert family myths. Who can have started it? And who, later, sustained it as she poured out her memories to her grand-daughter, if not Caroline Fleuriot herself? Being of noble origin, she had – to make up for the lack of roots – a *quality*: from afar, through blood, she belonged to the stable and certain order of a Great House. In short, she early gave herself up to this abstraction which provided her with an illusion of security: the guilty young girl, dry and empty, converting her sense of original sin into a superficial host of scruples, could only discover an Ego for herself in others and as another. There, in the families of Danyeau d'Annebault and Fouet du Manoir, her inner void found its true being and became a transient expression of the collective plenitude. Shy, timid, haughty and austere, made virtuous by necessity and assumed into that metaphysical being, the *noblesse de robe*, and in spite of all these compensations, lost – both in herself and in society. This was the sixteen-year-old who, in the Laumoniers' drawing-room, met a young anatomy instructor, Achille-Cléophas Flaubert. Small, slender and delicate, she had suffered a few years earlier from haemoptysis; all her life, she would remain nervous and impressionable, concealing her constant feeling of anguish beneath almost obsessive anxieties.

Hardly had the young people met, than they got engaged. For Caroline, it was love at first sight: this brilliant doctor, dispatched from Paris by the great Dupuytren, authoritarian, high-principled and hard-working, was nine years her senior. Most of all, he was an adult – at least, in her eyes; a strong man who carried weight: the father resurrected. Thanks to him, the vague, dark years at boarding-school and in exile dissolved into oblivion, she reknitted the thread broken by Dr Fleuriot's untimely death and found herself alone with her father in an empty house; in short, she turned back the clock and resumed her life from the age of ten. The Laumonier family had bewildered her, not so much because of their free morals, which were no temptation for her, but by the visible reciprocity of relationships: no one was in command. She would have found her place in a rigid hierarchy, but equality appeared to her as the ultimate in disorder: her unhappiness came from the dreadful failure of a couple; a conjugal family had formed itself and created her; then everything collapsed, leaving her alone, an absurd orphan. So, instead of the fragility of egalitarian love, which could be shattered instantly by death, she dreamed of order, strict and noble – here she could find her aim and the meaning of her life. For once, fate was on her side: she could not have found anyone better than Achille-Cléophas. Having only recently joined the ranks of the bourgeoisie, he had one principle (which, as we have seen, he derived from his peasant origins and his imperious pride): the husband alone captains the ship. From his future wife, he demanded what she longed for with all her heart: obedience and a relative existence – the wife is an eternal minor, her husband's daughter. She accepted and entered into a kind of complicity with him, as the peculiar episode of their engagement shows. He had seen and taken the measure of her: the young girl's austerity was brought out by the 'laxity' of her surroundings. Straight away, the fiancé appropriated the rights of her dead father and took it upon himself to send her back to boarding-school, only letting her emerge on the eve of their marriage. One may imagine that the Laumoniers could have asked for nothing better: this modest virgin must have been an embarrassment to them. In any case, where she herself was concerned, this assertion of authority was like being physically possessed: she felt that she had a master, and this intoxicating certainty even affected her sexually. The transfer was complete: in her near-monastic cell, patient and submissive, she waited until the time had at last come to sleep with her father. Much later, in old age and widowhood, she would still refer smugly to this stern measure. When Caroline Commanville writes, on this subject, that Achille-Cléophas was 'more far-sighted than she could have been', we can surely hear her grandmother's voice: 'My future husband, more far-sighted than I could have been . . .' In other words: there was something fishy there, liaisons that I did not know about or, perhaps, the threat of scandal, all of which I, in my naïvety, never suspected; but my fiancé did. I protested at first against his decision, sulked a little, then had the delight of admitting that I was wrong: as always, he knew best.

They were married in February 1812 and moved into No. 8, rue du Petit-Salut, where they were to stay for seven years. Madame Commanville writes: 'When I was a child, grandmother often used to take me by [the house] and, looking at the windows, say to me in a solemn, almost reverential voice: "You know, that is where I spent the best years of my life." '

This testimony seems to us to be highly significant. Seven years of happiness. Afterward, the misfortunes did not come all at once, there was a kind of intermission, but the storm clouds were gathering and, above all, her heart was no longer in it. So what were the important events in the couple's life between 1812 and 1819? Well, first of all, on the day before the first anniversary of the wedding, Achille was born. There is no doubt that he was well fed and cared for: the young mother loved this token of their love. And, apart from that, Achille-Cléophas had given him his own Christian name,

MATERNAL LOVE

indicating to those around him that he considered this firstborn child (there would be others) as his successor, the future head of the family: here is my son, which is like saying *myself*, today my reflection, tomorrow my reincarnation. The mother was made aware of this predilection and shared it: in her child she loved her husband's own tender, vulnerable childhood, long thought dead, but now at last reborn. The object of so much passionate care, Achille was a made-to-order child: healthy, obedient, bright. It was a pleasure for his mother, some time later, to teach him to read. Meanwhile, the progenitor made his wife pregnant on two further occasions and she gave him two more boys: two who came to nothing, because they died as infants. And here is what I find astonishing: in general, a single early death is enough to plunge parents into grief. The Flauberts experienced two, one after another – enough to distress them for a long time and to make them abhor this first house. Yet old Mme Flaubert, thirty years later, enjoys returning nostalgically to the rue du Petit-Salut, so that she can stop in front of her old dwelling and constantly recall that she experienced happiness here. If we are to divide her married life into two, as she suggests we should, we observe that *before* she went to live at the Hôtel-Dieu, she had three sons, only one of whom survived; while *after* she was living there, the ratio is reversed: of the three children she bore, only one died. However (and she tells us this herself), despite these dreadful misfortunes, she enjoyed real happiness in the seven years when she was living in the rue du Petit-Salut.

What can explain this? One thing seems to me certain: the dead were not able to inspire her with abhorrence for the first seven years, nor are the living able to make her feel affection for the ones that followed; so her offspring cannot have weighed heavily with her. Caroline Flaubert's happiness or unhappiness depended on a single person, and that was Achille-Cléophas. Gustave says so himself, in a letter to Louise: 'She loved my father as much as a woman has ever been able to love a man, not just when they were young, but right up to the final day which came after 35 years of marriage.' If we put this glowing tribute in context, it appears that the words are not without ulterior motive, as usual: he wants to offer his mother

95

as an example to Louise – you are jealous, my mother wasn't, she loved my father a thousand times more than you love me; that is the example to follow: love me and keep quiet. Moreover, having done it a few times oneself, one can recognize a note of hysteria, chiefly intended to convince others: the tone rises, there is an element of hyperbole to make-up for the lack of *pathos* in the statement. Perhaps he is exaggerating his mother's feelings. Fortunately we have further proof, which of course also originates with him, but which does not seem to be a falsehood: Mme Flaubert was a deist who had preserved her faith even though she had given herself to a non-believing doctor. There had to be a heaven – for the mother she had killed, for J.-B. Fleuriot, who died prematurely, for the little angels that God sent down to visit earth, then regularly called back to Himself before their time was up. And there had to be a little love, too, to moderate her feelings of guilt and to brighten the unrewarding virtues that she practised out of fear. She was one of those women who say: 'I have my own religion', or: 'I have my own God'; and who are content to cannibalize the Catholic faith here and there: they take its comforts, its incense, its stained glass and the organ, while leaving behind the dogmas. Caroline's deism, her super Superego, was to have recourse to God against the father; and it was also, no doubt, the poetry of a sensibility prematurely blighted: harmony, meditation, reflection, elevation. Lamartine was pleasing because he recorded thoughts that, though fragmentary, were so beautiful, in lines that would come into one's head during mass. The fact is that one attended and took the sacraments – if only because of the worthy clientele and through fear of the Congregation.[2]

One may be sure that Dr Flaubert made no effort to enlighten his wife; she would have abandoned her opinions at once had he given any indication of wanting her to do so. Her husband's tolerance allowed her to keep her beliefs, but without touching them: everything remained vague and poetic. In reality, after the complete success

---

2. *the Congregation*: an organization of Catholic ultra-royalists active in the 1820s. Liberals believed they were a conspiratorial secret society.

of the transference, she hardly had need of her super Superego. And I find it hard to imagine that she would have appealed to her God against a judgement passed by Achille-Cléophas. No matter; she prepared her children, or at least Gustave, to receive empty intuitions and calls from on high. The medical director did not interfere: religion is necessary in the nursery and the women's quarters; it's the best way to keep women in a state of childhood. As for his sons, at around the age of five or six he took them in hand and, with a single breath, blew away all the fine dust that the mother had left on their frontal lobes.

And yet, after the successive deaths of her husband and her daughter, Mme Flaubert suddenly lost her faith – the same faith that had not been disturbed by the loss of three children, given and absurdly taken away. No doubt, the shock was a dreadful one; but it did not demand that she should commit the sin of despair. It is usually in the event of such a loss that the non-believer is converted, needing help, needing to think that life is not a tale told by a madman, needing above all to believe that the dead are on a journey and that they will meet again. The first time that her father left her, Caroline was ten years old; she did what anyone else might do and strengthened her faith. The second time, she was more than fifty years old; this would have been the moment for her to fall into the hands of the priests, but no such thing happened. The widow reacted in an unusual way and broke with God. Can we say that she was driven to this mainly by the loss of her daughter? Of course, the two losses are inseparable; but it is the first that casts its dark light on the second. Nonetheless, the head surgeon had reached the age of sixty when he died; even in our time, this would not be too bad; and in those days such long lives were considered to be exceptional gifts of Providence. So, at first sight, God seems beyond reproach: in His goodness, He even went to the extent of not liquidating the father until the oldest son was of an age to replace him. Never mind that: this ageing wife of an old husband was not to be resigned. After thirty-five years of married life, the loss of Achille-Cléophas was, to her eyes, no less an intolerable outrage than the loss of his young wife, Anne Cambremer de Croixmare, must have been for young

Dr Fleuriot: such an appalling injustice is an indictment of the Universe, where evil is all-powerful. God does not exist. Gustave is right: she loves him as she did at the very start. For this relative being, the head surgeon naturally represented the sole source of happiness, but there is more to it than that: he justified her, absolved her, legitimized her existence and gave her a reason for living; he was Goodness. If Goodness dies, nothing is left on earth or in heaven: she reverted to the uncertainties of her youth, but this time without hope. She recalled her whole life, with all its griefs, and eliminated the Almighty in a furious act of revenge. Above all, she was converted to atheism as others are to revealed religion: out of loyalty to the dead person, to take him entirely into herself, to *become* him. She agreed never to see him again on condition that she might carry him inside herself, like a new child, by taking as her own the proud and hard beliefs that had contributed so much to her husband's eminence. While he was still alive, Dr Flaubert's atheism acted as guarantor of Caroline's religious leanings: in some vague way, she considered this faith without dogma as a minor enthralment, appropriate to her sex; her man was atheist for both of them. With Achille-Cléophas dead, she represented him; she spat out her Lamartinian sweetmeats and adopted the healthy cause of despair. What strikes me is this: she had to keep God, or else abandon any hope of rejoining the soul of the dear departed. She drove away the deceiving Almighty and, at the same time, knowingly, killed her husband for ever: if he had no soul, all that would remain were some white bones in the corrosive earth. This means that she preferred fidelity to hope: in the name of his own principles, the doctor-philosopher must turn to dust. She knew the implications of the doctrine, yet she adopted it even so: to meet her husband again in heaven was good; but to represent him on earth, in her own heart and for herself alone – she no longer went visiting – was better still. Can we speak of identification or reincarnation? No, rather of constancy; she would lapse towards death as the late Achille-Cléophas had done, knowing that the final calamity is complete and hoping to join her husband, with every heartbeat, *in this life*, rather than to meet him, *in the other*, as one of the elect in a Heaven in

MATERNAL LOVE

which he had not believed. None of this involved so much reasoning. Or, rather, there was no argument at all: she did what she could and became daily more like her man. Dried up, empty, anxious, bearing an infinite weight of misery that she poured out every day, but restrained from killing herself by the Flaubert utilitarianism: one must serve the family; as long as it still exists, one should not kill oneself.

This is what I call love; there are other kinds, but none stronger. Everything is there: this father dominated her, guided her, satisfying her needs for security, virtue and sex. She had everything: Goodness had taken her and put her in his bed, she had swooned beneath the weight of this mighty angel. In broad daylight, she was disturbed by the doctor's paternal severity: she saw it as the promise of new ecstasies; she was docile and easily swayed, feeling that her obedience was a voluptuous extension of her nocturnal submission.

I said that the Rouen branch of the Flauberts was constituted as a semi-domestic family: Achille-Cléophas constructed the family unit himself and, as we have seen, made it *as he himself was*, as he had been made and as he intended to be. But he was not solely responsible: his wife, chosen with care, suited him admirably; she did all the work, inside the little household, under his overall guidance. Not that she preferred this type of 'family unit' or rejected that one: she couldn't care less. What mattered in her eyes was the couple; and she wanted it as incestuous as possible. She endorsed her husband in his authority as *paterfamilias* so that she could feel, in her heart and in her body, that she had no other lover than her father. Her whole existence, from marriage to death, was marked, directed and permeated – at the heart of this patriarchy – by this conjugal love. She became the accomplice of the all-powerful progenitor in order to defend, from all, against all, the unity of this couple in which she found her sensual delight, her spiritual happiness, her place in the world, her being.

Of course, she did love the children: through them, she loved the father. *In them*, she loved the fecundity of the progenitor. And there was more to it than that: no doubt the little orphan had often dreamed in years past of the one means by which she might recover her lost family: she wanted to be married and to become a mother in her turn, to resurrect her mother in her own maternity. As one can see, the relationship was purely one with herself: in her eyes, the children, provided they were normal, had no other role than to bring her into possession of her maternal functions. Even in her most precise imaginings, they would remain vague. The brightest images in her fantasies were those that showed her in her new role: giving the breast, caring, bringing up a swarm of kids. Or, rather, no: what I have just said should only be applied to the boys. She would have as many of those as God would give her; but with girls, it was a different matter: she wanted *one*. A failed childhood, as we now know from psychoanalysis, has to be started afresh: it does so with another child. When Caroline had a baby girl, she was her own mother, giving birth to her. The love and care that she intended to lavish on her daughter were the very same that Mme Fleuriot had deprived her of, by her premature death. In short, another Caroline was expected: if the former orphan, having found herself a new incestuous father, could succeed in creating an improved version of her own childhood with a child of her own sex; and if, anticipating all the desires of this flesh of her flesh, she could succeed retrospectively in heaping happiness on these frustrated early years and filing down the claws of memories that were still ripping her apart, Mme Flaubert would have closed the circle: enjoying an eternal childhood under the paternal authority of her husband, she would uproot her own childhood – the real one – tearing it from her memory and making it a success through someone else. The proof of this deep desire is that she attributed her own name to the daughter that the medical director managed to give her after thirteen years. And it is no accident, either, that this daughter's daughter in her turn received this same first name: the essential thing, indeed, was to preserve the memory of the young mother who died giving birth to her, just as Mme Fleuriot had at the end of the previous century. No matter: what a strange dynasty these Carolines are, the first and last of them killing their mothers. To his firstborn, the progenitor had royally announced: '*This is me*, and to prove it I shall call him Achille.' Thirteen years later, the wife's intention was much the same, and doubtless inspired by her Master: 'This is me, repairing my own childhood, having a mother who lives only to love me.' This explains why Gustave's sister was undoubtedly her mother's favourite: in a way, she represented the only personal relationship that the doctor's wife maintained with herself, the only subjective intimacy to which the incestuous father did not have access. To the very act of breastfeeding (even though it was determined by objective considerations), she unconsciously brought a whole world that he could not fathom; *she made herself breast*, in order to eliminate in the present the indestructible frustrations of the past; she became love, so that she might at least *give* the tenderness that she had not *received*.

She waited for thirteen years for this opportunity which came too late; thirteen years in which Achille-Cléophas gave her five boys. She greeted the first with pleasure: the main thing was to assure the descent and the continuation of the family name. In any event, the wife's wishes came after those of the Master, and also it would not be good for the firstborn to be of the weaker sex. But with her second pregnancy, she started to expect. She was to be disappointed four times: Gustave was the third. In my view, this is what explains her strange indifference to the first two deaths. God had given her these sons, and she accepted them out of love for her husband and out of a sense of duty: the family must increase and multiply. But when God carried them off again, the mother remained dry-eyed: if He had taken them back, it was because they had been delivered to the Flauberts by mistake; they would just have to start again, that's all, and try to do better; they could always hope that the next offspring would be a girl. Even so, I imagine that she must have been affected: the infants died in her arms, despite the skilled care and vigilance that she provided; it was her task to make them live and to protect them; she was watchful, conscientious, fulfilling her duties to perfection, never sparing herself: however innocent she might be, the deaths became personal failures. She was her mother's killer and a relationship with death seems to have been her fundamental link to the world and to others, the original source of her feeling of guilt. The odds are strongly that she considered each of these sudden fatalities as a renewal of her original sin and, at the same time, as the effect of some obscure curse laid on her by her mother.

Luckily for her, Dr Flaubert had none of these refinements: of course, he preferred males and, most of all, whatever the sex, he wanted viable offspring. But for a long time his anxieties remained unfounded: the eldest was in good health, that was the main thing. As for the other children, they were each as good as the other, each represented the family, none could be its special incarnation. In short, he felt little attachment to the newborn children. In any case, at the start of the last century, it was not advisable to expend too much love on infants, since they died like flies. The first two deaths surely appeared regrettable, but not surprising: it was in the order of things. As soon as a child entered the world, Achille-Cléophas saw in it a statistical probability of survival. Unique and ill-fated dramas made an unfortunate start before his eyes, then blew up in his face, and all he could see in what had happened was a physiological accident. A lot of children are needed to carry on a line, he thought, and a lot of deaths to make one life. The conclusion was inescapable: a doctor, if he is also a philosopher on the side, must expect infant mortality and endure it with equanimity when it strikes his own family. This, as we know, amounts to saying: the individual is the inessential, ephemeral mode of being, the family group is the substance that produces the modes and reabsorbs them into itself. No doubt this slightly harsh philosophy had a good effect on Caroline: it must have explained to her that she was bringing into the world what (for want of a suitable word in French) I shall call *morituri*.* She knew them to be such in her very flesh when she was carrying them.

Sorrow, indifference: two burials, then, afterwards, a third son, Gustave. The mother had not taken off her mourning, or only just. But we know that she was melancholic and why: she could not accept any happiness not tinged with mourning. For her, black justified everything, or nearly everything: an orphan, the mother of

---

* So Goethe, when told of the death of his son, calmly remarked: 'I knew that I was fathering a mortal.'

still-born children, then a widow, she wore it more or less throughout her life. This explains why she spoke of those first seven years 'in a solemn, almost reverential voice'. Submission, respect, austerity and devotion to the head of the family – and, through him, to the future family itself; nocturnal pleasures, games of love and death: she needed this and nothing more; a brilliant, generous, fulfilling life would have reminded her of the Laumoniers' salon, and she would have rejected it with anxiety and frigidity. Her sons, on the earth or in it, always remained strangers to her: the father's authority insinuated itself between the wife and her children; boys belong to the father, that's the rule, as soon as they are old enough to leave the nursery. Achille, being his own father in nappies, delighted her. After a time, the father took him back. Even though she continued to take care of him, it was she who taught him his letters, but the little prodigy, the doctor's chosen one, escaped her: for her, he became merely the virile, foreign destiny that the father had in store for him. This explains the near-breakdown in relations between mother and son after the father's death: admittedly, she had a grudge against her daughter-in-law, and Achille was not very pleasant to her; but these causes would have been negligible had she felt for her eldest son the violent, mutual love that Mme Le Poittevin felt for Alfred. Twenty years later, misunderstandings and bad behaviour might well undermine such a powerful feeling, blight it with rancour and, sometimes, change it to hatred, but they could not prevent it from having left a mark on the heart, so that on occasion a memory will revive it in its first innocence and former strength. Mme Flaubert did not like the chief surgeon Achille – this is a fact that Gustave knowingly implies in his correspondence. But such indifference, tinged with blame, but without animosity, would not even be conceivable if she had once loved him. When he was small, what she did love was his father in him; when he became Achille, he no longer interested her. She never felt any possessive or jealous affection for either of her boys. The rights that she felt she had over them had first to be conceded to her by the father. She never took the initiative, or gave them an order in her own name: the sovereign will of her husband made her the vehicle of the *patria potestas*; she received the power, but her authority was only borrowed. This is what the chief physician demanded of his wife. But she, far from obeying out of habit, training or conformity with custom, delighted in submission and was all the more authoritarian with her children, the more submissive she was to the master. She did not pass their complaints on to him: a challenge to an order, objections raised by her sons, they would, in her mouth, have become *her own disrespect*. A 'no', whatever its origin, must not be spoken in front of the master: it would be a blasphemy *in any event*. The rest follows automatically: unlike so many other mothers, she never took her children's side against her husband; she was never tempted to defend them, so firm was her conviction that Achille-Cléophas' decisions were the best in the world. She loved him too much and too loyally to try to manipulate him; and I would suggest that her great merit was that, unlike so many wives, she did not know how to 'get round' her husband. But this is a *domestic* virtue: in order to acquire and keep it, she rejected all the complicities – more or less questionable, more or less successful – that unite mother and son in conjugal families. In taking virtue to the extreme (i.e. until it becomes vice), she never *interceded* on her children's behalf: right up to Achille-Cléophas' death, more fearful but more flexible when he exercised it himself, more rigid and bureaucratic when the wife acted as intermediary, the authority of the *paterfamilias* was imposed on the two boys with absolute sovereignty, but without the mother ever tempering it with her tenderness. How could she have done so, anyway? No doubt she loved them, but not tenderly, reserving her heart for the newcomer, Caroline, who was destined to be no less than the renewal of herself. And if one should ask what love is without tenderness, I would say that it was absolute devotion and collective valorization: I have no doubt that she would have ruined her own health to save her sons when they fell ill, and that she would have given her own life in place of either of theirs: this, in any case, is what she firmly believed. Yet she stated that she did not know what sacrifice was, or duty, for that matter. We must take her word for it, provided we understand what she means. What is implied is a criticism of some of her friends whose sour maternal generosity – ever panting, ever tearful, supported by a 'sense of duty' – aims at nothing more than to acquire rights for themselves, and if these are not accorded, ends in resentment. Caroline, for her part, has never *taken anything upon herself*; she acts because it pleases her or to defend the interests of the family. The only *valid* actions are those that arise from spontaneity. It is a good thing for a child that its mother should not pretend to be sacrificing herself for it when she wipes its bottom; what is *positive* here is the interest that Mme Flaubert took in the practical, routine tasks of being a mother. At least, she spared the two boys the unpleasant feeling that she did not come near them without having to overcome a sense of disgust. But we shall not follow her any further; it is true that, in this utilitarian age, she lacked any theory of virtue; and if, despite this deficiency, she was (like her husband) virtuous, it was not out of inclination (as Gustave says), but out of *need*. It was in carrying out set tasks that she found her balance and her earthly substance. Breastfeeding an infant, caring for it, spending her nights watching over it, she *took her bearings*: dead on course, position set, two hundred feet offshore. However, one must understand that she loved these familiar tasks for themselves and the accessories – nappies, cot clothes, cradle – rather than the child. From her first child, this anxious girl had undergone a complete reversal of means and ends: the newborn was no more than the *object* of her care, the indispensable means for her to become the best of mothers. Cared for *in general*, its individuality went by unnoticed; one asked nothing of it except to live. The accessories absorbed love and did not return it.

This generalization was also present in the act of enhancement. When she held one of the little mites in her arms, what she admired in him was the source of life that had fertilized her: the father's sperm become flesh. But whatever the child was, the seed remained the same: in the first months, they seemed interchangeable to her. In each of them – which, when it came down to it, was only a socialization of her unease – she also respected the Flaubert and Cambremer de Croixmare families, intimately mingled. But, in early infancy, none of them could be especially the incarnation of the families. We must revert to this: in her children she loved the eternal repetition – that is, the cyclical movement of virtue – the power of the father and the House of Flaubert. Not any individual quality. In modern bourgeois families, the mother, who is most in love, loves her son in part against her husband: that will be her revenge. No sooner is the child born than she starts to worship the peculiar features of this future progenitor; for both of them, an adventure is beginning, unique, unpredictable, and for that very reason endearing. Caroline, in 1830, had nothing with which she could reproach the philosopher-doctor: not that he was irreproachable, but she had decided, even before marrying him, that she would approve of everything that he did. This wife had not even the shadow of rebellion that would have made her a mother.

More wife than mother: almost a cliché. Should we apply it to Mme Flaubert? Not without reservations. If one were suggesting, in fact, that she made love more willingly than she made children, then one would be wrong: for her to take pleasure in the former, it was obviously necessary that she should consider it the only means to produce the latter. She came out of a sense of maternal virtue. It would be truer to say that, more than a mother, she was an incestuous daughter. There was nothing between her and her sons: we know that the ties that seem to unite them are borrowed and that what they unite are the young Flauberts to their father. Communication with the mother has been cut. In reality, she was her sons' secret sister: an older sister, in whose care they are left; she is responsible for them to the *paterfamilias*, she loves them in him as Christians love one another in God; but the only direct relationship of Caroline to her children is *cohabitation* – and by that, one must understand not only coexistence in a single place, but belonging to the same House.

This is why Mme Flaubert's conjugal happiness did not really suffer from the first deaths. Yet we know that it suffered a marked decline when she moved house. What happened? We cannot tell precisely, but the broad circumstances are known. The following, to start with, the first, which is the origin of all the rest: Caroline was so constituted that neither joy nor sorrow could affect her unless it came directly from Achille-Cléophas. In other words, she was smitten in her incestuous heart. Seven years is an age: snakes change their skins and many men change women every seven years. I am not saying that Achille-Cléophas changed his wife or that he was unfaithful to her, but simply that love, in the well-ordered life of the chief physician, took only a subordinate place. Caroline, on the other hand, *lived in* love; it was an immutable force, her axis and her sustenance; still more, it was the sacred sphere of repetition: through love, it became poetic and sacred to repeat, with obstinacy and (as we know) with only moderate success, the task of breeding and rearing. She wanted nothing, not even an intensification of the feeling – something that she would not have considered possible, or which would have terrified her. Just this: continuity; everything returns, each year recalls all previous years, repeats the same vows and guarantees that the future is no more than a memory to come; nothing changes. In short, this is happiness: first of all one must be a vassal, then the pattern of submission and of the lord's generosity must be fixed once and for all; one is granted one's place, one sticks to it. With reciprocity, happiness disappears; good riddance. I am not suggesting that Caroline was immediately aware of the master's every change of mood or feeling. But, when the young wife did notice it, we can be sure that it made her suffer or at the very least feel anxious. As soon as Achille-Cléophas changed, she would become vaguely aware that the special rule of her man was always to press forward and never to go back; in short that her conjugal happiness was profoundly in danger from the very person who provided her with it. There must have been premonitions of this sort during the first seven years, but they flashed across the life and consciousness of the wife like shooting stars, soon forgotten. Yet the philosopher-physician was not at all comparable to those rather uncouth taskmasters who, until the day of their death, mount their wives because they are *theirs* and they are determined to enjoy them – men who are at once disappointing and reassuring, who never change, but give nothing. A story told by Gustave casts an unusual light on his father: he must have adored women and charmed them, as courteous as a prince, as churlish as a country bumpkin, not doing anything that might spare his wife any of the pangs of jealousy:

'I remember, ten years ago, when we were all at Le Havre. My father learned that a woman whom he had known as a young man of seventeen was living there with her son. He thought he would go and see them. This woman, a celebrated local beauty, had once been his mistress. He refused to do what many middle-class husbands would have done: he did not disguise the fact, he was above that. So he went to pay her a visit. My mother and the three of us stayed standing outside in the street, waiting . . . Do you think this made my mother jealous or that she was at all upset by it? No.'

This narrative calls for some comment. Firstly: it may be that Mme Flaubert was neither upset nor jealous, but even if she had been dying the death of a thousand cuts, her children would never have guessed it. What Flaubert can tell us is that there was no scene in the street, and that his mother gave no visible evidence of resentment, either that day or on the following days; that's all. This is not surprising: Mme Flaubert was not especially outgoing and, even if she had been, would categorically have refused to inform her sons of their father's shameful behaviour. Moreover, on this as on every other occasion, the dutiful daughter must have made an effort to put up with it.

However, in this case, it is the father who interests me. There is a great deal of constancy and some delicacy of feeling in a man who is keen, after thirty years, to see a woman whom he loved; this is a tribute to his mistress that means: I have never forgotten you. Unfortunately, the same man is behaving like a complete boor towards his wife – though I agree that he should perhaps not have hidden his intentions from her; but one should understand the meaning of such frankness: if one person refuses to lie to his equal, nothing could be better, for the double reason that their equality is based on truth and that lying gains only a base, temporary superiority to the liar which conceals an enduring inferiority. But *above* lying? Perhaps he was telling the truth *in order to preserve* his superiority? The *paterfamilias* considered his wishes as orders and it was the family's duty to submit without argument. He wanted to see his former mistress: this was the king's whim, and therefore legitimate; he communicated it to his subjects so that they might serve his ends;

and, as for his great vassal, his wife, she would just have to reconcile herself to it. After that, he left her standing on the pavement with the children and forced her to kick her heels while he was indulging the other woman with his pleasantries. The churlishness takes one aback. For it to seem so spontaneous and for the youngest son to find it so natural, it must have been commonplace; and for Mme Flaubert not even to be put out by it means that this child-wife had been long trained, breaking her back in the constant exercise of docility.

Caroline Flaubert, *née* Fleuriot, deserved the happiness that she enjoyed for seven years: she knew how to take a punch. This difficult art is not learned overnight – though I accept that, being an orphan and respectful, she had a talent for it. But talent is not enough: she had to practise, from the very start, to stifle disgust, to choke back sobs, to smother resentment. Above all, she was required to approve everything, in advance and *a priori*; she managed it, like the peasant woman in the popular story who constantly repeats: 'What the old man does, is well done.' The wife of the philosopher-physician eventually became the very incarnation of unconditional acceptance. This is never accomplished without pitiless, exhausting effort: in the worn-out soul, some faculties become abnormally enlarged, others atrophy. The wife of Achille-Cléophas owed her Master's trust to the number of about turns she had made, in her eagerness to *ratify* the calluses on her heart and her deliberate insensitivity in certain areas. But one may turn and turn about as much as one likes; that is not to say that one can do it with impunity. De-Stalinization led to an increase in neuroses in Europe: one can only assume that the grievances repressed, lines of reasoning cut short, feelings muzzled and facts not mentioned were repressed, buried under the floorboards of the soul, without being abolished. Some are dead and stinking; others which were buried alive and have returned to the scene since the end of Stalinism, embittered to the point of madness: when the 'de-Stalinized' person opens his eyes, he finds himself rootless in a frightful, featureless world with no signposts. No more myths, only mortal, ephemeral truths: he has 'suffered like a Russian', and for nothing.

After seven years of domestic Stalinism, nothing so serious occurred in the Flaubert household. The husband did not die; he reigned on. But the story recounted above proves that he was capable of passionate impulses: one would almost suspect that he was capable of love; in any case, he kept in his heart the memory of some old flames, still burning, with disquieting fidelity: when he was giving Mme Flaubert a son, just *what* did he think about? And *of whom*? She must have realized early on that he 'had lived' and that he was attached to his past: the chief physician was 'above' sparing her the story of his loves. She accepted everything, she proclaimed herself proud to have the right of entry to this well-stocked memory. But as he was describing himself in this way, the husband, without ceasing to be a father, became a stranger: every episode of his life, every leaning, every taste put a distance between them. She felt him to be unattainable even in his physical presence: he escaped from her by defining himself; another Achille-Cléophas turned a dark face towards a past which he had lived alone and which was beyond her grasp. It might have amounted to nothing: however far a woman may take her identification with the man, or her alienation from him, and whatever the eagerness with which she may have cut herself off from herself and confined herself within the absolute being of her husband, he will always betray her, if only by simple exercise of his recognized sovereignty: he is the independent variable, as the wife wanted him to be in order to take the couple's integration to the limit; yet his independence, if he were to do nothing all his life but to assert it, becomes in him and through him the original sin, the choice that favours one sex at the expense of the other, the source of all infidelities. This means: in order to become one, it is necessary to be and to remain two. A doctor driven by ambition, wisely administering his little fortune, an imperious father and husband, Achille-Cléophas belonged to his wife. Yet, through some old enchantments lodged in the depths of his memory; through what one can sense of a sensibility that was bitter, dark, nervous and occasionally tender; through the tears that he shed for himself; and through a quite unusual and rarely conscious relationship to himself, he escaped her – all the more surely since she did not try to hold him back: what need had she, weak and racked with guilt, of his solitude and vulnerable weakness? Most daughters want *to be the object* of paternal love. Which of them wants the father, that absolute subject, to become permanently the object of her understanding or her sympathy?

So nothing changed in those seven years, except feelings. Without that curious glimpse of Achille-Cléophas, we might have thought that he remained the same until his death, not having time to become anyone else: between being an overworked doctor, a professor and a dogged researcher, when would he have had time for self-analysis? In reality, however, he was constantly changing: this restless being had his own dreams and his fidelity was bought at a price. In the tribute paid to his old flame we can catch sight of the sort of person he was at the time of their engagement and in the early days of the marriage: he overwhelmed Caroline with his austere gallantry and an imperious show of respect, shot through at moments with a bolt of passion. And the same story tells us about the development of his behaviour inside the marriage. At the end, he still respects his wife — enough at least to tell her the truth, but not enough to spare her a long wait in the middle of the street while he goes back to his youth, to shed a few tears over himself. Here, the two ends of the puzzle meet: the deterioration of relations is evident. Perhaps seven years are enough to bring things to such a pass, but the most probable explanation is that the death of Laumonier caught the young couple on some intermediate stage in this development. Achille-Cléophas was working harder and harder every day, more from preference than from necessity, and he would rest in the evenings, more and more frequently turning his thoughts in on himself. The wife accepted, or at least kept quiet, telling herself that everything was the same. The unchanging nature of the surroundings and the repetition of her tasks — she was both a mother and a housewife — helped to mask the imperceptible distance that, when it comes down to it, indicates nothing more or less than the death of love in a heart. Caroline was still in love, Achille-Cléophas no longer was; or, if you like, he loved her in a different way. The evidence of this change was all around, in minute details right in front of her eyes: the young woman saw them without being aware of them. They had come in uninvited and been buried, where they gnawed at her softly and she did not deign to feel their effects.

The change of house, which they had anticipated with dread, was a catastrophe: it threw a different light on everything. To start with, their new home was ghastly. It has often been described, to point out Gustave's peculiar familiarity, from the age of four, with corpses; but no one, as far as I know, has wondered how his young mother put up with their company. Having lost four of those closest to her, she now had death for a neighbour, naked, familiar. There were rotting corpses in the basement, severed limbs in the lecture halls, dying patients in the hospital wards. True, she was a doctor's daughter as well as a doctor's wife: if she wished, she could tell herself with pride that her husband was struggling with all his might to save human lives. But she didn't wish: this somewhat impoverished imagination did not have the resources needed to transform the missing father into a Galahad. And, then, the gallant knight was fighting his battles a long way from her, leaving her alone in dreary old lodgings that everyone who saw them agreed were hideous. One knows what these apartments in hospitals are like: however prettily done up they may be (and these weren't), one enters them with nostrils on the alert, sniffing for smells of phenol and of decomposition. In the morning, early, out of any window, one can see the paupers' hearse slipping out – and not empty; one can see men in prison uniform crossing the yard or gathering in the doorways, patients, pale and convalescent, who do odd jobs and sometimes serve at the director's table. Illness produces its own techniques and the techniques produce their own men; between the hospital walls, the interior of the doctor's home is penetrated by what lies outside it; public suffering stifles private life. For some years, surrounded by deaths that reflected her own losses back to her as particular instances of the national mortality rate, Caroline must have felt haunted, anonymous and alone. Her husband left her at daybreak. If he took lunch at home, he did not stay for long, but left again to return late and go to bed early. His new duties naturally meant a considerable increase in his responsibilities and his work. The evenings became shorter just when more effort and more perseverance were needed for the couple to recover their former intimacy. What does a housewife become when her home is transformed into a public crossroads? Mme Flaubert, who had long been secretive, closed up altogether. She was still submissive, still loving and loyal, and continued both to revere her husband and to lead a virtuous life; but resignation – not daring to speak its name – drove her back, giving her a kind of icy depth. It was with the benefit of this tiny distance that life appeared to her and demanded reconsideration: new habits, or merely the old ones transported to strange surroundings, showed her herself *from outside*. Was it a matter of perseverance or incongruity, this giving of life and nourishing it in the kingdom of death? Eventually, she decided on perseverance, but without managing to get rid of a sense of the absurdity of what she was doing. As for the husband, a familiar figure who stood out at set times against a strange, almost hostile background, he became involved, almost against her wishes, in this 'estrangement' around her. In short, what this meant was that she had lost the sense of immediacy: nothing could any longer be taken for granted, not even love. One would imagine that in the course of this silent reassessment, she discovered the true meaning of her recent, happy years: that the worm was already at the bud, that Dr Flaubert had drifted away from her well before Laumonier's death, that the love which women dream of is unchanging, while that of men is not. But, in my view, it would be dangerous to attribute too lucid an awareness to her. In the absence of any proof, there is another, more likely hypothesis: that she did not want to realize that her uneasiness had begun in the rue du Petit-Salut, and especially not that she had felt it without admitting as much to herself; she attributed full responsibility for her husband's distancing from her, for her anxieties and for her slight depersonalization to their new lodgings: it all dated from the moment when they had moved house; and at the same time, she was quite willing to pad out her thoughts by turning back to earlier years: there had been awkward moments, periods of silence, interludes, while Laumonier was still alive, which she had repressed and which now resurfaced; but although she felt them bitterly now, as prophecies that had come to pass, she refrained from dating and localizing them: rather than seeing them as stages along an unavoidable progression, she used them to support her indictment of the Hôtel-Dieu, that cemetery of the living which was taking away her husband. Achille-Cléophas came out of these inner deliberations as he had gone in: head high, innocent, his heart unchanged. It was universal death and the sufferings of mankind, like transparent windows raised between the two of them, that were separating the couple. This device rescued the years of happiness, but at the expense of the present. Caroline had projected everything – disappointment, anxiety, resentment, irritation with herself – on to the dark walls imprisoning her, and the walls reflected back her misfortunes as a single whole.

I have chosen the second hypothesis, others may prefer the first; no matter: in terms of what we are trying to achieve, they amount to the same. Whether more or less consciously, with more of true unhappiness or of bewilderment, the young woman found that the ice had entered her soul: it is death approaching her husband, who steps back. It is more or less certain that she passed on her anxieties to the chief surgeon. No sooner had they moved in, than he bought a country house at Butot, so that they could spend the holidays there. From 1820 to 1844, he lived in the summer at Déville, and in 1844 he bought the house at Croisset where he meant to live. In short, from the first year, the drawbacks of his winter home were compensated for by his summer ones. It is hard to believe that this scientific fanatic would, on his own initiative, have moved away from the place where he was doing his research: it must be that his wife's mood and perhaps her health had been affected, and he took note of this and questioned her. This nervous, passionate, utilitarian, reasonable pre-Romantic must have seen the Hôtel-Dieu through Caroline's eyes – not for more than an instant, but it was enough for him to judge that her request was valid. And it was, to the extent that their gloomy dwelling has been disused for the past half-century: no one lives there any more. We men have acquired the sensibilities of our great-grandmothers.

Masturbation

This is an extract from *Saint Genet* (1952), Sartre's mischievous, miscellaneous celebration of the life and art of Jean Genet. Moving by way of a thematic circuit that links luxury, fakery and bad taste, Sartre explores a subject that has attracted very little serious attention.

The true for God, the false for man. *True* luxury is a homage to creation, while *false* luxury, a human hell, does honour to production. True luxury has only ever existed in its pure state in aristocratic and agricultural societies; it was the opulent consumption of rare, natural objects by God's elect. It is true that legions of slaves were employed in discovering, transporting and refining these products of Nature. But human labour was still contemptible: upon contact with nature, it immediately degenerated into a natural activity. In the eyes of the Rajah, the pearl fisher was not much different from the pig who hunts for truffles; the lacemaker's work has never made lace a human product; on the contrary, it was lace that made the lacemaker into a laceworm. Truffles, diamonds, pearls, lace and gold, by the fact of appearing somewhere in the universe, naturally brought into being human instruments who would raise them to the highest degree of perfection. In such societies, the worker is neither man nor beast. His traditional techniques, their source lost in the mists of time, have become natural and sacred. An intermediary between man and nature, he fades into the background once he has put mankind in the presence of nature. Nothing remains of his work but a drop of blood, to heighten the sheen of the pearl and a little surface bloom that allows fruit and meats the better to release their scents. The Aristocrat devours nature and the product in the form in which he consumes it should have a slight odour of entrails or urine: wool is better when it preserves a slight redolence of suint, honey when it has a hint of wax, a pearl when it is not quite round. Strong and indistinct odours, the taste of cooked blood, the exquisite imperfection of forms and a discreet blurring of colours are the best guarantees of authenticity. One is a person of taste if, beneath a carefully contrived presentation, one is able to discern the carnal, tenacious, humble, organic, milky *taste* of the creature. The supreme end of the Universe, the king of Nature and himself a natural product, the luxury consumer uses the objects that he consumes to reflect back his sumptuous and sanguinary birth; through his commerce with the aristocracy of stones, plants and animals, the aristocrat realizes the communion of his human 'nature' with the great cosmic Nature. When he eats, magnificent and coarse, his fingers and beard dripping with gravy, the circle is complete and divine Creation takes pleasure in itself, in his person.

With industry arrives *antiphysis*; as soon as the worker asserts his rights, the reign of man ceases to be natural; by producing, man forges his own essence; by consuming, the consumer recognizes and is repeated *as a producer* in the object consumed: he consumes what, in other circumstances, he would have been able to produce and what attracts him in the merchandise is the unmistakable mark of human labour: a polish, a smoothness, a roundness, a clarity of colour that are not to be found in nature. With the birth of a manufacturing society, aristocracy, taste and naturalism vanish together, as one can already anticipate by the case of the Americans. Aesthetic sensibility will still have criteria, but they will be very different. For the moment, in our ambiguous society, at this strange period in our history, meanings crisscross one another, and naturalism and artificiality coexist; an argument may be started under the rules of artificiality and concluded according to naturalist principles. There are still people who play the aristocrat, who are inclined to like lace; but ask them *why* they like it. Well, it's because, even if a machine were to imitate the errors of the lacemaker, it could not replace her infinite patience, humble taste and eyes worn out at the work. In short, without realizing it themselves, they are contaminated by the ideology of the day and it is on human labour that they base the value of a luxury item. Hand lace is more beautiful because the worker works harder, longer and for less pay; we can stroke this exhausting work on the lace itself; fine folks might almost say that this is *pure labour* (meaning: without machines). So taste remains, but loses ground and takes the name of *good* taste, by opposition to pure artificiality, which becomes *bad* taste. Between the model and its imitation, the natural product and its synthetic reconstitution, the man of poor taste – with unfailing accuracy – instantly chooses the copy. But one should not think that he is short-sighted, blinkered, unable to distinguish true from false: if that were the case, he would get it right one time out of two. His admirable persistence in his error shows, on the contrary, that he likes the fake because it is a fake. This does not mean necessarily that he *recognizes* its falseness, but he is attracted by its *visible* characteristics. The violence of a scent, the blatant exaggeration of a colour are symbols of antiphysis. Admittedly, as Nature recedes, we are less inclined to admire the aspect of imitation in industrial products. As dentistry progresses, so true and false teeth will disappear together: cared for, nourished, worked over and transformed by the dentist, the tooth will be neither true nor false; there is no more good or bad taste. But, in this prehistory of industry, bad taste expresses the amazement that we feel at our own power: a synthetic pearl reminds us constantly by its shine that mankind, a creature who was still natural until recently, can produce in himself and outside himself a fake nature that is shinier and more accurate than the real one.

Let us be quite clear: Genet's bad taste is not that of an Oklahoma tinsmith; it is the opposite. The latter sees the electric corkscrew and the ballpoint pen as the antiphysis of which a *gadget* is the transitory expression, the other side of freedom of production, of the creative effort which transforms the world; in short, movement, progress, transcendence: this tinsmith is a humanist. And, surely, what attracts Genet in a clashing array of colours that nature could never have put together is *also antiphysis*. But for him, as for pimps, thieves, pederasts and the whole parasitic tribe, the work concentrated in the fake piece of jewellery is that of the Other; he cannot see in it the reflection of his own work, since he does no work. Since he steals them, or buys them with stolen money, he finds himself in the same relation to the glass diamond or the synthetic pearl as the aristocrat to the true one: the mediation of work is suppressed; and, just as nature was the very substance of the luxury product, so antiphysis becomes the pure essence given to the manufactured product; to Genet it does not exhibit either human transcendence or the arduous conquest of nature. Instead, a fake product of Society, it tells the young man nothing except the simple fact that it is against nature. It is *first of all* its being-against-nature that Genet perceives and values in fake jewellery. This child who was not born of woman sees himself reflected in a pearl which is not born of an oyster. He will make use of it to legitimize his perversions: if the cabochon is allowed to become a false diamond, why should Divine not make himself into a false woman? Violent perfumes justify the homosexual's artificiality: they depart as far from the imprecise smells of nature as the pederast wishes to remove himself from his species. But, above all, the fake jewel is *appearance*; because, to the extent that *it is*, it is not a jewel (it is only a piece of cut glass); and, to the extent that it appears to be a jewel, it *is not*. It reflects back on Genet his own nothingness, his inability to create a being. But, at the same time, it needs his gaze to exist. If Genet were to lose interest in jewels, the real diamond would remain a diamond, the false one would become a glass cabochon; only for human freedom, as it asserts its right to transcend being and to emerge into illusory nothingness, do fake diamonds exist. By choosing to prefer fake luxury over everything else, Genet is exercising the most profoundly human of activities, without raising a finger: he is becoming the one *by whom* and *for whom* there are specifically human objects which escape the eyes of God – the one who takes it upon himself to see a diamond where God only sees cut glass. Antiphysis reverses the roles: a whole society goes to work so that Genet's gaze can light up an imaginary diamond.

So the girl-queen, because she is a fake, surrounds herself with

MASTURBATION

sham knick-knacks and, because she is bad, wants to have bad taste. At once, falsity grows and multiplies. With Stilitano, bad taste is in some respect natural, a spontaneous expression of his condition. With Genet, the taste for fakes becomes fake bad taste. To caricature the true luxury of the true prince, Aldini, his aesthetic instinct obliges this false son of a fake prince to employ a false taste for false luxury that destroys itself. From clashing colours, vulgar scents and glass beads, a pure and secret refinement will draw a subtle quintessence, imposing the strictest and most classical unity on these pure, immaterial iridescences. We have already realized that this work of distillation must lead to the Word. We are sliding into the universe of absences, into language. Indeed, it is one thing to write: 'I love vulgar perfumes'; and another to scent oneself with them. But we have not reached that stage. For the time being, Genet takes pleasure in loving fake jewellery with a false love – the same false love that he has for Stilitano, the pretend tough. Here again, the imposture is taken to the limit: he imagines that he loves an appearance of jewellery. A false woman nurturing an imaginary passion for a simulacrum of a man and decking herself out, for him, with an appearance of jewellery: isn't that the definition of the pederast?

For appearances can only inspire an appearance of feeling; and that, too, is Evil. If I think I see a man in the night, I may feel afraid; but if I establish that the man is an illusion of my senses, my fear will vanish. So will the illusion: I cannot *see* the man from the moment when I have perceived it to be a tree; I cannot even understand how I might have seen him. If the apparition persists, it will become flat and ineffectual: I know that it comes from within me. So the person who, like Genet, delights in the appearance as such cannot obtain his feelings from it. What fear and what agitation could be provoked by these images which he is conscious of creating himself? And if, despite that, he wants to love, hate and tremble because of them, then it must be because he is affecting himself with love, fear or hatred, and because, through a new lie, he relates these feelings to the images as to their causes, while knowing full well that they come from himself. Hence the object is nothing, the feeling is faked and the relationship between them is imaginary: a triumph of perversity

– here is something to delight a man who, even where his passions are concerned, has a horror of passivity. Nothing disturbs him, nothing overwhelms him: there is nothing more in the image than what he wants and knows. To this, and to this alone, one may apply the famous maxim: *esse est percipi*. A creature of flesh and blood will surprise us, disappoint, thwart our plans, and always give more or less than we expect. But, confronted with these stereotypical phantoms, vaporous, patched around nothingness, Genet delights in almost managing to provoke agitation in himself. He imagines a handsome male, and strokes his prick from inside his pocket: the prick hardens beneath his fingers, his excitement rises and the image of the Pimp acquires a measure of solidity; but Genet insists that it is the image that is giving him an erection. It is not easy to picture this demoniacal labour: the appearance must first be restrained from vanishing altogether; beneath the cynical eyes that stare at it and know that they are producing it, it pales and is in process of dispersing; and yet, by a determined effort against himself, by a constant labour of re-creation, Genet manages to preserve a measure of objectivity in it. In short, he is once more desiring the impossible. This contradictory tension enchants him: his perversity likes to clench around a void; he knows that the image is empty and is careful not to forget it; and since that knowledge is indestructible, since it is the very given of 'I think', his faith in the objectivity of the appearance becomes itself imaginary: Genet unrealizes himself, playing the role of a fake Genet who is taken in by his own fantasies. He *knows* that they are nothingness, he *pretends to believe* that they have being. At the same time he hopes – or pretends to hope – that, in that strange site where the traitor becomes a Saint, where nothingness becomes being and where all contradictions are resolved, a solution will be granted to this new conflict of faith and knowledge. Over there, somewhere, belief is changed into knowledge, images become true, Genet discovers that he is the true hero of a royal adventure: 'Sometimes ... I really thought that a trifle would be enough, a slight and imperceptible shift in the plane on which I live, for this world to surround me, become real and really mine; that a slight effort of thought on my part would be enough

MASTURBATION

for me to discover the magic spells that would open the doors,' he writes in *Notre-Dame des Fleurs*. And, in *Le Miracle de la Rose*: 'Imagination surrounded me with a host of delightful adventures, perhaps intended to soften my collision with the bottom of this precipice – because I thought that there was a bottom, though despair has none – and, while I was falling, the speed of my fall accelerated the working of my brain and my tireless imagination wove away. It wove still further adventures and stories, faster and ever faster. Finally, carried away, exalted by violence, I repeatedly felt that it was no longer the imagination, but some other, higher faculty, a means of salvation. Increasingly, all the splendid and invented tales took on a sort of tangibility in the physical world. They belonged to the world of matter, though not here: I sensed that they did exist somewhere. It was not I who lived them; they lived elsewhere, without me. With some kind of exaltation, this new faculty, which had arisen from the imagination, but was higher than it, showed them to me, prepared them for me and arranged them so that they were ready to receive me. Little was needed for me to abandon the disastrous situation through which my body was passing, to leave my body (so I was right to say that despair gets us out of ourselves), and to project me into other consoling situations which were unfolding in parallel to my own poor one. Had I, thanks to my immense fear, started on the miraculous road to the secrets of the Indies?'

The secrets of the Indies, no – as Genet knows very well. If one day he were to succeed in believing *once and for all* that these fantasies were real, it would not mean that they had acquired a being, but that he had lost his. He cannot enter into the world of dreams because he belongs to the real one. But if he could complete the movement of de-realization that he has begun, detach himself altogether from being and become entirely imaginary, then the fictions that he imagines, without ceasing to be appearances, would *through this new fiction* become truths. The fantasies that I invent are lies *for me*, but for the people that I place inside them, they represent the extent of the real. For Stendhal, Fabrice and the Farnese Tower are equally imaginary. But *in the realm of the imaginary*, the tower in which he is imprisoned is, for Fabrice, a real tower. To be a Stendhal who, driving his imaginative effort to the limit, would transform himself into a jailmate of Fabrice: this is what Genet wants.* In one sense, it is entirely impossible, in another it is what happens to us day after day when we are asleep. In this way we discover the old dream of swooning away that Genet guards within himself. 'To sleep . . . perchance to dream,' says Hamlet. The annihilation of Genet, the impossible non-entity that he seeks, would not be a dreamless sleep: he would become one of the flat characters in his own nightmare.

But he stops himself in time. He *must not* pass out, he must realize the failure of his attempt to become unreal. He remains suspended between true knowledge and feigned belief, just as the image he is sustaining hovers between appearance and disappearance. And it is in this intermediary state that he produces phantom-feelings within himself: phantom-feelings, that is to say, actions and words, the void and abstract pattern of the emotion that he wants to feel. And this is precisely the state that he wished to achieve: the image is now only a thin film separating his freedom from itself. Normally, freedom cannot be grasped: if one is inactive, one cannot touch it; if one is involved and committed, one loses sight of it, being only aware of the undertaking and the tasks that have to be performed. But in this twilight moment when the image is about to be dispelled, in which the undertaking suggests no particular task because it is, in principle, impossible, then naked freedom, inactive and yet tensed, attains itself in its vain effort to confer being on nothingness, in its finitude, its failure, but also its fundamental affirmation, its challenge to being and to God. At last, we discover the secret of this imaginary life: the image is the inconsistent mediation that unites Narcissus with himself. The fabulous Opera results in masturbation.

All convicts indulge in masturbation, but normally this is because

---

* 'One day . . . he called over a boy who was playing. He had just painted a trompe-l'œil; it depicted a cloister with a wall on the left and an arcade on the right. The lad came in and stared, surprised by this cloister which he had not known to be there . . . He dashed at the wall, *purely and simply* penetrating the lie . . .' Cocteau, *Des beaux-arts considérés comme un assassinat*.

they have nothing better. They would prefer the most wretched whore to these solitary festivities. In short, they make good use of their imaginations: they are honest wankers. A French journalist, shocked by the puritanism of America, once haughtily announced in Cincinnati: 'I, a thirty-five-year-old, with the Croix de Guerre and five children, masturbated this morning.' There's a righteous fellow. But Genet wants to misuse masturbation. Making up one's mind to prefer appearances to all else, means as a matter of principle putting masturbation before any form of intercourse. Moreover, he was on the right track: flesh-and-blood hooligans played the role of the Pimp, lending him their reality. But, as Genet was already remarking: 'These boys I am talking about, who were the pretexts for my iridescence, then my transparency, and finally my absence, evaporated. All that was left of them was what was left of me.' Why not get rid of them altogether? *Images* will be amply sufficient to show the great essences of pederasty. This remark by Genet seems to me admirably to define his masturbation: 'I am only through them, and they are nothing, being only through me.'

A masturbator by choice, Genet prefers his own caresses because the pleasure received coincides with that given, the moment of passivity with that of greatest activity; he is at one and the same time the consciousness which 'curdles' and the hand which is getting annoyed at churning. Being, existence; faith, works; masochistic inertia and sadistic ferocity; petrification and freedom: at the moment of orgasm, the two contradictory components of Genet coincide, he is the criminal raping and the Saint allowing herself to be raped. On his body, a hand caresses Divine. Or else the hand that strokes him is the hand of Mignon. The person masturbated is de-realized, he is about to discover the magic formulae that will open the gates. Genet has vanished: Mignon is making love to Divine. Yet, victim or tormentor, caresser or caressed, in the end these fantasies must be reabsorbed into Narcissus: Narcissus fears men, their judgements, their real presence; he longs only to feel a dawn of love for himself; he asks nothing except to be able to stand back a little from his own body, and a light gloss of otherness on his flesh and his thoughts. His characters are melting flavours, their inconsistency reassures him and serves his sacrilegious ends: it is a caricature of love. The person masturbated is delighted at never being able to feel himself enough someone else, and at being able to produce all by himself the diabolical appearance of a couple that fades away as soon as it is touched. The failure of pleasure is also a sour pleasure in failure. A pure demonic act, masturbation sustains at the heart of consciousness an appearance of appearance: masturbation is de-realization of the world and of the masturbator himself. But this man who allows himself to be devoured by his own dream knows very well that the dream is sustained only by his own will; Divine does not cease to absorb Genet into herself, nor Genet to re-absorb Divine into him. And yet, by a reversal which will bring the ecstasy to its climax, this non-existent flesh will excite real events in the true world: erection, ejaculation, damp patches on the sheets: all these are caused by the imaginary. Simultaneously, the masturbator grasps the world in order to dissolve it and instils the order of the unreal into the universe: these images must *have being*, since they act. No, the onanism of Narcissus is not, as foolish people believe, a little homage done to oneself as evening comes, a sweet and playful little reward for a hard day's work: it aspires to be a crime. It is from its nothingness that Genet derives his pleasure; solitude, impotence, the unreal and the evil – directly and without having recourse to *being* – have produced *an event* in the world.

Homosexuality

Two further extracts from from *Saint Genet* (1952) follow, corresponding to pages 23–9 and 81–5 of the original French edition.

The child was playing in the kitchen, when suddenly he realized that he was alone; and, as usual, he was gripped with anxiety. So he 'absented' himself. Once again. He plunged into a sort of ecstasy. Now there was no one at all in the room: an abandoned consciousness reflects some cooking utensils. Now a drawer is opening. A little hand reaches out . . .

Caught in the act: someone has come in and is looking at him. Beneath that gaze the child comes back to himself. He was not yet anyone, and suddenly he becomes Jean Genet. He feels that he is dazzling, deafening: an alarm bell that will not stop ringing. *Who is Jean Genet?* In no time the whole village will know . . . When he is on his own, the child can't tell. He carries on with his alarm-clock racket with feelings of fear and shame. Suddenly:

a dizzying word
Rising from the depths of the world
Destroys the harmony . . .*

A voice declares publicly: 'You are a thief.' He is ten years old.

That is how it happened: like that, or differently. In all probability there were misdemeanours and punishments, solemn promises and relapses. No matter: the important thing is that Genet lived through this period of his life, and continues to do so, as though it only lasted an instant.

* Genet, *Poèmes*, 56.

It was an instant of awakening. The sleepwalking child opens his eyes and observes that he is stealing. They reveal to him that he *is* a thief and he pleads guilty, overwhelmed by a fallacy that he cannot refute: he stole, so he is a thief. What could be clearer? Genet is dumbfounded. He considers what he has done, looks at it from all sides: there is no doubt, it is a theft. And theft is an offence, a crime. What he *wanted* was to steal, what he *did* was a theft, what he *was* is a thief. A little voice still protests inside him: he does not *acknowledge* his intention. But the voice is soon silenced: the act is so clear, so sharply defined that there can be no mistake as to its nature. He tries to go back, to understand, but it is too late. He cannot find himself. The dazzling obviousness of this present gives its meaning to the past: now Genet *recalls* that he cynically decided to steal something. What happened? Almost nothing, in reality. An act undertaken without forethought, conceived and carried out in the silent and secret private place where he often hides, has just *passed into objectivity*. It is this *passing* that will determine the whole of his life.

The metamorphosis occurs instantly: he is nothing more than he was, yet he is unrecognizable. Driven from the paradise lost, exiled from childhood and from the immediate, condemned to see himself and suddenly provided with a monstrous and guilty 'I', isolated, separate, in short, changed into vermin. There had been a bad principle living inside him, unnoticed, and now it was revealed. This principle is the source of everything, it produces the slightest movement of his soul. The child used to live in peace with himself, his desires appeared simple and clear; now it seems that their transparency was deceptive; they were designed with a false bottom. Little Genet's shame reveals eternity to him: he is a thief from birth and will remain so until his death. Time is only a dream: his wicked nature is split into a thousand fragments, a thousand petty thefts, but it does not belong to the temporal order. *Genet is a thief*: there is his truth, his eternal essence. And, if he *is* a thief, he must be one always and everywhere, not only when he is stealing, but when he eats, sleeps, or kisses his foster-mother. Every one of his gestures betrays him and reveals his rotten nature in the full light of day; at any moment, the schoolteacher may pause in his dictation, look Genet in the eyes and exclaim out loud: 'We have a thief here!' It would be pointless for him to think he deserves indulgence because he confesses his sins or represses the perversity of his instincts: every impulse of his heart is equally guilty because each one expresses the essence of him.

If only the dizzying word had at least been spoken by his own father, then the discovery would have been made within the indestructible family cell, in other words within the unit of a single collective conscience. The young offender, isolated for a moment inside this conscience, like an intruding thought, would immediately have been taken back inside it: one cannot steal from one's family. But while at times the affectionate attitude of his adoptive parents gave Genet the illusion of being their son, that illusion vanished as soon as they became his judges. Because they considered him a thief, Genet *became* a foundling. Father and mother: unknown. No one wants to take responsibility for his birth; it is as though he produced himself, in spite of everyone, in a fit of ill will: Evil is one's cause. At the same time, his sins are explained by dark forces that go well beyond the time of his birth: 'Where does this little thief come from? He must take after someone. You have to be a real whore to abandon your child. Like mother, like son.' In the end, everything goes together, everything is clear: emerging out of nothingness, the child has nothing, is nothing; his being has the substantiality of non-being and if he exists, it is as a corroding acid. Does he exist elsewhere? Is he not merely the repulsive beast that dashes through the excited dreams of decent folk?

Jouhandeau, another outcast, has given a very good description of what might be called the 'ontological curse': 'The insult is perpetual. It is not only in the mouth of this one or that, and explicit, but on every lip that names me; it is in the very "being", in my being, and I find it in every eye that looks on me. It is in the hearts of all those who have dealings with me; it is in my blood and inscribed on my face in letters of fire. Always and everywhere it goes with me, in this world and in the next. It is myself and it is God Himself who utters it in uttering me, who gives me this execrable name for eternity, who sees me from that position of wrath.'

One cannot even have recourse to telling God: 'Since You made me, You are guilty.' Because, in this magical conception of the world, nature and freedom are the same: captive because he cannot change, the thief is free because he is condemned. It is like the Calvinist idea of predestination, which accords the sinner full responsibility for Evil, while denying him any possibility of doing Good. Being is here a subtle and fundamental perversion of freedom, a constant inclination to do wrong, a sort of reversal of grace, a weighting of free will that makes it always descend to the lowest level. In this criss-cross, freedom is responsible for being and being petrifies freedom. Free to be guilty, Genet is not free to change himself – because the wrath of the just wishes to go on for ever: if Genet were to become honest, then it would lose its object. This virtuous wrath is relentless: it is not enough to have murdered a child; it devises a future without hope for the monster that it has just made. He is told that prison and the penal colony await him; everything is decided: from an eternal cause, irremediable consequences flow in the temporal world: 'You will end on the scaffold!' In amazement, Genet contemplates the inescapable course of the universe and the chain of circumstances that will lead him to execution. Yesterday, everything was still possible: he was, perhaps, a prince's son; he might become a saint; it was an anarchy of desire, the graces of fortune smothered him with wishes, the future was not decided. Now everything is in order: he has been given a nature, a guilty freedom and a destiny. He is eleven years old and knows already, in the smallest detail, the life that he will have to savour drop by drop: 'The order of this world, seen back-to-front, appears so perfect in its inevitability that this world has only to fade away.'

Indeed, what is the sense in living? Time is merely a tedious illusion, everything is already here, his future is only an eternal present and, since his death is at the end – his death and only deliverance – since, in short, he is *already dead*, already guillotined, better to finish it straight away. To faint, to slip through their fingers, to drain away from the present through some waste hole, to be swallowed up by nothingness. Which among us, at least once in his life, caught by surprise, paralysed with shame, has not wanted to die on the spot? But it is no use: Genet remains alive, he has weight and volume, he is a scandal in the indignant eyes of the adults. Deep in his heart, however, he will keep that old, plaintive dream of vanishing away. Or, rather, more than that: like old Lapérouse – who, in Gide's *Les Faux-monnayeurs*, not having had the courage to kill himself, decides that he is dead – Genet will from now on date all subsequent events of his life from the day of his suicide. Then, later, in the funeral rites that reconstitute the original crisis, the rite of death will take first place.

Two sorts of people suffering from persecution complexes are found in asylums. One kind, who are called persecution maniacs, are the victims of a conspiracy. The whole world is secretly plotting their destruction. The passer-by in the street is a spy, a provocateur or a judge, who wants to dishonour them, imprison them or perhaps even kill them. At least, they remain free and sovereign in their inner beings. They despise their opponents and thwart their tricks; and they enjoy their solitude with pride and anxiety. But there are others who cannot take refuge within themselves, because the enemy is already there: they are said to be under the influence of a delusion. In the most secret region of their consciousness and the most private region of their inner life, their persecutors have placed their spies and their tormentors. Their thoughts are stolen, they are forced to say things that they abhor, and strange instruments are used to inspire them with wicked beliefs, dreadful convictions and atrocious desires which they do not recognize. I don't think there can be any suffering in the world worse than theirs: outside, they find horror, monstrous creatures and the hatred of a whole people, sometimes of the universe; but if they retreat into themselves, what they discover is still more horrible: the very things that they were fleeing have already arrived and are laughing as they wait.

These were the wretches whom the child Genet, suddenly, came to resemble. The contempt and anger of decent folks would have been bearable for him, if he could have returned blame for blame and hatred for hatred. No doubt that is what he would have done, if the 'accident' had occurred a bit later in his life. Had he been called a thief at seventeen, Genet would have laughed: this is the age when one is getting rid of the father's values. There would have been a thousand different possibilities to fall back on: he could have responded that his accusers were themselves guilty, shown them the evil everywhere and obliged it by its very excess to be swallowed up along with good in a sort of indifference and wretchedness, challenged the principles of public morality in the name of a Nietzschean or anarchist ethics, or denied the existence of values and deigned only to recognize the law of the jungle. But he was only a child, taken by surprise, a very small child, shy, respectful, conventional in his outlook. Having been brought up to believe in God and follow the best precepts, he had acquired such a passionate love of Good that he aspired to sanctity rather than fortune. Nor did he have the means to defend himself by returning an accusation: adults were gods for this righteous little soul. He is caught like a rat in a trap: he has been so imbued with the morality in the name of which he is being condemned that it has become part of him: they have penetrated to the depths of his heart and installed a permanent delegate, who is Genet himself. He himself will be both the court and the accused, the policeman and the robber; he is the one who will commit the crime, hand down the sentence and apply it. If he should wish to return into himself, in order to escape the blame of those around him, he will find a more severe accuser still: himself. Ardent persecutor of himself, from now on he will experience his emotions, moods, thoughts and even his perceptions in terms of conflict. The most simple and legitimate desire will be perceived by him as a thief's desire, and so guilty. The adults have triumphed and found an accomplice who is none other than the accused himself. Such luck doesn't happen every day. Better still: had the child grown up normally, he would have freed himself little by little from this crude morality, or at least made it more flexible, expanded it, perhaps replaced it by anarchism, but slowly, without violent clashes or internal catastrophes. But the dreadful blow that has just struck him will forever prevent this friendly dissolution. Don't imagine that Genet would change: in the worst of his aberrations, he was to remain loyal to the moral code of his childhood; he might flout it, perhaps, hate it, try to drag it down with him into the mire; but

HOMOSEXUALITY

the 'fundamental crisis' has branded him with it like a hot iron. Henceforth, whatever happens, whatever escape route he may find, one thing will remain forbidden to him: *to accept himself*. The law of his conscience is a tearing apart. Until the 'crisis', he lived in the 'sweet confusion' of the immediate present and was not aware of being a person: he learned that he was and, at the same moment, that this person was a monster.

'Guilt,' he was later to write, 'first of all makes for singularity.' Beneath the accusing finger, it is the same thing for the little thief to discover that he is himself and that he is different from all others. No doubt, many other people have affirmed that they discovered their own individuality around their tenth year, with astonishment or distress. There was Gide, as a child, weeping in his mother's arms and crying that he 'was not like other boys'. But normally this discovery occurs without much harm being done; adults are not involved; the child is playing alone; a slight change in the landscape, an event or a fleeting thought are enough to set off this reflected moment of awareness that reveals our Ego. And that Ego, as I have shown elsewhere, is still nothing for itself but the empty and universal form of individuality. Not being like others is being like everybody, since each is the same as oneself in being different from all. If this reflective operation takes place normally, far from preventing reciprocal relationships, it produces them. I feel that I am different from Pierre and I know that Pierre is like me because he feels himself to be different from me. But the otherness that Genet discovers in himself, on the contrary, is exclusive of all reciprocity. This is not an empty and universal form, but a singular distinction that simultaneously affects both form and content. There is Genet and there is everyone else. And, by a nice irony, the child's dreadful solitude creates a more perfect understanding among those who condemn him: when they baptize an evil-doer, decent people have a field day: they stand shoulder to shoulder to block his way and almost come to like one another. Genet can see clearly that he is an offering and that his sacrifice serves to unite his sacrificers: *all others*, whatever the differences that divide them, recognize themselves as similar in – thank God – not being thieves; *all others*, whatever their conflicting interests, see themselves as fellows because each can read in his neighbours' eyes the horror that Genet inspires. They become only a single and monstrous conscience judging and damning: it is frightful to 'conceive' unanimity, to see suddenly that it is possible, that it is there, that one is touching it, that one has produced it and to know at the same time that it has been created against oneself. It would be pointless for him to try to turn against the others and exclude them in his turn: there is not a square metre on earth from which he could drive them away; he has nothing of his own. So the revulsion that he inspires is one-way: he disgusts right-thinking people, but he cannot feel disgust for them. The only feeling he has in his heart is love. A humiliated, forbidden love that shamefully and humbly seeks out opportunities to express itself. Notre-Dame-des-Fleurs, in the Court of Assizes, looks for the first time at the presiding judge who will condemn him to death: 'It was so sweet to love that he could not avoid melting in a sweet, confident affection for the judge: "He's not such a bad lot," he thought.' The child loves his accusers, tries to get closer to them and to dissolve – to the point of unconsciousness – in the unanimity that he has created. He can find no other way except to share in the disgust that he inspires in them, and to despise himself with their contempt. The trick works, Genet tears himself apart, he has become an absolute object of horror.

There was once in Bohemia a flourishing industry which seems to have gone into decline: people would take children, split their lips, compress their skulls and confine them day and night in boxes to prevent them from growing. By this and similar treatments they were turned into very entertaining and profitable monsters. To make Genet required a more subtle proceeding, but the result was the same: they took the child and made a monster of him, for reasons of social utility. If we want to find those who are really guilty in this affair, we should turn to the right-thinking, decent people and ask what peculiar cruelty they used to make a scapegoat of a child.

* * *

Through his original crisis and the decision that follows, Genet finds himself thrust into a situation that might be called pre-pederastic;

even if he had subsequently never slept with a man or even imagined doing so, he was marked, one of the chosen; he would have been henceforth, like so many others, one of the Vestals of homosexuality: like that banker, smartly turned out, preening, neat and elegant, whom everyone thought was a pansy and who carried on half-hearted affairs with women without even suspecting the existence of 'forbidden love', before learning about it through a chance encounter at the age of forty which changed him, retrospectively, into what *he was*. Sexually, Genet is first and foremost an abused child. That first rape was the other's gaze, which took him by surprise, penetrated him and transformed him for ever into an object. Let us be clear: I am not saying that his original crisis was *like* a rape; I am saying that it *was* one. The events that mark us take place at the same time on all levels of our mental life and, on each level, are expressed in a different language. In our moral consciousness, a true rape can become an unjust, yet inescapable condemnation; and, conversely, a condemnation can be experienced as a rape. Both transform the guilty person into an object and he feels this objectivization in his heart as a feeling of shame and in his sexual being as a subjection to coitus. From now on, Genet is deflowered; an iron grasp has made a woman of him: all that remains is for him to get used to *being*. He is the village whore, anyone can enjoy him whenever he likes: unclothed by the eyes of decent folk as women are by the eyes of males, he bears his sin as they carry their breasts and their rumps. Many women hate their backs, that unseen, public mass that belongs to everyone before it belongs to them; when a hand brushes them from behind, they feel both excitement and shame well up inside them. Genet is the same: as he was caught stealing *from behind*, it is his back that he feels become vulnerable when he steals, and his back that expects to be looked at and awaits catastrophe. After that, what is surprising about the fact that he feels himself to be mainly an object in his rump and the small of his back, or if he makes these the focus of a sort of sexual cult? As a guilty man unmasked and possessed, it is as a guilty man that he will experience excitement and desire; and since he wishes to become what people have made him – that is, an object – that wish will even have an effect on the way in which he feels his body and the erection of his penis. For the man who has made himself a hunter, his penis is a knife; but, for one who sees himself as an object, his sexual organ is a still life, a *thing*, which only hardens to provide a better grip and make it easier to handle. Proust, typically, never called the male organ a 'prick' or a 'plonker' like our village romeos, but a 'tendril'.* The same tumescence that the male experiences as the aggressive stiffening of a muscle, Genet will feel to be like the expanding of a flower. Whether it is the swelling of an inert air chamber or the unsheathing of a sword, nothing is fixed in advance: the whole choice that one makes of oneself gives a meaning to this intimate perception, and while one person experiences his transcendence in his penis, another will feel his passivity. And, by the same token, while it is quite true that erection is a hardening and a projection, it is also true that the stiffening is involuntary: the basic fact is ambiguous and its meaning depends on each individual. But the male descends on the female, carries her off, forces her submission and feeds her: even his way of making love reflects his economic situation and his pride in earning a living. So whence do you expect Genet to derive such pride? He doesn't earn a living: he loses it. Where is he to find that mixture of generosity and oppressive imperialism that nowadays characterizes male sexuality, being the parasite of a society that denies him salvation through action, and excluded from all its works? It is rare for a male to try and seduce through his physical qualities: these he has received, not made. He forces his wife to love him for his strength, his courage, his arrogance and his aggression; in short, to desire him as a force without a face, a pure power to take and do, not as an object soft to the touch; and in her submissive eyes he looks for the reflection of his infinite freedom. But for Genet, who does nothing, who undoes, who acts only in order to be, the effects of his actions are only apparent: they do not reveal his strength, but his essence. They are *gestures*. Of Divine, he writes: 'She sought to adopt masculine poses . . . whistled, put her hands in her pockets; and all this play-acting was so ineptly performed that in a single

---

* 'A slug', another homosexual called it, in a fine but unpublishable short story.

evening she seemed to be five or six people at once.' Divine is Genet himself. He shows himself, makes himself an object. After that, how could he possess someone? And what need does he have of a woman, that other competing object? They could only dance around one another, each wanting to be taken, not to take, and to be seen, not to look.

This priority, right inside the subject, of object over subject leads, as we have seen, to passivity in love; and when this concerns the male, it gives him a tendency to homosexuality.

In short, Genet decides to *realize* his being and knows that he cannot achieve this on his own, so he turns to the mediation of others. This means that he makes his objectivity for others the *essential* and his reality-for-himself inessential. What he desires is to have himself passively moulded by the Other so as to become an object in his own eyes. Every man who puts his truth in his Being-for-others finds himself in a situation which I have just called 'pre-pederastic'; and this is true, for example, of many actors, even if they only enjoy sleeping with women.

But, in Genet's case, there is more: there are other factors inclining him to homosexuality. Indeed, before any sexual determinacy, Genet reacted to his condemnation by a general, ethical inversion: he was, he says, turned inside out like a glove. Sent back to nothingness, it was to nothingness alone that he wished to belong. He was the monster, the exception to the rule, the improbable, or better still, the impossible. Undesirable, he was not born of man but of some incubus. He cannot start a family: so not only is he exiled from the fields, woods and streams, he is excluded from *his own nature*. We bask in our lives, our blood, our sperm; our bodies are a very dense liquid which supports us and all we have to do is to let ourselves go. A trivial Venus, barely distinguished from digestion, breathing and the beating of the heart, gently inclines us to love women. All we have to do is to trust in her and this obedient goddess will take charge of everything: of our pleasure and of the species. But Genet *is dead*: his life is no more *natural* than his birth; it haunts a corpse. He clings on only by strength of will; if he should pay some attention to the muffled sensations that reach him from his organs, he feels himself to be impossible and plunges into astonishment. He can find in himself none of those powerful instincts that support the desires of ordinary men; the only one he knows is the death wish. His sexual desires are like his life itself: ghosts. Whatever their object, they are condemned in advance; he is *from the outset forbidden* to desire. All societies castrate those who won't fit in; it is merely that this castration can be real and physical, or work by persuasion: the result is the same. Condemned, unnatural and impossible, Genet's desire becomes a desire for what is impossible and against nature. And since this accursed child is only an appearance, his sexuality must also be a pretence, an illusion of nothingness. None of the usual devices can explain it, it doesn't derive from universal nature or sink its roots there; in truth, it is air, a purely diabolical imitation of legitimate emotions. By accepting his situation, Genet comes to stand on his absolute singularity; he shall be beholden only to himself; and this upheaval even affects his sexuality. Tensed, nervous, acidic, his desire arises only from itself; it cannot have a normal relationship with its object. And since Genet's sincerity is a demand for artifice, his emotion will be all the more sincere the more it feels artificial and free. He has no knowledge of abandonment or swooning with pleasure: if he were to let himself go, he would plunge into an abyss; so he does not *abandon himself* to sex; on the contrary, it appears at the highest point of tension: at the supreme moment of passion it has a taste of ashes and freedom. And since negative freedom and Evil are the same thing, his sexual life is a new field open for his perversity. Desire for nothingness, nothingness of desire, an exhausting effort of the whole being, sterile, rootless and insatiable, Genet's sexual appetite contains in itself a fierce demand for autonomy and singularity against the rules, against nature, against life, against the species and against society: he will be reflected in his entirety on the level of the flesh.

This is the situation that has been created for him. And, though it gives him a tendency towards homosexuality, it has not yet decided whether Genet will be an active or a passive homosexual. It is here that the upheaval we have mentioned plays its role: as the scapegoat of the young gang bosses in the reformatory, Genet turns into a lover, that is a woman. But why? We can see what the loved one gains by his role: he is magnified in the lover's heart; he is safe, he has found a refuge. But what about the lover? Why does he demand the disgust, the rebuttals and the indifference of the Other, the tortures of jealousy and finally the despair that comes from the certainty of not being loved? Yet he must have some benefit from it. What lies underneath? For Genet, the answer is clear: love is a magic ceremony by which the lover steals his being from the loved one, in order to become a part of it:

'The most distant form of love that I can remember, is my desire of *being* that pretty boy . . . whom I saw going by.'*

The most distant, perhaps; but Genet was to pick it up for use later. Doesn't Divine say to Gabriel: 'You are myself'; and Gabriel, a well-meaning lad, smiles fatuously without realizing that his blood is being sucked. In the same way, the wild, passionate love of the lieutenant for Querelle is a desire to tear off his testicles and his cock in order to graft them on to himself.

To those who are well-balanced, the righteous, the decent, such an identification can seem pointless and absurd. But I would first of all ask them if they are so sure of being themselves. How do I know if this peace that reigns in them has not been obtained by submission to a foreign protector who rules there in their place? I do know that anyone whom I hear saying the words: 'We doctors . . .' is in a state of slavery. That *we doctors* is his Self, a parasite sucking his blood. And if he were only himself, there are still a thousand ways of being delivered to oneself as to wild animals, and to nourish with one's own flesh an invisible and insatiable idol. Because no one is allowed to speak these simple words: I am myself. The best and freest can say: I exist. This is already too much. For the rest, I suggest they use a formula like: 'I am Oneself,' or 'I am so-and-so *in person*.' If they do not consider changing skins, it is because the grip that rules them does not leave them the leisure to do so, and

---

* Compare Cocteau, in *Le Grand écart* (*Œuvres complètes*, vol. I, p. 15): 'Since his childhood, he had felt a desire to be those whom he considered beautiful, but not to be loved by them.'

above all because society recognized a long time ago and sanctified this symbiosis, by according glory or simply honourability to the couple formed by the sick man and his parasite: it is a legitimate hell. For myself, I keep away from them if I can: I do not like possessed souls. But I can understand that the children of Cain, who are driven by a ruler whom society condemns, should wish to change their masters. And it is no more ridiculous to aspire to become 'that gentleman walking by', as Fantasio did, than to be *the doctor* when one practises medicine. The two processes are the same in kind and in both failure is assured. If, for yourself, you are already the Other, if you suffer from a perpetual absence in the depth of your being, then you can experience this absence as though it were that of any other person: the other will never be more absent than you are. For the manner in which he is not oneself (that is to say, in which he is, for himself, an Other), the way in which you are not yourself and the one in which you are not him, do not differ a great deal.

Revolutions

What do we make of what happens to us? How do we live out the possibilities and the impossibilities which the age imposes? An anarchist by inclination, schooled in an individualist tradition, Sartre was jolted by the events of 1940 into a deeper and more dynamic understanding of collective historical experience. His emphasis was always libertarian and critical. It was also increasingly activist.

To grasp the sense of the century in which he found himself, Sartre had to understand the decay and failure of Europe's political ideals. Why did 1789 lead to 1793? Why did the Bolshevik revolution of 1917 produce Stalin's Soviet Union? Would the Liberation of 1944 engender a socialist Europe? Would the revolutions in China, Algeria, Cuba and Vietnam follow the dismal Soviet path into authoritarianism?

Sartre was uniquely placed to pursue these questions. *Les Temps modernes* was a clearing-house of socialist argument and information. Sartre could travel to Italy, to Cuba, to China, to Brazil. In his conversations with Castro and Che Guevara, with the Italian Communist leader Togliatti and with the Algerian militant Fanon, he sustained a unique critical intellectual dialogue with activists of the radical left. He could also lend the immense cultural prestige of his name to the causes that he favoured. His mere presence could focus attention and spark debate.

In his last years, before failing eyesight paralysed intellectual activity, Sartre's most cherished political project was the founding of *Libération*, an independent socialist daily newspaper. Described as 'the one signal success in the recent history of the daily press',[1] *Libération* is the kind of practical monument Sartre might have relished.

---

1. *The New Oxford Companion to Literature in French*, 641. Under the item entitled 'Press'.

The Liberation of Paris

Published in the journal Clarté *on 24 August 1945, the first anniversary of the Liberation of Paris, this article sketches out a connection between the events of 1944 and those of July 1789.*

Nowadays, if you don't proclaim that Paris liberated herself, you are taken for an enemy of the people. Yet it seems obvious that the city would not even have considered an uprising if the Allies had not been quite close. And, since the Allies themselves would not even have considered landing in France unless the Russians had tied down and defeated the greater part of the German Army, one must draw the conclusion that the Liberation of Paris, an episode in a war that covered the whole world, was a joint action on the part of all the Allied armies. In any case, one cannot be said to expel people who are leaving of their own accord, and when the uprising occurred, the Germans had already started to evacuate the city. The aim of the Resistance was precisely the opposite of the one that is now attributed to them: they tried to slow down the enemy retreat and to shut Paris up like a trap around the occupying forces. And then, most of all, they wanted to demonstrate to the future victors that the Resistance was not a myth, as foreigners still seemed too inclined to believe; confronted with governments who for a time considered having their own officers administer the liberated countries, they sought to assert the sovereignty of the French people and realized that they had no other means to legitimize an authority devolving from that sovereignty, except to shed their own blood. As a result their undertaking owed its greatness to its limitations. The fate of Paris was being decided fifty kilometres away, by the German and

American tanks. But the men of the Resistance refused to bother about that, they did not even want to know the outcome of the struggle in which they were involved. By giving the order for the uprising, they unleashed vague and powerful forces which might crush them from one moment to the next. And it was this that gave that week in August the appearance of a classical tragedy. But what these men intended was precisely to reject destiny. It was not up to them whether the Germans did or did not blow up the Senate and an entire district around it. It was not up to them whether the retreating divisions dropped back on Paris and turned our city into another Warsaw. What did, however, depend on them was to bear witness through their actions – regardless of the outcome of the unequal struggle in which they were engaged – to the will of the French people. Thus each one of them refused to place any hope except in himself. Parisians who were not fighting anxiously wondered from one moment to the next whether the Allies would arrive soon. The combatants never discussed the matter, and it was even as though a tacit agreement forbade them to speak about it: they did whatever they had to do. One afternoon in that week, while I was on my way to see a friend who was publishing a resistance newspaper in offices that he had just occupied, someone came to inform him that the Germans were breaking through around the building. 'If they attack tonight,' he told me, 'we shall be caught like rats in a trap. There are only two ways out, neither of them secret.' 'Do you at least have some weapons?' He shrugged his shoulders and answered: 'No.' So, in the midst of obscure and encroaching danger, these journalists were doing their job, which was to print a paper. As for the rest – in other words, everything to do with their personal safety, and their chances of getting out of this situation alive – they did not want to think about it. Since they could not change anything by their actions, they considered that none of all that concerned them.

So the other aspect of the Parisian uprising is the festive air that has not left the city. Whole districts have been decked out in their Sunday best. And, when I ask myself what is being celebrated in this way, I realize that it is mankind and his powers. It is comforting that the anniversary of the Parisian uprising should fall so close to the first appearance of the atomic bomb. What that represents is the negation of mankind, not only because it risks destroying the whole of humanity, but above all because it makes the most human qualities void and ineffective: qualities like courage, patience, intelligence, initiative. On the contrary, most of the Forces Françaises de l'Intérieur (FFI) in August 1944 had a vague feeling that they were not only fighting for France against the Germans, but also for mankind against the blind forces of the machine. Hadn't we been told often enough that the revolutions of the twentieth century were bound to be different from those of the nineteenth, and that a single plane or a single gun would be enough to tame a rebellious crowd? Hadn't they told us often enough about the ring of German guns around Paris? Hadn't it been proved to us often enough that there was nothing we could do against their machine-guns and their tanks? Well, that August, the fighters that one met in the street were young men in shirtsleeves; their only weapons were revolvers, some rifles, some grenades and bottles of petrol; and, faced with this enemy who was wrapped in iron, they were intoxicated as they felt the freedom and the lightness of their own movements. At every instant, their discipline, made up on the spot, triumphed over learned discipline; they measured and helped us to measure the naked power of mankind. And one could not help thinking of what Malraux, in *L'Espoir*, calls the exercise of the Apocalypse. Yes, it was a triumph of the Apocalypse, that Apocalypse which is always defeated by the forces of law and order, which, for once, was victorious, within the narrow limits of that street battle. The Apocalypse: that is, the spontaneous organizing of the revolutionary forces. All Paris, that August, felt that man still had every chance, that he could still defeat the machine; and even had the outcome of the struggle been the crushing of the forces of resistance, as in Poland, those few days would have been enough to prove the power of liberty. For that reason, it is not really important whether the FFI literally liberated Paris from the Germans, because at every moment, behind each barricade and on each paving-stone, they exercised freedom for themselves and for every French person.

So what will be commemorated every year – officially and in due order – will be an explosion of liberty, a break-up of the established order and the invention of a new one, effective and spontaneous. It is to be feared that the festival will quickly lose its meaning. Yet there is a particular aspect of the uprising that may continue in our celebrations. When the crowd in 1789 stormed the Bastille, it was unaware of the significance and the consequences of what it was doing; it was only afterwards, bit by bit, that they became aware of this and raised it to the status of a symbol. But our age knows that it is making history. What was most striking in August 1944 was that the symbolic nature of the uprising was already fixed, even before the outcome had been decided. Choltitz, by hesitating to destroy Paris, the Allies, by agreeing to bring forward the date of their entry into the capital, and the Resistance, by choosing it as the site of the great battle, all decided that the event was to be 'historic'. They all remembered the great angers of Paris. All of them considered it as one of the crucial stakes of the war. And every member of the FFI, as he fought, felt that he was writing history. The whole history of Paris was there, in that sun, on those loose paving stones. So this tragedy, this risky affirmation of human freedom, was also something like a 'ceremony'. A pompous and bloody ceremony, the ordering of which was strictly laid down and which would inevitably end in the death of some, rather like a human sacrifice. It is this triple aspect of tragedy rejected, of apocalypse and of ceremonial that gives the uprising of August 1944 its profoundly human character and the power that it still has to touch our hearts. Is it not still, today, one of our chief reasons for hope? It is silly and pointless to imagine and to shout out that we liberated ourselves by our own strength alone. Are we trying to find a roundabout way back to Maurras, so that we can keep on repeating with him that ridiculous: 'France, France alone . . .'? And in the same way it is pointless to stamp one's foot, to strike magnificent poses and to keep daily demanding a place in the meeting-place of nations that we are daily refused. But, confronted with the outsized powers that the war has thrown up, and which are in danger of crushing us one day, doesn't the uprising of 1944 show us our real strength? In that disproportionate and ceremonial battle, Paris asserted the power of mankind against the German tanks. Is it not still our task to defend the human, without any great illusions or too much hope, in the face of those somewhat inhuman young forces that have just emerged victorious?

Is This a Democracy?

> This was first published in *Les Temps modernes* in April 1952, the year in which Sartre began to move towards a more sympathetic dialogue with the communist movement. It was reprinted in *Situations VI* (1964), a volume with the subtitle *Problems of Marxism*.

It was ridiculous to die for Danzig, but it would be reasonable to die for democracy – at least, that is what they keep telling us. I am not arguing about the principle: if one doesn't give one's life for 'something', one ends up giving it for nothing. But before I die for democracy, I'd like to be certain that I am living in one. It appears that this is the very regime that operates in my country; fair enough, but whenever I look for proofs, I observe that they all depend on the evidence of others. I have *read* on postage stamps and over the doorway of town halls that the French State describes itself as a Republic; I can *read* the Constitution, the constitutional laws and the legal codes; but historians have long known that the study of written laws is not a description of the way in which institutions actually operate. As a child, I was given an optimistic view of history, based on the myth of progress. According to this officially sanctioned view, the sufferings and labours of our ancestors, from Cro-Magnon Man to the Battle of Valmy, bore the human race forward towards the sacred moment in which the bourgeoisie would finally take power. I am not entirely free of this optimism and, since I have been persuaded that every historical period accomplishes a degree of progress over the preceding one and contains the seeds of future progress, I am still inclined to believe that the Fourth Republic is inevitably more democratic than the Third, and that the Third was more so than the Second. Unfortunately for us, this key no longer opens any doors: while the bourgeoisie was rising, progress was the universal explanation. Now that it is declining, all the locks have been changed, and the confusion in people's minds is such that the bourgeoisie describes fascist governments as *regressive*, even though they have arisen from its very heart, and calls 'progressive' the people's parties that are replacing an optimistic myth of evolution by a tragic and catastrophic faith in revolution. But, if I can no longer believe in progress, who is to assure me that democracy is not in decline? Do I know how it works in Algiers, in Goa or even in Le Creusot?[1] In short, I know the regime in France, where I live, by hearsay, just as I know the relief map of Afghanistan, where I have never set foot.

However, a lot of people claim to have a persistent and practical sense of what our institutions mean. For them, democracy is taken for granted: they become aware of it every day in the actual course of their lives, when they have their rights respected and even when they fulfil their duties. You can come and go, think and say what you think; you vote; you are informed of events by a free press, and you are protected against arbitrary action by the State or by individuals: that's democracy.

But as far as I am concerned, it's not so simple. Certainly, I can see that – just like any other members of any other national community – we are in possession of certain rights and subject to certain duties. But as soon as I try to assure myself that I really do have the rights that have been granted to me, the picture is less clear. Undeniably, I have the right to vote. But can I be sure that my vote will not be pinched from me? Suppose the country to which I belong is forced to align its foreign policy with that of a more powerful nation that 'protects' it: then what difference does it make, if my ballot helps to bring this party or that one 'to power'? What difference, since in reality there is no more power and all governments are pursuing the same policy? To find out if I *truly* do have the right

---

1. *Le Creusot*: an industrial town in eastern central France, specializing in iron and steel production.

to vote, I must first of all determine whether France has preserved or lost its sovereignty. Another example: every morning, I open my paper to find accurate news about what happened the day before. I have faith in the press because I know that it's 'free'. That means that it is not subject to censorship and the government of my country does not have a direct means of exerting pressure on it. But suppose the situation in France and in the world does not allow this press to achieve the economic and social conditions which would assure it of genuine freedom; suppose that, without the titles even being sold off, the main daily newspapers were constrained by historical circumstances to abdicate their independence; suppose that the very ideas of truth and objectivity were to lose their sense in a society torn apart by class struggles and in a world divided into two hostile blocs. If I were suddenly to realize this, then my trust would evaporate and all at once I should find myself surrounded by a wall of lies. In that event, the *ideal* for the press would be objectivity, but the *reality*, constant myth-making. If we continue to buy the paper every morning, that means we have refused on principle to ask the question. In short, we believe that we have a continual awareness of our freedoms and our rights, because we have first of all been persuaded that we live in a democratic regime. But if, instead of really exercising my right to vote, I were simply to take part in the ludicrous ceremonial of the voting booth and the ballot paper – in other words, if my *actions* as a citizen were secretly to be transformed into mere empty gestures – then I would not notice that it had happened, because I have been so well indoctrinated. And if, despite that, some vague feeling of unease made me sense that everything was not quite right, then I would accuse individuals, not the regime.

It's quite true that I do have some genuine powers; but who is to say if they come to me from the Constitution or from the fact of my belonging to the privileged class? I am free to travel abroad, and Soviet citizens are not: agreed; but nor are French workers. They have an abstract right to cross frontiers; but can you imagine them as tourists? And if they want to emigrate, national or international bodies will make a ruling on their case. In short, everyone has the same rights, but everyone does not have the right to enjoy them.

IS THIS A DEMOCRACY?

The regime under which I live is much more democratic *for me* than for a manual worker; isn't this the same, in a different form, as the old division of free citizens into 'passive' and 'active'? We could be inclined to judge the laws according to our own prejudices. I have known some intelligent people who considered the law on electoral groupings very democratic. After all, they would say, if the Communist Party – or the Gaullist MRP – is not happy, let it join an alliance. They claimed that the isolation of the Communists was just some kind of sulk. And when you proved that this was not so, they would shrug their shoulders: the Gaullists and the Stalinists are seditious; a law that protects democracy cannot be anti-democratic. However, they were quite happy to accept that the scales should be tilted. It had been decreed, at a stroke of the pen, that a vote for one of these parties should be worth less than a vote for the others; it had been decided that some opinions had less right to be represented; yet they called themselves democrats and had no complaints.

For these reasons and many others, I felt that we must try to clear away some of the myths. From today onwards, we will be undertaking an inquiry into the *real* workings of French democracy. Does the historical situation, in its social, economic and international dimensions, permit the free functioning of democratic principles? What is the gap between rights and realities in the crucial areas of the press, colonial administration, the law, the police, parliament, etc.? Is France still a sovereign nation? Is universal suffrage the *real* method of election? Does the administration in the colonies conform to the undertakings entered into by the government? Do we really enjoy the rights known as *habeas corpus*? And so on. Obviously, it is too early to determine precisely the true structure of present-day French society (though it is quite certainly not either a democracy, nor a disguised totalitarian regime). But I feel it is possible, right now, to *make an assessment*. We will be devoting a series of articles to sorting out the complex mixture of facts and measurements, myths and realities, progress and reverses, myths and facts. Our readers have a positive contribution to make: we are addressing them, because the exercise will only make sense if it is a collective one. So, if they are interested, they should inform us of any facts that might be appropriate – from either side, we are not biased. We shall take into account any criticism or suggestions that they send us and, if there are so many that we cannot publish them in full, we shall in any event devote special articles to them.

One final word, to clear up any misunderstanding: there can be various, conflicting interpretations of the shortcomings that we may find. For example, it could be argued that there is, in some Platonic heaven, an ideal republic which only the imperfections of human nature prevent us creating here on earth. One may also argue that the normal operation of our democratic institutions has been distorted by *external* events and that the machine can be repaired. And, finally, one may argue that the golden age of democracy is already past: the breakdown of the regime is merely an early symptom of the imperial order that normally follows a republican era, according to comparative historians.

None of these points of view is our own; and, moreover, we are not concerned here with philosophical reflections on history. For us, democracy is a bourgeois regime and the contradictions we may note in it are inherent in bourgeois society. There is no such thing as an ideal democracy; there is a liberal regime which engenders contradictions from the outset because it assumes that the problem has been resolved: that is, on paper; the reality of class and the class struggle is denied, and they claim only to consider the individual, abstract citizen, in relation to the State or to other individual citizens. If there was a golden age of political liberalism, and if some simple-minded people consider themselves entitled to refer to it nowadays to condemn the 'decay' of our institutions, it is because for a time the visible signs of class struggle were repressed through the electoral system or through the crushing of a still inadequately organized proletariat by the armies of the bourgeoisie. The proletariat, silent or bewildered, did not at that time appear to be an historical actor, with the result that the government, parliament and the organs of judicial power appeared effectively to derive from a classless society: the bourgeois class alone produced them, controlled them and employed them to its advantage, so they were unable to reflect the contradictions of a society that they did not entirely express. We

IS THIS A DEMOCRACY?

shall see that the constantly widening gap in certain fields between the principle and the reality shows on the contrary the resistance of *the real*, that is to say the simultaneous shift in Europe and its bourgeoisie, and the appearance within the framework of the nation-state, of an organized and self-conscious working class. The instability of the government and its constant, fruitless search for a parliamentary majority are not due, as we are told by the Right, to perversity on the part of our members of parliament; but the class struggle is reflected in the parliamentary arena, thus causing a breakdown in a body that was expressly designed to reflect the harmony of the 'middle ranks' in society and to allow them to accord their interests. We shall also observe that, in other areas, there have been democratic measures that represent an advance on the pre-war situation; but at the same time we shall see that this very progress, because of the consequences deriving from it, is helping to destroy the regime that brought it about: it is as though the total accomplishment of bourgeois democracy had to coincide with its total destruction. This should not surprise anyone: to the very extent that liberal thought denied the existence of classes, with the barely concealed intention of disguising the real problem, so it was bound to produce a clear image of a classless society, which would be the *truth* of bourgeois democracy and contribute to its downfall.

The Genesis of Stalinism

A glitteringly aphoristic critique of the cult of the personality, this is an extract from *The Ghost of Stalin*, a polemical essay sparked by the Soviet suppression of the Hungarian rising of October 1956. The essay was published in *Les Temps modernes* in January 1957 and reprinted in *Situations VII* (1965). An earlier English translation appeared in 1968.

In our bourgeois lands, we know the price that had to be paid to accomplish 'primitive accumulation': we have not forgotten the huge waste of human lives, the forced labour, the poverty, rebellion and repression. It appears that industrialization in the USSR was less costly; yet, what a fearful effort it did demand: how much sweat, how much blood. It was a race against time in an under-developed, almost entirely agricultural country, under siege, having to equip itself despite an economic blockade and the constant threat of armed attack. No one will ever be able to say to what extent this 'besieged fortress' might have been able to reduce the pain and suffering of its inhabitants, without risking total destruction; what we do know for sure is that the Communist leadership assumed full responsibility for the regime, in both its greatness and its defects. The bourgeois liberal pleads not guilty: *he* did not make the world and, like everyone else, he only obeys the pitiless laws of economics; but the Soviet revolutionaries, after a few years of wavering, eventually realized that socialism is inseparable from planning. Moreover, the immediacy of the danger and the lack of education among the masses forced the Russian government to opt for an authoritarian form of planning; and, consequently, the leaders became identified with the Plan, the Plan assumed their faces, their voices, their hands, it became itself the true government. This alienation of the leadership in its enterprise could only have the effect of accentuating the fundamental contradiction of Soviet society: the long-term interests of socialist construction were contrary to the immediate interests of the working class. Now, in a bourgeois democracy, as Marx says, the proletariat is by itself and as a specific class, 'the decomposition of society'; and in that negative situation, its immediate reactions are so closely suited to its historical task that the masses themselves set an example of radicalism: their spontaneous demands have the effect of hastening the breakdown of capitalist society, while at the same time expressing the profound character of the proletarians, 'the secret of their very existence'. In this way, the oppressed class acquires 'a universal character through its universal sufferings' and Marx can use the term 'duty', which he borrows from ethical philosophy, to describe demands which have their origin in immediate interests. In other words, the worker's needs in a capitalist regime – for example, his tiredness, his hunger – are in their very nakedness socialist in character: as the outcome of exploitation, these needs cannot be expressed without indicting exploitation, and they cannot be satisfied without reducing profits and endangering capital. But in Soviet Russia, the leaders' main concern will be to create the necessary material conditions to allow it to resolve the problems created by the revolution – and the spontaneous reactions of the masses retain their negative character with respect to the general needs of the economy. In the period of post-revolutionary reconstruction, at a time when the socialist state is trying to equip the country with an industrial base, a movement of mass protest puts everything at risk: the worker may refuse to do long hours, or ask for rises in salary, for clothing, shoes, a housing policy. In a word, his immediate interest drives him to demand the development of consumer industries in a society which will perish unless it can first supply itself with heavy industry. His protest, which was universal in bourgeois society, becomes particularized in a post-revolutionary one, yet his situation has not changed. It is true that he is no longer exploited, but 'the contradiction between his human nature and his vital existence' has not vanished: revolution, of whatever kind, does not accomplish miracles, it inherits the deprivation created by the Old Regime. Of course, this conflict is not confined to opposing the Plan, a necessary condition of progress towards socialism, and the worker as a force for work and as a system of needs. The conflict exists in each person, because the worker wants socialism to be created, while at the same time wanting the satisfaction of his needs. He will agree to compromise the latter in the name of the former; one can demand considerable sacrifices of him. But what happens is a displacement of his aims: under a capitalist regime, he was aiming at the overthrow of the bourgeoisie and the dictatorship of the proletariat through his concrete demands: the distant goals gave *meaning* to the immediate needs, while the immediate needs gave an actual and immediate content to those goals. The worker was in agreement with himself, and the leaders, while they were *organizing* the mass movement, could not escape the control of the masses: they could not lead them anywhere except where they wanted to go. In the period of post-revolutionary construction, the worker's socialism rests on a sure foundation: the socialization of the means of production;* he knows that his efforts must sooner or later profit the working class itself and, through it, the whole population; work no longer seems to him an enemy force, but a concrete link between the different layers of society; a rational understanding of the situation and its necessities, the desire to avoid endangering what has been acquired and fidelity to principles, to the goal: all this predisposes him to contain his needs as far as he can and to consider his exhaustion as a particular event which concerns himself alone – while, in the period of bourgeois exploitation, he saw it as an expression of the universal exhaustion of his class. The fact remains that his socialist goals no longer appear through the lived necessity on which his protest was based; even if he wants to work harder, in order to relieve his sons from the constraints of need, it is with

---

* Even after the collapse of the planned economies in Hungary and Poland, the proletariat felt it had gained something for which it was ready to fight: in neither country did it call socialism into question or tolerate its being called into question. What it denounced was a particular *policy* (and in Hungary it went so far as to condemn the Party responsible for that policy), but it remained loyal to the *regime*.

their needs and not his own that he associates the development of industrialization. This is not to say that the split would have been as clear-cut if the revolution of October 1917 had taken place in Germany or England, rather than Russia: in these already industrialized countries, the rhythm and distribution of investments would have been different in kind. But since the USSR needs *above all* to tool up, it will be quite a long time before the efforts and sacrifices of individuals have the *visible* effect of raising living standards. This means that the worker is really torn apart in this first stage of building socialism – a fact oddly underlined in the new Poland by the existence in some factories of management committees and trade union bodies elected by the same workers. Bourdet asked whether there was not a danger that one of these organizations might replicate the work of the other. The workers said no: 'The management committee, even though it derives directly from us, is driven by the general march of the economy; it represents us at the broad national level as socialist workers, and for that very reason may underestimate our concrete needs and immediate interests: this is why we must have trade unions.' Hence the contradiction of socialism demands that the same workers be doubly represented: the permanent clash between the management committee and the union simply brings out a conflict which each individual experiences obscurely, and shows it in the clear light of objectivity. This objectivization may even allow the contradiction to be transcended: in the USSR, in the heroic epoch of the first five-year plans, it was inconceivable. The proletariat was expanding day by day with a mass of illiterate peasants, dragged away from the countryside by the demands of concentration. The Civil War had decimated the élite of the working class, and these vague masses, devoid of political education, had no clear sense of their task or of their future. The conflict between the universal and the particular existed in them only at an embryonic stage: over-worked and underfed, they were chiefly characterized by their needs. By contrast, at the level of the leadership, the contradiction was patent; but it appeared chiefly a problem to be resolved within the framework of the Plan: human needs were seen as a factor of prime importance, but a negative one, tending to hold back production; it is human and politic to make the broadest concessions to these needs, in view of the vital demands of the Soviet economy. During this first stage, the masses lose the power to declare their own needs; experts decide what is proper for them. In the pre-revolutionary period, the party cadres and hierarchy – however authoritarian they may have been – were still controlled by the working classes, but after the revolution, the socialist experiment partly escapes human control, and tends to replace it by technical criteria. Being forced to *decipher* the objective contradictions of economic progress, the leaders become detached from the condition of the workers; they are confined to a pure understanding of objectivity and to the authoritarian actions that solve problems. In this way, the masses become the passive and unconscious object of historical contradictions, while the leaders make a veritable rational calculation to decide investment, working norms and living standards.

Around the same time, industrialization created a demographic upheaval which demanded an increase in agricultural productivity. These changes suddenly bring out the contradictions between the interests of industrial workers and agricultural workers: the former can only make up for the inadequacy of their pay by a fall and imposed stabilization in agricultural prices, while the latter want the fall in prices to apply to manufactured goods. The government finds itself constrained to impose rural collectivization by force: large-scale enterprises are more profitable and easier to manage. The working class unrestrainedly supports this violent approach since it serves the interests of the urban areas; in addition to which, industrial workers consider nationalization of industrial enterprises the greatest victory of the proletariat: collectivization of agriculture seems to them to be a necessary consequence of socialization of industry. Country people, on the other hand, even if they belong to a prosperous kolkhoz, will continue to resist what they view as expropriation. In reality, both groups were subject to the unconditional authority of the Plan, yet the fact remains that socialist construction necessarily brought about a situation which meant a veritable class struggle between workers and peasants, and that it was aggravated to the point of civil war. Deportations and executions are ineffective in suppressing this struggle: from 1930 onwards, the Soviet leaders have been obliged to exercise, in the name of the proletariat, an iron dictatorship over a hostile peasantry.

Stalinism was born out of this double contradiction. Firstly, the Plan created its own instruments: it developed a bureaucracy of experts, technicians and administrators, just as rationalization, in the capitalist countries, developed the 'tertiary sector'.* It is absurd to pretend that this bureaucracy is *exploiting* the proletariat or that it constitutes a *class* – otherwise, the words no longer have any meaning. Nor is it true to say that its one concern is to defend its own interests. Its members are far too well-paid, but they exhaust themselves with their efforts: they put in longer hours than the workers. Their privileges are the fruit of the Plan and legitimized by the Plan: their personal ambition is indistinguishable from their devotion to socialism viewed as abstract planning, that is to say, in the end, as a continuous growth in production. This total alienation allows them to consider themselves as the instruments of the universal to the very extent that the Plan demands their efforts to set it up; the demands of the masses, in contrast (even if they should take them into account), they view as particular and accidental, and strictly negative in character. The result is that their situation is, in itself, contradictory, because it is true that they represent the universal to the extent that they want to lead the whole country to the building of socialism, but it is also true that they represent a simple *particularism* to the extent that their function has cut them off from the Russian people and its everyday life. Between these 'organizers' and the masses, the party claims to play the part of mediator. Hence, it ceaselessly chastises the bureaucracy; through endless persecution, reshuffles and 'purges', it keeps it on its toes and prevents it from settling down; but the party, in itself, is the political expression of planning. A creator of myths, specialized in propaganda, it controls, stirs and urges on the masses: it can unite them for a time in a unanimous movement, but it is no more able than are the unions

---

* To the same extent that it cuts the leadership off from the masses, it inevitably develops the only power that can ensure its realization: the police.

to reflect their immediate interests, their demands and the streams that carry them this way or that. The working classes close in on themselves and their real life slips into a kind of clandestinity: this distancing creates mutual mistrust. Much later, the leadership will ask itself how to interest the masses *as such* in the productive process (this is a question they were considering in 1954, when I was in Moscow); but one only formulates problems when one has the means to resolve them. Today, the extraordinary achievements of the Soviet economy make it possible to consider real solutions: a deep unity of long-term objectives and short-term goals is characteristic of the revolutionary movement in a capitalist regime, but this unity defines it as something negative; at a certain level of socialization, however, the Soviet economy may make it easier to unify the people's goals in a positive process of construction. But, in the period after the revolution, pre-revolutionary unity gives way to an insurmountable contradiction, so it becomes necessary to create a working-class élite for whom the growth in productivity will at once be translated into an improvement in living standards, and which will see its most short-term interests in carrying out the Plan and exceeding its norms. This linkage of immediate well-being to the building of socialism is purely artificial: it is imposed from above, for a few only, by subtracting from disposable surplus-value. These 'Heroes of Labour' are held up everywhere as an example, but the example is false: their prosperity is a function of their small number; yet, their very existence is enough to bring about a general rise in norms, sometimes without the masses realizing it. The demands of socialization incline the leadership to underestimate the revolutionary strength of the proletariat; the leaders work on it from the outside, through propaganda, through generalized constraints and through emulation, while in any case preferring the Stakhanovites[1] who, like them, are a product of the Plan and, like them, alienated by the growth in production. The working masses, for their part, support the regime, but do not trust the bureaucracy. Admittedly, between an alienated

---

1. *Stakhanovites*: élite Soviet workers, named after Alexei Stakhanov, the legendary model worker.

bureaucracy and a crushed peasantry, industrial workers are the only ones who have kept some kind of independence and even – within well-defined limits – some right to criticize. But the fact remains that they feel they are being ruled from outside. The proletariat is no longer a subject of history, but it is not yet the concrete goal of socialization: it feels itself to be *the main object* of concern in the administration and *the essential means* for building socialism. For that very reason, socialism remains its 'class' duty, while ceasing to be its reality. However, the bureaucracy works away at itself and relentlessly pursues unification. The contradictions of socialism, in particular the conflict between the proletariat and the peasantry, force the leadership to make hurried U-turns, to change direction constantly, constantly to be correcting earlier deviations; the existence of rightist and leftist factions within the administration would be a serious danger to planning: what should only be a tactical withdrawal or a temporarily tougher stance, would be turned into a triumph for *one* political line, that is to say, one team and its policies. In reality, the Plan is only a hypothesis, continually subject to testing against experience: it should be possible to correct it without further committing oneself, purely in relation to experience itself. The urgent need for corrections implies total agreement among the organizers; only such an agreement will prevent a momentary change of direction from becoming a party line, it alone will allow the repeal of any harmful measure, even one which has just been decreed, it alone will permit the leadership's constant submission to objective reality. Meanwhile, there are increasingly well-defined threats from abroad; then the silent and hostile rural masses refuse to rally to the cause; constraints have to be tightened; and a dictatorial group needs first of all to exercise its dictatorship on itself. Hence, the danger from outside and resistance within demand an indissoluble unity among the leaders. Having no deep roots or genuine support, the group of 'organizers' can only maintain its authority and ensure national security if it achieves its own security, *from inside*, by itself and on itself; events oblige it to push its own integration to the limit. But this limit can never be reached, because the best image of it is furnished by the biological and mental unity of the individual. The result of this is a strange contradiction: each individual becomes suspect in the eyes of every other, and even in his own eyes, for the sole reason that his unity defeats the aim of absolute integration; but *only* an individual is capable of becoming the example, agent and ideal goal of a social process of unification. At the very moment when each individual considers himself inessential with respect to the group, considered as a totality, this totality must remain a simple working concept, or else the great mass of mankind must transcend itself and come together in the sacred unity of one essential individual. The cult of personality is thus, above all, the cult of social unity in one individual. And Stalin's function was not to represent the indissolubility of the group, but *to be* that indissolubility itself and, simultaneously, to create it. No one should be surprised at the emergence of this idolatry in a regime which denounces and rejects bourgeois individualism, because it is precisely the product of that rejection. Every bourgeois is like every other in that he insists on his own, specific individuality and the value of his own person; these unsocial, savage assertions cancel one another out; the apparent reciprocity of the relationships universalizes them; the bourgeois respects the absolute dignity of the human being in himself, and claims to respect it in others – whereupon, the cult becomes an abstraction; since everyone is sacred, no one is; under cover of this respect, a realistic appreciation of oneself and others will depend on the particular content of the universal form: ability, actions, character. These material elements can form the basis of a hierarchy, but not of a cult, because none of them is given value *a priori*. Thus, individualism excludes any possibility of idolatry. The star, the 'great' man or woman, those indispensable adjuncts of bourgeois ceremonial, are surely not intended to demonstrate the absolute superiority of a few over the many; for each individual, they are the incarnation of his own potential; they are laden with honours, at the summit of fame and power: their very existence achieves more than the most adept propaganda: in the face of reality, it persuades him that the highest honours are within reach of the humblest citizen. Function – as an abstract force – is identified with personality as a pure form; this entity is the object of the cult, it is sacred; but the *real* qualities of the individual are not taken into consideration: every slightly pretty girl respects the star in Brigitte Bardot, but remains persuaded that the actress's qualities cannot entirely justify her eminence; there is such a gap between the actual individual and what I shall call the 'function-personality', that only luck can cause the former to be moulded into the second. And luck *is nothing*; so, in this way, every famous actress reflects back to every woman in France her own potential for becoming sacred.*

By subordinating himself to the group, the Soviet avoids the ridiculous vices of bourgeois individualism. But, at the same time, the constantly more pressing need to maintain and reinforce unity drives his individual reality into clandestinity; despite the Constitution, it is deprived of any status and remains a simple factor of multiplicity, a potential source of disunity and the object of latent mistrust. However atrocious the struggles may be, they remain at the level of objectivity: there are solutions and plans which conflict with one another, but ambition and self-affirmation remain implicit, never coming out into the open: the Plan envelops and absorbs them. Denied the possibility of expressing themselves, the will of individuals cannot either be recognized or balanced in a system which claims to be a universal guarantee against any abnormal growth in the cult of personality. As a matter of fact, Stalin does not at first appear as an individual superior to others, but substantially similar to everyone else. What he represents is not the dignity of the individual, but social integration taken to the very limit. This indissolubility – which *happens* to be that of the individual – makes him the only possible agent of unification, because unity alone can unite multiplicity; he is indentified with the coercive action which the group exercises over its own members, he will carry out the

---

* Bourgeois propaganda very cleverly emphasizes the fact that public figures, prestigious in their public activity, have very ordinary private lives, just like anyone else. They are shown at home, seeing the New Year in with their wives (a very modest little party) or playing with their children. We are told about their lives and they are shown when they were young, ambitious, champing at the bit, just like any other young people, when suddenly, *opportunity knocks . . . !* So, in his early career and in his home life, the leader, the great man and the star equal: *myself plus good luck*.

sentence that the bourgeoisie pronounces on itself, he resumes and interiorizes the vague distrust of the revolutionary collective; in the name of all, he will be mistrustful of each; but the group is not mistrustful of him; had he been at the heart of the bureaucracy, he would merely have represented plurality and division; but, once he is placed above, he reflects back on the bureaucracy the impossible ideal of collective unity; Stalin's right hand is not mistrustful of his left, or his left ear of his right one. Stalin cannot spy on Stalin, or cease to be in agreement with himself. The group cannot survive without confidence; it is not enough to say that it trusts in Stalin, but it makes its own confidence out of the confidence that Stalin has in himself. Nobody *enjoys* this confidence except Stalin in person, but everyone knows that up there, in Stalin, the bureaucratic collective exists in a form of higher integration and that it is reconciled. Hence, every member of the bureaucracy, far from seeing in Stalin an exalted form of the human being, discovers in this concentrate of collectivity a radical negation of his own person for the benefit of unity. In this way, the upward movement that leads from the group to Stalin is characterized by the total destruction of individuality. Contrariwise, there is a downward movement: Stalin can only resolve the problem of integration by taking the social hierarchy to the extreme. From the top of the ladder to the bottom, directly or indirectly, those in authority owe their power to him. Thus one sees the rebirth of the *individual*, the *person*. But this has nothing to do with the bourgeois individual; it doesn't owe its existence to some universal status, but to the single being whom the demands of integration place above the group; his reality, always revocable, derives from his very function; in his relationships with his peers, it remains a factor of multiplicity and so an object of mistrust; while, to his subordinates, in contrast, it is a hypostasis of Stalin, hence a factor of unification and a cult object. At every level of the hierarchy, we find the same contradiction; biological and mental autonomy seems to be an element of plurality and a symbol of integration; the same individual sets himself up as a synthetic force with regard to his subordinates and denies his living reality in his relations with his leaders. In any event, what creates and destroys the Soviet individual is the unattainable unity of the group. Stalin, alone, is pure unity: he is the act itself. It is not his individual qualities that people worship in him, still less some 'charismatic' power or other, like the one that the Nazis attributed to Hitler. There is nothing mystical about his cult: he addresses a unity which is real in so far as it is a force for unification. Moreover, he is inseparable from the terror: as the incarnation of collective mistrust, Stalin can only defeat multiplicity by trying to reduce it. The negative counterpart of hierarchization is the ever-shifting terror that the bureaucracy exercises over itself, through Stalin, taking the form of 'purges' and deportations.

'Socialism in one country', or Stalinism, is not a deviation from Socialism: it is a path imposed on it by circumstances; the rhythm and development of this defensive construct were not decided merely by taking account of Soviet resources and needs, but also by the relations of the USSR with the capitalist world; or, in a word, by circumstances external to socialization which constantly oblige it to compromise on its principles. The contradictions of this first phase initiate a class conflict between workers and peasants, and cut the leadership off from the working masses; an authoritarian, bureaucratic system is set up in which everything is sacrificed to productivity. The contradictions of this system are reflected in its ideological superstructures: it calls itself 'Marxist-Leninist', but this is a façade that barely conceals a double value judgement on mankind and on socialism. On the one hand, propaganda and the rose-tinted novels of 'socialist realism' subscribe to a sickly form of optimism: everything in the socialist countries is good, the only conflict is between the forces of the past and those who are building the future; the latter must inevitably triumph. Failure, pain, death – all this is revised and salvaged by the progress of history. It even seems advisable for a while to write novels in which there are no conflicts at all. In any event, a positive hero is immune to internal difficulties and contradictions; without weakening and without making mistakes, he contributes to the building of socialism; his model is the young Stakhanovite; if he is a soldier, he never feels fear. These industrial and military idylls call themselves Marxist: they depict the happiness of a classless society. On the other hand, meanwhile, the exercise of dictatorship and the internal contradictions of the bureaucracy inevitably create a pessimism that dare not speak its name: since they are governed by force, men must be wicked; the most shining virtues of these Heroes of Labour, of these most devoted higher civil servants, of these party militants – so upright and so pure – can be extinguished by a puff of wind: now they are counter-revolutionaries, spies, agents of capitalism; habits of honesty, probity, thirty years of loyal service to the Communist Party, nothing can defend them from temptation. And if they veer from the party line, it is soon found that they were guilty *at birth*. Suddenly it is discovered that the great deeds which won them such honours, such praise, were crimes: one must be ready to withdraw any judgement and to despise the man whom one previously lauded to the skies, without showing any surprise at having been so long mistaken about him: in this confused and obscure world, today's truth must be proclaimed all the louder, the more chance it has of becoming tomorrow's error. The State, far from withering away, must be reinforced: its withering will come when authoritarian education has internalized the constraints that it imposes in each individual; it is not the emancipation of mankind that will make it obsolete, but their self-domestication and their internal conditioning: it will not disappear, but be carried into their hearts and minds. It is this mistrust of mankind that is expressed in the famous 'theoretical error' of Stalin: the class struggle is intensified in the period of building socialism. It has been claimed that he tried cynically to justify what he 'practised'. Why? Practice, in this case, engenders its own theory. Moreover, the same pessimism is to be found in foreign policy. The USSR did not want war, but expected it: rightly so, since Hitler's armies were to invade in 1941. But these quite justified fears led to a gross simplification of the problems: the capitalist world, beyond reach, little understood, became a purely destructive force, mercilessly bent on the extermination of the Soviet people and the liquidation of the armies of socialism: they still speak of its contradictions, of the conflicts that these might bring about, of the forces of peace that are in opposition to the forces of war in the West. They speak about them, but they no longer believe in them, especially after the failure of the Popular Front: because the only certain policy, given the state of isolation in which socialist Russia finds itself, is to arm, and to arm continually, *as if war were just around the corner*. This means that internal and external policy must always be determined by the risk of catastrophe, never with regard to the chances of peace. Until it catches up with the Western powers, the USSR must adhere to the pessimistic principle: *Si vis pacem, para bellum*; or, in plain language: 'Always expect the worst.'

Czechoslovakia 1968

This is an extract from an essay first published in 1970 under the title *The Socialism That Came in from the Cold*. It was Sartre's preface to a book about the Soviet invasion of Czechoslovakia, which took place in August 1968 in response to the months of political reform known as the Prague Spring. It was reprinted in *Situations IX* (1972).

The trials, the confessions, the diseased thoughts, the institutionalized lying, the atomization and the universal mistrust – no, these were not mere abuses; they were the inescapable consequences of prefabricated socialism. No accommodation or patching up could make them go away and, whatever the team in power, it would have been petrified in its turn or broken, for all its good will, unless Czechs and Slovaks had fallen on the machine in unison with hammers and thumped away like madmen until it fell apart, smashed beyond repair. They learned the true content of their thought in the heat of it, at the end of 1967, when their writings had the honour of drawing down upon their heads the wrath of an exhausted regime: gagged (for a short while), they watched their ideas go down into the street where the students – that generation of whom they were so suspicious – had seized on them and were waving them like banners. The victory of reformism in January 1968 was by then no longer their victory, despite the provisional alliance between the masses and the technocrats: their real triumph came later when the working class, roused from its torpor, without at first really being aware of what it was doing, returned to its old maximalist demand, the only one that truly emanated from it: power to the soviets. It was debated in every workplace, where people learned about direct democracy; in some factories, the workers did not even wait for the law to be passed to throw out the manager and put his *elected* successor under the control of a workers' council. The new leaders were overtaken by the people and had to redraft their bill to allow for popular pressure. Too late. It became clear that the process of democratization would not be halted. In this great popular movement, the intellectuals recognized the radicalization of their ideas and, at once, radicalized themselves, though without hostility towards the new ruling group, and intensified their struggle against the system. Never were any press and radio freer than in Czechoslovakia in the spring of 1968. But what is striking for someone from the West is that the battle of the intellectuals for complete freedom of expression and information was supported by the workers, who very rapidly came to the conclusion that the right to be completely informed was among their fundamental demands. It was on this basis that the union of workers and intellectuals was sealed* – which goes to show how much the problems of a people's democracy differ from our own. French workers would not go on strike if our government were to attack the freedom of the press and, in the present situation, this is understandable: the authorities seldom need to gag the newspapers, the profit motive does that for them. Workers read *Le Parisien libéré* without believing a word of it, thinking that the problems of the press will be solved purely and simply with the abolition of profit. They may realize that there is censorship in the USSR and in Poland, but they don't lose any sleep over it: in those countries, they have been told, the proletariat exercises its dictatorship: it would be a crime to allow counter-revolutionary

---

* The alliance was still in force when I went back to Prague in November 1969. The students had occupied some university premises to protest against the effective reimposition of censorship. However, one could still speak quite frankly about the occupation and I was able, at the request of a student, to tell a packed room that I considered the intervention of the five powers as a war crime; they demanded freedom of information in the context of the maximalist demand that I mentioned above. The government, without much conviction, was thinking of clamping down, when the staff of some important Czech factories put an end to its ditherings by letting it be known that they would come out on strike immediately if the students were harmed.

newspapers, in the name of abstract principles, and bourgeois ones at that, to poison the air with their lies. Yet in 1968, after twenty years of Stalinism, Czech and Slovak workers saw things quite differently. Firstly, they too had had their fill of lies; they had never realized just how much, and were only just learning. The dictatorship of the proletariat was the dictatorship of a party that had lost all contact with the masses; and as for the class struggle, how were they to believe that it had intensified with the advance of socialism, when they could very well see that the latter, since it had been installed, had only regressed? In their view, censorship was not even a lesser evil, because it was a case of lies censoring the truth. On the contrary, to the extent that they became aware of their maximalist demand, total truth became an absolute necessity for them, both as theoretical and as practical knowledge, for the simple reason that workers' power cannot even be exercised in the workplace if it is not constantly provided with information at all levels. This demand, as one may imagine, did not only concern the broadcasting, day by day, of national and international news through the mass media. On closer examination, it acquired its true meaning: in order to direct, improve and monitor production; in order to situate their activities in the context of the country and of the world; and in order to remain in permanent contact with each other, despite the distance between them, Czech and Slovak workers were demanding that they should participate fully and entirely in the scientific and cultural life of the country. This demand which, at the time of the Prague Spring, had barely begun to gain an awareness of itself, would sooner or later have caused a revolution in culture and teaching. Consequently, at the heart of a vast revolutionary movement, workers and intellectuals were one towards the other, by reciprocity, a permanent factor of radicalization: the latter had convinced themselves that they could not fulfil their function – the search for truth – except in a socialist society where power is exercised by everyone; and the former, seized with enthusiasm by the arguments in the newspapers, had persuaded themselves that they would not achieve socialism without breaking the monopoly on knowledge (which exists in the East as in the West) and without ensuring the widest possible distribution of truth which, being inseparably both theoretical and practical, could only achieve full development in the dialectical unity of these two formulations. There is no doubt that the agents of this process were far from understanding, in every case, where they were going and what they were doing; but there is also no doubt that they were trying to *build socialism* by liquidating the system and establishing new relationships of production. The group in power, left behind but still lucid, was quite aware what was going on, as we can see from the timid proposal for a 'Revision of the Party Statutes' published in *Rude Pravo* on 19 August 1968, which forbade the joint holding of public offices in the Party and the State.* It was bureaucracy itself that had been forced to apply the first of the hammer blows that would smash the machine.

We know what happened then: this socialism was still in process of being born when it was suffocated by counter-revolution. This is what *Pravda* keeps on saying, and I am entirely in agreement with the Soviet press except on a small matter of compass bearings: it was not from the West that the counter-revolutionary forces came; for once, it was not Western imperialism which crushed the movement towards democracy and used force and violence to re-establish the reign of the Thing. The leaders of the USSR, appalled at seeing socialism once more on the move, sent their tanks to Prague to stop it. The system was narrowly saved and another group, quickly brought in, prolonged the existence of institutionalized lying by publicly congratulating itself on the Soviet intervention. Nothing has changed, except that the donated socialism, by becoming oppressive socialism, has unmasked itself: official speeches are delivered in the midst of the silence of fourteen million people who do not believe a word and those who proclaim it from the heights are as alone as collaborators under the German occupation of France: they know

---

* Indeed, the idea was not new, nor was it revisionist. It is stated quite openly in the statutes of the CPSU. But I have shown why, in the USSR, it was never remotely applied. What matters here is the desire to go back to the beginning, to revive a forgotten principle and to give back a revolutionary role to the Communist Party.

that they are lying and that the Thing is the enemy of mankind; but the lie has taken hold of them and will not let go. The invitation to become an informer is in the logic of the system: if it is to endure, it needs everyone to mistrust others and himself; but mistrust of oneself is over. After the 20th Congress and the invasion of 1968, the Czechs and Slovaks will not give in to it; all that remains is to make of everyone, in spite of himself, a possible informer and so suspect in the eyes of his neighbours. Apart from a few precautions, in any case ineffective, the five invaders have not even tried to disguise the eminently *conservative* nature of their intervention. Our Western bourgeoisie understood that very well: the arrival of the tanks in Prague *reassured* it: why not put an end to the Cold War and enter into a Holy Alliance with the USSR that would maintain order everywhere? This is the point we have reached: the cards are on the table; there can be no more deception.

And yet, we are still cheating. The Left *protests*, becomes indignant, blames or 'regrets'. *Le Monde* often publishes articles inspired by virtuous wrath, followed by a long list of signatories among whom one keeps on finding the same names – mine, for example. Let's sign! Come on! Anything is better than a silence that might be taken for acceptance. But we must not use this moral stance as an alibi. And, indeed, what the Five did was not well done: they should be ashamed! And do you know: they don't give a damn! More than that: if they did care about the European Left, they could ask nothing better than for it to stamp its foot and shout: Boo! As long as we confine ourselves to the realm of deontology, the system will sleep easy: they are guilty, they didn't behave as *socialists*? That means that they could have done so: they alone are implicated, the regime is not in question. But if we read these interviews and if, through them, we decipher the Czechoslovak experience, we shall soon realize that the Soviet leaders, recruited and trained by the system, since they exercise power in the name of the Thing, could not have behaved otherwise than they did. It is the regime we should blame, the relationships of production that formed it, which have been reinforced and frozen by its action: where it is concerned, since August 1968, we have had to abandon the haven of moralism and the reformist illusion: the machine will not be repaired, the people must seize hold of it and throw it on the scrapheap. The revolutionary forces in the West have now only one way in which they can help Czechoslovakia (in the long term, but effectively). This is to listen to the voices that talk to us about the country, gather documents, reconstruct events, try to make a profound analysis of them, beyond mere conjecture, to the extent that they exhibit the structures of Soviet society, those of the people's democracies, and the relationship of the two with each other, and to use this analysis to rethink the European Left, without presupposition or bias – its aims, its tasks, its potential, its various types of organization – with a view to answering the fundamental question of the time: how can we unite, liquidate the old, ossified structures, and how can we produce new ones to prevent the next revolution from giving birth to *that kind of socialism*?

After Colonialism

> First published in 1961, this was Sartre's preface to *The Wretched of the Earth*, Frantz Fanon's revolutionary critique of European colonialism and of the psychological aspects of black oppression. The book and its uncompromising preface had a great influence on the anti-colonial and anti-racist movements of the 1960s.

Not so long ago, the earth had 2,000 million inhabitants – which is to say, 500 million men and 1,500 million natives. The former had use of the Word, the latter borrowed it. Between one and the other, acting as intermediaries, was a kind of ready-made pseudo-bourgeoisie, composed of corrupt petty rulers and feudal lords. In the colonies, the truth was openly displayed, but the inhabitants of the 'mother country' preferred it in disguise: the native had to love them – in a way, like mothers. The European élite set about making a native élite. Young men were chosen, branded on the forehead with the principles of Western culture and had fine-sounding gags thrust down their throats: great doughy words that stuck to their teeth. After a short stay in the mother country, they were sent back home, counterfeit. These living lies were left with nothing to say to their brothers; they gave off an echo. From Paris, London and Amsterdam, we proclaimed the words: 'Parthenon! Eternity!'; and, somewhere in Africa or in Asia, lips opened: '. . . thenon!' . . . nitty!' This was the golden age.

It came to an end. The mouths opened on their own. Yellow and black voices still spoke of our humanism, but now it was to reproach us with our inhumanity. We were not displeased when we heard these polite expressions of bitterness. First of all, there was proud astonishment: Goodness! Can they speak by themselves? Just look what we have made of them! We did not doubt that they accepted our ideals, because they were accusing us of having betrayed them. At this point, Europe believed in its mission: it had hellenized the Asians and created a new race, Greco-Latin negroes. And, among ourselves, being practical, we added: why not let them kick up a fuss, if it makes them feel better? A barking dog doesn't bite.

Another generation came along and moved the premises of the question. Its writers and poets tried, with incredible patience, to explain to us that our values were not entirely applicable to the reality of their lives, that they could neither altogether reject them nor assimilate them. Broadly speaking, what it meant was: You are making monsters of us, your humanism claims that we are universal while your racist practice particularizes us. We listened to them, quite unperturbed: colonial officers are not paid to read Hegel, so few of them do read him, but they do not need any philosopher to tell them that a troubled consciousness becomes entangled in its own contradictions. Efficiency: nil. So, let's perpetuate their unease: nothing will emerge except wind. The experts tell us that if there were the shadow of a real demand in their sighing, it would be for integration. Of course, there was no question of granting it: that would have ruined the system which, as you know, is founded on exploitation. But it would be enough to hold this carrot in front of their eyes, and they would gallop onwards. As for rebellion, we were quite easy on that score: what evolved native would go about massacring the fine sons of Europe, just in order to become a European like them? In short, we encouraged these melancholy musings and did not feel it improper, once, to award the Goncourt Prize to a negro. This was pre-1939.

1961. Listen: 'Let us not waste time in sterile litanies or disgusting mimicry. Let us leave behind this Europe, which is constantly talking about humankind, while massacring humanity wherever it finds it, on its own streetcorners, in every corner of the world. It has been centuries now . . . that [Europe], in the name of some so-called "spiritual adventure", has been stifling three-quarters of mankind.' The tone is new. Who dares to speak in this way? An African, a man of the Third World, from a former colony. He adds: 'Europe has reached such a crazy speed . . . it is going helter-skelter towards the abyss, which is something better avoided.' In other words, it's done for. This is a truth better left unsaid, but one which – don't you agree, my dear fellow-continentals? – we all accept, in our heart of hearts.

However, there is one reservation to be made. When, for example, a Frenchman says to another Frenchman: 'We've had it!' – something which, to my knowledge, has happened more or less daily since 1930 – this is a speech from the heart, burning with fury and love: the speaker is putting himself in the same boat as all his compatriots. Then, usually, he will add: 'Unless . . .' You see what's going on: there's no room for any more mistakes; if his recommendations are followed to the letter, then and only then will the country not fall apart. In short, this is a threat followed by a piece of advice, and the words are all the less shocking because they spring from the collective unconscious of the nation. But when Fanon, on the contrary, says that Europe is rushing to destruction, what he offers is not a cry of alarm, but a diagnosis. This doctor is not, on the one hand, uttering a definitive condemnation – miracles have been known to happen – nor is he offering a cure: he is stating that Europe is in its death throes. From outside, based on the symptoms that he has managed to observe. As for treating it, no; he has other things to worry about; he doesn't care one way or another if it lives or dies. This is what makes his book scandalous. And if you mutter, with an embarrassed laugh: 'He's really letting us have it!' then the real nature of the scandal is lost on you, because Fanon is not 'letting you have' anything at all. His book, which burns so fiercely for others, remains icy cold to you. It often speaks about you, but never to you. No more black Goncourts and yellow Nobel prize-winners: the days of the colonized laureate are over. A 'French-speaking', former native is turning the language to new ends, exploiting it and addressing the colonized alone: 'Natives of every under-developed land, unite!' What degradation! For the fathers, we were the only people they could talk to; and now the sons don't even consider us valid partners in the discussion: we are the objects of their discourse.

Of course, Fanon mentions, in passing, our notorious crimes: Sétif, Hanoi, Madagascar; but he does not waste time in condemning; he uses them. If he analyses the tactics of colonialism, the complex network of relationships that unite and oppose the colonials and those in the 'mother country', he does so *for his brothers*; the aim is to teach them how to foil us.

In short, the Third World discovers *itself* and speaks to *itself* through this voice. We know that this Third World is not homogeneous, that it consists of peoples who are still subject, others who have acquired a kind of pseudo-independence, others who are struggling to gain their autonomy, and still others who have won their freedom, but live under the constant threat of imperialist aggression. These differences are the product of colonial history, that is to say of oppression. In one place, the Motherland has been satisfied with paying a handful of feudal lords; in another, dividing to rule, it has artifically manufactured a bourgeoisie from the ranks of the subject people; elsewhere, it has scored a double hit, making a colony which is one of both settlement and exploitation. In this way, Europe has multiplied divisions and oppositions, created classes and sometimes forms of racism, lured on by every expedient to instigate and to intensify the stratification of colonized societies. Fanon does not gloss over anything: in order to fight us, the former colony must fight itself. Or rather, the two struggles are the same. All internal divisions must melt in the heat of battle. The impotent bourgeoisie of speculators and *compradores*, the urban working class, which is always privileged, the *lumpen-proletariat* of the shanty-towns: all of them must align themselves with the standpoint of the rural masses, the real reservoir of the national, revolutionary army. In these countries, where development has been deliberately held back by colonialism, it is the peasantry which, when it rebels, very soon appears as the *radical* class: it has experienced naked oppression, suffers much more from it than the workers in the cities and, to avoid starving to death, it requires nothing less than the breaking down of all structures. If it triumphs, then the national revolution will be a socialist one; but if its forward march is restrained, and the colonized bourgeoisie takes power, then the new state, even though it has formal autonomy, will remain in the hands of the imperialists. This is rather well demonstrated by the example of Katanga. So the unity of the Third World has not been accomplished: it is an undertaking still in progress which proceeds via the unity of all the colonized in each country, both before and after independence, under the command of the peasant class. This is what Fanon explains to his brothers in Africa, Asia and Latin America: either we shall achieve revolutionary socialism, all together and everywhere, or else we shall be defeated one by one by our former masters. He disguises nothing: neither weaknesses, nor divisions, nor mystifications. Here the movement has made a false start; there, after brilliant success, it is losing speed; elsewhere it has stopped: if it is to resume its progress, then the peasants must drive their bourgeoisie into the sea. The reader is warned against the most serious forms of alienation: the leader, the cult of personality, Western culture and, just as much, a return to the distant past of African culture. The real culture is the revolution; and that means it must be struck hot from the fire. Fanon speaks out loud; we, Europeans, can hear him: witness the fact that you have this book in your hands. Isn't he afraid that the colonial powers will take advantage of his sincerity?

No. He's not afraid of anything. Our methods are obsolete: they may sometimes hold back emancipation, but they cannot stop it. And let us not imagine that we can update our methods: neo-colonialism, that lazy dream of the mother countries, is pure moonshine. Those 'Third Forces' either do not exist or else they are the phoney bourgeoisies that colonialism had already established in power. Our machiavellian schemes are not very effective against the high degree of alertness in this world which has already detected our lies one by one. The colonialist has only one resort, which is force, if he has any left; the native has only one choice: servitude or sovereignty. What does it matter to Fanon whether or not you read his book? It is for his brothers that he gives away our old tricks, certain that we have none to replace them. It is to them that he is saying: Europe has got its hands on our continents, so we must hack away at them until it lets go. The age works in our favour: nothing happens in Bizerta or Elizabethville or in the Algerian *bled* without

AFTER COLONIALISM

the whole world knowing about it. The major power blocs support different sides, they are keeping each other at bay, so let's take advantage of this paralysis, let's step into history – and let our entrance make it for the first time universal. We must fight: since we have no other weapons, the slow working of the knife will be enough.

Europeans, open this book, go into it. After taking a few steps in the dark you will see some strangers gathered around a fire; go up to it and listen: they are talking about the fate they have in store for your trading posts and the mercenaries that defend them. They may see you, but they will go on talking among themselves, without even lowering their voices. This indifference strikes one to the heart: the fathers, creatures of the shadows, *your* creatures, were dead souls; you supplied them with light, they spoke only to you and you did not even bother to answer these zombies. The sons ignore you: they have a fire which lights them and gives them warmth, which is not your fire. You, staying at a respectful distance, feel stealthy, nocturnal, chilled. Everyone has a turn: out of this darkness will come another dawn, and the zombies are you.

In that case, you may say, let's throw this book out of the window. Why read it since it was not written for us? For two reasons, the first being that Fanon explains you to his brothers, and for their benefit analyses the workings of our alienations: take advantage of it to reveal yourself to yourself in your reality as an object. Our victims know us through their wounds and their chains: that is what makes their testimony irrefutable. It is enough for them to show us what we have done to them for us to realize what we have done to ourselves. Is there any point in that? Yes, because Europe is in great danger of dying. But, you may say, we live in the motherland and we condemn excesses. That's right, you were not colonials, but you are no better than they are. Those are your pioneers, you sent them overseas and they made you rich. You did warn them: if they spilled too much blood, you would formally dissociate yourselves from them: in just the same way, a State – any State – maintains droves of agitators, *agents provocateurs* and spies in foreign countries, then disclaims them if they are caught. You who are so liberal and so

177

humane, you who take your love of culture to the brink of affection, pretend to forget that you have colonies and that people are massacred there in your name. Fanon reveals to his comrades – especially to some of them, who have remained a little too Westernized – the solidarity of those in the mother country and their colonial agents. Have the courage to read it, for this reason: it will shame you, and shame, as Marx said, is a revolutionary feeling. You see: I, too, I cannot give up my subjective illusions. I, too, am saying to you: 'Everything is lost, unless . . .' As a European, I am stealing an enemy's book and making of it a means to heal Europe. Take advantage of it.

We have first to confront an unexpected show: our humanism doing a striptease. Here is it, naked and unlovely: it was just a deceitful ideology, an exquisite justification for pillage; its sentimentality and its niceties sanctioned our aggression. They cut a fine figure, don't they, the advocates of non-violence: neither victims nor torturers! Come, come! If you are not victims, when the government that you voted into office, and the army in which your younger brothers served, without hesitation or scruple, are responsible for 'genocide', then you are unquestionably torturers. And if you choose to be victims, to risk a day or two in jail, all you have done is to choose to sit this hand out. But you can't sit it out: you must play to the end. So you might as well learn this: if violence had only come into existence this evening, and if exploitation and oppression had never existed on this earth, then perhaps a display of non-violence might settle the dispute. But if the whole regime, up to and including your non-violent thoughts, is conditioned by thousands of years of oppression, then your passivity serves no purpose except to place you on the side of the oppressors.

You know quite well that we are exploiters. You know very well that we have taken the gold and the metals, and then the oil, of these 'new continents', and taken them back to our old homelands. To excellent effect: palaces, cathedrals, industrial capitals; and then, when a crisis loomed, the colonial markets were there to absorb the shock or to deflect it. Europe, gorged with wealth, accorded humanity *de jure* to all its inhabitants: a man, for us, means an accomplice, because we have *all* profited from colonial exploitation. This fat, pale-skinned continent is eventually lapsing into what Fanon correctly describes as 'narcissism'. Cocteau used to be annoyed with Paris, 'that city which talks always about itself'. And what else does Europe do? And that super-European monster, North America? What chatter: liberty, equality, fraternity, love, honour, patriotism, and heaven knows what else. This didn't stop us at the same time from racist talk: dirty nigger, dirty Jew, dirty Arab. Well-thinking people, soft-hearted and liberal – in short, neo-colonialists – claimed to be shocked by this lack of consistency, which was a mistake or hypocrisy: nothing is more consistent, for us, than racist humanism, because the European has only been able to make a human of himself by creating slaves and monsters. As long as the state of 'native' existed, the imposture behind this could remain concealed; one could posit an abstract notion of universality in the human race which served as a cover for more realistic practices: beyond the seas lived a race of sub-humans who might, perhaps in a thousand years, thanks to us, come to share our state. In short, the species was confused with its élite. Now, the native has revealed his truth, and at the same time our highly selective club reveals its weakness: it represented nothing more nor less than a minority. Worse was to come: since the others have become men against us, it appears that we are the enemies of the human race. The élite reveals its true nature: it is a gang. Our cherished values are brought back to earth; if we look closely, we shall see that not one among them is untainted with blood. Do you need an example? Remember those fine words: 'how generous France is . . .' Generous? Really? What about Sétif?[1] And what about the eight years of savage war that cost the lives of more than a million Algerians? Not to mention torture. But you must realize that we are not being reproached with betraying some mission or other, for the very good reason that we

---

1. *Sétif*: a province of northern Algeria. In 1945 the town of Sétif was the site of a spontaneous outburst against French colonial rule. More than 100 Europeans were killed. 8,000 Muslims were massacred in retaliation.

had no mission. It is generosity itself that is in the dock, that fine-sounding word that means just one thing: status granted. For the men over there, fresh and freed, no one has the power or the authority to give anything to anyone. Everybody has every right, over everyone; and our human race, when one day it brings itself into being, will not define itself as the sum of the inhabitants of the globe, but as the infinite unity of their reciprocal relations. At this point, I will stop: you can continue the task without difficulty. All you need to do is to look our aristocratic virtues straight in the face, for the first and last time: they drop dead. How could they outlive the aristocracy of sub-humans who engendered them? A few years ago, a bourgeois (and colonialist) commentator could find nothing better to say in defence of the West than this: 'We are not angels, but at least we do feel remorse.' What an admission! In former days, our continent had other things to keep it afloat: the Parthenon, Chartres, the Rights of Man, the swastika. Now we know what they amounted to, and no one now has any suggestion how to prevent us sinking, except the most Christian sense of our guilt. As you can see, it's all over: Europe is leaking on all sides. So what has happened? Quite simply this: once we were the subjects of History, now we are its objects. The balance of power has been reversed, decolonization is in progress; the best that our mercenaries can hope for is that they will delay its completion.

Even then, the old 'mother countries' will have to throw themselves into the fray, committing all their forces to a battle which they are bound to lose. The old colonial brutality which ensured the dubious glory of men like Bugeaud[2] can be seen once more, at the end of the saga, vastly increased, but still insufficient. The regular army and conscripts are sent to Algeria, they are kept there for seven years and have achieved nothing. The meaning of violence has changed. When we were victorious, we employed it apparently without this having any effect on us: it decomposed others, while we – the humans – kept our humanism intact. United by profit, the inhabitants of the

---

2. *Bugeaud*: Thomas-Robert Bugeaud, the French general who led the army that broke Algerian resistance to French conquest in the 1830s.

AFTER COLONIALISM

motherlands baptized their common crimes 'fraternity' and 'love'. Nowadays, the same communality, which is blocked everywhere, comes back against us through our soldiers, is internalized and possesses us. Involution begins: the colonized man recomposes himself and we, both ultra-rightists and liberals, colonists and inhabitants of the home countries, are decomposed. Already, fury and fear are nakedly displayed: one can see them openly in the *ratonnades*[3] when Arabs are attacked in Algiers. Where are the savages now? Where is the barbarity? Everything is there, down to the tom-toms: while the Europeans are burning Muslims alive, the car horns hammer out *Algérie française*. Not so long ago, as Fanon reminds us, conferences of psychiatrists bemoaned the extent of criminal behaviour among the natives: these people kill one another, they said; it's not normal, the Algerian cortex must be under-developed. In Central Africa, others have decided that 'the African makes very little use of his frontal lobes'. These experts would do well to continue their investigations in Europe, especially among the French, because we too must have been afflicted with lazy lobes for the past few years: our Patriots kill their compatriots from time to time; and, if they happen not to be at home, blow up the concierge and the house. Yet our lobes seem to be in perfect order: is it not rather that, since we are unable to crush the natives, our violence turns in on itself, accumulates inside us and looks for some way out? The unity of the Algerian people has produced a disunity of the French: throughout the territory of the former 'mother country', the tribes are dancing and getting ready to fight. Terror has left Africa and settled here: because there are some people who are quite simply enraged, who want to make us pay with our blood for the shame of having been defeated by natives, and then there are the rest, all the rest, who are just as guilty – after Bizerte[4] and after the lynchings

---

3. *ratonnades*: this means something like 'nigger-hunt'. *Raton* was a pejorative term for a North African. *Ratonnade*, coined in the early 1950s, was the word for organized violence directed against the *ratons*.

4. *Bizerte*: a prosperous port on the east coast of Tunisia. French forces were evacuated from Tunisia after independence in 1956. However, forces remained stationed in Bizerte.

in September, who went down into the street to say: *enough*? – but not so worked up: the liberals, the tough guys of the soft Left. Their blood is rising, too; and their aggression. But how scared they are! They disguise their anger behind myths and complicated rituals. To hold off the moment of truth and the final settlement of accounts, they have put a Grand Wizard over us, whose function is to keep us in the dark at all costs. No use. The violence that is hailed by some, repressed by others, goes round and round, one day exploding in Metz, the next day in Bordeaux; it has been here, it will be there, it's a game of pass the parcel. And now we are the ones who, bit by bit, are turning into natives. But for us to become entirely natives, our soil would have to be occupied by the people of the former colonies and we should have to be starving. It won't happen: no, we are in the grip of colonialism in decline and soon it is what will drive us on, senile and haughty: there you have it, our *zar*, our *loa*. And when you read Fanon's final chapter, you will be persuaded that it is better to be a native at the lowest point of poverty, rather than a former colonialist. It is not right for a police officer to be obliged to torture people for ten hours a day: at that rate, his nerves will crack, unless in their own interests torturers are forbidden to do overtime. When you want to use the full rigour of the law to protect the morale of the nation and the army, it is not a good idea for the latter systematically to demoralize the former; or for a country with a republican tradition to put hundreds of thousands of its young men in charge of the instigators of military coups. It is not a good idea, my fellow-countrymen, you who know all the crimes committed in our name, it really isn't a good idea to whisper a word of them to anyone, even to your own soul, for fear of having to judge yourselves. At the start, you were unaware, I accept that, then you had your doubts, and now you know; but you are still silent. Eight years of silence is damaging. And for nothing: today, the blinding sun of torture is at its height, shining on the whole country. In such a light, every laugh sounds hollow, every face is made up to hide anger or fear, every action betrays our disgust and our complicity. It is enough now for two Frenchmen to meet for there to be a corpse between them; and when I say, one corpse . . .

There was a time when France was the name of a country; we must beware, in 1961, that it doesn't become the name of a neurosis.

Will we recover? Yes. Violence, like Achilles' lance, can cauterize the wounds it makes. Today, we are chained, humiliated, sick with fear, at our lowest ebb. Fortunately even that is not enough for the colonial aristocracy: it can only achieve its reactionary aims in Algeria if it can first complete the colonization of the French. Every day we retreat from the fight, but we can be sure that you won't avoid it altogether. The killers need it: they want to have a go at us and give us a good hiding. This will be the end of the days of sorcerers and fetishes: you will either have to fight, or rot behind in camp. This is the last stage of the dialectic: you condemn the war, but don't yet dare to declare your solidarity with the Algerian freedom fighters. Don't worry, you can count on the colonialists and the mercenaries: they will get you to take the plunge. Then, perhaps, when your backs are against the wall, you will at last let loose the new violence that is aroused in you by those old festering crimes. But that, as they say, is another story. The story of humankind. I have no doubt that the time is coming when we shall join those who are writing it.

Modern Times

Though his deepest roots were in the literature of the nineteenth century, Sartre was the enemy of all forms of cultural nostalgia. Temperamentally and politically he was committed to the modern. His near-contemporaries, the generation we might describe as the class of 1925, were Graham Greene, Walt Disney, George Orwell, Marlene Dietrich and W. H. Auden. The cosmopolitan modernism of his Parisian youth was accordingly a mix of French, European and American ingredients: jazz and cinema, Dos Passos and Hemingway, Surrealism, Céline and Charlie Chaplin. This was the matrix of his early writings.

After 1940 he moved away from the experimentation of *Nausea*. The heroic era of aesthetic vanguardism was over. Populist literary and cultural forms now complemented socialist politics. The effort to renovate collective values led Sartre away from fiction towards journalism, biography, drama and the editorship of an eclectically independent socialist journal entitled *Les Temps modernes*.

Surrealism

In this extract from *What is Literature?* (1947) Sartre takes issue with the radical pretensions of his immediate literary predecessors. The whole essay was first published in *Les Temps modernes* between February and July 1947, and later included in *Situations II* (1948). This extract corresponds to *Situations II*: 214–27.

The second generation reached maturity after 1918. Of course, this is a very broad definition, since it is appropriate to include Cocteau, who made his début before the war, while Marcel Arland, whose first book as far as I know did not appear until after the armistice, has definite affinities with the writers about whom we have just spoken.[1] The evident absurdity of a war, the real causes of which would take thirty years to emerge, brought a renewed feeling of negativity. I shall not have much to say about this period which Thibaudet so correctly classed as one of 'decompression'. It was a fireworks display, and now that it has passed, so much has been written about it that it seems we know all there is to know. It is, however, worth noting that the most splendid of its rockets, Surrealism, harks back to the destructive tradition of the writer-consumer. These unruly young bourgeois wanted to wreck culture because they had been cultured; their chief enemy was the Philistine according to Heine, Monnier's Prudhomme, Flaubert's bourgeois; in short, their own father. But the violence of the preceding years made radicals of them. While their predecessors had been content to fight the utilitarian ideology of the bourgeoisie through *consump-*

1. Sartre has been discussing Gide, Claudel and Proust.

MODERN TIMES

tion, they made a more profound identification of the search for utility with the human project, that is to say with conscious and voluntary life. Consciousness is bourgeois, the Ego is bourgeois: Negativity must first of all be directed at this Nature which, as Pascal says, is only a first habit. To begin with, one must abolish the accepted distinction between conscious and unconscious life, between dream and wakefulness. This means the dissolution of subjectivity. Subjectivity starts, in point of fact, when we recognize that our thoughts, emotions and desires come from ourselves, at the moment when they appear, and when we deem both that it is certain that they belong to us and that it is only probable that the exterior world is modelled on them. The Surrealist abhorred this humble certainty on which the Stoic had based his morality; it displeased him both because of the limits that it assigns to us and the responsibilities that it imposes. Any means is valid to escape this consciousness of oneself and, consequently, of one's situation in the world. The Surrealists turned to psychoanalysis because it showed consciousness being invaded by parasitic excrescences having their origin elsewhere, and they rejected the 'bourgeois idea' of work, because work implies conjecture, hypothesis and projects, hence a perpetual recourse to the subjective. Automatic writing is above all an annihilation of subjectivity: when we practise it, we undergo a spasmodic bombardment by clots that tear through us; we do not know their origin or their nature until they have taken their place in the world of objects, which means that we must then look upon them with the eyes of strangers. So it is not a matter, as has often been said, of putting their unconscious subjectivity in place of consciousness, but of demonstrating that the subject is a flimsy, transparent delusion at the heart of an objective universe. However, the Surrealist's next move is to abolish objectivity. The idea is to blow up the world, and since no amount of dynamite would be enough – and, apart from that, a *real* destruction of all existing things is impossible, since it would merely convey this totality from one *real* state to another, equally *real* – they will try instead to break down particular objects; in other words, to abolish the very structure of objectivity in these exemplary objects. This is an operation which clearly cannot be performed on *real*, predefined existences, the essence of which is indeformable, so they would produce imaginary objects, constructed in such a way that their objectivity abolishes itself. The basic model of the process is provided by the fake sugarlumps which Duchamp actually cut out of marble, so that they would surprise by their unexpected weight. The visitor who felt them in his hand was to have an immediate and dazzling revelation, feeling the destruction of the objective essence of sugar by itself; he was to experience that same fundamental disappointment, the same malaise, the same sense of being out of kilter that, for example, one has with practical jokes: the teaspoon that melts in a cup of tea or the sugar (this is the opposite of the trick invented by Duchamp) that resurfaces and floats. Through this intuition it was hoped that the whole world would reveal itself to be a radical contradiction. Surrealist painting and sculpture have no other goal except the multiplication of these local and imaginary explosions, which are like plugholes through which the whole universe can empty itself. Dalí's paranoid critical method is only a perfected and more complex version of the process; in the end it too offers itself as an attempt to 'contribute to the total discrediting of the world of reality'. Literature would endeavour to make language suffer the same fate, destroying it by telescoping of words. In this way, sugar refers to marble and marble to sugar, and the soft watch challenges itself by its softness; the objective is abolished and suddenly brings us back to the subjective, since reality is discredited and one is happy to 'consider the very images of the external world as unstable and transitory' and to 'make them serve the reality of our own minds'. But the subjective in turn collapses, revealing behind it a mysterious objectivity – all this without even the beginning of a single act of real destruction. On the contrary: by means of its symbolic annulment of the ego by sleeping and automatic writing, the symbolic annulment of object by the production of evanescent objectivities, the symbolic annulment of language by the production of absurd and erratic meanings, and the destruction of painting by painting and literature by literature, Surrealism undertook the curious enterprise of achieving nothingness through an excess of being. It invariably destroyed by *creating*, in other words by adding pictures to existing pictures and books to already published books. Hence the ambivalence of its works: each of them can be seen as the savage and magnificent invention of a form, an unknown being, an unexpected phrase, and so become, as such, a deliberate contribution to culture; and since each one of them is a project to abolish all reality, and itself with the rest, Nothingness hovers around it, a Nothingness that is merely the endless flickering of contradictions. And the *spirit* that the Surrealists want to attain over the ruins of subjectivity, that spirit which it is not possible to envisage except through an accumulation of self-destructive objects, also hovers, flickering in the reciprocal and hard-set annihilation of things. It is neither the Negativity of Hegel, nor hypostasized Negation, nor even Nothingness, though it comes near to that: it is more appropriate to call it *the Impossible* or, if you prefer, the imaginary point where dream and wakefulness, real and fictitious, objective and subjective are confused with one another. This is confusion, not synthesis: synthesis would present itself as an articulated existence, dominating and controlling its internal contradictions. But Surrealism does not wish for the appearance of such a novelty, which would have to be challenged in its turn. It wishes rather to maintain itself in the state of nervous tension induced by the pursuit of an unrealizable intuition. At least Rimbaud wanted to see a drawing-room in a lake. The Surrealist wants to be constantly on the point of seeing both lake and drawing-room: if by chance he should encounter these, either he finds he is sick of them, or he takes fright and goes to lie down, with the blinds drawn. In the end, he paints a lot and blackens a lot of paper, but never really destroys anything. As a matter of fact, Breton acknowledged as much in 1925 when he wrote: 'The immediate reality of the Surrealist revolution is not so much to change anything in the physical and apparent order of things, as to create a movement in the mind.' The destruction of the universe is the object of a subjective undertaking, very similar to what has always been known as philosophical conversion. This world is constantly annihilated, without a grain of wheat or of sand being touched, or a feather on one of its birds: it is quite simply placed *in parenthesis*. It has not been enough appreciated that the constructions, paintings and object-poems of Surrealism were the tangible realization of aporia which the Sceptics of the third century BC used to justify their state of perpetual *epochē*. After which, certain that they would not compromise themselves by unwisely attaching themselves to anything, Carneades and Philo lived like everyone else. In the same way, the Surrealists, once the world has been destroyed and miraculously preserved by its own destruction, can indulge themselves shamelessly in their enormous love of the world. This world, the everyday world, with its trees and its roots, its women, seashells and flowers – yet haunted by the impossible and by nothingness – is what is known as *le merveilleux surréaliste*: the Surrealist fantastic. I cannot help thinking of that other process of marginalization by means of which the conscripted writers of the previous generation destroyed bourgeois life and preserved it, with all its nuances. Isn't the 'Surrealist fantastic' that of *Le Grand Meaulnes*, but radicalized? Admittedly, the passion here is sincere, as are the hatred and disgust directed against the bourgeois class. Only the situation has not changed: one must get by without smashing anything – or, at least, only in a symbolic way – and cleanse oneself from the original stain without giving up the advantages of one's position.

The fundamental question is the necessity, once again, of finding a coign of vantage for oneself. The Surrealists, more ambitious than their fathers, are counting on the radical and metaphysical destruction that they have undertaken, to confer on them a status a thousand times superior to that of the parasitic aristocracy. It is not a matter of escaping from the bourgeoisie: one must leap outside the human condition. What these scions of the family want to destroy is not the family heritage, it is the world. They have reverted to parasitism as a lesser evil, all with one accord abandoning studies and jobs; but it has never been enough for them to be the parasites of the bourgeoisie: their ambition is to prey on the whole of humankind. However metaphysical it may have been, it is clear that their loss of class came from above and that their priorities strictly forbade them to find an audience in the working class. Breton once wrote: 'Marx said: change the world. Rimbaud said: change life. For us these two slogans are one and the same.' This itself is enough to reveal the bourgeois intellectual in him: it is a question of knowing which change precedes the other. For a Marxist militant, there is no doubt that only social transformations can make possible radical changes in thought and feeling. If Breton thinks he can go on with his interior experiments on the fringes of revolutionary activity and in parallel with it, he is condemned from the start, because this would be the same thing as saying that liberation of the mind is conceivable while one is captive, at least for some people, thus making the need for revolution less urgent. This is the very treachery of which revolutionaries have always accused Epictetus, and Politzer[2] only the other day accused Bergson. And if one were to claim that Breton meant, with this statement, to announce a progressive and closely linked metamorphosis of the social state and personal life, I should reply by quoting another passage: 'Everything leads us to think that there is a certain point where the mind ceases to perceive life and death, reality and fantasy, past and future, the communicable and the uncommunicable as contradictory . . . In vain does one seek any other motive for Surrealist activity than the hope of determining this point.' Is this not to proclaim his divorce from his working-class readers far more than his bourgeois ones? The proletariat, which is caught up in the struggle, if it is to succeed in its aims, must constantly distinguish past from future, reality from fantasy and life from death. Breton did not mention these particular contraries at random: they are all categories of action, and revolutionary action needs them more than any other. And Surrealism, just as it radicalized the negation of utility to transform it into a rejection of projects and conscious life, radicalizes the old literary demand for gratuitousness, to make this a rejection of action through the destruction of the categories of action. There is such a thing as Surrealist quietism. Its quietism and permanent violence are two complementary aspects of a single position. Because the Surrealist has deprived himself of the means of mounting any kind of enterprise, his whole activity is reduced to impulses in the here and now. Here, darkened and weighted, we find the Gidean moral stance: the instantaneity of the

---

2. *Politzer*: Georges Politzer (1903–42), communist philosopher and psychologist, prime mover of the intellectual Resistance.

gratuitous act. There is nothing surprising in this: there is an element of quietism in all parasitism and the favourite *tempo* of consumption is the present instant.

However, Surrealism declared itself to be revolutionary and offered its hand to the Communist Party. This was the first time since the Restoration that a literary school had explicitly identified with an organized revolutionary movement. The reason is clear: these writers, who were also young people, wanted chiefly to destroy their families – the uncle in the army, the cousin in the church – just as Baudelaire, in '48, saw the February Revolution as an opportunity to set fire to General Aupick's[3] house. If they were born poor, they also had certain complexes to get rid of: envy, fear ... Then, too, they were rebelling against external constraints: the war, which had just ended, with its censorship, military service, taxes, the sky-blue chamber, brainwashing; they were all anti-clerical, no more and no less than old Combes[4] and the pre-war radicals, and generously disgusted by colonialism and the war in Morocco. This indignation and these hatreds could be expressed abstractly, through a concept of radical Negation which, *a fortiori* and without the need to make it the object of a particular act of will, would bring about the negation of the bourgeois class. And since youth, as Auguste Comte realized, is the metaphysical age *par excellence*, this abstract and metaphysical expression of their rebellion was obviously the one that they would prefer. The only trouble is that it was also the one that left the world altogether intact. It is true that they appended to it a few sporadic acts of violence, but these scattered demonstrations would succeed at the most in stirring up feelings of outrage. The best that they could hope for was to set up as a clandestine, punitive association on the model of the Ku Klux Klan. So they got to the point of hoping that others, outside the orbit of their spiritual experiments, would accept responsibility for carrying out real acts of destruction by the use of force. In short, they wanted to be the

---

3. *General Aupick*: Baudelaire's hated stepfather.
4. *old Combes*: Émile Combes (1835–1921), French premier who presided over the separation of Church and State in the wake of the Dreyfus affair.

clerics of an ideal society, the temporal function of which would be the permanent exercise of violence.* This is why, after praising the suicides of Vaché and Rigaut[5] as exemplary acts and having presented a gratuitous massacre ('emptying one's revolver into the crowd') as the most straightforward of Surrealist acts, they turned for help to the yellow peril. They could not see the profound contradiction that distinguished these brutal and partial acts of destruction from the poetical process of annihilation that they had undertaken. In reality, every time an act of destruction is partial, it is a *means* for achieving a positive and more general end. Surrealism was prepared to stop at this means: making it into an absolute end, it refused to advance any further. But, on the contrary, the total abolition that it dreams of harms no one, precisely because it is total. It is an absolute, situated outside history, a poetic fiction – and one which includes, among the realities that are to be abolished, the very aim that, for the Asians, for revolutionaries, justifies the violent means that they have been obliged to adopt. For its part, the Communist Party, hunted down by the bourgeois police, very much smaller in numbers than the SFIO [Section française de l'Internationale ouvrière], with no hope of taking power except in the very long term, and uncertain of its tactics, was still at the negative stage. Its priority was to win over the masses, to infiltrate the Socialists and to incorporate whatever elements it could detach from this collective that rejected it: its intellectual weapon was criticism. So it was not improbable for it to see in Surrealism a provisional ally, which it was preparing to reject when no longer needed: negation, the essence of Surrealism, is only a stage for the CP. It did not agree even for an instant to consider automatic writing, hypnotic trances or objective chance,

---

* Making oneself the cleric of violence implies the deliberate adoption of violence as a method of thought, that is to say commonly having recourse to intimidation and to the authority principle, haughtily refusing to argue through or to discuss. This is what gives the dogmatic texts of the Surrealists a purely formal, but disturbing similarity to the political writings of Charles Maurras.

5. *Vaché and Rigaut*: Jacques-Pierre Vaché (1895–1919), anarchist and dandy, one of the precursors of Surrealism, an early associate of Breton. Jacques-Georges Rigaut (1898–1929), founder member of the Paris Dada group.

except in so far as they might contribute to the breakdown of the bourgeoisie. It may appear, then, that what we had here was a recurrence of the identity of interest between the intellectuals and the oppressed classes that was the good fortune of writers in the eighteenth century. However, the appearance is deceptive. The deep source of the misunderstanding resides in the fact that the Surrealist cares little about the dictatorship of the proletariat and sees the pure violence of revolution as an absolute end, while communism aims at the taking of power and uses this end to justify the blood that it sheds. Apart from that, the link of Surrealism with the proletariat is indirect and abstract. The strength of a writer resides in his direct action on his audience, through the anger, the enthusiasm and the thoughts that he inspires with his writings. Diderot, Rousseau and Voltaire remained in continual contact with the bourgeoisie, because the latter read what they wrote. But the Surrealists have no readership in the proletariat: they barely manage to communicate from outside with the party or, rather, with its intellectuals. Their audience is elsewhere, in the cultured bourgeoisie, and the CP knows it, using them simply to stir up unease in the ruling groups. Hence their revolutionary statements remain purely theoretical, since they change nothing in their attitude, do not win over a single reader and find no response among the workers. They remain the parasites of the class that they insult, and their rebellion stays on the fringes of the revolution. Breton eventually recognized this himself and reclaimed his cleric's independence, writing to Naville: 'There is not one among us who does not wish for power to pass from the hands of the bourgeoisie to those of the proletariat. Meanwhile, however, we believe that it is no less essential to continue our experiments on the inner life and to do so, naturally, without external control, even by the Marxists . . . The two problems are quite different in kind.'

The conflict was to become more acute when Soviet Russia and, consequently, the French Communist Party went on to the stage of constructive organization; Surrealism, having remained in essence *negative*, was to break with it. This was when Breton turned to the Trotskyites, precisely because, being in a minority and having their backs to the wall, they were still at the stage of critical negation.

The Trotskyites, in their turn, used the Surrealists as a means of splitting the movement: there is a letter from Trotsky to Breton that leaves no doubt on the matter. If the Fourth International had also been able to proceed to the constructive phase, it is clear that this would have been the cause of a further break.

So the first approach by the bourgeois writer to the proletariat remained utopian and abstract, because he was looking not for an audience, but for an ally; and because he preserved and reinforced the division of the temporal and the spiritual, confining himself within the limits of a clerical sect. The agreement in principle between Surrealism and the CP against the bourgeoisie never went beyond the formal stage: they were united only on the formal notion of negativity. Indeed, the negativity of the Communist Party is provisional, a necessary historical moment in its great enterprise of social reorganization; while Surrealist negativity, whatever one may say, situates itself outside history, at once in the present moment and in the eternal: it is the absolute goal of life and art. Somewhere, Breton states that the spirit struggling against its demons and the proletariat struggling against capitalism are identical, or at least parallel, with reciprocal symbolization; which comes down to a reaffirmation of the 'sacred mission' of the proletariat. But the point is precisely that this class, when considered as a legion of exterminating angels, with the CP as a wall defending it against any approach from the Surrealists, is nothing truly for these authors but a semi-religious myth; and they appease their consciences by assigning to it a role similar to the myth of the people for well-meaning writers in 1848. The originality of the Surrealist movement is its attempt to take in everything at once: the breaking down of classes from above, parasitism, the aristocracy, the metaphysics of consumption and an alliance with the revolutionary forces. The history of the experiment shows that it was condemned to failure. But, fifty years earlier, it would not even have been conceivable: the only relationship that a bourgeois writer then could have had with the working class was to write for it and about it. What made it possible even for a moment to consider the conclusion of a provisional pact between an intellectual aristocracy and the oppressed classes is the emergence of a new factor: the party as a mediator between the middle classes and the proletariat.

I readily admit that Surrealism, with its ambiguous elements of literary clique, spiritual college, church and secret society,* is only one of the products of this interwar period. We ought to talk about Morand, Drieu la Rochelle and many others. But if the works of Breton, Péret and Desnos seemed to us the most representative, it is because all the works by those other writers implicitly contain the same characteristics. Morand is the model consumer, the traveller, the passer-by. He cancels out national traditions by setting them up against one another, following the well-established procedure of the Sceptics and of Montaigne. He throws them like crabs, into a basket, then leaves it up to them to tear each other apart. The whole enterprise is to do with finding a certain *gamma* point, very like the *gamma* point of the Surrealists, where differences of language, custom and interests are abolished by a process of total non-distinction. Here *speed* plays the same role as the paranoiac-critical method. *Europe galante* is the annihilation of countries by railway, *Rien que la terre* the annihilation of continents by plane. Morand puts his Asians in London, Americans in Syria, Turks in Norway; and he presents our customs through their eyes, as Montesquieu did through the eyes of his Persians – which is the surest way of depriving them of any *raison d'être*; but, at the same time, he does it in such a way that these visitors have lost much of their original purity and entirely reject their own customs, without altogether having adopted ours: at this particular moment in their transformation, each of them is a battlefield in which their picturesque exoticism and our mechanical rationalism destroy one another. Full of superficial brilliance, like glass beads, and of strange, fine-sounding names, Morand's novels, despite this, are the death-knell of exoticism. From them derives a whole literature that sets out to abolish local colour, either

---

* This is another thing that makes it similar to l'Action Française,[6] about which Maurras said that it was not a political party, but a conspiracy. Aren't the Surrealists' punitive expeditions comparable to the pranks played by the royalist Camelots du Roi?
6. *L'Action Française*: right-wing political movement formed in 1899 at the height of the Dreyfus affair. It was royalist, nationalist and antisemitic.

by showing that the distant cities about which we have dreamed since childhood are as depressingly familiar and banal to the eyes and the hearts of all their inhabitants as the Gare Saint-Lazare or the Eiffel Tower are for our hearts and eyes; or else by revealing the play-acting, the trickery and the lack of conviction behind ceremonies which travellers in previous centuries described with greater respect; or else by letting us perceive the universality of capitalist mechanism and rationalism behind the worn screen of the Oriental and African picturesque. Nothing is left but a world which is uniformly similar and monotonous. Never have I felt the deep meaning of this method more acutely than I did one day in the summer of 1938, between Mogador and Safi, where I was in a motor coach which overtook a veiled Muslim woman pedalling along on a bicycle: a Muslim woman on a bicycle – there's a self-destructive object that could equally well belong either to the Surrealists or to Morand. The precise mechanism of the bicycle counters the leisurely harem dreams which one imagines, as one passes by, to be those of this veiled creature; but at the same time the remnants of voluptuous and magical shadows behind those painted eyebrows and that narrow forehead are a counter to the mechanics, and suggest a beyond, enslaved, defeated and yet virulent and enchanting, behind the uniformity imposed by capitalism. Phantom exoticism, the Surrealist impossible, bourgeois dissatisfaction: in each of these three cases, the real collapses, while behind it one tries to maintain the irritating tension set up by contradictions. In the case of these travelling writers, the trick is clear: they suppress exoticism because one is always exotic in relation to someone else, and they do not wish to be so: they destroy tradition and history in order to escape from their own historical situation; they want to forget that the most lucid consciousness is always grafted on to something; they want to bring about a fictitious liberation, through an abstract form of internationalism, and to create a transcendent aristocracy by means of universalism.

Theatre and Cinema

This piece was first published in *Un Théâtre de Situations* (1973)

[Notes for a lecture given on 6 May 1958 at the sanatorium in Bouffémont]

[Among the many lectures that Sartre gave on the theatre, one remains in the form of notes and is of particular interest, both by its form and the ideas developed in it (the contrast between theatre and cinema and the definition of Brecht's theatre). The text that follows stays close to the manuscript, but does not respect all its breaks: we have added a few linking words here and there to make it easier for the reader].[1]

1. Theatre is a social art which produces collective facts. It is thus characterized *as much* (and more) by the part of society that controls it as by the author.

While in a film we are dealing with actors and actions preserved, theatre is an actual event, a 'hot jam session', a unique, daily event.

2. But this event has a particular structure, not perhaps *everywhere*, but *today*, in most of our societies. This is what I shall call *presentation*.

The audience takes part in a *social event*, but for that very reason they do not take part in *the story being told*. The latter is *presented* to them. Participation in a film is greater than in the theatre: one is directly confronted with the film.

---

1. Paragraph added to Sartre's text by the editors of the original anthology, *Un théâtre de situations* (1973).

Nonetheless, the actors are live, but:

(a) The cinema actor is closer: close-ups, nudity of faces. Example: Robert Aldrich's *Kiss Me Deadly* (1955).

(b) The cinema actor dominates the audience, he is above them. The spectator is crushed: low-angle shots. In the theatre there is not this 'superman' aspect that makes us feel people in their full size and weight.

(c) *Guided vision*. I am shown what someone wants me to see: our perception of the images is *directed*.

In the theatre, on the contrary, one looks at whatever one wants. This is why it is *so hard* for an actor to keep an appropriate expression while another is speaking.

So: *greater freedom*.

(d) The result of the absolute proximity of cinema: the person is strictly adapted to his role ... Appearance and reality are confused.

In the theatre, it hardly bothers us for a minute if Madeleine Renaud is a twenty-year-old widow. Because what matters is not *being* the twenty-year-old widow, but *playing* it. In that, where *are* beauty and youth? She *is not*. She is *the meaning of the gestures* – not a presence, but a sort of absence, an intangible ghost; the absent object is enfolded in the gesture and we feel that it is still there.

(e) But what then are these gestures that create the appearance of the person making them?

A film is a landscape. The California desert in Stroheim's *Greed* (1925) is a thing, a real, tangible object, a milieu. Then come the characters who are going to die there. In a sentimental film, the landscape is a state of mind which creates its interpreters.

Cinema depicts men in the midst of the world and conditioned by it. In the theatre, the contrary is true: Beckett and pantomime. Cinema décor takes a man and either breaks him or saves him. In the Peking Opera, river, boats, danger and night are significations suggested by the action.

So the theatre *presents* a man's actions to the human spectators and, *through this action*, the world in which he lives and the person performing the action. This does not mean voluntarism, it means that *everything*, even failure, impotence and death, must manifest itself as the signification of actions.

But what is an action?

1. An unusual situation directly or indirectly puts an individual or a social group in danger.

2. The individual or social group project a goal for themselves: making such changes outside themselves that the danger no longer exists.

3. The action or plot is the totality of operations performed on the outside world, and through it on the individual or the group itself, to obtain this goal by specified means.

Through the action of a body on itself, it involves bringing to light the determining circumstances, the ends and the means. Action is movement and gesture in the theatre, not in the cinema.

We do not have a real action or effect on real objects, but a presentational gesture which gives the action as its first sense and through it the world (in perspective) as the second sense. Puppets. All things, even beauty and youth, come from the movement/gesture and are appearance.

(a) Theatre in the theatre.

Men play-act in front of a fake audience; this time it is the acting itself which is appearance.

(b) Genet and *Les Bonnes*.*

At the same time as he denounces illusion, Genet wants it to keep its character of pure presentation. Here we have presentation of man himself as an appearance to real men who exist in the play.

Hegel and 'pathos'.

Action in the theatre reveals feeling. The hatred, jealousy and desperate love of Hermione appear in the action which makes her send Orestes to kill Pyrrhus.

* Play commissioned by Louis Jouvet and performed at the Théâtre de l'Athénée in 1947.

The clearest gesture, that is to say the clearest representation of action, is the word. But we must understand: the word in the theatre is necessarily the presentation of an act. Eloquence in the theatre.

So the theatre is a presentation of man to men through imaginary actions.

The result: a *distance*. A personal example: *Morts sans sépulture* was too violent. But this distance of presentation gives a new coherence to the universe which is presented. It is out of reach, one cannot act upon it or make it cease. In this way, it shows us our impotence in relation to it.

I can, with a few others, organize a plot against a play and prevent the actors from coming on stage, but this would simply be to prevent an actual thing, a social and economic fact. In the same way, I might break a gramophone record.

But I cannot break the symphony on it;* nor the dramatic object. This is whence it derives its reality.

And if there is no participation, at least there is discovery, sometimes painful, of a man beyond our reach – who is dashing towards his destruction, for example, while we are powerless to intervene. In the cinema we *are* the hero, we participate in him, we dash to our own destruction.

In the theatre, we remain outside and the hero is destroyed in front of us. But the effect on us and on our feelings is all the stronger since, at the same time, this hero is ourselves outside us.

THE PLAYS OF BRECHT

His aim is to show the man of today to us, his contemporaries, through the gestures that present his actions.

(a) Distancing. It is a matter of using this contradiction: the man present is myself outside my control. This means: making us discover

---

* See *L'Imaginaire*. Conclusion: II. The Work of Art.

ourselves *as others*, as if other men were looking at us; in other words, to obtain that objectivity that I cannot obtain by my own reflection.

In the cinema, today, participation excludes observation and explanation. In the theatre, the opposite is the case.

(b) Choice of subject: epic theatre.

Replacing the conflicts of classical theatre by contradictions.

Thus, the man who is made present before us is ourselves as social beings. But at the same time, he is shown to us in unfamiliar surroundings. Hence, I grasp my contradictions – that is to say, those of my time – through a figure who is foreign to me and does not touch me.

For Brecht, our intimate contradictions and the contradictions that set us in opposition to other individuals are never accidental: in their origin, they express the contradictions of society.

So it is a question of the actions of individual characters presenting our world to us to the extent that it is riven with social contradictions. In short, to the extent that individuals and individual actions *demonstrate* the major social currents and their meaning. It is never just the drama of a single person. Through it, we see the drama of society.

For example: the servant in *The Caucasian Chalk Circle* does not have a word to say of love, but only gestures. Maternal love is a permanent explanation, but one to be found, not to feel.

Brecht and the Classics

This theatre programme note was published in April 1957, the year after Brecht's death, as part of a brochure entitled *International Homage to Berthold Brecht*. The Berliner Ensemble, Brecht's company, were visiting Paris at the time.

In some respects, Brecht is one of ours. The richness and originality of his work should not prevent French people from finding in it their own old traditions, buried by the romantic and bourgeois nineteenth century. Most modern plays try to convince us of the reality of the events taking place on the stage. On the other hand, they pay hardly any attention to the truth of these events: if someone can make us expect and fear the final revolver shot, and if it resounds deafeningly in our ears, what does it matter that it is improbable? We will 'go along with it'. And it is not so much the precision of an actor's playing that the bourgeois admires, but that mysterious quality, his 'presence'. Whose presence? The actor's? No, his character's presence: if Buckingham appears in flesh and blood, we let him say whatever nonsense he likes. The bourgeoisie only believes in particular truths.

As far as I know, Brecht was not subject to the influence of our great dramatists, or the Greek tragedians who served them as models: his plays suggest Elizabethan dramas rather than classical tragedies. Yet he does have something in common with our classical writers and with the classical writers of Antiquity, which is that he has available to him a collective ideology, a method and a faith: like them, he puts mankind back in the world, that is to say, in truth. In this way the relationship of truth and illusion is reversed: as with

BRECHT AND THE CLASSICS

the classics, the event that is shown denotes its own *absence*: it took place some time previously or else it never happened at all; reality dissolves into pure appearance; but these pretences reveal to us the true laws that govern human conduct. Yes, for Brecht, as for Sophocles and for Racine, there is such a thing as Truth: the theatre's job is not to *tell* it, but to *show* it. And this proud undertaking of showing man to man without having recourse to the dubious sorcery of desire or terror is undoubtedly what we call classicism. Brecht is classical because of his concern for unity: if there is a total truth, which is the true object of theatre, then it is the event as a whole that mixes social classes and people, which makes individual chaos a reflection of collective chaos, and which by its violent unfolding brings to light both conflicts and the general order that conditions them. For this reason, his plays have a classical economy: of course, he is not concerned with the unities of place and time; but he leaves out anything that might distract us and rejects elaboration of details if it risks distracting us from the whole. He does not want to *move* us too much, when this might deprive us of our entire freedom to listen, to see and to understand at every moment. Yet he is telling us about a terrible monster: ourselves. But he wants to talk about it without terrorizing us. You will see the result: an image that is at once unreal and true, airy, elusive, many-coloured, in which violence, crime, madness and despair are made the object of calm contemplation, like those monsters 'imitated by art' that Boileau mentions.

So, should we assume that we are to remain impassive on our seats while people are shouting, torturing and killing on stage? No, since these assassins, these victims and these torturers are none other than ourselves. Racine, too, spoke to his contemporaries about themselves; but he was careful to exhibit them through the large end of the telescope. 'My tragic characters should be seen with different eyes from those we ordinarily turn on people whom we can view so closely. It may be said that the respect we feel for the hero increases the further away he is from us ... The distance that separates us from the country in some way makes up for the too great proximity in time.' This is a good definition of what Brecht, in his turn, calls the 'distancing effect'; because the respect that

205

Racine speaks of – with reference to the sanguinary Roxane in his play – is above all, even exclusively, a manner of burning bridges. We are shown our loves, our jealousies and our dreams of murder, and we are shown them cold, separated from us, inaccessible and fearful, all the more foreign for being ours, so that we imagine we can control them, while they develop beyond our reach, with a pitiless rigour that we simultaneously discover and recognize. Brecht's characters are the same: they surprise us as much as Papous and Kanaks, and we see ourselves in them without any lessening of astonishment. These grotesque or dramatic conflicts, these sins, these weaknesses, these pettinesses, these complicities: all ours. If at least there were a hero. The spectator, whoever he is, likes to identify with these élite characters who bring about – within themselves and on behalf of everybody – a reconciliation of contraries and the destruction of Evil by Good. Even when he has been burnt alive or cut into small pieces, he can walk home, if the night is fine, whistling, reassured. But Brecht doesn't show us heroes or martyrs: or rather, if he does describe the life of a new Joan of Arc, she is a ten-year-old child; we shall not be able to identify with her, far from it: heroism, locked up in childhood, seems all the more inaccessible to us. This is because there is no individual salvation: Society as a whole must change, and the dramatist's function remains the 'purification' that Aristotle spoke of: he reveals to us what we are, victims and accomplices at the same time. This is why Brecht's plays move us. But our emotion is a very unusual one, a perpetual unease – since we are the play suspended in contemplative calm and since we are the audience. This unease does not vanish when the curtain falls. On the contrary, it grows, it merges with the everyday unease which we do not recognize in ourselves, which we experience in bad faith and flight – and shows it up. Today, 'purification' has another name: awareness. But was there not a coming to awareness – in another time, with a different social and ideological context – in that calm and serious unease created in the seventeenth century by *Bajazet* and *Phèdre* in the mind of a woman spectator who would suddenly discover the inflexible law of human passions? This is why Brechtian theatre, that Shakespearean theatre of revolutionary denial, also seems to me – though its author never intended it – to have been an extraordinary attempt in the twentieth century to reach back to the classical tradition.

Seriality: The Bus Queue and the Radio Broadcast

Taken from *The Critique of Dialectical Reason* (1960), this corresponds to pages 308-25 of the original French edition.

We must illustrate these concepts with an example, of the most banal and everyday kind. Here we have a group of people on the Place Saint-Germain; they are waiting for the bus, at the stop in front of the church. I am using the word 'group' here in a neutral sense: this is a gathering, but I cannot yet tell if it is, as such, the inert result of separate activities, or of a common reality which by its nature governs everyone's actions, or of an agreed or contractual organization. These people – whose age, sex, class and background are very different – are giving reality, in a banal and everyday fashion, to the relationship of solitude, reciprocity and unification from outside (and massification from outside) which is characteristic, for example, of the citizens of a large city when they find themselves joined together, without being united in work, struggle or any other group activity which they share. The first thing, in fact, that we must note is that this is a plurality of solitudes: these people are not concerned with or for one another, they do not speak to one another and, in the main, do not observe one another; they exist, side by side, beside a post marking a bus stop. At this level, I can note that their solitude is not an inert status (or the simple reciprocal exteriority of the organisms), but that it is *in fact* experienced in each person's project as its negative structure. Or, if you prefer, the solitude of the organism as an impossibility of uniting with Others in an organic whole reveals itself through solitude experienced as a provision negated by each of the reciprocal relationships with Others. This

SERIALITY: THE BUS QUEUE AND THE RADIO BROADCAST

man is not only isolated by his body as such, but by the fact that he is turning his back on his neighbour who, moreover, has not even noticed him (or else has discovered him in his practical field as a general individual defined by the fact of his waiting for the bus). And this attitude of semi-ignorance has as its practical conditions a real belonging to other groups (it is morning, he has just got up and left home, he is still connected to his children, who are ill, and so on; moreover, he is going to the office, he has a verbal report to give his boss, he is thinking what he will say, he is muttering under his breath, and so on) and his being-in-the-inert (that is to say, his interest). So this plurality of separations can be expressed in a way as the negative of the integration of the individuals into separate groups – or which are separate *at this time* and *at this level* – and, through that, as the negative of each person's projects as determinants of the social field on the basis of specific conditions. But, conversely, if one considers the question from the viewpoint of groups, interests, etc. – in short, social structures to the extent that they express the fundamental social order (mode of production, realtionships of production, etc.) – then, on the contrary, each solitude can be defined by the disintegrating forces exercised by the whole of society on individuals (and which are, of course, the correlatives of the integrative forces that we shall speak about later). Or, if one prefers, the intensity of solitude, as a relation of exteriority between the members of a provisional and contingent gathering, expresses the *degree of massification* of the social ensemble, to the extent that it is produced on the basis of given conditions.* At this level, the reciprocal solitudes as a negation of reciprocity signify the integration of the individuals in a single society and, *in that sense*, can be defined as a certain manner (conditioned by the totalization in progress) of living in interiority and as reciprocity at the heart of the social, the exteriorized negation of all interiority: 'No one helps anyone else, it's each man for himself'; or, on the contrary, in sympathy, as Proust wrote: 'Each person is very much alone.' Finally, in our example, for each person and by him or her, solitude becomes

---

* When I say that it 'expresses', I mean that it does so in a purely indicative way.

a real, social product of large cities. In fact, for each member of the group waiting for the bus, the city is present (as I showed in the first part) as a practico-inert whole in which there is a movement towards interchangeability of men and the instrumental-whole; it has been present since the morning as exigency, instrumentality, milieu, etc. And, through it, we take as given the millions of people who make it up and whose entirely invisible presence makes of each individual a polyvalent solitude (it has millions of facets) and, *at the same time* an *integrated* member of the city (a 'native Parisian', a '*Parisien de Paris*', and so on). Let us add that the way of life inspires every individual to *solitary behaviours* (buying the newspaper as he leaves home, reading it in the bus, etc.) which are often operations for switching from one group to another (from the intimacy of the family to the public life of the office). So solitude is a project. Moreover, as such, it is relative to particular individuals at particular moments: cutting oneself off in order to read the newspaper means using the national collective and ultimately the totality of living humans, in so far as one belongs to it and depends on all, to isolate oneself from a hundred people who are waiting for or using the same public transport vehicle. Organic solitude, involuntary solitude, experienced solitude, solitude-as-behaviour, solitude as the social status of the individual, solitude as the exteriority of groups conditioning the exteriority of individuals and solitude as a reciprocity of isolations within a society that creates *masses*: all these types and all these oppositions can be found at once in the little group under consideration, to the extent that isolation is an historical and social behaviour of man in the midst of a gathering of men.

But at the same time the relationship of reciprocity remains in the gathering itself and between its members, and the negation of solitude through *praxis* preserves it as negated: it is, in fact, purely and simply the practical existence of men among men. Not only do we find it as a lived reality – since each person, even if he turns his back on the Others and even if he is unaware of their number or their appearance, knows that they exist as a finite and indeterminate plurality *to which he belongs* – but, even outside the real relationship

SERIALITY: THE BUS QUEUE AND THE RADIO BROADCAST

of each to the Others, the totality of *solitary* conducts, to the extent that they are conditioned by historical totalization, implies on all levels a structure of reciprocity: reciprocity must be the most constant possibility and the more immediate reality if the social models in use (clothes, hairstyles, etc.) are to be adopted by everyone (though of course this is not in itself sufficient) and if each individual, on discovering something amiss with his or her dress, is to put it right as soon as possible and, as far as possible, without being seen; this means that solitude does not take one outside the visual and practical field of the Other and that it is realized objectively in this field. At this level, we can find the same society which just now was serving as an agent of massification, in so far as its practico-inert being serves as a conductor for inter-individual reciprocities: these separate people form a group *to the extent that* they are all standing on a single pavement which protects them from the cars driving across the square, *to the extent that* they are grouped around the same bus stop, and so on. And above all these individuals form a grouping because they have a *common interest*, that is to say to the extent that, separated as organic individuals, they share a structure of their practico-inert being which unites them to the exterior world. They are almost all working people, who use this line, know the timetable of the buses and their frequency, and who are consequently waiting for the same vehicle: the 7.49 bus. To the extent that they are dependent on it (on its failures, breakdowns, accidents), this object *is their present interest*. But this present interest – since they all live in the area – refers back to wider and deeper structures of their general interest: improvement of public transport, maintenance of fare levels, etc. The bus they are waiting for unites them through being their interest as individuals who *this morning* have business on the right bank; but as the 7.49 bus, it is their *interest as passengers*. Everything is temporalized: the passing individual becomes an *inhabitant* (i.e. he is referred to the five or the ten previous years) and at the same time the vehicle is characterized by its daily, eternal recurrence (in fact, it is indeed the *same*, with the same driver and the same conductor). The object adopts a structure that transcends its pure inert existence and as such is provided with a passive future and past which makes it appear to the passengers as a (minute) part of their destiny.

However, to the extent that the bus designates the passengers who are there, it constitutes them in their *interchangeability*: each of them is produced by the social whole as united to his neighbours to the extent that he is strictly identical to them; in other words, their being-outside (that is to say, the interest that they have as users of the route) is single, as a pure and indivisible abstraction and not as a richly differentiated synthesis: it is a simple identity designating the passenger as an abstract generality by a defined *praxis* (hailing the bus, getting on board, taking one's ticket) in the development of a broad, synthetic *praxis* (the enterprise that joins driver and conductor every morning in that temporalization which is one particular route across Paris at one particular time). At this moment in the experiment, the group has its unit-being outside itself in an object to come and every individual, to the extent that he is defined by the common interest, is not distinguished from every other except by the simple materiality of the organism. And already, while he is characterized in his temporalization as waiting for his being in so far as it is the being of all, the abstract unity of the future common being manifests itself as *being-other* with respect to the organism which he *is in person* (or, if one prefers, which he *exists*). This moment cannot be one of conflict, it is already that of reciprocity and one must consider it quite simply as the abstract stage of identity. To the extent that *they have the same objective reality* in the future (one minute more, the same for all of them, and the bus will appear at the corner of the street), the *non-justifiable* separation of these organisms – to the extent that it derives from other conditions and another realm of being – is determined as *identity*. Identity exists when the *common* interest (as determination of the generality by the unity of an object within the framework of particular practices) is evident and when the plurality is defined precisely *in relation to this interest*. In short, at this moment it is not especially important that the passengers differ in their biological and social characteristics: to the extent that they are united by an abstract generality, they are identical as separate individuals. Identity is the practico-inert unity to come to the extent that it reveals itself at the moment as a *separation void of meaning*. And, since all lived characteristics that might serve for a definition of interiority fall outside this determination, the identity of each with each Other is their unity there, elsewhere, as being-other and here and now their common alterity. Each is the same as the Others to the extent that he is Other than himself. And identity as alterity is a *separation of exteriority*; or, if one prefers, the impossibility of achieving the transcendent unity to come through the body, to the extent that one experiences this unity as an irrational necessity.*

It is precisely at that level that the material object will determine the serial order as the social reason for the separation of individuals. The practico-inert demand here comes from scarcity: there is *not enough space for all*. But, aside from the fact that scarcity as a contingent, but fundamental relation of man to Nature is the context of all experience, this *particular* scarcity is an aspect of material inertia: whatever the demand, the object remains passively what it is. So one must not think that material demand is necessarily a special scarcity, directly experienced: we shall see other practico-inert structures of the object, as a *being distinguished from the generality* which conditions other serial relationships. I chose this example for its simplicity, nothing more. So the particular scarcity (the number of people in relation to the number of seats), aside from any particular *practice*, identifies each of them as surplus, which means that Other will rival Other by the very fact of their being identical; separation would become contradiction. But, except in the case of panic, when in effect each individual is fighting *himself in the Other*, in the twisting madness of an abstract unity and concrete, but unimaginable singularity, the relationship of reciprocity, emerging or re-emerging in exteriority of identity, establishes interchangeability as an impossibility of deciding *a priori* what is surplus and inspires some practice which has as its sole aim

---

* In fact, it is perfectly rational if one goes back over the stages of the entire process. The fact remains that the conflict beween interchangeability and existence (as a single, lived *praxis*) must be experienced at some levels as *a scandalous absurdity*.

avoiding conflict and arbitrariness by some order or other. While waiting for the bus, the passengers have taken tickets numbered in order. This means that they accept *the impossibility of deciding the surplus on the intrinsic qualities of the individual*; in other words that they remain on the ground of common interest and identity of separation as a meaningless negation; positively, this means that they seek to differentiate each Other from the Others, without adding anything to his nature as Other as the sole social determinant of his existence: so *serial unity* as common interest is imposed as a demand and overcomes all opposition. Admittedly, the order number refers to a temporal determination. But this is just what makes it *arbitrary*: the time in question is not a practical temporalization, but the homogeneous medium of repetition: each, in taking an order number on arrival, does what the Other does; he carries out a practico-inert *demand* of the whole; and, since the individuals are going to different jobs and have distinct aims, the fact of getting to the stop first confers *no particular distinguishing character*, but just the right to get into the bus first. All material justifications of this type, in fact, only take on meaning after the event: getting there first confers no merit; having waited longest confers no rights (one could well, in fact, think of fairer classifications: for a young man, it is easy to wait, but tiring for an old woman; moreover, the war wounded go ahead in any event, and so on). The real, essential transformation is that alterity as such (that is to say, pure alterity) is no longer either a simple relation to the common unity, nor the shifting identity of the organisms: as a means of ordering, it becomes a negative principle of union and of determination of the fate of each person, as Other, *by every Other as Other*. So it is very important to me to have the tenth rather than the twentieth order number. But I am tenth *through Others* to the extent that they are Others than themselves, that is to say to the extent that they do not in themselves possess the Reason for their order number. If I come after my neighbour, that may be because he failed to buy his newspaper this morning, or because I stayed longer at home. And the fact of our having numbers 9 and 10 depends on us and on all the Others, those in front and those behind.

SERIALITY: THE BUS QUEUE AND THE RADIO BROADCAST

On this basis we can grasp our relations to the object in all their complexity. On the one hand, we remain general individuals (to the extent that we belong to the gathering, of course). Hence, the unity of the gathering of passengers is to be found in the vehicle for which they are waiting: it *is* that vehicle itself as a mere potential means of transport (not of *all*, because we have nothing to do together, but of each of us). So, in appearance and as a first abstraction, there does indeed exist a structure of universality in the group, and each is identical to the Other to the extent that he is also waiting. However, their 'waits' are not a common fact, in that they are experienced separately as identical instances of the same act. From this point of view, the group is not structured, it is a gathering and the number of individuals remains contingent: this means that any different number was *possible* (though purely to the extent that the people are considered as anonymous particles and that their coming together is not the effect of any common dialectical process). It is at this level that conceptualization will occur; that is to say that the concept is founded on the molecular appearance of the organisms and on the transcendent unity of the group (the common interest).

But this generality as the fluid homogeneity of the gathering (to the extent that its unity is outside it) is only an abstract appearance since in fact it is constituted in its very multiplicity by its transcendent unity as structured multiplicity. In this notion, each is the same as the Others to the extent that he is himself. In a series, on the contrary, each becomes himself (*as Other than self*) in so far as he is other than the Others, that is to say, equally, in so far as the Others are others than him. No *concept* can be formed of the series since each member is serial through his place in the order, so through his alterity to the extent that it is posited as irreducible. This can be seen in arithmetic by simple consideration of number, as a concept and as a serial entity. All full numbers can be the object of a single concept, in so far as they all present the same characteristics; in particular, all full numbers can be represented by the symbol $n + 1$ (with the proviso that $n = 0$ when it is a question of a single unit). But *for that very reason*, the arithmetic series of full numbers, to the extent that they are constituted by the addition of one unit to the previous number, is a practical and material reality, constituted by an infinite series of uncomparable entities, and the uniqueness of each resides in the fact that it is, in respect to the number preceding it, what that number is to the one that preceded *it*. In the case of ordinals, alterity also changes in meaning: it shows itself in concept as common to all and designates each as a molecule identical to all others; but in series, it becomes a rule of differentiation. And, whatever procedure is used to put in order, seriality comes from practico-inert matter, that is to say from the future as a whole of inert possibilities, each equivalent to the others (equivalent, here, because no means of forecasting them is given): the possibility that there is one place, or two, or three, etc. These rigid possibilities are inorganic matter itself in so far as it is non-adaptability. They keep their rigidity when passing into the serial order of separate organisms: in fact, they become for each, according to his having such and such an order number, a totality of possibilities which are peculiar to him (he will find a place if ten or more than ten persons can get into the bus; he won't find one if nine people can do so, but he will be first for the next bus). And it is these possibilities and these alone which, inside the group, constitute the real content of his alterity. However, one must note here that this constitutive alterity necessarily depends on all the Others and on the real possibility which will arise, and that in this way the Other has his essence in all the Others, to the extent that he is different from them.* Moreover, this alterity, as a principle of ordering, naturally becomes a *link*. And this link between men turns out to be an entirely new kind compared with those which we have previously met: on the one hand, it cannot be explained as reciprocity, since the serial movement in the example we have given excludes a relationship of reciprocity: each is the Reason of the Being-Other of the Other, in so far as an Other is his reason for being; in a sense, we have another type of material exteriority, which is not surprising since unorganized materiality decided the series. But, on the other hand, in so far as the order was the product of *a practice* and this practice included

---

* In so far as he is *the same*, he is simply and formally *an other*.

reciprocity in it, it contains a *real interiority* for it is *in his real being* and as an integral part of a whole which has totalized itself outside, that each is dependent on the Other in his reality. Or, if one prefers, reciprocity in the context of identity becomes a false reciprocity of relations: what *a* is to *b* (the reason for being other than his being), *b* is to *c*, and *b* and the entire series are to *a*. By the opposition of the Other and of the same in the context of the Other, alterity becomes the following, paradoxical structure: the identity of each to each as an action of serial interiority of each on the Other. At this, *identity* (as a simple absurdity of non-signifying dispersal) becomes synthetic: each is identical to the Other in so far as he is made, by the Others, into an Other action on Others; the formal and universal structure of alterity will constitute *the Rationale of series*.

In the formal, strictly practical and limited case that we have been considering, the adoption of the serial mode remains a simple convenience without any particular influence on the individuals. But this elementary example has had the advantage of showing us the appearance of new practico-inert characteristics: in short, in this example we discover two charactersitics of *a non-active human gathering*: the visible unity, here, at this moment of the gathering (that totalized reality that they make up *for* anyone who looks at them from a window or from the opposite pavement), is only *apparent*; for each observer who discovers this totality, its origin is the integrating *praxis* in so far as it is the practical organization of *its* dialectical field and, in practico-inert objectivity, the general and inert bond between all the people in a field restricted by its instrumentality, in so far as it is social – that is, in so far as its inert, instrumental materiality finally refers back to the order in historical movement – joined to their true being-outside-themselves in a certain practical object which is not in any way a *symbol*, but on the contrary a material being producing their unity in itself and imposing it on them through the inert practices of the practico-inert field. In short, the visible unity of a gathering is a result produced *in part* by accidental factors (accidental at the level of experience and which will find their unity in a wider movement of totalization), and *in part* by the *real* but *transcendent* unity of a practico-inert object, in so far as this unity in the development of a directed process *is produced* as the real and material unity of the individuals in a particular multiplicity which it defines and limits itself. I have already said that this unity *is not* symbolic, and now we can see why: it is because it has nothing to symbolize, since *it itself* is the unity of all. And if, at times, in very special circumstances, one were to find a symbolic relation between the gathering as a visible assembly of discrete particles (where it appears in visible form), and its objective unity, it would be the little, visible crowd which by its assembled presence, would *become the symbol* of the practical unity of its *interest*, or of any other object which arose as its inert synthesis. As for this unity, as a practico-inert, it can be given to individuals through a wider *praxis* of which they are at once the inert means, ends or objects, which constitutes the true synthetic field of their gathering and which creates them in the object with their new laws of unified multiplicity. This *praxis* unifies them by producing the object in which they are already inscribed, where their forms are determined negatively; and it is this *praxis* – to the extent that it is already itself other (affected by all the inertia of the matter) – which produces them in common in other unity.

The other point to be made is that the apparent absence of structure in the gathering (or of apparent structures) does not correspond to objective reality: even were they all to be unaware of one another and to take their social conduct of solitude to the limit, the passive unity of the gathering *in the object* demands and produces an *ordinal* structure out of the multiplicity of the organisms. In other words, what appears to one's perception as a sort of organized totality (men together, standing close to one another and waiting), or as a dispersion, does (as a gathering of men brought together by an object) possess a basic structure that is quite different, transcending by its serial ordering the conflict between external and internal, unity and identity. In the context of the institution-activity (we shall see the precise meaning of these terms later), represented in Paris by the RATP,[1] this little

---

1. *RATP*: Régie Autonome des Transports Parisien, the Paris transport authority.

gathering that forms bit by bit around a bus stop – and, it seems, by simple addition – had *already* been given its serial structure: it was produced *in advance* as the structure of some grouping or other by the machine that distributes order numbers which is fixed to the post marking the stop. Each individual realizes it for himself and confirms it for the Others by means of his own individual *praxis* and his own ends: this means not that he is contributing to the creation of an active group by freely defining the aim, the means and the differentiation of tasks with other individuals, but that he is *actualizing* his being-outside-himself as a reality common to several and *which already is, which awaits him*, by an inert practice, denoted by instrumentality, the meaning of which is to integrate him into an ordered multiplicity by assigning him to a place in a prefabricated seriality. In that sense, the non-differentiation of the beings-outside-oneself in the passive unity of an object is produced between them as a serial order, as separation-unity in the practico-inert environment of the Other. Or, if one prefers, there is a fundamental, objective relation between collective unity as a transcendency *coming to the gathering* of the future (and of the past), and seriality as the practico-inert actualization by each individual of a relationship with Others in so far as this relationship determines him in his being and *already awaits him*. The thing as *common being* produces seriality as its own practico-inert being-outside-oneself in the plurality of practical organisms; each individual realizes himself outside himself in the objective unity of interpenetration in so far as he constitutes himself in the gathering as an objective element in a series. Or, again, as we shall see more clearly later on, whatever the series is and whatever the circumstances, it is constituted from the object-unity and, conversely, it is in the serial environment and through serial behaviour that the individual realizes his membership of the common being, both in practice and in theory. There are serial behaviours, there are serial thoughts and feelings; in other words, *the series is a mode of being of individuals in relation to one another and in relation to the common being*; and this mode of being changes them in all their structures. In that sense, we must distinguish serial *praxis* (as the *praxis* of the individual to the extent that he belongs to the series and as *praxis* of the total series, or the series totalized through individuals) from common *praxis* (*group action*) *and individual constituent praxis*. Conversely, one will discover in every non-serial *praxis*, a serial *praxis* as the practico-inert structure of that *praxis*, to the extent that it is social. And since there is a *logic* of the practico-inert layer, there are *also* structures proper to the thought which is produced at this social level of activity; and, if one prefers, there is a *rationality* of theoretical and practical behaviours of the agent as member of a series. Finally, to the extent that *the series* represents the use of alterity as a link between men under the passive action of the object, and since this passive action defines the general type of alterity which serves as a link, in the last resort alterity is the practico-inert object itself, in so far as it is produced in the context of multiplicity with its particular demands. In fact, every Other is Other than himself and Others to the extent that their relations constitute him and constitute Others in accordance with an objective, practical and inert rule of alterity (in a formal particularization of that alterity). So this rule – the *Rationale of series* – is common in all to the very extent that they are differentiated. I say 'common', not 'identical', because identity implies separation while the *Rationale of series* is a dynamic schema for determining each by all and all in each. Hence the Other, as Rationale of series and as a factor in each case of particular alterity, thus becomes a being common to all (as interchangeability denied and preserved), over and beyond his structure of identity and his structure of alterity. At this level, beyond the concept and the rule, the Other is myself in every Other and every Other in myself, and each as Other in all the Others; in short, it is the passive unity of multiplicity in so far as it exists in itself, it is the reinteriorization of exteriority by the human whole, it is the being-one of organisms to the extent that it corresponds to the unity of their being in oneself in the object; but, to the extent that the unity of each with the Other and all the Others is never given in itself and in the Other in a true relation based on reciprocity, to the extent that this *interior* unity of all is always and in each in all the Others in so far as they are others, and never *in itself* except *for Others*, in so far as it is other than them, this unity

– which is *always present, but always elsewhere* – becomes once more interiority experienced in the environment of exteriority; it no longer has any relation to molecularity, *it is really a unity*, but it is the unity of a flight; and it will be understood if one thinks that in an active, contractual and differentiated group, each can at the same time consider himself subordinate to the whole and as essential, as a practical presence of the whole here, in his own particular action. On the contrary, in the alterity link, the whole is a totalization of flight, the Being as a material reality is the totalized series of *not-being*, it is what each makes the other become, like its double, out of reach, without acting directly on it and by its own simple transformation under the action of an Other. Alterity as unity of identities is necessarily always elsewhere. *Elsewhere* there is only an Other, always other than oneself which, as soon as it is thought by the ideal thoughts of real others, seems to engender them by logical scissiparity, that is to say to produce the Others as indefinite moments of its alterity (when in fact it is precisely the opposite that occurs). Can we say that this hypostasized serial reason merely refers back to *the practico-inert object* as the unity outside oneself of individuals? No, since on the contrary it engenders it by multiplicity as a certain practical interiorization of being-outside. So must we then make it an Idea, that is to say, an *ideal category*? Surely not: *the* Jew (as a serial unit within Jewish multiplicities), *the* colonist, *the* career officer, and so on, are not ideas; nor is *the* militant or, as we shall see, *the* petit-bourgeois and *the* manual worker. The theoretical error (not practical, since the *praxis* really did constitute them in alterity) was to conceive these beings as concepts, when – as the fundamental basis of extremely complex relationships – they are *first of all* serial unities. In fact, the being-Jewish of each Jew in a hostile society that persecutes Jews, insults them and sometimes opens up to them, only to reject them immediately, cannot be the only relation of every Israelite with the antisemitic and racist society around him. It is this relationship in so far as it is lived by every Israelite in his direct or indirect relationship with all other Jews and in so far as it constitutes him by all of them as Other and puts him in danger in and by Others. To the extent that, for any Jew who is lucid and aware, his being-Jewish (which is his status *for non-Jews*) is interiorized as his responsibility with respect to all other Jews and his being-in-danger, out there, from some possible act of imprudence caused by Others who are nothing to him, on whom he has no influence and all of whom are themselves like Others (in so far as he makes them exist as such despite himself), *the* Jew, far from being *the model* common to each separate example, on the contrary represents the perpetual *being-outside-oneself-in-the-other* of the members of this practico-inert group (which I call such *in so far as* it exists inside societies with a non-Jewish majority and to the extent that each child – even if he should afterwards proclaim it with pride and by a concerted practice – must first of all *endure* his status). This is how, for example, in a society suffering a crisis of anti-semitism, which has started to reproach its Jewish members with 'taking all the best jobs', for every Jewish doctor or professor or banker, the other banker, doctor or professor will constitute him as dispensable (or the other way about). Moreover, one understands the necessity for this: alterity, as the interiorization by each person of his common-being-outside-oneself in the unifying object cannot be grasped as the unity of all except in the form of common-being-outside-oneself-in-the-other. This is because totalization, as *an organized form of social relations* assumes (in the abstract and in extreme cases, of course) an original synthetic *praxis* of which the aim is the human production of unity as its objectivization in and by men. This totalization, which we shall describe below, comes to men through themselves. But the totality of the gathering is only the passive action of a practico-inert object on what was dispersed. The limitation of the grouping to *these* individuals is only an accidental negation (since, in principle, their number as identities is not set) and the transformation into a totality never becomes the aim of a *praxis*, but reveals itself in so far as the relations of the men are governed by object relations, that is to say in so far as it comes to them as a practico-inert structure of which the sealed exteriority is unveiled as an interiority of real relations. From this point, in the framework of *demand* as an objectivity to be carried out, it is plurality which becomes unity, alterity which becomes spontaneity of myself in the Other and of all in me, it is the reciprocity of flights (as a pseudo-reciprocity) which becomes the human relationship of reciprocity. We have only cited this simple and narrow example of the bus passengers to show serial structure as the being of the most everyday, banal groupings: indeed, this structure, as the fundamental constitution of sociality, tends to be neglected by sociologists. Marxists know of it, but hardly mention it and prefer in general to attribute the difficulties that they encounter in the *praxis* of emancipation and agitation to organized forces, rather than to seriality as a material resistance of gatherings and masses to group action (and even to the action of practico-inert factors). But, if we want to encompass the world of seriality, if only in a brief glance, and if we want to point to the importance of its structures and practices – to the extent that finally they constitute the foundation of all sociality, even that which seeks to bring mankind back to the Other through the organization of *praxis* – then we must abandon the example we have chosen and consider the facts in the field where this elementary reality reveals its true nature and its effectiveness to experience. What I describe as *collective* is the two-way relationship of a material, inorganic and worked object with a multiplicity that finds in it its unity of exteriority. This relationship defines a *social object*; it has two directions (a false reciprocity) because I can both grasp the inorganic object as a materiality gnawed away by serial flight and also the totalized plurality as materialized outside itself as a common demand of the object; and, conversely, I can go backwards from material unity as exteriority to the serial flight as a determinant of the behaviour which will characterize the social and material environment of the original seal of seriality, or else start from serial unity and define its reactions (as a practico-inert unit of a multiplicity) on the common object (that is to say the transformations that it produces in the object). Indeed, from this point of view, one can consider the false reciprocity between the common object and the totalized multiplicity as an interchangeability of two material statuses in the practico-inert field; but one must at the same time consider it as a continuing transformation of each of the practico-inert materialities by the Other. From this point onwards, in any event, we can clarify the meaning of serial structure and the possibility of applying this knowledge to the study of the dialectical intelligibility of the social.

To conceive the rationality of alterity as a rule of the practico-inert social field, one must conceive that this alterity is more concrete and more complex than in the superficial and limited example in which we have seen it produced. By continuing the experiment, we can discover new characteristics which are produced when seriality occurs in a wider field and as a structure of more complex collectives. Indeed, the first thing that we must note is that practico-inert objects produce assembly – according to their own structure and their passive action – as a direct or indirect relation between the members of the multiplicity. We shall describe as *direct* a relationship that is based on *presence*. And I shall define *presence*, in a society which has at its disposal determined tools and techniques, as the maximum distance that allows two individuals to establish immediate relations of reciprocity. (It is clear that the distance is variable. In particular, there is a *real presence* of two people who telephone one another, one in relation to the other; and in the same way an aircraft remains in a permanent relation of *presence*, through its radio, with all the technical services responsible for its security.) Naturally, there are different types of presence and these types in fact depend on *praxis* (certain undertakings demand the presence of each within the perceptual field of the Other – without the intervention of any instrument); but in any event we shall define an assembly through the co-presence of its members, not to the extent that there exist necessarily between them relations of reciprocity, or a common and organized practice, but in so far as the possibility of this common *praxis* and of the relations of reciprocity on which it is based is an immediate given. Housewives queuing in front of the baker's shop, at a time of shortage, may be characterized as an assembly with a serial structure; and this assembly is *direct*: the possibility of a sudden unitary *praxis* (a riot) is an immediate given. On the other hand, there are practico-inert objects of perfectly defined structure which themselves constitute, among the indeterminate multiplicity of men (of a town, a country or the world), a certain plurality as an *indirect* assembly.

SERIALITY: THE BUS QUEUE AND THE RADIO BROADCAST

And I shall define these gatherings by *absence*: by this I mean not so much the absolute distance (in a given society, at a given moment in its development) – which in reality is only an abstract view – but the impossibility for the individuals of establishing relations of reciprocity between each other, or a common *praxis*, to *the extent that* they are defined by this object as members of the grouping. Indeed, it is not very important whether a given radio listener himself possesses a transmitter and can, as an individual, *later* get in touch with any other given listener in another city or another town: the very fact of *listening to the radio*, that is to say of receiving a particular broadcast at a particular time, establishes a serial relation of *absence* between the various listeners. In that case, the practico-inert object (and this is valid for all the so-called *mass media*) not only produces unity outside itself in the inorganic matter of the individuals: it determines them in separation and, to the extent that they are separated, ensures *their communication through alterity*. When I 'receive' a broadcast, the relationship that is set up between myself and the speaker is not a human one: I am passive, in fact, in relation to the thought expressed, the political commentary on the news, and so on. In an activity that develops on every level and over a period of years, this passivity can be counterbalanced *to a certain extent*: I can write, protest, applaud, congratulate, threaten, etc. But one must immediately point out that all these reactions together only carry weight if the majority (or a large minority of listeners) do the same thing, without knowing me, with the result that, here, reciprocity is from an assembly to a voice. Moreover, radio stations represent the viewpoint of the government, or certain interests of a group of capitalists, so one may imagine that the very action of the listeners (on the programmes or the opinions expressed) will remain ineffective. It quite often happens that political and social events that occur on all levels throughout the country can alone bring about the modification of a broadcasting schedule or tendentious commentary. From this point of view, the listener who disagrees with the policy of the government – even if in other places, in the midst of organized groups, he may make some effective protest against this policy – will understand his passive activity (his 'receptivity') as powerlessness. And, to the extent that this voice gives him exactly the limits of his powers (if it is a *truly* dreadful drama or musical programme, then the audience can act; but not entirely: there have been plenty of examples) to the extent of his indignation – or his enthusiasm: I take the negative case because it is simpler, but the same powerlessness applies if I am delighted by a lecturer or a singer on the radio, and demand that he should be given a regular programme or offered the microphone more often – is only the lived experience of his powerlessness as a man *with respect to another man*. Because, in a sense, this voice, with its quite individual inflexions and accent, is the particular voice of a particular person; and this person has prepared his audience by a series of precise, individual actions. And, in addition, there can be no doubt that he is addressing me. To me, and to Others, the voice says: 'Dear listeners . . .' But, though the speaker in a meeting is addressing all those present, each of them can contradict or even insult him (though of course, in certain cases, there may be some risk involved, but with a more or less clearly defined prospect, according to circumstances, of 'changing people's minds'). So the public speaker is really addressing *us*, in so far as one can imagine both individual reciprocity (*I* shout out my approval or disapproval) and collective reciprocity (*we* applaud him or boo him). While on the contrary, in principle, in its reality as a human voice, this radio announcer's voice is mystifying: it is based on reciprocity of discourse, hence on human relations, and it is in reality a reifying relation in which the voice presents itself as *praxis* and constitutes the listener as object of the *praxis*, in short it is a univocal relationship of interiority, like that of the organism interacting with the material environment, but in which I, as an inert object, am subjected as an inorganic materiality to the human work of the voice. However, if I like, I can press the switch and turn off the radio, or change stations. But this is where we get a gathering at a distance, because this purely individual activity changes absolutely nothing in the work of the voice. It will continue to sound in millions of rooms before millions of listeners. I am the one who plunges myself into the ineffective and abstract solitude of private life, without changing anything in the objective fact. I have not denied the voice, I have denied myself as an individual in the gathering. And, especially when it is an ideological broadcast, it was deep down *as an Other* that I wanted the voice to be silent, that is to say, for example, to the extent that it can harm Others who listen to it. I may perhaps be perfectly sure of myself, I may perhaps even be perfectly sure of an active political group, all of whose ideas I share and all of whose positions I adopt. However, the voice is unbearable to me *to the extent that* it is listened to by Others – Others who are precisely *the same* in that they are listening to the radio and Others in so far as they belong to different milieux. I tell myself that it might *convince them*. In truth, I feel that I could answer the arguments face-to-face with these Others, even if they do not think as I do; but precisely what I experience is *absence*, as my mode of connection to these Others. This time, my powerlessness resides not only in the impossibility of stopping the voice, but in convincing, *one by one*, the listeners whom it is haranguing together in this common solitude which it has created for all as their inert link. As soon as I imagine any practical action against what the speaker is saying, I can only consider it as serial: one would have to take the listeners one after another ... Obviously, this seriality is the measure of my powerlessness and, perhaps, that of my party. In any case, if the latter did consider counter-propaganda, it would be obliged to adapt to the serial structure that the mass media have created (and supposing the listener were to be a journalist who the following day was to express his indignation in his newspaper, he would be fighting one serial action with another: he would be addressing four hundred thousand of the separate radio listeners in the town to the extent that they can be reached as separate newspaper readers). So the powerless listener is constituted by the voice itself as *other-member* of the indirect gathering: a lateral relationship of indefinite seriality is established between him and *the Others* with the very first words. Naturally, this relation had its origin in a knowledge produced by language itself to the extent that it is a medium for the mass media. It is the newspapers and the radio itself that inform each person of the frequency of French radio stations. But this knowledge (which is itself serial in kind by its origin, its content and its practical aim), has long since been transformed into a fact. Every listener is objectively defined by this real fact, that is to say by this structure of exteriority which has been interiorized as knowledge. And, at the very instant when, in a given historical situation and in the context of the struggles that it creates, he is listening to the voice in a state of powerless indignation, he no longer listens to it *on his own account* (we have accepted that he was sure to be impervious to the arguments) but *from the point of view* of the Others. Which Others? This depends on the circumstances and the individual, with his own experience and his past: perhaps he is putting himself in the place of the Xs, his friends who are easily influenced and seemed to him, the previous day, less decisive than before. Perhaps he will be trying to listen as some abstractly defined listener, known to him in general terms (the half-hearted, the weak; or, far more precisely, one who has some particular interest or other and who is being cleverly flattered, etc.). But in any case the abstract individual whom he imagines, in his alterity, has for a long time also been a notion-fact (a type forged both by experience and by the stereotyping of the mass media); and, conversely, the hesitant family whom he takes as a point of reference cannot truly cause him anxiety except to the extent that it represents the first item in a series, that is to say that it is itself stereotyped as Other. There is no point here in describing the curious attitude of the indignant listener (everyone can consider his own experience) and the dialectic between three moments: the (triumphal) one in which he refutes the argument (or thinks he refutes it; that doesn't make any difference), *for the Other* (but to the extent that a relation of reciprocity ought to exist); the moment (of powerless indignation) when he realizes himself to be a member of a series in which the members are united by the sole link of alterity; and the moment (of anxiety and temptation) when, placing himself in *the Other's point of view*, he allows himself to be convinced as an Other – up to a point – in order to feel the strength of the argument. This third moment is one of unease and fascination: I am at the same time the person who knows how to refute this nonsense and the one who is letting himself be convinced by it. And by this I do not mean that I am at once myself and the Other: perhaps the triumphal attitude of the one who knows is only another form of alterity (I have confidence in Others who can refute the argument and I identify myself with them because I share their opinion). What counts most of all is that my powerlessness to act on the series of *Others* (who may be convinced) rebounds on me to make *those Others* my destiny. Not, of course, in connection with this single broadcast, but because it is produced in the context of a certain propaganda which mystifies and lulls them. Hence, the voice becomes for each person *dizzying*: it is no longer the voice of a person (even if the announcer is named), since reciprocity has been destroyed. But it is *doubly* a collective: on the one hand, as we have just seen, it produces me as an inert member of a series and as Other in the midst of Others; on the other hand, it appears in itself as the social result of a political *praxis* (of the government, if we are talking about a State radio) and as *sustained* in itself by another serial cross-section of listeners: those who are already convinced, and whose interests and leanings it expresses. Thus in it and through it, the Others (supporters of that policy) influence Others (waverers, neutrals); but this influence is itself serial (what is not serial, of course, is the government's political action and its propaganda activities) since each person listens in place of the Other as Other, and since the voice itself is Other: Other for those who reject the policy which inspires it, as an expression of certain Others and action on Others; Other for the undecided who are *already* receiving it as an opinion of Others (of those all-powerful Others who control the mass media) and who are already influenced by the mere fact that this policy has the power to make a case for itself publicly; Other, finally, for those who support government policy, in that *for each of them* in their solitude it is backed by the approval of Others (those who are of their opinion) and by the action that it exerts on the undecided; for the former, it is their thoughts that the voice expresses, but it is their thoughts as Other, that is to say in so far as they are *spoken* by another, and *formulated in other terms* (better or differently from the way in which they would have done it) and to the extent that it exists at the same moment *for all the Others* as Other-Thought.

Any behaviours to which the Other-Thought, as a meaning of the Other-Voice, gives rise in all its listeners are always *behaviours of alterity*. By this, one should understand that these behaviours have neither the immediate structure of individual *praxis*, nor the concerted structures of common and organized *praxis*. They are stimulated *immediately* – like the free reactions of the individual – but he cannot produce them under the influence of the collective except in so far as they are in themselves lateral totalizations of seriality (indignation, ironic laughter, impotent rage, fascination, enthusiasm, a need to communicate with Others, outrage, collective fear,* etc.). In other words, the individual, as a member of the series, exhibits *altered* behaviour patterns, each of which in him is the action of the Other, which means that they are by themselves a recurrence taken to the utmost limit (i.e. to infinity).

By developing this example, we have enriched our understanding of seriality. From the very fact that certain objects can establish indirect links of alterity between individuals who are unknown to one another as such, we can envisage the possibility that a series may be finite, indefinite or infinite. When multiplicity, although numerically determined in itself, remains practically indeterminate as a factor of the gathering, it is indefinite (this is the case, for example, with the radio: there are a definite number of individuals listening at this moment to a particular broadcast, but it is as an indeterminate quantity that the broadcast constitutes the seriality of its listeners as the relation of each with the Others). When multiplicity is brought together by a pattern of circular recurrence, we are dealing with a practically infinite series (at least, for as long

---

* Collective fear, to the extent that it is exhibited as serial behaviour in an isolated listener, appears if the broadcast seems daring or shocking; fear is then the fear of anger or the fear of others, it is a sacred fear, because it is the fear that these words have been spoken in the indefinite context of seriality and also the fear, with respect to the Other, of having been a *listener* to these words. These others, in myself, condemn the moment of receptivity in which, by my individuality as a practical organism, these words existed *here*, in this room. Alterity condemns my personal reality in me, while the Other passes judgement on the Same.

as the circular pattern continues). In effect, each term (to the extent that it produces the alterity of Others) becomes itself Other to the extent that the Others produce it Other, and contributes in its turn to modifying them in their alterity.

However, we have also noted that pure, formal alterity (of the kind shown in our first examples) is only an abstract moment in the serial process. It is true that it can be found in all groups which, for example, are *ordered* in some manner or other (groups of purchasers, for example, when there is a shortage of products for sale or a shortage of staff). But formal purity is here maintained by deliberate action: one refuses to distinguish the individuals by anything other than alterity, which itself is constituted as a rule of succession. In all other cases, that is to say when alterity is not itself a means of selection, the individuals produce themselves in the serial context with some characteristics peculiar to them, which differ from one to the other or from one example to another. Of course, the fundamental structure remains unchanged: the radio listeners make up at that moment *a series* to the extent that they are listening to the common voice that constitutes each of them in their identity as an Other. But it is precisely for that reason that an alterity of content appears between them. This alterity still remains very formal, since it constitutes them on the basis of the object (the voice) and according to their possible reactions to the object. It goes without saying that in order to establish the basis for these reactions, one would have to find out more about the differences, find other collectives, other interests and groups, and finally totalize the historical moment with its past. But to the extent that the gathering is created by the radio, it remains on the level of practical alterity of *listening behaviours*. It is from here that alterity, as the Rationale of the series, becomes a constitutive force of each and of all: because in each, the Other is no longer a simple, formal difference in identity; in each, the Other is a different reaction, a variant behaviour; and each is conditioned in the fleeting unity of alterity by these different behaviours of the Other *in so far as* he cannot modify them in the Other. So each is as effective in his action on the Other as if he were to establish a human relationship with him – direct and reciprocal, or organized

– but his passive and indirect action derives from his *very powerlessness*, to the extent that the Other lives it in himself as his own powerlessness as Other.

The Man with the Tape-recorder: A Psychoanalytic Dialogue

A literary hoax in the spirit of 1968, this 'document', supposedly the transcript of a psychoanalytic session, was first published in *Les Temps modernes* in April 1969. Sponsored by Sartre and attributed to an author known only as A., the text was the cause of a public disagreement between Sartre and two of his editorial collaborators, Pontalis and Pingaud, who subsequently resigned. The piece was included in *Situations IX: Miscellany* (1972). The style strongly suggests that it was written by Sartre.

We were deeply divided over the question of A.'s text. Then we reached a compromise agreement that I hope will last.* I was to say why, from the start, I felt that it should be published; Pontalis and Pingaud, who think the opposite, were to tell us why they were opposed to publication. So here is the evidence, sandwiched between our two articles.

Firstly, a few words to avoid one probable misunderstanding: I am not a 'false friend' of psychoanalysis, but a critical fellow-traveller, and I have no intention — and, what is more, no means — of making it look ridiculous. The dialogue that follows will make people smile: one always likes to see Mr Punch beating the policeman. Personally, I don't find it funny, either for the analyst or for the former subject of analysis. Of course, the latter has the best part and I shall say in a moment why I find him exceptional; but the former, when all's said and done, came away without glory (who could do more, unless he were a judo expert?), but without suffering

---

* It did not last (7 October 1970).

a disaster: he did not speak. Moreover, I am happy to acknowledge that the discussion took place in the context of a psychoanalytical narrative: what is in question, it seems, is first and foremost a particular interpretation which, according to A., Dr X. had been imposing on his patient for some years and had then suddenly repudiated: it goes without saying that we shall not commit ourselves either way on this interpretation or on the recantation, since the tape-recorder did not record the start of the conversation. A., moreover, is the first to recognize this when he entitles the document: 'Psychoanalytical dialogue'. The title is ironic: he is giving us to understand that, as Merlin says, 'the one who seeks to analyse another, often analyses himself'. Dr X. is supposed to have projected his own 'childhood problems' on A. This idea belongs to A. alone, and in any case is not what matters for us: I wish to emphasize that because it shows the *problematic* aspect of the dialogue. A. refers to Freud on two occasions with genuine respect; he doesn't come to any conclusion about whether the practice of analysis, *as such*, has failed or whether a better analyst would have cured him. In any event, *for us*, that is not the question: even if a mistake was made, we may well understand that A., who was the victim of it, might be indignant about that; but, in our opinion, psychoanalysis cannot be blamed for this isolated case any more than Uruffe's crime can be said to threaten the Church in the eyes of a believer: analysis is a discipline which aspires to scientific rigour and aims to cure; moreover, it is not one single matter, but several; if it were to raise any objections (which, moreover, would not be directed at the principles, but at certain aspects of the practice), then one would have to apply as much rigour to the discussion as the practitioners who adhere to it, put into their clinical and therapeutic methods.

So why did this dialogue fascinate me? Well, because it highlights in the most conspicuous way the sudden and violent entry of the *subject* into the analyst's study; or, rather, the reversal of the unequivocal subject–object relationship. And, here, what I mean by 'subject' is not the I or the Ego, that semi-object of the reflection, but the agent: in this brief adventure, A. is the subject in the sense that Marx says of the proletariat that it is the subject of history. Let us be clear: A. acknowledges that he 'needed help', he reproaches Dr X. for 'not having cured him', of having kept him in a state of dependency by 'promising' one day to give him 'permission' to recover his health. He talks about Dr X.'s clients as 'patients', in inverted commas, meaning: those whom analysts *consider to be* ill, but not those whom they have made ill. You have aggravated my condition, he says. So, he does not present himself as a perfectly free and healthy subject – who is? – or like those whom Jones calls 'adults' – a frightful term when one considers that Mme Freud, in his eyes, was an adult, and Freud was not – but as an injured subject or, if you prefer, as the subject of his injury, as an individual tormented by grave, intangible problems, who has come to ask others to help him find a solution to them. Having said this, with what does he reproach Dr X.? Let him speak: 'One cannot cure somebody on that . . .' (pointing to the psychiatrist's couch). 'You do not dare to look people in the face. Just now, you began by speaking of "facing up to my fantasies". I should never have been able to face up to anything! You forced me to turn my back on you. That's not how to cure people. It's impossible because . . . living with others means being able to face up to them.' Is he challenging the method, the couch, the studied silence of the great professional listeners? Yes and no: for years, he devoted his energies to expressing himself, exposing himself, while being aware that what he said, apparently freely and randomly, referred back to an obscure, hidden text that he had to construct, as it happens, rather than discovering it, and which was contained in the spoken word, in the sense, as Éluard says, that: 'There is another world, and it is in this one.' But in that strikingly concise formula of 'facing' and 'turning one's back', he reveals his profound experience to us: by his very presence, this invisible and silent witness of what he is saying – or more precisely what he is saying and what he makes himself say by the indispensable intermediary of a subject – transforms the word in the patient's very mouth into an *object*, for the simple reason that, between this turned back and the seated man, invisible, elusive, there can be no reciprocity. I know: the 'patient' ought to emancipate himself, it is up to him to discover *himself* little by little. The trouble, as A. tells us, is that it is understood *from the start* that he will discover himself as a passivity, through that look which he cannot grasp, which measures him up. The man with the tape-recorder is convinced that the road which leads him to independence (facing up to his fantasies, to other people) cannot pass through absolute dependency (transference and frustration, and at least a tacit promise – 'I shall cure you' – together with waiting for 'permission'). True, he is disappointed, he has a grudge against his doctor and some people will talk about an inadequately resolved transference; but what can we tell him if he says that the so-called patient's cure should start face to face and become a joint enterprise in which each of them takes his own risks and assumes his own responsibilities? He has been castrated? Very well. He wants someone to tell him so, looking him in the eyes. Let someone offer this interpretation, to *him*, to A., in the course of a long joint exploration, internalized, and not have it 'handed down', anonymously, impersonally, like a graven oracle. This subject wants to understand himself as an injured, deviant subject. Failing to obtain an intersubjective collaboration, he 'resorts to action', as they say: this means reversing the *praxis* and the situation at the same time. In this 'Psychoanalytical Dialogue', the roles are reversed and the analyst becomes the object. For the second time, the meeting of man with man fails to take place. This story, which some will consider a farce, is in fact the tragedy of unattainable reciprocity.

The result is violence, says Dr X.; and there is no doubt of it. But is it not, rather, a form of counter-violence? A. puts the question admirably: this 'interminable psychoanalytic relationship', this dependency, this transference that they bank on, and instigate, this feudality, this long travail of the man prostrate on the couch, reduced to babbling like a child, stripped bare: is that not the original form of violence? I know that Dr X. would answer him – and would have answered, were it not for the presence of the tape-recorder: 'We never use force, everyone comes and goes as he pleases; when a patient wants to leave us, we may try to dissuade him – because we know that this break can be damaging – but if he persists, we accept; and to prove it, three years ago, I reluctantly let you go.' This is true and in my view it is not the analysts who are under attack. But A. would not accept defeat. He tells us so: if one abstracts the men and considers only the situation, the weekly or twice-weekly abdication of the person under analysis, in favour of the analyst, becomes an increasingly imperative need. This means that the state of being an object has its advantages. Violence is ever latent and insinuating: being a subject is so tiring and, on the couch, everything invites one to put aside the agonizing responsibility of being alone and to replace it with the anonymous society of impulses.

The reversal of the *praxis* clearly demonstrates that the analytical relationship is *in itself* violent, whatever doctor-patient couple we can conceive. In fact, when violence turns the situation about, the analyst immediately becomes the analysed, or rather analysable: this is because the putsch and his own powerlessness put him artificially in a situation of neurosis. A. fully expected this, after considering his putsch for three years. Listen to what he says: 'Up to now, you were in the habit of completely controlling the situation, and suddenly here is something foreign which has arrived and taken up residence with you.' And the analyst's reply proves that he has suddenly become the *patient*. Now it is his speech that has to be decoded: 'I am not used to physical violence.' What an odd phrase: why doesn't he simply say 'violence'? So is he used to non-physical violence? And how is it that as an example of physical violence, he offers the fact of 'getting that tape-recorder out now'. I am not trying to exaggerate the importance of those few words, uttered at a time of quite understandable uneasiness; I should just like to put across the idea that violence breaks up what is being said, so that every word becomes ultra-significant because it means either too much or too little. The sudden transformation of Dr X., subject of the analysis and therapeutic agent, into an object plunges him into a crisis of identity: how is he to *recognize himself*? This is the reason for the strangeness – 'estrangement', Lacan would say, translating the Freudian term *Unheimlichkeit* – that he suddenly feels and for the desperate resistance he puts up against A.: he will not speak into the tape-recorder. The reason must lie firstly in the deontology of the profession. But is that enough? Does it explain the horror that he feels for the recorder? Doesn't he discover, like the object of a course of analysis, that his words, which he guarded so jealously and which fly away so lightly, at times, in the silence of the cabinet – a 'patient' is not a witness – are going to be engraved, set down for ever: they were only the joyous murmur of his sovereign thoughts, now they risk becoming the petrification of the same. Inert, they will bear witness. This tape-recorder enrages the mildest among them, because it corresponds to the warning given by British justice to an accused: henceforth, whatever you say may be taken down and used in evidence against you. Dr X. makes one last attempt to intimidate A., to treat him as a object in order to remind him of his dependency: 'You are dangerous because you're out of touch with reality'. But he only elicits the inspired response: 'What is reality?' Yes, what is reality, when analyst and patient are face to face, when with the aid of violence the analyst can no longer decide, alone and in complete control, what is real – in other words, privilege a certain concept of the world? What is reality when the patient no longer agrees to speak? Or when, in a farcical kind of antagonistic reciprocity, each of the two men is psychoanalysing the other; or rather, when they are applying the same models to one another: you are imitating your father; no, you're the one imitating *your* father; you're behaving like a child; no, you are . . . ? When the language of analysis, doubled up, repeated parrot-fashion, anonymous, seems to be becoming mad?

This extreme situation – and I may add that other analysts have found themselves in it: it is one of the risks of the profession – allows us to ask the true question: do we have to choose between the *subject-being* of the 'patient' and the psychoanalyst? Look at the man with the recorder, look at how he has deliberated over these three years – no matter whether he is wrong or right; how he has plotted his move and carried it out; listen to him speaking, feel his irony and also his pain ('I must have a nerve to do such a thing . . .'); and the ease with which he manipulates the concepts that have for so long been applied to him by others. Now I ask you: *who* is he?

Who is this A.? A blind process, or the transcendence of that process by an act? I don't doubt that the last of his words or all of his actions may be interpreted analytically – provided one restores him to his status as an analytical object. What will vanish with the subject is the inimitable and singular quality of the scene: its synthetic organization, in other words, the action as such. And don't tell me that it is a 'sick person', a 'patient' who is organizing it: I accept that, and I accept that he is organizing it as a 'patient'. Nonetheless, he does organize. Analysts may give the motivation for the 'transition to action', but they have not so far bothered to take account of the act itself, which interiorizes, transcends and preserves the morbid motivations in the unity of a tactic, the act which gives meaning to the meaning which has occurred. The reason is that one would have to reintroduce the idea of the subject. In England or in Italy, A., the undeniable subject of this brief narrative, would be able to engage in a valid dialogue: a new generation of psychiatrists is trying to create relations of reciprocity between themselves and the people they treat. Without giving up anything of the huge body of understanding that psychiatry has acquired, they first of all respect in each of their patients the diverted freedom to initiate – each patient as agent and subject.* It does not seem impossible that one day conventional psychiatrists will join them. Meanwhile, I offer this 'Dialogue' as a benign and beneficial provocation to controversy.

PSYCHOANALYTIC DIALOGUE

A.
I would finally like to clear something up. Up to now I have followed your rules, but now you must try . . . In any case, I don't see why . . .

---

* I am not underestimating the difficulties that they will encounter: 'in-depth psychology', as Lagache calls it, requires relaxation, abandonment, a degree of resignation, hence the couch; while face-to-face analysis demands vigilance, sovereignty and a degree of tension. But one cannot make progress without grasping the nettle.

Dr X.

Now if you want . . . We've agreed. There. If we stop here, it will be all the worse for you.

A.

Are you really afraid of this recorder?

Dr X.

I don't want that. I'm not going along with it.

A.

But why not? At least explain that: are you afraid of the recorder?

Dr X.

I'm cutting off here!

A.

Cutting? Now, that's interesting: you're back to cutting. Just now you were speaking about cutting off the penis. And now you are the one wanting to cut off suddenly.

Dr X.

Listen to me! we're finished with that recorder!

A.

What exactly is finished?

Dr X.

Either you leave the room, or the session is finished! We've agreed! I'm happy to explain what I was going to explain to you, but right now either that recorder goes outside, or I shall not say another word. I'll be sorry to have to do it, but I won't go along with that.

A.

I think you're afraid! I think you're afraid and you're wrong, because what I'm here to do is in your interest. Without seeming to, I am taking a great risk, and I'm doing it for you and for lots of other people. But I want to get to the bottom of this mystification and I intend to continue.

Dr X.

All right, as you like . . .

A.

No, Doctor! Stay there! Stay there and don't touch your phone. Stay there, and above all don't try having me sectioned.

A PSYCHOANALYTIC DIALOGUE

Dr X.

I won't have you sectioned if you leave this room.

A.

I'm not leaving the room! I have matters to settle with you, important matters, and you're going to answer to them. And I'm not putting this to you in my name alone, but in that of ... Now, now, be good enough to sit down. Let's not get worked up! You see, it won't hurt. I'm not going to bugger you around. Just cool it! Sit down ... Don't you want to sit down? All right, stand up.

So, this 'cutting off the penis'. Right? My father wanted to ... No? What was it again?

Dr X.

Now listen to me! Right now, you're in no state to discuss this.

A.

Oh, yes, I am! You're the one who doesn't want to discuss anything. You are the one who is in no state ...

Dr X.

I asked you to put away your recorder.

A.

But my recorder is not a spy, you know! It's a listener, which is following you with the best will in the world.

Dr X.

I was just explaining something to you ...

A.

Fine, carry on!

Dr X.

And at that moment, rather than trying to understand, you ...

A.

Because you wanted to drop something vital, something that you've been drilling into my head for years, and that's why I didn't want you to try and get out of it by skirting round the problem, I mean, once again, the problem of your responsibility.

Dr X.

Of yours!

A.

What?

Dr X.

Right now, you're trying to make me responsible for things which are your responsibility.

A.

Not at all! At this moment, I'm working, scientific work!

Dr X.

Maybe.

A.

So, let's go on. You know that it works much better when we record scientific investigations, because that way we are free, we don't have to take notes. We can get on with it.

Dr X.

What we have here is not a scientific investigation.

A.

Yes, it is! I thought I was talking to a scientist. In any case, I confided in one and I should like to know just what science precisely is involved, because I'm not at all sure that this so-called science is not quackery.

Dr X.

Well, I have the right not to have to talk into a recorder.

A.

Of course you do, and you keep telling me so. Many thanks . . . You feel you are in the dock and you are talking like some American who refuses to speak unless his lawyer is present . . . Sit down!

Dr X.

I'm ready to talk to you and to explain.

A.

Well, let's get started then.

Dr X.

But I am not prepared to talk into a recorder.

A.

But why were you about to phone someone?

Dr X.

Because I'd have asked you to leave if you kept that recorder running.

A.

And so? Why? Why were you going to phone?

Dr X.

Because I'd have asked you to leave if you kept that recorder going. I don't want to have you sectioned, but . . .

A.

But why did you . . . You can't have me sectioned, you know! Because if anyone ought to be sectioned, it's you, if it was really a case of deciding which of us is unbalanced.

Dr X.

I . . . I . . . In any case . . .

A.

But listen. I'm fond of you, I have no wish to harm you. On the contrary . . .

Dr X.

Well, we're agreed on that. Put down the recorder.

A.

We're having fun now, but I would like you to stop feeling afraid.

Dr X.

I'm not having fun.

A.

But you are afraid. And what about your libido? Do you think I want to cut off your willy? No, no! I've come to give you a proper one: it's great to have a real one! At last! You've waited so long for this little celebration! Now, admit that you're managing very well. Doctor!!! Doctor, I have your interests at heart, but you don't.

Dr X.

Right now, you are . . .

A.

I have your interests at heart, but . . . but . . . I really feel you're going too far! You, you go too far, you've gone much too far with me! I might even say that you've swindled me, if we have to use the legal term, because you haven't fulfilled your obligations, you haven't fully cured me. In any case, you're not able to fulfil your obligations, because you don't know how to cure people; all you know is how to make them a little more mad. You know . . . One has only to

243

talk to your other patients, well, I say 'patients': I mean, the ones you call 'patients', those who come to you for a bit of help and don't get any, who just get to wait . . . Now, do sit down! Let's be calm about this! Calm down! Come now! Are you a man or a wimp? Are you a man?

Dr X.

Once more, I tell you, I've said it for the last time, you have a recorder there, and I don't want this attitude.

A.

I'm sorry, I'll tell you one more time why I brought up the recorder – using your phrase, 'bring up' – it's because I don't at all like the way you suddenly insisted that I should drop the question of castration.

Dr X.

I'm only too happy to talk about castration, if that was the real problem here, but I don't want to talk into a recorder.

A.

Very well, we won't talk about it. We'll wait until you change your mind. Now, you're on the spot.

Dr X.

What do you expect to gain by putting me on the spot?

A.

I've nothing to lose!

Dr X.

Maybe.

A.

You're afraid! Come, come, Jack! Lighten up! What? No? You won't?

Dr X.

Don't you think this is a serious situation?

A.

Terribly serious. That's why it would be much better if you pulled a different face from the one you're pulling.

I must have a nerve to do such a thing! I really must be very sure . . .

Dr X.

No! It's not a question of being sure. If you were sure you wouldn't act in this way! Now, let me out. This is a very dangerous situation!

A PSYCHOANALYTIC DIALOGUE

A.
Dangerous?
Dr X.
Yes, you are dangerous.
A.
Not at all! You're the one that says so! You are constantly trying to convince me I'm dangerous, but I'm not at all!
Dr X.
You are dangerous because you're out of touch with reality!
A.
Not at all!
Dr X.
You're out of touch with reality!
A.
I'm a little lamb! I've always been a little lamb!
Dr X.
You're out of touch with reality!
A.
You're the one who's dangerous! It's the one that says it, that is it.
Dr X.
You're out of touch with reality.
A.
And what is 'reality'?
Dr X.
Right now, you're dangerous because you're out of touch with reality.
A.
But what is 'reality'? We must understand one another, first of all. Now I know one thing, from the point of view of your reality, which is that you are very angry, you are trying hard to keep a hold on yourself, but you're not succeeding and you're certainly going to explode. It will burst, you're under pressure. You're definitely going to lose your temper, and there's nothing to gain by that. I mean you no harm, you don't need to get angry, I'm not your father!
Dr X.
Do you have your recorder there?

A.

I'm not your father.

Dr X.

You've got your recorder.

A.

So what?

Dr X.

Let's stop now.

A.

Come, come! It's not hurting you, is it? Are you afraid of it? It's not a revolver.

Dr X.

Let's stop now!

A.

What does that mean? Stop what?

Dr X.

I don't want this kind of discussion.

A.

Tell me, would you like a spanking?

Dr X.

You see: you are dangerous!

A.

Do you want a spanking?

Dr X.

You see: you are dangerous!

A.

No, I'm asking you a question: whether you want to stop behaving like a child.

Dr X.

And I'm afraid you're going to demonstrate it.

A.

No, I'm not going to demonstrate it.

Dr X.

Let's stop here.

A.

But what does it mean: stop here?

Dr X.

I've nothing to say to you. You are dangerous.

A.

What do you mean, nothing to say to me? You owe me an explanation.

Dr X.

I asked you to leave.

A.

Sorry, you're wrong!

Dr X.

You see, you are dangerous.

A.

You owe me an explanation!

Dr X.

You see, you are dangerous!

A.

I'm not dangerous. I'm just raising my voice, and you can't take it. If someone shouts, you're afraid, aren't you? If you hear someone shout, you don't know what's happening, it's dreadful, it's horrible, it's the daddy shouting [for the last few moments the two have been only twenty centimetres from one another], but, Jack, I'm only shouting here to show that this time it's not serious. You see, now you're overcoming your fear already. There you are! You've got over your fear! There, that's better, you're getting used to it. Very good. That's much better. You see, it's really not so serious. I'm not your father and I can shout again. But I won't! There, that's enough.

Dr X.

Are you imitating your father here?

A.

No, not mine: yours! The one I see in your eyes.

Dr X.

You're trying to play the role . . .

A.

I don't want to take any role with you. I just want to be free of my traumas. You're the one who's shitting himself just now. Of course. Look at you: why are you crossing your arms like that: you're defending yourself. Do you really think I want to hit you? What on earth makes you think I want to hit you? I'm far too well-behaved! I'm controlling myself, I don't want to do what you want me to. That would be so much simpler: I'd hit you, I'd be in the wrong, I'd have started it, I would have done something that would give you the power to . . . I don't know what . . . to be the doctor, to play the doctor, no? The psychiatrist.

If I'm dangerous, I'm not dangerous for little Jackie, I'm dangerous for the doctor, for the sadistic doctor, not for Jack. He's suffered too. I've absolutely no wish to hit him . . . but as for the doctor, the psychiatrist, the one who has taken the father's place: that one deserves a kick up the arse.

Now let me explain. Sit down. No, you don't want to?
Dr X.
You can talk. I'm not going to. I told you, I'm not . . .
A.
Very well, then, I'll talk. At last! Thank goodness! In any case, I was going to tell you as soon as I got out the recorder, I was only getting it out so that I could talk, because I was going to talk. Of course, you can be recorded if you like. And, if you want, I'll make you a copy, it should be extremely interesting for you. Well, perhaps. I hope so, for your sake. Now, there we are! One can't be cured on that! [He nods towards the psychiatrist's couch.] It's impossible! And you're not cured, either, because you've spent too many years on it. You don't dare look people directly in the eye. Just now, you began by talking about 'facing up to my fantasies'. I'd never have been able to face up to anything! You forced me to turn my back on you. That's not the way to cure people. It's impossible, because in fact, living with others means learning to face them. What do you expect me to learn on that? Quite the opposite! You unlearned me any taste I had for even trying to live with other people or for looking anything in the face, and that's your problem! That's why you make people like that, because you cannot face them, you can't cure them, you can only pass on your problems with your father, which you can't resolve; and from one session to the next you drag victims along like that with the problem of your father, huh? Do you see what I'm saying? And I had

a lot of trouble understanding and getting out of it and turning myself round. Of course, you got me to do mental gymnastics. Well, a bit anyway, but you must admit it was pretty expensive, if that's all I got! But there's worse to come: you made me forget how to face things by promising me, and I relied on you; but since I couldn't see you, I couldn't guess when you were finally going to give me what I had come to you for. I was waiting for permission. Yes, that's it! You would have been very silly to have given me permission, no? – to have turned me round, to have freed me, since I was feeding you, you were living at my expense, you were pumping me, I was the patient, you were the doctor; and you finally got round to your childhood problem, your problem with being a child in relation to your father . . . Because you have the right, you do, uh, the right for example if you want to confer with others, I don't maybe, but you do have the right to confer with other people.

Dr X.

I'm going to phone 609 and have you taken away, 609, the police, and they'll throw you out.

A.

The police? Dada? That's it! Your dad's a policeman! You're going to phone daddy to come and get me.

Dr X.

Because, in my opinion . . .

A.

Listen, this is getting interesting. Why do you want to call the police? You would have missed all that . . . Admit it!

Dr X.

You're a doctor in law . . .

A.

Yes, I was right to stop you.

Dr X.

When someone doesn't want to leave your house, you turn to the police.

A.

Oh, yes! There we have it! You brought me to your place, you lured me into your little home, into your cave . . .

Dr X.

I asked you to leave.

A.

Listen! If you're going to speak out and say such things, then why not let me carry on, because otherwise we'll get annoyed and waste time. No, won't we?

If you really have something important to say, then you must say it, OK, you must definitely get it out. It's true, you're full of repressions ... But if all you want is to tell me that you'll call the police or that you'd like to have called them, then that is something you should analyse.

Right now, is that better? [Very calmly and softly.] Better?

Dr X.

No, no. [He gets up.] You can go away and listen to your recorder.

A.

No, no, no, no, that's not what matters right now. Just look how you reacted: what madness! You got worked up and annoyed simply because I got out a little machine which will help us to understand what's going on here. It's ridiculous. In any case, you haven't really managed to explain why you don't want a recording. Or, at any rate, you don't want to tell me. Why are you so cross? Because suddenly I took control of something? So far you have got used to being totally in control of the situation and suddenly this unusual thing enters and takes up residence.

Dr X.

I'm not used to physical violence.

A.

What do you mean: physical violence?

Dr X.

It's a violent act, getting that recorder out now.

A.

An act of physical violence? [Extreme astonishment.]

Dr X.

And you realized it very well ... You only have to see where my phone is to see that it's a case of physical violence. [The phone has

A PSYCHOANALYTIC DIALOGUE

indeed been lying on the floor since the first case of: 'Don't touch your phone.']
A.
But hang on: are you serious? Do you enjoy saying what you've just said? Are you happy now? I'd like to be assured of your well-being. Are you feeling good? Are you in good shape? Tut, tut . . . [Friendly, as if addressing a child.] Doctor! [Very soft and low.] Cuckoo . . . So, you don't want to answer, you won't tell me? Come, come! Just consider the situation for a moment! It's ridiculous! Let's try to behave with a modicum of decorum.
Dr X.
One moment: what you said a moment ago, what you've just told me . . .
A.
Yes? What?
Dr X.
It might be a good idea if you listened to it again.
A.
Indeed, and if you listened to your silence . . . The trouble is you can't speak because you're repressed. Someone gets out a recorder and you're cut off immediately! That's what you said: 'I'm cutting off.' And you cut yourself off, didn't you, in the sense of the murderer who 'cuts' himself, who reports himself. I didn't cut anything, on the contrary, I want to go on and I want us to move further towards the truth . . .
Dr X.
The time I allocated you is over, you must go.
A.
No! Time doesn't exist.
Dr X.
Yes, it does.
A.
No, it doesn't. Now the best time is just beginning, I promise you.
Dr X.
But you explained something and all you have to do is learn the lesson from it: you explained something . . .
A. Yes?

Dr X.

... that you should have understood a long time ago.

A.

What?

Dr X.

Your attitude.

A.

What do you mean: my attitude?

Dr X.

Yes, of course, as you explained.

A.

You're the one with an attitude ... [ring at the doorbell] ... of cutting off.

Dr X.

What you have just explained is your attitude. Now, listen, there's someone else expecting me.

A.

I don't give a damn! The next victim is in no hurry.

Dr X.

But I do give a damn.

A. [in an insistent and emphatic tone]

We won't get out of this impasse until we are clearer about what happened and on the problem of your obligations and your non-fulfilment of them. Above all, don't talk about physical violence, because it's you who started the physical violence by forcing me to turn round on the couch, you were the one who twisted, who made me turn my head the other way. You were the one who distorted the situation, don't you realize that? Don't you realize how ridiculous you've become suddenly? There is something that goes beyond this present moment. There's something shameful and infantile in the way you're behaving!

Dr X.

You see: you're dangerous. I said you were dangerous.

A.

Dr X., you're a puppet ... and you're a sinister puppet! You're evading the question ... How many years did I come here two or three times a week, and what did I get out of it? If I am mad and dangerous, as you're now saying, you will only be reaping what you have sown, what you put in with your misleading theories. Understand that. And, basically, you'd come pretty well out of it with the little fright I'm giving you at the moment and the little reflection I'm asking you to make, just a bit of an exercise you're being asked to do, a little exercise, nothing too bad! It won't harm you! Come, come, give us a smile, why don't you; don't put on that sulky face. You know it's very important to look after curing people, to be a doctor, and they write loads of books about psychoanalysis; it's worth thinking about and worth us trying to explain frankly to ourselves and understand what went on between us, because we might perhaps get something out of it for other people, and I'm not dangerous, so don't tell me I am all the time, because you're just trying to put us off like that! You took advantage of an existing situation, you're a privileged person, you came after Freud, someone paid for your studies, and you managed to stick a brass plate on your door and now you're buggering up loads of people and have the right to do so, and so you think you're getting away with it. You're a failure and you'll never do anything with your life except to pin your own problems on others . . .

Right . . . Now that's all over and done with, you understand? You'll be very pleased with what I'm putting you through now, because I'm not subjecting you to anything, not subjecting you to anything at all.

Dr X.

Yes, you are. You're subjecting me to your presence.

A.

I'm not subjecting you to my presence, I want you to stay sitting down.

Dr X.

Physical violence!

A.

I want you to sit down.

Dr X.

Physical violence! Physical violence!

A.

Not at all! I'd just like you to stay seated.

Dr X.

Physical violence!

A.

Come on, sit down.

Dr X.

Physical violence!

A.

No, no [in a fatherly, reassuring tone of voice].

Dr X.

Physical violence!

A.

No, this is play-acting.

Dr X.

You're subjecting me to physical violence!

A.

Not at all, I'm not subjecting you to physical violence.

Dr X.

I've given you an opportunity to explain yourself.

A.

And now I'd like you to explain yourself.

Dr X.

I've given you the opportunity to explain yourself and I suggested . . .

A.

Not at all. You cut me off, you interrupted the explanation that I was trying to give you.

Dr X.

Only because I didn't want to talk into a recorder.

A.

But to start with I didn't ask you to talk, I asked you to let me talk.

Dr X.

No, you asked me to talk.

A.

You interrupted me, that's what happened. Suddenly, you began talking to me about the police.

A PSYCHOANALYTIC DIALOGUE

Dr X.
Now the discussion is closed.
A.
No kidding! Do you want to bet? I say it isn't.
So, who's going to make the first step towards physical violence?
Dr X.
That's just what you're doing.
A.
Not at all. I'm fine here. I'm like a Southern senator who won't leave the lectern.
Dr X.
You are really very dangerous. Yes, and you're certainly very well ... [The doctor goes over to his window: the study is on a ground floor, but above street level. A very loud sound of shutters opening.]
A.
Are you going to jump out of the window? Amazing! You're actually going to do it? [Further sound of A. closing the shutters, and laughing]. You see: this really is play-acting.
Dr X.
This will end in tears.
A.
It will end dramatically! A bloody ending! There'll be blood.
Dr X.
Yes, there'll be blood.
A.
Whose blood?
Dr X.
There'll be blood.
A.
No, no, there won't, that's not how it will end. It will all end very amicably. We're having a good time.
Dr X.
It will end in violence.
A.
No, no, it won't end in violence, surely.

255

Dr X.
Let me open the door and leave . . .
A.
You mean you're scared? Are you starting that again? Boo!
Dr X.
You see: you are dangerous.
A.
No, I just need to let off steam.
Dr X.
A funny way of letting off steam, you're frightened.
A.
You're trying to scare me.
Dr X.
You're dangerous because you're afraid.
A.
Dangerous? What does it mean: dangerous?
Dr X.
You are acting physically by staying here.
A.
Is that what's dangerous?
Dr X.
That's right!
A.
And mental torture! What about that?
Dr X.
You're acting in a physical way.
A.
Listen, when slaves rebel, obviously there is sometimes a bit of blood spilt, but you can see for yourself that no one is bleeding yet.
Dr X.
You're resorting to physical action.
[We should note that A. has taken up a strategic position, with his back to the only door of the room.]
A.
You're shitting yourself.

Dr X.
You'd like me to be shitting myself.
A.
Not at all. I'm just observing that you are shitting yourself.
Dr X.
You think you're on to something . . . You think you're bugging me . . .
A.
No, I'm not bugging you. I have no intention of doing so. I'd like you to start talking seriously.
Dr X.
Well, I am talking seriously to you; it's time.
A.
Time?
Dr X.
It's time. I've got others to attend to.
A.
It's time? What do you mean? Time to settle accounts! Quite right, time's come.
Dr X.
I'm very sorry.
A.
What's that, you're very sorry? I beg your pardon. I'm the one who's very sorry, you really don't know how sorry! You drove me crazy, you turned me mad for years! For years! And you want to draw a line under it!
Dr X.
Help! Help!
[From here on the doctor will shout 'help!' about ten times, getting louder and louder, in the carefully modulated tones of a self-satisfied pig having its throat cut].
Murder! Heeelp! Heeelp! Heeelp! Heeelp!
A.
Shut up and sit down.
Dr X.
Heeeeelp! Heeeeelp!

A.

Shut up, or I'll put a gag on you!

Dr X.

Heeeeeeellllp! [Long-drawn-out cry.]

A.

Poor sod! You poor idiot! Sit down.

Dr X.

Heeelp! [Very weak murmur.]

A.

What are you afraid of?

Dr X.

Heeeeellp! [The cries resume.] You see: you are dangerous.

A.

No, I'm not.

Dr X.

Heeeelp!

A.

Are you scared I'll cut off your willy?

Dr X.

Heeeeeelllllpppp! [This is the loudest cry of all.]

A.

What a funny recording it will be.

Dr X.

Very funny! Help! Help! Help! [This time, it's the final, mournful shout of a windbag emptying like some burst animal – then a long silence.]

A.

Come, now, my good man. Pick up your glasses.

Dr X.

They're broken. [Not true.]

[Further silence.]

A.

Well, I didn't expect you to behave like such a prick, I really didn't! You're an absolute baby! You're definitely the one who started the fight. Sit down. And you a scientist! Well I never, it's a fine thing,

your science! A fine thing indeed; Freud would be delighted. He never managed to get himself all worked up like that.
Dr X.
Now, let's call an end to it, if you don't mind. They know about this outside, so perhaps it's better for you to leave.
A.
I'd be delighted if you could go on to the very end.
Dr X.
You risk being sectioned, and it won't be my fault.
A.
Fine, fine, delighted. I'm not worried about sectioning. I'm just curious to know if you will go that far. And meanwhile we're writing a fine chapter in the history of psychoanalysis.
Dr X.
What else can I tell you?
A.
Well then let's sit right down here and wait for the police, for your daddy to arrive. Sit down, calm down, you're awfully overwrought, Dr Jekyll ... Huh ... Mr Hyde is never far away. Hmm ... and to think that I meant to do you a favour ... [Pause.] I'm not dangerous, I'm very nice.
Dr X.
Yes, of course, never doubt it.
A.
No, no ... We are now going to start the trial of psychoanalysts and see something of what happens and what they do in their studies and how they stand with their clients, we'll see and I think it will be fascinating as a discovery, to find out whose head is really screwed on. What? You want to leave? You want to take to your heels? Coward! [In the distance the doctor can be heard asking his wife: 'Lulu, would you please phone 609!']
A.
[Imitating the doctor's voice and tone]. I beg you, be quick ... Good, then, we're off ...

You've nothing more to say, doctor, before we leave one another?

Dr X.
Next time...
A.
Yes?
Dr X.
Today, I shan't speak, I'd still like to talk to you, but from now on I shall only speak in front of people who can control your violence.
A.
Very well!
Dr X.
But I'm quite willing to talk it over with you without a recorder and in front of people who can restrain you.
A.
Fine! That's all you have to say? Is it over then? Shall we cut it off? End the session?
Dr X.
Yes!
A.
Very well, we're ending the session. That was the first session. See you next time. Goodbye, doctor.

Portraits

How can biography be anything other than the obliging accomplice of bourgeois individualism?

Sartre's first fictional hero, Antoine Roquentin, is trying to write a biography of the Marquis de Rollebon, a devious late-eighteenth-century diplomat. He eventually gives the thing up in disgust. Gazing upon the great men depicted in statues and oil-paintings, Roquentin scoffs at all conventionally edifying portraiture. Perhaps biography is a lost cause.

In a series of idiosyncratic artist-biographies Sartre endeavoured to put the whole genre back on its feet. The Sartrean biography is a bulky, hybrid creature. It bulges alarmingly, having swallowed down great cratefuls of philosophy, but then it always glides with surprising grace and style across the deepest abyss of speculation. Genet, who read *Saint Genet* before it was published, wondered if he had been embalmed alive. Such empathy, such sustained powers of identification, could be weirdly predatory.

Alongside these larger biographies, Sartre also practised the more urbane art of the contemporary portrait. He was an accomplished writer of prefaces and of intimate intellectual obituaries, both affectionate and hostile. Whether celebrating Fanon or Togliatti, attacking Mauriac or Céline, defending Nizan's reputation or making amends to Camus, Sartre had a rich and ever-vivid sense of the human physiognomy of discourse.

Baudelaire

Sartre's disparaging remarks about Baudelaire scandalized critics when they were first published. In 1944 Sartre wrote an essay on Baudelaire which was intended as the preface to an edition of the poet's *Intimate Writings*. Part of that essay was published as *Fragment of a Portrait of Baudelaire* in *Les Temps modernes* in May 1946 and the whole piece, with a dedication to Jean Genet, was published in book form in 1947. The character of Philippe in *Roads to Freedom* is evidently based on Baudelaire.

Baudelaire's biographers and critics have often stressed his horror of Nature. They generally look for the source in his Christian upbringing and the influence of Joseph de Maistre.[1] The effect of these two factors cannot be denied: Baudelaire himself refers to them when he tries to explain himself: 'Most errors with respect to the beautiful originate in the false concept of the eighteenth century with respect to morality. At that time, nature was taken as the basis, source and model of all possible good and all possible beauty. The denial of original sin played a not inconsiderable part in the general blindness of that age. However, if we are content to refer merely to visible facts, to the experience of every age and to the *Gazette des tribunaux*,[2] we shall see that nature teaches us nothing, or almost nothing; that is to say, she *constrains* mankind to sleep, drink, eat

---

1. *Joseph de Maistre*: influential theorist of the Counter-Revolution. De Maistre (1753–1821) saw the public executioner as the key figure in the social order.
2. *Gazette des tribunaux*: daily newspaper devoted to verbatim accounts of court proceedings. It was first published in 1825.

and to protect itself, as best it can, against the inclemencies of the atmosphere. She it is, too, that drives a man to kill his neighbour, beat him, imprison him and torture him ... Crime, something for which the human animal acquires a liking in his mother's womb, is natural in origin. Virtue, on the other hand, is *artificial* and supernatural, since at all times and in every nation gods and prophets have been needed to teach it to animalized humanity, and mankind, *on its own*, would have been powerless to discover it. Evil is done without effort, *naturally*, by fate; good is always the product of art.'*

At first sight, this passage seems conclusive, but it is less convincing when you re-read it. Baudelaire identifies Evil with Nature: the words could have been written by the Marquis de Sade. But if we are to rely on them entirely, we can only do so by ignoring the fact that the true Baudelairean Evil, the Satanic Evil which he evokes a hundred times in his work, is the deliberate product of Will and Artifice. So, if Evil may be either distinguished or vulgar, what the writer abhors must be vulgarity, not crime. And the matter is more complicated than that: while Nature, in several of his writings, seems to be identified with original sin, there are many passages in Baudelaire's letters where the term 'natural' is synonymous with 'legitimate' or 'just'. To quote one, picked at random (though there are a hundred others):

'This idea,' he writes on 4 August 1860, 'was the product of the most natural and most filial intention.'

So we must deduce that there is a degree of ambivalence in the concept of Nature. His abhorrence of it is not so strong as to prevent him invoking the concept to justify or to defend himself. On examination, we shall find layers of very different meanings in the poet's attitude, the first of which – to be found in the passage from *L'Art romantique* quoted above – is literary and factitious (the influence of de Maistre on Baudelaire is chiefly for show: the writer considered it 'distinguished' to claim that it existed); and the last of

---

* *L'Art romantique: Le peintre de la vie moderne*. XI; In Praise of Make-Up.

which is concealed, perceptible only through the contradictions that we mentioned earlier.

What seems to have had an influence on Baudelaire's thought far deeper than that of de Maistre's *Soirées de Saint-Pétersbourg* is the great anti-naturalist current running from Saint-Simon to Mallarmé and Huysmans, through the whole of the nineteenth century. The combined effect of the Saint-Simonians, the Positivists and Marx was to create, around 1848, the dream of an Anti-Nature: the very term *anti-nature* comes from Comte; in the correspondence of Marx and Engels, we find *antiphysis*. The theories are different, but the ideal is the same: to set up a human order in direct opposition to the errors, injustices and blind mechanisms of the Natural World. What differentiates this order from the 'City of Ends' that Kant devised at the end of the eighteenth century, also in opposition to strict determinism, is the introduction of a new element: labour. Man no longer imposes his order on the universe by the sole light of Reason, but by labour, and more specifically by industrial labour. Far more important to the birth of this anti-naturalism than some outmoded doctrine of grace, is the nineteenth-century industrial revolution and the advent of the industrial machine. Baudelaire is carried forward on the wave. Admittedly, he is not greatly interested in workers; but labour does interest him because it is like *thought* impressed upon matter. He was always attracted by the idea that things are thoughts objectified and, as it were, solidified: in this way, he could see himself reflected in them. But natural realities have no meaning for him. They signify nothing. And we can be sure that one of the most spontaneous reactions of his mind is the disgust and ennui that overtake him when confronted with the vague, mute, disordered monotony of a landscape.

'You are asking me for some verses to put in your little book, verses about *nature*, is that it? About the woods, great oak trees, greenery, insects – and the sun, presumably? But you know very well that I am incapable of any affection for plants, and that my soul revolts against this new religion which, it seems to me, will always be slightly *shocking* to any *spiritual* being. I shall never believe that *the soul of the Gods lives in plants* and, even if it did, it would not bother me greatly: I should consider my own soul of much higher price than that of any sanctified vegetable.'*

'Plant', 'sanctified vegetable': the words clearly indicate the contempt in which he holds the insignificant world of plants. He has a sort of profound intuition of that formless, obstinate contingency that is life – and it inspires horror because to his eyes it reflects the gratuitous nature of his own consciousness – and this, he wants to dissimulate at any cost. A town-dweller, he loves geometric shapes which have been subject to human rationalization. Schaunard tells that he would say: 'Free water is unbearable to me; I want it imprisoned, fettered, between the geometrical walls of a quayside.' He wanted labour to impress its stamp even on fluidity and, since he was unable to endow it with a solidity that was incompatible with its nature, he wanted to contain it between walls, in horror at its tendency to disperse, its vagrant ductility, and to shape it geometrically. This reminds me of a friend who, when his brother was filling a glass of water from the kitchen tap, asked him: 'Wouldn't you rather have some *proper* water?' – and went to get a jug from the sideboard: proper water was water defined and, as it were, redesigned by its transparent container so that, instantly, it lost its dishevelled appearance and all the stigmas attaching to its promiscuity with the sink, to enjoy the transparent, spherical purity of the work of human hands. This was not untamed water, uncertain water, oozing water, stagnant or streaming, but metal collected at the bottom of the jug, humanized by its receptacle. Baudelaire is a town-dweller: *proper* water, to him, like *proper* light and *proper* heat, is found in towns. They have become manufactured goods, unified by a dominant idea. Human labour has given them a function, and a place in the human scheme of things. A natural reality, once it has been worked upon and transferred to the rank of utensil, loses its unjustifiability. A utensil exists as of right to the man who observes it; a barouche in the street, or a windowpane, exist just as Baudelaire wants them to exist: they provide him with the image of realities which came to be such through their function, which arose to fill a void, on

---

* Letter to F. Desnoyers, 1855.

the urging of the very void they were destined to fill. Man panics when he is enveloped by Nature, because he feels trapped in a vast, amorphous, gratuitous existence: its very gratuity turns him to ice. He has no place anywhere, he finds, he has been put on earth, without any goal or *raison d'être*, like some tuft of heather or sprig of broom. In the midst of a town, on the other hand, surrounded by precious objects whose existence is determined by their role and each of which is wreathed in a value or a price, he feels reassured, because they reflect back what he himself aspires to be: a *justified* reality. And Baudelaire, in so far as he wishes to be a thing in the midst of Joseph de Maistre's world, dreams in precisely this way of existing in the moral order, with a function and a value, just as a fine leather suitcase or some water tamed in a jug exist in the hierarchy of utensils.

Above all, though, what he calls Nature, is life. What he invariably mentions when he talks about it are plants and animals. Vigny's 'impassive Nature' means the entirety of physical and chemical laws, while Baudelaire's is more pervasive, a great, warm, abounding force that penetrates everywhere. He is revolted by this warm dampness and abundance. It was inevitable that the prolixity of Nature, which reproduces the same model in millions of examples, should offend his love of the rare. He too said: 'I like what will never be seen a second time' – meaning to praise absolute sterility. What he cannot stand about paternity is the continuity of life, from progenitor to descendants, which means that the latter compromise the former, who continues to have a life of secret humiliation in them. This biological eternity seems unbearable to him: the rare individual takes the secret of his making to the tomb; he wishes to be entirely sterile: this is the only way in which he can attribute some price to himself. Baudelaire took this feeling even to the extent of rejecting spiritual paternity. In 1866 he wrote to Troubat, after a series of flattering articles on Verlaine: 'These young people are certainly not devoid of talent, but what sillinesses, what inaccuracies! What exaggerations! What a lack of precision! To tell you the truth, they scare the wits out of me. I like nothing so much as to be alone.'*

* Letter of 5 March 1866.

Creation, which he worships, is the opposite of giving birth. It involves no compromise: of course, it is another form of prostitution, but in this the cause, the spirit – infinite and inexhaustible – remains unaltered when it has produced its effect. As for the object created, it is not alive, but imperishable and inanimate, like a stone or an eternal truth. Even then, one must not be too prolific in one's creation, or one may come to resemble Nature. Baudelaire often exhibits his repugnance for Hugo, with his gross temperament. He himself wrote little, but not through sterility: his poems would have seemed less of a rarity if they had not been the outcome of exceptional mental acts. Their small number and perfection were meant to stress their 'supernatural' character; what Baudelaire sought throughout his life was *infecundity*, and what most appealed to him in the world about him were the hard, sterile forms of minerals. In his *Poèmes en prose*, he writes:

'This city is on the edge of the sea; they say it is built of marble and that the inhabitants so hate the vegetable kingdom that they pull up all trees. Here is a landscape to my liking, a landscape made of light and minerals, and liquid to reflect them.'*

Georges Blin makes the pertinent remark that he 'fears nature as a reservoir of magnificence and fecundity, [and] in its place puts the world of his imagination: a metallic universe, that is to say, coldly sterile and luminous'.

The reason is that for him metal and, in general, minerals reflect the image of the mind. Because the power of our imagination is limited, all those who, in contrasting the mind with life and the body, have been led to describe it in non-biological terms have inevitably had recourse to the realm of the inanimate: light, cold, transparency, sterility. Just as Baudelaire found his wicked thoughts acquiring objective shape in 'foul creatures', so steel, the most brilliant and most polished metal, with the surface that offers the least grip, will always seem to him a precise objectification of his Thoughts as a whole. If he has an affection for the sea, that is because it is a moving mineral. Brilliant, inaccessible and cold, with

* *Anywhere out of the world.*

a movement that is pure and almost immaterial, with its successive shapes, change without anything changing, and occasionally in its transparency, the sea provides the best image of the mind; *it is* the mind. So it was because of his hatred of life that Baudelaire came to choose symbols of the immaterial among what is purely material.

Above all, he is afraid of feeling this vast, soft fecundity in himself. Yet nature is there, his needs are there, and they 'oblige' him to assuage them. One has only to re-read the text that we quoted earlier to see that what he hates above all is this *obligation*. One young Russian woman used to take stimulants when she wanted to fall asleep: she could not agree to let herself be overwhelmed by this sly and irresistible demand on her and suddenly to be drowned in sleep, to become merely a sleeping animal. Baudelaire is the same: when he feels nature rising up in him like a flood – the nature that we all share – he clenches his fists and stiffens, he holds his head above the water. This great muddy flood is the essence of vulgarity: Baudelaire is annoyed at feeling in himself these stodgy waves, so unlike the subtle combinations he dreams about; he is annoyed, most of all, at feeling that this irresistible and sugary force is trying to force him to 'do as everybody does'; because nature in us is the contrary of what is rare and exquisite, it is *everybody*. Eating like everyone else, sleeping like everyone else, making love like everyone else – what madness! Each of us chooses those components in himself of which he will say: that's me; and he knows nothing about the others. Baudelaire chose not to be nature, but to be that constant, straining rejection of his 'natural being', that head rising out of the water and watching the flood rise with a mixture of contempt and terror. Most of the time, this free, arbitrary choice that we make in ourselves is what people call our 'lifestyle'. If you accept your body and let yourself go, if you like to surrender to a sense of contented exhaustion, to your needs, to sweat and all the other things that relate you to the rest of mankind, if yours is a humanism of nature, your gestures will possess a kind of roundness and generosity, an abandoned ease. Baudelaire hates abandonment. From dawn to dusk, he doesn't experience a moment's relaxation. His slightest desires and his most spontaneous urges are repressed, filtered and acted out rather than

269

lived: they are only let through when they have been duly artificialized. This partly explains the cult of appearance and dress, to hide his all-too-natural nakedness; and also occasional whims, such as painting his hair green, which border on the ridiculous. Even inspiration fails to find favour in his eyes. Of course, he must trust in it to some extent: 'In art – and this is something too seldom pointed out – the part played by the human will is much smaller than one thinks.' But inspiration is nature, again. It comes when it wants, spontaneously. It is like a need; one must transform it, work on it. He claims only to believe 'in patient work, in the truth expressed in good French and in the magic of the *mot juste*'. In this way, inspiration becomes simply a raw material to which the poet consciously applies the techniques of his craft. There is a good deal of play-acting and taste for artifice in this frenzied search for the *mot juste*, as Léon Cladel recalls:* 'From the first line – no, before the first line, at the first word, you had to start unpicking! was that word exactly right? Did it render precisely the desired shade of meaning? Careful! One must not confuse "agreeable" with "affable", "alluring" with "charming", "pleasant" with "kindly", "amiable" with "gracious" – oh no! These different words are not synonymous; each has its own very precise connotations; they belong more or less in the same class of ideas, without saying exactly the same thing! One must never, but *never*, use one in place of the other ... We who are workers in literature, and only that, must *always* find the ultimate means of expression, or else lay down our pens and take up plastering ... Search, search! If the word doesn't exist, invent it; but let's find out first if it does exist. And the dictionaries of our own tongue were seized upon and instantly consulted, leafed through, probed with fury and with love ... (After that) came the vocabularies of foreign languages. We had recourse to the French-Latin dictionary, then the Latin-French. The hunt was relentless. Nothing among the Ancients? Then let it be the Moderns! And the dogged etymologist, to whom most living languages were as familiar as most dead ones, digging his way into the English, German,

---

* Quoted by E. Crépet, *Charles Baudelaire*.

Italian and Spanish lexicons, pursued the refractory, elusive phrase, eventually creating it himself if it did not exist in our language.' In this way, while not categorically denying *the poetic fact* of inspiration, our poet dreams of replacing it with pure technique: this lazy man felt that the writer's prerogative was sheer hard work, not creative spontaneity. His taste for the minutiae of artificiality helps us to understand why he would spend such long hours correcting a poem, even a very old one and quite alien to his mood, in preference to writing a new one. When he came fresh and, so to speak, as a foreigner, to a work that was already written, which he could no longer get inside – when he knew the workmanlike pleasure of changing a word here or there for the sheer joy of rearranging something – then he felt at the furthest remove from nature, at his most gratuitous and – since time had delivered him from the constraints of feeling and the particular circumstance – at his most free. At the opposite end of his concerns, at the very bottom of the ladder, it is only in terms of a disgust at his animal needs that one can explain his unfortunate pretension to a liking for the art of cooking, which he did not at all understand, and his endless conversations with piemen and pastry-cooks. He had to disguise his hunger; he would not deign to eat to satisfy an appetite, but to use his teeth, tongue and palate to appreciate a particular sort of poetic creation. I would wager that he preferred meat in sauces to grilled meat, and tinned vegetables to fresh ones. The perpetual control he exercised over himself explains why he made contradictory impressions on people. The air of ecclesiastical unctuousness that was often attributed to him came from the unremitting guard he imposed on the flesh; but his tight, short, stiff gait – in appearance so far removed from the gentle manner of a cleric – has the same origin. In any event, he cheats nature and refines it. Softly mannered and ready to bless as long as it is asleep, tensed up when he senses that it is reawakening, he is always the one who says *no*, who buries his meagre body in thick clothing and disguises his meagre desires behind a carefully fabricated contrivance. I am not even sure that this is one source of Baudelaire's perversions. It seems that women aroused him chiefly when they were clothed; he could not stand their naked bodies.

He boasts, in *Portrait de maîtresse*, at having 'long ago reached the climacteric era of the third degree when beauty itself was not enough, unless spiced with scent, ornaments *et cetera*'. Apparently he entered this 'climacteric era' right from the start, according to a passage in *La Fanfarlo*, an early work, which reads like a confession:

'Samuel saw the new goddess of his heart approach him in the radiant and sacred magnificence of her nudity.

What man is there who would not give up even so much as half his life to see his dream, his true dream, standing unveiled before him, and the adored phantom of his imagination cast aside one by one all the clothes designed to protect her from the gaze of the mob? But Samuel, seized by some eccentric whim, began to shout like a spoiled child: "I want Colombine, give me back Colombine; give her to me as she looked the evening when she drove me mad, with her fanciful attire and her acrobat's bodice."

La Fanfarlo was at first astonished, but happy to indulge the fancy of the man whom she had chosen, and Flora was called for . . . The chambermaid left and Cramer, remembering something, hung on to the bell and cried in a resounding voice:

"Please . . . Don't forget the rouge!"'

If we compare this text with the famous passage from *Mademoiselle Bistouri*:

'"I want him to come and see me with his instruments and his gown, with even a little blood on it . . ." She said this in a very open manner, as a sensitive man might say to an actress, when he was in love with her: "I want to see you dressed in the costume that you wore in that famous part you played . . ."'*

– then there seems to be no doubt that Baudelaire was a fetishist. Surely he confessed as much himself in *Fusées*:

'A precocious love of women. I confused the smell of fur with the smell of woman. I remember . . . Anyway, I loved my mother for her elegance.'†

---

* *Petits poèmes en prose*, ed. Conard, p. 163.

† *Fusées*. See also in Baudelaire's notebooks (*Carnets*, ed. Crépet, p. 110, the note on Agathe).

Meat disguised, masked by sauces full of spice; water contained in geometrical basins; a woman's nakedness concealed beneath furs or theatrical costumes which still have a lingering hint of scent, a glimmer of the footlights; inspiration reined in, chastened by hard work: these are all different aspects of his disgust with nature and the everyday. We are far removed here from the theory of original sin; and when Baudelaire, from his horror of nudity, his liking for hidden, half-glimpsed lusts and pleasures, and purely cerebral titillation, demanded that Jeanne should be dressed for making love, one can be sure he was not thinking of the *Soirées de Saint-Pétersbourg*.

But, as we said, the idea of nature for Baudelaire is ambiguous. As he puts his case, appealing to our emotions as to his motives, he presents his feelings as the most *natural* and legitimate in the world. Here, his pen betrays him. Is it really true that, deep down in himself, he identifies nature with sin? Is he altogether sincere in making it the origin of crime? No doubt it means conformity, first and foremost. But for that very reason, it is the work of God – or, if you prefer, of Goodness. Nature is the first impulse, spontaneity, the instantaneous, kindness, direct and uncalculating; it is above all the whole of creation, a hymn rising towards its Creator. If Baudelaire had been *natural*, he would no doubt have been lost in the crowd; but, by the same token, he would have had a clear conscience, he would effortlessly have obeyed God's commandments, he would have been at home and at ease in the world. This is just what he does not want. He hates Nature and tries to destroy it *because it comes from God*, precisely as Satan tries to undermine Creation. Through pain, frustration and vice, he tries to construct a place apart for himself in the universe. He yearns for the solitude of the damned and the monster, of what is 'against Nature', for the very reason that Nature is everything and everywhere. And his dream of craft and artificiality is indistinguishable from his desire for sacrilege. He lies, and lies to himself, when he compares virtue to the construction of something artificial. For him, Nature is the transcendent Good, to the extent even of becoming a *given*, a reality surrounding him and insinuating itself into him without his consent. It demonstrates the ambiguity of Good, a pure value in so far as it *is* without my having chosen it. And Baudelaire's horror of Nature is combined with a profound attraction to it. This ambivalence in the poet's attitude is found in all those who have neither agreed to exceed all Norms through their choice of themselves, nor to submit entirely to an external Morality: submitting to Good to the extent that he sees it as a Duty to be carried out, Baudelaire rejects and despises it to the extent that it is a given quality of the Universe. Yet, one and the other are the very same Good, since Baudelaire, once and for all, has chosen not to choose it.

This explains Baudelaire's cult of frigidity. First and foremost, cold is *himself*, sterile, gratuitous and pure. Unlike the soft, warm mucous membranes of life, every cold object reflects back his own image. He developed a complex about cold, identifying it with polished metal, but also with precious stones. *Cold* means great flat expanses without vegetation, and these smooth deserts are like the surface of a metal cube or the facet of a jewel. Coldness becomes confused with pallor. White is the colour of cold, not only because snow is white, but mostly because this absence of colour is a clear enough sign of infertility and virginity. That is why the Moon becomes an emblem of frigidity; this precious stone, alone in the sky, looks down on us with its chalky steppes and, in the chill of night, sheds over the earth a white light that kills what it shines on. The light of the Sun appears nourishing; it is golden, thick, warming, like bread; but moonlight is comparable to pure water. It serves as the means to combine transparency – an image for lucidity – with frigidity. We may add that the Moon, with its borrowed light and its constant opposition to the Sun that illuminates it, is a passable symbol for the satanic Baudelaire, lit by Good and giving Evil in return. This is why there is always something unhealthy even in this purity. The Baudelairean cold is an environment where no spermatozoa or bacteria or any germ of life can survive; it is at the same time a white light and a transparent liquid, both verging on the limbo of consciousness, where microscopic life and solid particles are dissolved. It is the clarity of the Moon and liquid air, it is the great mineral power that freezes us to the mountain tops in winter.

It is avarice and impassibility. Fabre-Luce quite rightly remarks, in *Écrit en prison*, that pity always wants to give warmth; in that sense, the Baudelairean cold is pitiless: it freezes whatever it touches.

Naturally, Baudelaire plays out this elemental force in his approach to life. With his friends, he *is* coldness: 'many friends, many gloves'. He displays a ceremonial, frigid attitude of politeness with them, because he must be sure of killing off those germs of warm sympathy, those living effluvia that try to pass from them to him. He deliberately surrounds himself with an impassable no man's land, reading his own coldness in the eyes of those close to him. We may imagine him like a traveller arriving, one winter's night, at an inn: he has on his person all the ice and snow from outside. He can still see and think, but he no longer feels his body: he is desensitized.

It is Baudelaire's very natural reaction to project this frigidity that envelops him on to the Other. And here the process becomes complicated, because now suddenly Another – that foreign consciousness which observes and judges – has this chilling power attributed to it. The lunar light becomes that of the gaze. It is the look of the Medusa that freezes and petrifies. Baudelaire can hardly complain: isn't the function of the Other to transform him into a *thing*? Nonetheless, it was only women (and a certain type of woman, at that) to whom he ascribed this frigidity. He would not have stood it from men: that would have meant recognizing that they had some kind of superiority over him. But woman is an inferior animal, a 'latrine': she 'is on heat and wants to be fucked'; she is the opposite of the dandy. Baudelaire can make her a cult object without danger; in no event will she become his equal. He is not in any way taken in by the power that he attaches to her. Presumably, as Royère says, he sees her as 'the living supernatural'; but he knows very well that she only represents a pretext for his dreams, for the very reasons that she is absolutely *alien* and impenetrable. So this puts us in the realm of games; and, besides, Baudelaire never met a cold woman. Jeanne wasn't, if we are to believe *Sed non satiata*; nor was Madame Sabatier, whom he accused of being 'too jolly'. In order to realize his desires, he had to put them artificially in a state of coldness. He would choose to love Marie Daubrun because she loved another man. So this warm and passionate woman would adopt an attitude of the most icy indifference, at least in her relations with him. One can see that he anticipated it with pleasure, in the letter which he wrote to her in 1852:

'A man who says: "I love you," and who implores a woman who replies: "Love you? Never! A single man has my love, and woe upon him who comes after; he will have nought from me but indifference and contempt." And this same man, in order to have the pleasure of looking longer into your eyes, lets you speak to him of another, to speak only of him, to burn only with passion for him and when thinking of him. For me, the outcome of all these confessions is a quite singular fact, which is that, to me, you are no longer simply a woman whom one desires, but a woman whom one loves for her openness, her passion, her boldness, her youth, her folly.

I have lost much in giving these explanations, because you were so peremptory that I had to give in at once. But you, Madam, have gained much: you have inspired me with respect and profound esteem. Always remain as you are and preserve this passion that makes you so beautiful and so happy.

Come back, I beg you, and I shall be mild and modest in my desires . . . I cannot say that you will find me without love . . . But have no fear: for me you are an object of worship and it is impossible for me to defile you.'

This letter tells us a lot, first of all about Baudelaire's lack of sincerity. The passionate love that he swore would last no more than three months: in the same year he began to send anonymous, but equally passionate letters to Mme Sabatier.*

---

* In this second case, the process is the same: firstly, Baudelaire chooses a happy, well-loved and attached woman. With both of them, he pretends to have the greatest esteem for the official lover. He worships both 'as a Christian worships his God'. But since Mme Sabatier appears easier to him and, after all, might risk falling into his arms, he remains anonymous. In this way he can enjoy his idol at his ease, love her in secret and be overwhelmed by her contemptuous indifference. No sooner has she given herself to him than he departs: he is no longer interested in her and cannot keep up the play-acting. The statue has come to life, the cold woman is warming up. It even seems probable that he was unable to perform with her, his own impotence thus making up for the coldness which had suddenly failed La Présidente.

This is an erotic game, nothing more. People have gone into raptures over these two loves of Baudelaire's, but anyone who reads his letter to Marie Daubrun and his missives to La Présidente one after another will find that the repetition of these expressions of platonic adoration have an obsessive quality. This becomes even clearer if one refers to the famous poem 'Une nuit que j'étais près d'une affreuse juive' ['One night, as I lay beside a hideous Jewess . . .'], which, according to Crarond, goes back to the time of Louchette: in it, Baudelaire, unacquainted either with Marie or with Mme Sabatier, is already starting to explore the theme of feminine duality and depicts himself, beside this fiery demon, dreaming of a frigid angel:

> 'Je me pris à songer, près de ce corps vendu
> A la triste beauté dont mon destin se prive . . .
> Car j'eusse avec ferveur baisé son noble corps . . .
> Si quelque soir, d'un pleur obtenu sans effort,
> Tu pouvais seulement, ô reine des cruelles,
> Obscurcir la splendeur de tes froides prunelles.'

['I fell to thinking, beside this body I had bought/Of the sad beauty that my fate declined/For I would eagerly have kissed that fine body,/Most cruel mistress, if one evening you had caused/A single unforced tear to rise/And dim the icy pupils of your eyes.']

So what we have here is a pattern established *a priori* in the Baudelairean sensibility which functions for a long time in the void, but is later able to find concrete realization. The cold woman is the sexual incarnation of the judge:

'When I do something really foolish, I think: Good heavens, if she knew about it! And when I do something good, I tell myself: now I am getting closer to her in spirit.'*

Her coldness demonstrates her purity: she is released from original sin. At the same time, he identifies her with his alien conscience: she signifies incorruptibility, impartiality and objectivity; she is, at the

---

* Letter of 18 August 1857.

same time, a look, that pure look of clear water and melted snow, which is never surprised, which does not express pain or irritation, but puts everything back in its proper place; which *thinks* the world and Baudelaire in the world. It is certain that this frigidity he yearns for imitates the icy strictness of a mother who surprises her child 'doing something silly'. But as we have seen, it is not so much an incestuous love for his mother that makes him look for authority in the women that he desires: on the contrary, his need for authority led him to choose his mother, with Marie Daubrun and La Présidente, as judge and object of desire. He writes of Mme Sabatier that 'nothing can equal the gentle sweetness of her authority'. And he acknowledges that, going from one extreme to another, he thinks about her in the midst of his debauchery:

> 'Quand chez les débauchés l'aube blanche et vermeille
> Entre en société de l'idéal songeur,
> Par l'opération d'un mystère vengeur
> Dans la brute assoupie, un ange se réveille.'

['In debauchees, when white and rosy dawn/Encounters the pensive ideal,/Then through some vengeful mystery/An angel wakens in the slumbering brute.']

What is involved, as we see, is an *operation*, the mechanism of which is revealed in another passage:

'What makes one's mistress dearer, is debauchery with other women. What she loses in sensual pleasure, she gains in adoration. An awareness of the need for forgiveness makes a man more agreeable.'

We have here a common feature of pathological platonism: the patient, who worships a respectable woman from afar, conjures up the image of her at the moment when he is engaged in the most base occupations: when he is in the lavatory, when he is washing his genitalia. At this moment she appears to him, silently observing him with a stern look. Baudelaire sustains the obsession at will: it is when he is lying beside 'a frightful Jewess', dirty, bald and pox-ridden, that he evokes within him the image of the Angel. The Angel varies; but whatever woman he has chosen to fulfil the role, there is always *someone* watching him – no doubt at the very moment of orgasm. The result is that he no longer knows whether he is calling on a chaste, stern figure to increase the pleasure he takes when he is with a prostitute, or whether his hasty encounters with tarts are merely the means to conjure up the chosen woman and bring him into contact with her. In any event, this great, frigid figure, silent and unmoving, is for Baudelaire the eroticization of the social prohibition against what he is doing: she is like one of those mirrors which some sophisticated lovers use to reflect the image of their pleasures. She lets him watch himself making love.

But still more directly, he is guilty for loving her since she does not love him; and more guilty still if he desires her and defiles her. By her very frigidity she stands for what is forbidden. If he swears, with the most solemn oaths, that he will respect her, this is in order that his desires shall be the greater crimes. Here once more is the sin and the sacrilege: the woman is there, she walks across the room with that indolent, majestic bearing which Baudelaire himself affects and which, in and of itself, signifies indifference and freedom. She more or less ignores Baudelaire: if by chance she does consider him, he is nothing special in her eyes. He passes through her look *as glass passes through the sunlight*. Speechless and some way from her, he feels insignificant and transparent – an object. But at the very moment when the eyes of the lovely creature put him in the place in the world that her gaze dispassionately dictates, he escapes, he desires her, he sinks deeper into sin. He is guilty, he is *different*. The 'two simultaneous postulations' instantly fill his soul and he is invaded by the double presence of those inseparables: Good and Evil.

At the same time, the woman's frigidity spiritualizes Baudelaire's desires and transforms them into *voluptés* – sensual delights. We have seen what sort of pleasure – restrained, lightened by the spirit – he seeks. As we said, it is a matter of the merest of touches. This is the pleasure that he promises himself in the letter to Marie Daubrun. He desires her in silence and his desire will altogether enfold her at a distance, without leaving a trace, without her even noticing:

'You will not be able to prevent my mind from straying around your arms, your lovely hands, those eyes in which your whole life resides and all your beloved fleshly being.'

So the coldness of the desired object achieves what Baudelaire has been trying to obtain by any means: solitude of desire. This desire, which lingers from afar on beautiful but indifferent flesh, which is only a caress with the eyes, takes pleasure in itself because it is unknown and not recognized. It is altogether sterile, it stirs no feeling in the beloved. We know about the communicative desire that Proust describes with reference to Swann, which appears with such dramatic suddenness that the desired woman is left momentarily limp and shattered by it. This is exactly what Baudelaire loathes: it creates a disturbance, it enlivens and gradually warms the originally icy nudity of the desired object; it is a fertile, communicative, hot desire, comparable to the warm abundance of nature. Baudelaire's desire, on the other hand, is entirely sterile and *without consequence*. He is, from the start, master of himself, because 'the cold majesty of the sterile woman' can only arouse a cerebral love, represented rather than experienced. And since the object of his desires is unaware of them, this pretended turmoil, feigned as much as felt, does not commit him. Baudelaire remains alone, trapped in his masturbatory avarice. Moreover, if he were to make love with one of these inaccessible beauties – which he is very careful not to wish for, since he prefers the nervous itch of desire to its fulfilment – it would be on the express condition that she should remain icy until the end. He wrote: 'The woman that one loves is the woman who does not feel pleasure.' And he would be appalled if he were to give it; but if, on the contrary, the statue stays fixed in marble, the sex act is, so to speak, *neutralized*; Baudelaire has had no relations except with himself, he has remained as solitary as a child masturbating, the sensual pleasure that he felt has not been the cause of any external event, he has *given* nothing, he has made love to a block of ice. Because she did not conserve her icy coldness, because she showed that her flesh was too sensitive and her temperament too generous, La Présidente lost her lover in a single night.

But, as with the idea of the natural, there is an ambivalence here. The sexual act with a frigid woman does indeed represent a sacrilege and a soiling imposed on Good which leaves Good as pure and virginal and unpolluted as before. It is a *white* sin, blank, sterile, which evaporates into thin air at the very moment of its commission, leaving no memory and having no effect, but at the same time ratifying the inalterable everlastingness of the law, and the eternal youth and the eternal availability of the sinner. But this white magic of love does not exclude black magic. Since he is unable to transcend Good, as we have seen, Baudelaire slyly sets out to depreciate it from beneath: hence the fact that the masochism of frigidity is accompanied by sadism. The frigid woman is a feared judge, but in addition a victim. For Baudelaire, while the act of love involves three people – if the idol appears before him at the moment when he is indulging in his vices in the company of a prostitute – this is not only because he needs an observer and a strict witness; it is also because he wants to make her ridiculous. She is the one that he is striking when he penetrates his paid whore. He is deceiving her and polluting her. It is as though Baudelaire, from a horror of exercising any direct action on the universe, were seeking for magic (that is, long-distance) influences, no doubt because they are less compromising. In this way, the frigid woman becomes the *respectable wife* whose very respectability is faintly ridiculous, and whose husband is unfaithful to her with common tarts. This is what is implied by the peculiar Fanfarlo: here, coldness becomes clumsiness and inexperience; and when the loving wife forces herself to engage in sexual practices which revolt her in order to keep her husband, there is even something obscene about her frigidity. In the same way, the 'blank' sexual act of the woman who does not experience sexual pleasure – possession in a void, almost at a distance and without pollution – is sometimes transformed purely and simply into rape. Like Mme Aupick, like Marie Daubrun, all Baudelaire's heroines 'love someone else': this is the guarantee of their coldness. And this happy rival is endowed with every good quality. In *La Fanfarlo*, M. de Cosmelly is 'noble, honest'; people talk about 'his finest qualities'; he adopts with everyone 'a commanding manner that was at once amiable and irresistible'. In *L'Ivrogne*, an outline for a play that was never written, the drunkard's wife was attracted to 'a young man, quite rich, from a higher social sphere and respectable, who admired her virtue'. In *La Fanfarlo*, this leads to a peculiar twist in the plot: Mme de Cosmelly, rejected and ridiculed by her husband with La Fanfarlo, gets the same treatment for the second time, at her own request, with the same woman from Baudelaire himself, under the name 'Cramer'. The barely disguised subject of the tale is that of the respectable woman scorned and magically violated in the person of a magnificent prostitute; it is frigidity humiliated. But, in *L'Ivrogne*: 'A working man will gladly seize upon the excuse of his over-excited jealousy, to hide from himself the fact that what he chiefly resents in his wife is her resignation, her gentleness, her patience and her virtue.' Here, the hatred of goodness is quite openly expressed. It would lead directly to rape: in the version of 1854 (see his letter to Tisserand) murder is substituted for rape at the last moment, in a fairly absurd manner, as if covering something up: 'Here is the scene of the crime. The man arrives first at the meeting-place which he has chosen. Sunday evening. Dark road or level common. In the distance, the sound of a dance band. A sinister and melancholy landscape on the outskirts of Paris. A love scene as sad as can be imagined between this man and that woman. He wants her to forgive him, he wants her to let him live and come back to her. Never has he thought her so beautiful . . . His expressions of affection are sincere. He is almost in love with her again, he desires her, he begs her. She is all the more interesting for being so pale and thin: this almost acts as a stimulant to him. The audience must guess what is going on. Although the poor woman also feels a return of her former feelings, she rejects his wild passion in such a place. The rejection annoys the husband who attributes her chastity to some adulterous affair or the defence of a lover: "We must have done with this; but I shall never find the courage, I cannot do it myself."' We know what happens. He sends his wife along the road, at the end of which is a well; she falls down it. 'If she escapes, so much the better; if she falls into the well, then God has condemned her.'

One can see the symbolic richness of this fantasy: the crime is premeditated and it sets the underlying tone of the relationship between Baudelaire, the drunkard, and his wife (his mother, Marie

Daubrun, etc . . .). So everything that follows takes place against a background of crime, in such a way that the drunkard's feelings of tenderness are poisoned from the very start: he represents that common occurrence, the sex murderer who weeps over his victim. But, in addition, Baudelaire/The Drunkard approaches the frigid woman *asking for her forgiveness*, so the love theme is primarily the 'blank' one of masochism. The wife's pallor and her thinness excite him (see the themes of frigidity and the 'hideous Jewess'); we know that a thin body appeared 'more obscene' to Baudelaire than a well-covered one. This is the moment of the switch to sadism. The Drunkard wants to violate that coldness, to pollute it and to attack in the woman the more fortunate lover who represents morality (he 'forbade' her to resume her sexual relations with her husband). At the same time, rape = murder: he wants to complete the decomposition of this body, already presaged by its thinness. He wants to oblige this gentleness, this chastity to become obscene. And he wants to take this woman on the spot, here, like the lowest of whores, at this crossroads (and, note, fully dressed: we are back with the fetishism of *La Fanfarlo*). Since she refuses, he kills her. Or rather, since he does not have the strength to carry out a direct act of murder, he puts the onus of getting rid of her on to chance and magic (this is the theme of impotence and sterility: one does not act oneself, one makes things happen). The crime is brought in to disguise the rape, both because there is an affective equivalence between them and because Baudelaire was afraid of himself: rape is too obviously erotic, while murder conceals its sexual implications. He kills her in order to penetrate her and pollute her, in order to attack the Good in her. But he fails to accomplish this possession in hot blood and she dies behind him, in the darkness, from a death that he has merely prepared with words. The fantasy haunted Baudelaire for a long time. He was not altogether satisfied with this underhand crime, because Asselineau tells us that he dreamed up another version: 'Baudelaire was describing (to Rouvière) one of the chief scenes in the part, where the Drunkard, after killing his wife, felt renewed tenderness for her and a desire to violate her. Rouvière's mistress objected to this atrocious situation. "Well,

Madame," Baudelaire told her, "anybody would do the same. And any man who is not like that is very much the exception." *

This story may predate the letter to Tisserand and Baudelaire may have shifted the moment at which desire is awoken, so that the woman was still *alive*, from fear of the theatrical censors and also, no doubt, to bring some action into the scene. Moreover, it is plausible now, because he has thought up a new ending, namely the indirect murder, whereas if he was to give any meaning to the temptation of necrophilia, the presence of the body would be indispensable. So, originally, the Drunkard was to strangle or stab his wife, and then rape her. With this, the insensibility, sterility and unattainable coldness of the frigid woman acquire their ultimate meaning and perfect realization: the extreme case of the frigid woman is the corpse. It is when confronted with a corpse that sexual desire would become at once most criminal and most solitary; however, at the same time, disgust for the dead flesh would imbue that desire with a profound nothingness, make it more willed, more intentional and more artificial; and would, so to speak, 'chill' it. In this way frigidity, which is originally sterilization by cold, finally discovers its true environment: death; and its depiction varies – as Baudelaire himself oscillates between masochism and sadism – from the icy and incorruptible lunar metal to the corpse as it loses its animal warmth. Absence of life or the destruction of life: the spirit of Baudelaire is situated between these two extremes.

---

* Asselineau, *Recueil d'Anecdotes* (first published *in extenso* by E. Crépet, *Charles Baudelaire*).

Gide

This tribute to André Gide, written just after his death, appeared in *Les Temps modernes* in March 1951 and was reprinted in *Situations IV* (1964).

We thought of him as sanctified and embalmed; then he dies and we discover how much alive he still was; the embarrassment and resentment that one can sense behind the funerary wreaths, being woven with such bad grace, show that he still gave offence and will continue to do so for a long time to come. He managed to create a united front of right-wing and left-wing conformists ranged against him and one can well imagine the joy with which certain eminent and venerated mummies are saying: 'Thank you, Lord! So he really was wrong, since I am the one who has survived.' One has only to read in *L'Humanité* that 'what has died was a corpse', to know the weight of this eighty-year-old, who had more or less given up writing, in the scales of contemporary literature.

There is a geography of the mind. Just as a Frenchman, wherever he goes, cannot take a single step abroad without *also* getting either nearer to France, or further away, so any intellectual step *also* took us either closer to Gide, or further from him. His penetration, his lucidity, his rationalism, his rejection of pathos, licensed others to embark on more troubled and risky intellectual ventures: we knew that in the meantime a luminous intelligence was upholding the rights of analysis and purity and a particular tradition. If we were to founder in a voyage of discovery, we should not take the mind down with us in our shipwreck. All French thought over the past thirty years, like it or not, and regardless of its other points of reference – Marx, Hegel, Kierkegaard – had *also* to define itself in relation to Gide.

As far as I am concerned, the mental reservations, hypocrisy and, to put it bluntly, the abject stench of the obituaries that have been written about him have disgusted me too much for me to consider setting down here the things that separated us; better, instead, to remind ourselves of the inestimable amount that we owe him.

I have read articles by some fellow-journalists (who never yet astonished me by their daring), that he 'lived dangerously, beneath three thicknesses of flannel'. What a ridiculous jibe! These fainthearts have discovered a peculiar way of defending themselves against the courage of others: they only admit that it exists if it is exhibited at the same time in every sphere. They might have forgiven Gide for venturing his thought and his reputation, if he had ventured his life – and, oddly, if he had risked a cold on the chest. They pretend ignorance of the fact that there are forms of courage, which are different from one person to another. Well, yes, Gide was cautious, he weighed his words, hesitated before signing anything and, if he did take an interest in a current of thought or opinion, was careful to give only conditional support, so that he could stay at the edge, ready to retreat. But this same mind dared to publish his declaration of faith in *Corydon* and the indictment of *Voyage au Congo*. He had the courage to align himself with the USSR when it was dangerous to do so and the still greater courage to reverse his opinion when he thought, rightly or wrongly, that he had been mistaken. It may be this very mixture of circumspection and daring that made him an example to us: generosity is only admirable in those who know the price of things and, in the same way, considered temerity should touch us most deeply of all. Had it been written by a mere booby, *Corydon* would have been just a matter for the vice squad; but, since the author is this wily Jesuit who weighs everything up, the book becomes a manifesto, a *testimony*, the significance of which far exceeds the outrage it inspires. This cautious daring should be a 'Rule for the Guidance of the Mind': withholding judgement until everything is clear and then, when one is firm in one's conviction, agreeing to pay for it to the last farthing.

Valour and caution: a judicious mixture of the two explains the inner tension of his work. Gide's art tries to achieve a compromise between risks and rules. In him, there existed a balance between Protestant precepts and a homosexual's non-conformity, between the proud individualism of the upper middle class and a puritanical liking for social constraints; a certain dryness, a problem in communicating and a basically Christian humanism; a strong vein of sensuality, which laid claim to innocence: in him, observance of the rules coexists with a quest for spontaneity. These weights and counterweights are the basis of the immeasurable service that Gide performed for the literature of our time: he was the one who lifted it out of the rut of Symbolism. The second generation of Symbolists was convinced that a writer demeaned himself if he ventured beyond a very small number of subjects, all most elevated; but that, on these clearly defined subjects, he could express himself in any way he pleased. Gide freed us from this naïve concentration on the thing named: he taught us, or reminded us, that *everything* can be said – here he was daring – but according to certain rules of good writing – here he was cautious.

This cautious daring was the source of his constant about-turns, his swings from one extreme to the other, and his passion for objectivity – one might even say, his 'objectivism' (which, I admit, is very bourgeois), which led him to seek for right and reason even among his opponents and meant that he was fascinated by other people's opinions. I am not saying that these attitudes, so characteristic of him, could be advantageous to us now, but they allowed him to conduct his life as a rigorous experiment and can be assimilated by us without any preparation. In a word, he *lived* his ideas, one above all: the death of God. I cannot imagine that a single believer today was brought to Christianity by the arguments of St Bonaventure or St Anselm; but neither do I think that a single unbeliever has been turned away from the faith by the opposite arguments. The problem of God is a human problem, connected with relations of human beings among themselves, a total problem, to which each one of us applies a solution for his whole life and the solution which one applies reflects the attitude one has chosen towards others and towards oneself. Gide's most precious gift to us was his decision to experience the agony and the death of God right to the end. He could well, like so many others, have taken a chance on how he felt and, at the age of twenty, chosen between faith and atheism, and stuck to it all his life. Instead of that, he wanted to *test* his relationship to religion, and the living dialectic that brought him ultimately to atheism was a path which others can follow in his footsteps, but which cannot be fixed in notions and concepts. His endless debates with Catholics, his outpourings, his shafts of irony, his flirtations, his sudden breaks, his advances, his marking time and his withdrawals, the ambiguity of the word 'God' in his work, his refusal to abandon it even when he no longer believed in anything except mankind: in short, this whole rigorous experiment, did more to enlighten us than a hundred reasoned arguments. *On our behalf*, he lived a life which we have only to relive as we read him; he lets us avoid the pitfalls into which he fell, or to get out of them as he did; the opponents whom he discredited in our eyes, if only by publishing their correspondence with him, have no further power to attract us. Every truth, Hegel says, has a history. One is too inclined to forget it: one sees the end, and not the journey, imagining that an idea is a finished product, not seeing that it is nothing more than its own slow process of maturation and a succession of necessary mistakes which have to be corrected, of partial views which are completed and expanded. Gide offers an irreplaceable example because he, on the contrary, chose to *become his truth*. If it had been settled upon at the age of twenty, his atheism would have been false; but, slowly consolidated, as the culmination of a half-century's quest, this atheism becomes his concrete truth, and our own. On that basis, the men of today can become new truths.

Reply to Albert Camus

First published in *Les Temps modernes* in August 1952, this piece was reprinted in *Situations IV* (1964). Having each reviewed the other's early fiction, Sartre and Camus met in June 1943 and became intimate friends. Growing political differences between the two men came to a head when Camus published *The Rebel* in 1951. The argument spilt over in a bitter printed polemic that ran from May until September 1952.

For us, you were – and tomorrow may be again – the same admirable conjunction of man, action and writings. That was in 1945: we discovered Camus, the resistance worker, as we had discovered Camus, author of *The Outsider*. And when we compared the editor of the underground newspaper *Combat* with the character of Meursault, who took honesty to the extent of refusing to say that he loved his mother and his mistress, and whom society condemned to death – and, most of all, when we knew that you continued to be both of these things, the apparent contradiction increased our understanding of ourselves and of the world – then you were little short of exemplary, because you summed up within you the conflicts of the age, and you transcended them through your eagerness to experience them. You were a *person*, the most complex and rich of persons, the latest and most welcome heir to Chateaubriand and the assiduous defender of a social cause. You had every kind of luck and every merit, joining a feeling for grandeur to a passionate feeling for beauty, and *joie de vivre* to an awareness of death. Already, before the war, you had chosen to defend yourself against the bitter experience of what you called *the Absurd*, with the weapon of contempt, but you believed that 'every negation contains a flowering of *yes*' and at the heart of rejection you sought to find consent, 'to consecrate the harmony of love and rebellion'. According to you, man is not entirely himself except when he is happy; and 'what is happiness, except a simple concordance between a being and the life that he leads; and what concordance can more legitimately unite a man to life than the double awareness of his desire to survive and his mortal destiny?' Happiness is not precisely a state of being nor an action, but the tension between these forces of death and forces of life, between acceptance and rejection, through which man defines the *present* – that is to say, both the instant and the eternal – and becomes himself. Thus, when you described one of those 'privileged moments' which achieve a provisional harmony between man and nature (and which, from Rousseau to Breton, have been one of the major themes of French literature), you managed to introduce an entirely new note of *morality*. Being happy means doing one's job as a man: you showed us 'the duty of being happy'. And this duty was combined with the statement that man is the only being in the world who has this feeling, 'because he is the only one who demands it'. The experience of happiness, similar to Bataille's *Supplice*, but richer and more complex, made you stand up before an absent God as a reproach, but also as a challenge: 'Man must assert justice in order to struggle against eternal injustice and create happiness to protest against the universe of misery.' The universe of misery is not *social*; or, at least, not primarily. It is Nature, empty and indifferent, in which man is an outsider, and condemned to die; in a word, it is 'the eternal silence of the Divinity'. In this way, your experience closely united the ephemeral and the permanent. Aware that you were perishable, you wanted to be concerned only with truths 'that were destined to rot'. Your body was one such. You rejected the trickery of the Soul and the Idea. But since, as you yourself put it, injustice is *eternal* – that is to say, since the absence of God is a constant through all the changes of history, this means that the relationship (immediate, constantly renewed) of man to this God – man, who demands to have a meaning (that is to say, to be given one), to this God who remains eternally silent – is itself transcendent with respect to History. The tension by which man realizes himself (which is, at the same time, intuitive enjoyment of being), is thus a veritable conversion which wrenches him from the agitation of everyday life and from 'historicity', and finally reconciles him with his condition. One can go no further; no progress can have any place in this instantaneous tragedy. An Absurdist before Absurdism, Mallarmé was already writing: '(The Drama) is immediately resolved, taking no longer than the time needed to show the defeat which occurs in a flash'; and he seems to me to have given us in advance the key to your own plays when he wrote: 'The Hero *releases* the (maternal) hymn which creates him and is restored in the theatre which this was – out of the Mystery in which this hymn was shrouded.' In short, you are part of our great classical tradition which, from Descartes onwards (though with the exception of Pascal), is entirely hostile to History. But you finally achieved a synthesis between aesthetic pleasure, desire, happiness and heroism, between contented contemplation and duty, between the fulfilment of Gide and the dissatisfaction of Baudelaire. You completed the immoralism of Menalchius with an austere morality; the content was unchanged: 'There is only one love in this world. To embrace the body of a woman is also to hold against oneself that strange joy which descends from the sky to the sea. In a short while, when I shall plunge myself into glasses of absinth in order to penetrate my body with their scent, I shall be aware – despite everything that people may think – that I am fulfilling a truth which is that of the sun and will also be that of my death.' But since that truth belongs to all of us, since its extreme singularity is precisely what makes it universal, since you were breaking the shell of the pure present in which Nathanaël searches for God and opened it out to 'the profundity of the world' – that is, to death – at the end of this dark and solitary pleasure you discovered a universal ethic and the solidarity of man. Nathanaël is not alone; he is 'aware and proud of it' that he shares his love of life, which is stronger than death, 'with a whole species'. Of course, everything ends badly: the world swallows up the unreconciled libertine. And you liked to quote this passage from Obermann: 'Let us perish while fighting against it, and if what awaits us is oblivion, let us ensure that we do not deserve it.'

So, do not deny it: you did not reject History because you suffered from it and were horrified to discover its face. You rejected it without any experience of it, because our culture rejects it and because you were investing human values in the struggle 'against heaven'. You chose yourself and created yourself as you are by meditating on your own personal misfortunes and anxieties, and the solution that you found for them was a bitter wisdom that endeavoured to deny time.

However, war came and you devoted yourself unreservedly to the Resistance. You carried on an austere struggle, without flourishes and without renown. The risks were not exhilarating: worse than that, there was the danger of being shamed and degraded. This effort, which was always demanding and sometimes solitary, appeared to you *necessarily* as a *duty*. And your first contact with History took, for you, the form of *sacrifice*. As it happens, you said the same yourself when you wrote that you were struggling 'for that small distinction which separates sacrifice from mysticism'. Don't misunderstand me: when I say, 'your first contact with History', it is not because I am suggesting that I had a different one or that it was any better. The only one, as intellectuals, that we had was that contact; and if I refer to it as *yours*, it is because you experienced it more profoundly and more entirely than many of us, including myself. That does not alter the fact that the circumstances of that particular struggle entrenched you in the belief that one must sometimes pay one's tribute to History, so that one may subsequently return to one true duties. You accused the Germans of having torn you away from your struggle against Heaven and forced you to engage in the temporal battles of mankind: 'For so many years, you have been trying to *make me enter into History* . . .' And further on: 'You did what was necessary, and *we entered into History*; and for five years it was no longer possible to enjoy the song of the birds.'* History was war; for you it was *the folly of others*. It does not create, it destroys: it prevents the grass from growing and the birds from singing and men from making love. Indeed, it so happened that external circumstances seemed to confirm your point of view:

---

* *Lettres à un ami allemand*. Emphasis added.

in peace you had been waging a timeless struggle against the injustice of our fate, and the Nazis, in your eyes, took the side of that injustice; allied to the blind forces of the universe, they were trying to destroy mankind. You were struggling, in your words, 'to save *the idea* of mankind'.* In short, you didn't think of 'making History', as Marx says, but of preventing it being made: the proof is that, after the war, you only thought about a return to the *status quo*: 'Our condition has not ceased to be desperate.' The meaning of the Allied victory seemed to you to be 'the acquisition of two or three small changes which may perhaps be of no use except to help us to die better'. After picking up your five years of history, you thought that you (and all mankind with you) could return to the despair in which man must find his happiness and 'prove that we did not deserve such injustice' (in whose eyes?) by resuming the desperate struggle that man wages 'against his repulsive destiny'. How we loved you in those days. We, too, were the neophytes of History and had endured it with loathing, without realizing that the war was only another form of historicity, neither more nor less so than the years that preceded it. We applied Malraux's statement to you: 'Let victory belong to those who made war without liking it.' And we felt a little sorry for ourselves as we repeated the words. This was a time when, like you, in you, we were under threat, without realizing it. It often happens that a culture produces its richest works when it is about to vanish, and these works are the fruit of a fatal marriage between the old values and new ones which seem to be fertilizing them, but in reality kill them. In the synthesis that you were attempting, happiness and assent derived from our old humanism; but rebellion and despair were intruders; they came from outside, from an outside where unknown eyes full of hatred were watching our spiritual festivities. You borrowed that look from them to turn it on our cultural heritage; it was their simple, naked existence that raised doubts about our calm enjoyment; the challenge to destiny, the rebellion against the absurd, all this, of course, came from you or was directed through you; but thirty or forty years earlier, you

---

* *Lettres à un ami allemand*. Emphasis added.

would have been cured of these bad manners; you would have joined the Aesthetes or the Church. Your Rebellion only took on the importance that it did, because it was whispered to you by that vague mass: you hardly had time to direct it against the heavens where it vanished. And the moral demands that you brought out were only an idealization of very real demands that were welling up around you and which you picked up. The balance that achieved could only be produced once, for a single moment, in a single man: it was your good fortune that the common struggle against the Germans symbolized, in your eyes and in ours, the unity of all men against the inhuman fates. By choosing injustice, the Germans had voluntarily sided with the blind forces of Nature and, in *La Peste*, you could assign their role to microbes, without anyone being aware that this was mystification. In short, for a few years, you were what one might call the symbol and the proof of solidarity between the classes. This is also what the Resistance appeared to be, and what you demonstrated in your first works: 'Men rediscover solidarity in order to enter the struggle against their repulsive destiny.'

In this way, a combination of circumstances, one of those rare moments of concord which make a life the image of a truth, allowed you to disguise from yourself that the struggle of man against Nature is at once the cause and the effect of another struggle, equally ancient and more pitiless: the struggle of man against man. You rebelled against death while, in the iron belts that ring our towns, other men were rebelling against the social conditions that raise the rates of death. A child died, and you would rise up against the absurdity of the world, and that deaf and blind God whom you had created, so that you could spit in His face; but the child's father, if he was an unemployed man or a workman, rose up against other men: he knew very well that the absurdity of our human condition is not the same in Passy as it is in Billancourt. And, finally, men almost hid the microbes from him: in working-class districts, children die in twice the numbers that they do in well-off areas; and, since a different distribution of wealth could save their lives,* half the

---

* This is not entirely accurate. Some are condemned in any event.

deaths, among the poor, are like executions, with microbes acting simply as executioners. You wanted to realize the happiness of all through a *moral* tension, in yourself, by yourself; but the crowd, the dark mass which we were beginning to discover, demanded that we should give up being happy so that it might become a little less unhappy. Suddenly, the Germans no longer counted; one might even have said that they never had counted; we thought that there was only one way to resist and we discovered that there were two *ways of seeing* resistance. And, while for us you still represented the incarnation of the immediate past, and perhaps even the incarnation of the near future, you had already become a privileged being for ten million Frenchmen who did not identify their all-too-real protest with your ideal rebellion. This death, this life, this earth, this rebellion, this God, this no and this yes, this love, they told you, were princely amusements; some went as far as to call them circus tricks. You wrote: 'Only one thing is more tragic than suffering and that is the life of a happy man'; and: 'A sort of continuity in despair can produce joy'; or again: 'I was not sure that this splendour of the world was not (the justification) of all men who know that there is an extreme form of poverty which always reaches a point where it joins the luxury and riches of the world.'* Naturally, being like you one of the privileged few, I understand what you meant and I believe that you bought the right to say it. I should guess that you have been closer than many men to a kind of death and a kind of destitution, and I think that you must have known real poverty, if not utter deprivation. These statements, coming from you, do not have the same meaning as they would in a book by M. Mauriac or M. de Montherlant. And also, when you wrote them, they appeared natural. But, now, today, the point is that *they no longer appear so*: we *know* that, to discover luxury in the depths of destitution, one must possess leisure, or at least culture, that inestimable and inequitable form of wealth. One feels that you were chosen, even in the most painful circumstances of your life, to bear witness that personal salvation is attainable by everyone; and the thought that

---

* These three quotations are from *Noces*.

dominates in everyone's mind, charged with threat and hatred, is that this is only possible for a few. There is hatred in the idea; but what can be done about that? It gnaws away at everything. Even you, who did not want to hate the Germans, show evidence in your books of a hatred of God, and it has been said that you were even more an 'anti-theist' than an atheist. An oppressed person invests all the value that he may still have in his own eyes, in the hatred that he directs against others. And his friendship for his comrades is conditioned by his hatred for other men. Neither your books nor your example can do anything for him: you profess an art of living and a 'science of life', you teach us to rediscover our own bodies; but his body, when he rediscovers it in the evening – it has been stolen from him for the whole day – is nothing more than a vast misery that weighs him down and humiliates him. Such a man is *made* by other men; man is his number one enemy; and if the strange nature that he finds in the factory or the building site still speaks to him of mankind, it is because men have transformed them into a penal colony or labour camp especially for him.

What should you have done? You should have changed yourself in part to keep some of your old loyalties, while satisfying the demands of these oppressed masses. You might have done this, had not their representatives insulted you, in their usual way. You slammed the brakes on the shift that was taking place in you and, in a new gesture of defiance, you persisted in brandishing before everyone the idea of class solidarity, and that men are united in the face of death, when already the classes had resumed their struggle before your eyes. So, what had been for some time *an exemplary reality* became the utterly vain statement of an *ideal* – all the more so, since this deceptive solidarity had been transformed into struggle even in your own heart. You contradicted History and rather than interpreting its course, you chose instead to see it as merely another absurdity. Basically, all you did was go back to your original position. You borrowed some idea or other about the 'deification of man', from Malraux, from Carrouges, and twenty other writers, then, condemning the human race, you took your place beside it, but not as part of it, like the last of the Mohicans. Your personality, real and vital for as long as it was nourished by events, became a mirage; in 1944, it was the future, in 1952, the past; and what seems to you the most repellent injustice is that all this is happening to you from outside, without your having changed at all. It seems to you that the world offers the same riches as before and that it is men who refuse to see them; well, reach out your hand, and see if it doesn't all vanish: Nature itself has changed in meaning because the relationship of men to it has changed. You are left with your memories and a language which is increasingly abstract. You are only half living among us and you are tempted to leave us altogether, so that you can retire to some solitary place where you can rediscover a drama which was supposed to be that of mankind and which is no longer even your own; in other words, to a society that has remained at a lower stage of technical civilization. What is happening to you is, in one sense, quite unfair; but, in another sense, entirely just: you had to change if you were to remain yourself, and you were afraid to change. If you feel that I am being unkind, don't worry: very shortly, I shall be speaking of myself in the same manner. There is no point in you trying to attack me; but you can trust me to pay the price of all this – because you are quite unbearable, but you are also my 'neighbour', by the force of circumstances.

Caught up, like you, in History, I do not see it in the same way as you do. I do not doubt that it wears an absurd and terrible face, for those who look at it from Hell: that is because they no longer have anything in common with the men who make it. And, if this were a tale of ants or bees, I am sure that we should depict it as a farcical and macabre succession of infamies, mockeries and murders. But if we were ants, perhaps we should judge things differently. I did not understand your dilemma – 'either History has a meaning, or else it has none . . .' etc. – until I re-read your *Letters to a German Friend*. Then everything became clear when I found this remark, addressed by you to a Nazi soldier: 'For years, you have been trying to force me into History.' 'Good heavens,' I thought, 'since he considers himself to be *outside*, it's normal for him to lay down conditions before coming in.' Like a girl putting a toe in the water and wondering: 'Is it warm?' you look at History with mistrust, poking a finger into it and asking yourself: 'Has it a meaning?' You did not hesitate in 1941; but then you were being asked to make a sacrifice. It was simply a matter of preventing the Hitlerite madness from destroying a world where solitary elation was still possible for a few, and you were willing to pay the price for your future moments of elation. Today, things are different. It is no longer about defending the *status quo*, but changing it: this is what you are not willing to accept without the most precise guarantees. And if I thought that History was a pool filled with mire and blood, I expect I should do what you have done and look at it twice before jumping in. But suppose that I am there already, suppose that, from my point of view, your holding back is itself a proof of your historicity. Suppose someone were to answer you as Marx does: 'History does nothing . . . It is man, real and alive, who does everything; History is only the activity of mankind pursuing its own ends.' If that is true, then the person who thinks he is distancing himself from it will cease to share the ends of his contemporaries and will be aware only of the absurdity of human endeavours. But if he rants against them, by the very fact of doing this, against his will, he returns into the historical cycle, because without wanting to he is supplying that one of the two sides which finds itself ideologically on the defensive (that is, the side whose culture is dying), with arguments designed to undermine the opposing one. On the other hand, the person who adheres to the concrete ends of mankind will be obliged to choose his friends, because in a society rent apart by civil war, one can neither share the aspirations of all people, nor reject all of them at one and the same time. But as soon as he does choose, everything acquires a meaning: he knows why the enemy is resisting and why he is fighting. For it is in historical action that one gains an understanding of History. 'Does History have a meaning?' you ask. 'Does it have a purpose?' For me, the question is what has no meaning, because History, apart from man who makes it, is merely an abstract, stagnant concept, and there is no saying whether it has any purpose or not. The problem is not to *know* what the purpose is, but to *give* it one. In any case, nobody acts *solely* with respect to History. In fact, men are involved in short-term projects, lit by distant hopes. And there is nothing absurd about these projects: here we have the Tunisians in revolt against colonialism; there, miners striking to support their own demands or in solidarity with others. We needn't discuss whether or not there are values which transcend History: one may observe simply that, *if there are*, they reveal themselves in human acts which are, by definition, historical. And this contradiction is part of the essence of mankind, who becomes historical in order to pursue the eternal and discovers universal values in the concrete action that he takes in order to achieve a particular outcome. If you say that this world is unjust, you have lost the match: you are already outside, comparing a world without justice to a Justice without content. But you will discover Justice in every effort that you make to govern your business, to divide the tasks up among your comrades, to submit yourself to discipline or to apply it. And Marx never said that History would have an end: how could he have said that? One might as well say that man, one day, will be without any objectives. He merely spoke of an end to prehistory, that is to say an end that will be attained in the midst of History itself, and then surpassed, as all goals are. It is not a matter of knowing whether History has a meaning and if we deign to take part in it, but since we are in it up to our ears, trying to give it the meaning that seems best to us, by not refusing our assistance, however feeble it may be, in any concrete action that may be required.

Terror is abstract violence. You became a terrorist and violent when History – which you rejected – rejected you in its turn, because you were only the abstraction of a rebel. Your suspicion of mankind made you assume that every accused person is *above all* a guilty one: hence your repressive attitude to Jeanson. Your morality changed first of all into moralizing, and is now nothing more than Literature; tomorrow it could well be immorality. I don't know what will become of us: perhaps we shall find ourselves on the same side, perhaps not. Times are hard and mixed. In any event, it is good that I can tell you what I have been thinking. The review is open to you if you wish to reply to me, but I shall not reply to you.

I have said what you were for me and what you are now. Whatever you may say or do in response, I refuse to fight with you. I hope that our silence will lead to this debate being forgotten.

Albert Camus

> When Camus died in a car crash in January 1960, Sartre wrote this brief
> obituary piece which was published in *France-Observateur* on 7 January
> 1960. It was reprinted in *Situations IV* (1964).

Six months ago, or even yesterday, we were wondering: 'What will
he do?' For the time being, riven by contradictions which we ought
to respect, he had chosen silence. But he was one of those rare beings
for whom one can be bothered to wait because they choose slowly
and stick by their choice. One day, he would speak. We did not
even dare venture to speculate on what he would say. But we thought
that, like each one of us, he was changing as the world changed,
and that was enough for him to remain a living presence.

We had quarrelled, Camus and I. A quarrel is nothing – even
though we were not to see one another again; just another way of
living *together*, without losing sight of one another in the narrow
little world where it is our lot to live. It didn't stop me thinking
about him, feeling his eyes fixed on the page of the book, or on the
newspaper that I was reading, and wondering: 'What has he to say
about that? What is he saying about it *now*?'

Sometimes, I considered his silence too cautious, sometimes painful, according to circumstances or my mood; but it was a quality of
every day, like heat or light, though human. One lived with his
ideas or against them, as they were revealed to us in his books –
particularly, *La Chute*, the finest and least well understood – but
always through them. This was an adventure peculiar to French
culture: we tried to pinpoint the different phases of the movement
and to predict where it would eventually lead.

He was the current heir, in this century and at odds with History, to that long line of moralists whose works represent perhaps what is most original in French literature. His humanism, unyielding, narrow and pure, austere and sensual, engaged in a dubious struggle against the mighty and misshapen events of our time. But, conversely, through the stubbornness of his opposition, in the heart of our age, against the Machiavellians and the sacred cow of Realism, he asserted the existence of morality.

One might say that he *was* that unwavering assertion. One had only to read or to reflect, to come up against the human values that he held in his fist: he called political activity into question. One had to bypass him or to assault him: he was, in a word, indispensable for the tension that creates intellectual life. There was even something positive about his silence, these last years: this Cartesian of the Absurd refused to abandon the sure ground of morality and to venture into the uncertain paths of *practice*. We guessed that this was the case and we also guessed at the struggles which he kept to himself: because morality, taken on its own, at the same time demands rebellion and condemns it.

We waited, we had to wait, we had to know: whatever he might eventually have done or decided to do, Camus never ceased to be one of the main forces in our cultural field, and to represent in his own way the history of France and of this century. But we might perhaps have known and understood his itinerary. He had done everything, a whole body of work, and as always everything still remained to be done. He said so, himself: 'My work is ahead of me.' It is finished. The particular scandal of this death is the abolition of the order of mankind by the inhuman.

The human order is still no more than a disorder: it is unjust, precarious; it encompasses murder and starvation; but at least it is founded, maintained and protected by men. That is the order in which Camus had to live: this man, always on the move, called us into question and was himself a question looking for an answer. He was living *in the middle of a long life*; for us, for himself, for those men who preserve the existing order and for those who reject it, it was important for him to emerge from his silence, to take a decision, to reach a conclusion. Others might die of old age, others (always on parole) may die at any moment without this changing the meaning of their lives, or of *life* itself. But for us, who are disoriented and unsure, it was necessary for the best of us to reach the end of the tunnel. Rarely have the characters of his works and the conditions of the historical moment so clearly demanded that a writer should live.

The accident which killed Camus is a scandal, because it demonstrates at the heart of the human world the absurdity of what we demand in the depths of our being. At the age of twenty, suddenly stricken with a malady which was to alter his life, he discovered the absurd – a senseless denial of mankind. He came to terms with it, he thought out his unbearable condition, and he survived. Yet one would think that only his first works tell the truth about his life, since this cured patient has now encountered an unpredictable death, which struck him from outside. The absurd is the question that no one asks him any longer, which he no longer asks anyone, this silence that is not even now a silence, which is absolutely *nothing* any more.

I don't believe it. As soon as it manifests itself, the inhuman becomes part of the human. Every life that stops – even that of such a young man – is *at the same time* a smashed gramophone record and a completed life. For all those who loved him, there is an unbearable absurdity in this death. But we must learn to see this mutilated body of work as the writer's entire works. To the very extent that Camus' humanism contains a *human* attitude towards the death that was to overtake him, to the extent that his proud search for happiness implied and demanded the *inhuman* necessity of death, we may recognize in these works, and in the life that is no longer separable from them, a pure and victorious attempt by a man to reclaim every instant of his existence from his death to come.

Genet

> Sartre's closing vindication of Jean Genet and of his subject-matter, this extract from *Saint Genet* (1952) explores the themes of betrayal, guilt and complicity.

Here is what I have tried to do: to show the limitations of a psychoanalytical interpretation and a Marxist critique, and to prove that only freedom can account for the totality of a person; to reveal this freedom grappling with fate, at first crushed by its misfortunes, then turning against them to absorb them bit by bit; to prove that genius is not a gift, but a means of escape from desperate circumstances; to discover the choice that a writer makes of himself, his life and the meaning of the universe, down to the formal aspects of his style and his composition, down to the structure of his images and the peculiarities of his tastes; and to trace in detail the story of a liberation. The reader must say whether or not I have succeeded.

As I draw to an end, I feel a misgiving: have I been fair to Genet? As far as the man is concerned, I think I have defended him against everyone, sometimes even against himself. Have I been firm enough in defence of the writer? This essay was meant to introduce his work; but suppose it were to turn people away? I know what they might say: 'Let him write what he likes. Do we have to read him? His poems are premeditated crimes; he is trying to base his own salvation on our destruction and to trick us with words: that is a good reason for admiring his books from a distance, while not buying them.'

I admit, Genet does treat his readers as a means to an end; he uses others to talk to himself about himself, and this peculiarity may drive us away from him. When he asks himself: 'Should I steal?' why should he expect the reply to interest *us*? What I write, this writer tells us, is valid only for me; and the public replies: what I take the trouble to read should be valid for everyone. Why doesn't he defend theft? At least we might have an impassioned debate, taking sides for or against his arguments. But he doesn't say that one ought to steal: quite the contrary, he knows that he is wrong to do so, and that he steals in order to be wrong. But he is not even asking us to put ourselves in the wrong; he is not asking anything of us at all. If anyone were to suggest becoming his disciple, I am sure he would reply: 'How could anyone act like me without being me?' This poet 'speaks to us as an enemy': is it worth overcoming the horror he inspires only to discover in the end that he is the only person to whom his message is addressed, and that he pretends to communicate with others only in order to depict himself to his own eyes in his uncommunicable singularity?* Just consider my problem: if I should reveal that there is something to be gained from his works, I am urging people to read them, but betraying him; while if I insist on his singularity, I am again liable to betray him: after all, if he publishes his poems for a wide audience, then he wants to be read. One betrayal against another, I have opted for the first: at least I shall be faithful to myself. I have no criminal record and no liking for young boys; and yet Genet's writings touched me. If they did so, that is because they concern me; and if they concern me, I can profit by them. So let's try to define what is the right way to 'use' Genet.

His work is a game of 'who loses, wins', and you are playing it with him: you will only win if you agree to lose. Let him trick you: above all, don't try to defend yourself by striking poses: it would be quite pointless to put yourself in a state of Christian charity, to love him in advance and to accept the pus that streams from his books with the self-denial of a saint kissing the lips of a leper. Some fine souls have bent over this infected soul; it rewarded them with

---

* In contrast to Montaigne, who also depicts himself in his peculiar individuality, but *for others* and with the idea of communicating with them.

a fart, and was right to do so, because their forced benevolence was only a device to disarm his wiles. You deplore the misfortunes that he suffers only to hide from yourself his free will to cause harm; and it is helping a thief to find excuses for him, while to look for excuses for the poet is to wrong him. And don't try to take refuge in aestheticism, because he will flush you out. I've seen people reading the crudest passages without batting an eyelid: 'These two men sleep together? Then they eat their own excrement? After that, one of them goes and reports the other to the police? So what? It's so well written.' They went no further than Genet's words, to avoid entering his delirium; they admired the form to prevent themselves from *grasping* the content. But form and content are one: the content demands *this particular* form; and if you are content to play the card of amoralism, you will never get beyond the threshold of the work. So what, then? So you must let yourself go, let yourself be taken in, remain yourself, feel naïve indignation. Don't be ashamed to appear foolish: since this fanatical challenge to humanity and all it holds dear is expressly designed to shock, be shocked, and don't fight against the horror and uneasiness that he is trying to create in you; you will only appreciate the pitfalls set by this sophist if you fall into them. 'But, if I express indignation,' you may ask, 'then what difference is there between me and M. Rousseaux?' I know what you mean: M. Rousseaux's fulminations are pathetic, and his criticism manages to sustain such a level of incompetence that one is tempted to adopt the opposite stance to everything that he says. However, this is a necessary test: if we want to win the game, we must take humility to the point of becoming like M. Rousseaux.

This is the only road out of hell: you will be delivered by the horror that Genet inspires in you, provided you use it correctly. What M. Rousseaux is unable to see, and what M. Mauriac, who is more subtle, can see clearly, but conceals, is that horror is *recognition*. If monkeys are petty thieves and dogs are pederasts, you can laugh at it. But Genet disgusts us: therefore he compromises us. And by that I don't mean only that he lights up the murky depths that we would prefer to hide: even if you were as pure as the driven snow, devoid of any repression; even if you were to be as naturally inclined to virtue as the moth to the flame or M. Rousseaux to error, Genet would still disgust you; hence you would still be compromised.

We ask writers to tell us their ideas about general situations. And we, 'normal people', only know 'deviants' from the outside; and if we happen to find ourselves 'situated' with respect to them, it is as judges or entomologists: we were amazed to learn that one of our friends stole the regimental funds or that a shopkeeper in our neighbourhood took a little boy into the back of his shop; we passed judgement on them, condemned them and firmly announced that we 'didn't understand'. If we do sometimes allow a novelist the right to describe these noxious creatures – 'since they exist, since we do come across them' – it's on condition that he contemplates them from outside, as a species.* This amounts to a ban on thieves talking about theft or homosexuals about love. Someone who laughs till he cries when Charpini appears on stage, might not be able to stand reading a single page of *Pompes funèbres*: that's because Charpini is merely an act; but when he expands on the quirks of the homosexual, he makes him into an insect: laughter will provide release. We may, at a pinch, agree for a reformed sinner to confess his sins, but only on condition that he rises above them: the *good* queer has been separated from his vice by remorse and disgust; he no longer indulges in it: he was a wrongdoer, but he has ceased to be one; he speaks of what he was as though he were *Another*, and when we read his confessions, we feel ourselves to be *totally other* than the wretch in question. Proust himself had the slightly cowardly guile to speak of homosexuals as though they were a natural species: he pretends to make fun of Charlus or to feel sorry for him; and, speaking to Gide, he regretted 'the indecision that, in order to give greater weight to the heterosexual part of his book, made him transpose into the realm of *les jeunes filles en fleur* all the grace and tenderness and charm that his own homosexual memories evoked in him, so that only the grotesque and base remained for Sodom'.†

---

* This does not mean that he cannot show us what they think or feel, as long as he employs his art to suggest that an insuperable barrier separates us from them.
† André Gide, *Journal*, Pléiade, p. 694.

After that, what was the point of protesting that he had not 'wanted to stigmatize homoerotic love'.* The fact is that he became the accomplice of his readers. What matters to us, in reality, is that we should not be made to hear the voice of the criminal himself, that sensual and unsettling voice that seduces young men, that breathless voice murmuring in the throes of love, that crude voice recounting a night of pleasure. The pederast must remain an object, flower, insect, an inhabitant of ancient Sodom or distant Uranus, an automaton leaping around in the footlights – anything you wish, except my neighbour, my image, myself. Because we have to choose: if every man is all men, then this deviant must either be merely a pebble, or he must be *me*.

Genet refuses to be a pebble; he never sides with the public prosecutor, he never speaks to us about the pederast and the thief, always as a pederast and a thief. His voice is one of those that we hope never to hear; it is not designed to analyse anxiety, but to communicate it. Speaking of Shakespeare, J. Vuillemin once wrote: 'He sometimes manages to repress the divinity of the spectator . . . In Hamlet, the actor's point of view becomes true . . . the spectator's point of view is transformed in its turn; and while the distinction between stage and auditorium does not vanish, it is blurred. *We participate, instead of seeing.*' And this is just what Genet does: he invents the pederastic *subject*. Before him, the homosexual was the plaything of external forces; whatever he said and thought, we were led to believe that his thoughts and words were effects rather than the expression of a psycho-physiological mechanism. It was enough to show him for us to be reassured: since he was in essence an object for human beings, he fell outside the realm of the human. But Genet justifies himself, contemplates himself and contemplates the world; you can try, if you will, to reduce his vice to a physiological defect: even when you have established that there is something wrong with his glands, you won't have touched this absolute consciousness that approves of itself and chooses itself. A child who had once seen Fernandel a dozen times on the screen met him one day in the street.

* Id., Ibid.

'What!' he exclaimed. 'Does he *exist*?' Reading Genet, we are equally tempted to ask ourselves: 'Does it *exist*, a pederast? Does it think? Does it pass judgement, pass judgement on us, does it see us?' If such a thing exists, everything changes: if pederasty is the choice of a consciousness, it becomes a human possibility. *Mankind* is homosexual, thief and traitor.* Deny that and you deny yourself your finest achievements: you were pleased to break the sound barrier with that pilot, with him *you* stretched the limits of human achievement and, when he appears in public, it is *yourself* that you are cheering. Nothing wrong with that: any human exploit, however unusual it might appear, involves the whole of humanity: this is what Catholics call reversibility of merit. But then you must accept the reversibility of crime, and agree to groan with every queen in some cheap bed or to blow a safe with every cracksman in the world. Remember the story of the child from the state orphanage fostered by brutal peasants who beat him and starved him. At the age of twenty, he couldn't read, so they made him a soldier. When he left the Army, he had learned nothing except how to kill. So he killed. He said: 'I'm a wild animal.' When they asked him at the end of the trial if he had nothing to add, he said: 'The prosecutor asked for my head, and will doubtless have it. But if he had led my life, then perhaps he would be in my place and I, if I had led his, would be putting the case against him.' The court was appalled: everyone in it had glimpsed an abyss, something like a naked existence, undifferentiated, able to be anything and which, according to circumstances, became Hoffmann, Solleilland or the Public Prosecutor – human existence. I am not saying that this is true: it isn't *that* judge who would become *that* criminal. But the argument carried weight and will continue to do so – and the murderer proved it retrospectively: he was pardoned, learned to read, did read and changed. But

---

* Of course, he is *also* heterosexual, honest and loyal. In Antiquity, it was dogmatically argued that, since he can be honest and a thief, then he is neither; the result is that man is nothing. Contemporary thought, seeking the historically concrete, sees concrete humanity as the sum of its contradictions. Since there are lawful forms of sexual relations, there is a human possibility of refusing them and resorting to vice. Conversely, since there are vices, then licit relations become *normal*.

what is important in all this is the vacillation of the self that occurs when certain consciousnesses open before our eyes like a gaping maw: what we had thought to be our most intimate being suddenly takes on the appearance of something contrived. We feel that only an incredible piece of luck has allowed us to escape the vices that disgust us the most in others; in horror we recognize the existence of a *subject*; he is our truth as we are his; our virtues and vices are interchangeable.

Genet invents betrayal and homosexuality for us, they are brought into the human world, the reader sees them as a personal way out, the emergency exit made specially for him. We will not derive any *knowledge* from these poems, either about ourselves or about others: one can only know objects; here, groping our way through the labyrinth of pederastic sophistries that we are obliged to take on board before even understanding them, we are changed into homosexual subjects for ourselves. What remains, once we have shut the book? A feeling of void, darkness and awful beauty, an 'eccentric' experience that we cannot weave into the pattern of our lives, but will always be 'marginal', unabsorbable, the memory of a night of debauchery when we gave ourselves to a man and took pleasure in it. There are books that are addressed to everyone in each of us: when we enter them, we feel that we are the crowd. Genet's books are brothels into which one only slips through a half-open door, hoping not to run into anybody; and once inside, one is all alone. And yet it is from this rejection of universality that they derive their universality: the universal and incommunicable experience that they offer each of us, individually, is that of solitude.

At first, this may not appear to be a very novel theme. A lot of writers have complained of being alone, in what are often agreeable terms: no one could perceive their merits, their genius lifted them so high that they were beyond the reach of others, and so on. But such isolation in pride or melancholy is of interest only to students of comparative literature: spiritual solitude among the great Romantic poets, the solitude of the mystics, solitude in Europe in the Enlightenment, solitude in the Eastern provinces, 1798–1832, or in the French sonnet, in the precursors of Malherbe . . . these are fine essay subjects.

man, quite rich, from a higher social sphere and respectable, who admired her virtue'. In *La Fanfarlo*, this leads to a peculiar twist in the plot: Mme de Cosmelly, rejected and ridiculed by her husband with La Fanfarlo, gets the same treatment for the second time, at her own request, with the same woman from Baudelaire himself, under the name 'Cramer'. The barely disguised subject of the tale is that of the respectable woman scorned and magically violated in the person of a magnificent prostitute; it is frigidity humiliated. But, in *L'Ivrogne*: 'A working man will gladly seize upon the excuse of his over-excited jealousy, to hide from himself the fact that what he chiefly resents in his wife is her resignation, her gentleness, her patience and her virtue.' Here, the hatred of goodness is quite openly expressed. It would lead directly to rape: in the version of 1854 (see his letter to Tisserand) murder is substituted for rape at the last moment, in a fairly absurd manner, as if covering something up: 'Here is the scene of the crime. The man arrives first at the meeting-place which he has chosen. Sunday evening. Dark road or level common. In the distance, the sound of a dance band. A sinister and melancholy landscape on the outskirts of Paris. A love scene as sad as can be imagined between this man and that woman. He wants her to forgive him, he wants her to let him live and come back to her. Never has he thought her so beautiful . . . His expressions of affection are sincere. He is almost in love with her again, he desires her, he begs her. She is all the more interesting for being so pale and thin: this almost acts as a stimulant to him. The audience must guess what is going on. Although the poor woman also feels a return of her former feelings, she rejects his wild passion in such a place. The rejection annoys the husband who attributes her chastity to some adulterous affair or the defence of a lover: "We must have done with this; but I shall never find the courage, I cannot do it myself."' We know what happens. He sends his wife along the road, at the end of which is a well; she falls down it. 'If she escapes, so much the better; if she falls into the well, then God has condemned her.'

One can see the symbolic richness of this fantasy: the crime is premeditated and it sets the underlying tone of the relationship between Baudelaire, the drunkard, and his wife (his mother, Marie and a soiling imposed on Good which leaves Good as pure and virginal and unpolluted as before. It is a *white* sin, blank, sterile, which evaporates into thin air at the very moment of its commission, leaving no memory and having no effect, but at the same time ratifying the inalterable everlastingness of the law, and the eternal youth and the eternal availability of the sinner. But this white magic of love does not exclude black magic. Since he is unable to transcend Good, as we have seen, Baudelaire slyly sets out to depreciate it from beneath: hence the fact that the masochism of frigidity is accompanied by sadism. The frigid woman is a feared judge, but in addition a victim. For Baudelaire, while the act of love involves three people – if the idol appears before him at the moment when he is indulging in his vices in the company of a prostitute – this is not only because he needs an observer and a strict witness; it is also because he wants to make her ridiculous. She is the one that he is striking when he penetrates his paid whore. He is deceiving her and polluting her. It is as though Baudelaire, from a horror of exercising any direct action on the universe, were seeking for magic (that is, long-distance) influences, no doubt because they are less compromising. In this way, the frigid woman becomes the *respectable wife* whose very respectability is faintly ridiculous, and whose husband is unfaithful to her with common tarts. This is what is implied by the peculiar Fanfarlo: here, coldness becomes clumsiness and inexperience; and when the loving wife forces herself to engage in sexual practices which revolt her in order to keep her husband, there is even something obscene about her frigidity. In the same way, the 'blank' sexual act of the woman who does not experience sexual pleasure – possession in a void, almost at a distance and without pollution – is sometimes transformed purely and simply into rape. Like Mme Aupick, like Marie Daubrun, all Baudelaire's heroines 'love someone else': this is the guarantee of their coldness. And this happy rival is endowed with every good quality. In *La Fanfarlo*, M. de Cosmelly is 'noble, honest'; people talk about 'his finest qualities'; he adopts with everyone 'a commanding manner that was at once amiable and irresistible'. In *L'Ivrogne*, an outline for a play that was never written, the drunkard's wife was attracted to 'a young could be at once subject and object, some for others and some through others, and if we could abolish ourselves together in an objective totality, or if we were always, as in the Kantian 'City of Ends', subjects recognizing ourselves as subjects, then the divisions would fall away. But one cannot go to the extreme in either direction: we cannot all be objects, except for one transcendent subject, nor all subjects unless we were firstly to undertake the impossible task of liquidating all objectivity. As for absolute reciprocity, it is concealed by historical conditions of class and race, by nationality, by social hierarchies; a boss is never an object to his subordinates, or he is lost; he is rarely a subject for his superiors. So, normally, we live in a sort of familiar and unconsidered state of indistinctness: we pass by unnoticed; in our jobs, in our families, in the party, we are neither entirely objects nor altogether subjects. The Other is the instrument that obeys commands, regulates, divides, distributes and is, at the same time, the diffuse, warm atmosphere surrounding us; this is what we are, too, for others and consequently for ourselves. However, this immediate lack of distinction contains the seed of disequilibrium: you are with everyone, you write for everyone, you appeal to God to witness, or to humanity, or history, or your next-door neighbour; you are the tame instrument of a family, a milieu, a profession, a party, a Church; you get your thoughts from outside, through the papers, the radio, lectures and speeches, then immediately redistribute them; you don't stay an instant without speaking or listening, and you never say or hear anything except the things that any other person would have said or heard in your place; from dawn to dusk you suffer the tyranny of the human face; you have no secrets, and no mystery, and you don't want to have any – and yet, in a certain fashion, you are alone. And I am not locating this solitude in private life, which is only a sector of public life, or in our tastes, which are social and shared: I find it everywhere. Being a negation, it is the negative of our loves, our actions, our personal and political life. It is neither subjectivity as such nor objectivity, but the relationship of one to the other when this is experienced as a failure. It arises at the very heart of communication, like poetry at the heart of all prose, because the most clearly expressed

Those people were not alone – or else we should have to believe in the solitude of adolescents 'whom nobody loves and nobody understands'; invisible armies gathered about their heads and future hands were crowning them with laurels. Stendhal was not alone: he anticipated 1880 and the 'happy few'; Keats more so: 'My name is writ on water'; but the desperate words that he had engraved on his tomb were still addressed to *others*. You are not truly alone as long as your thoughts are communicable, even if misfortune prevents you from communicating them, nor if you believe you are right, even against everyone, nor if you are sure that you are doing Good, nor if you succeed in your endeavours; you are not truly alone as long as you have a secret court to absolve you. For a long time we believed in the social atomism that we inherited from the eighteenth century, and thought of man as a solitary entity from birth who only subsequently entered into relationships with his fellow beings. In this way, solitude appeared as our original state; in favourable cases, one might emerge from it, but with a little bad luck, one could slip back. We know now that this is balderdash. The truth is that 'human reality' is 'being-in-society' as it is 'being-in-the-world'. Hence it is not nature, nor is it a state, but a becoming. Since a child knows himself first of all as son, grandson, nephew, worker, bourgeois, French, etc., and since he defines himself bit by bit through his behaviour, solitude is a certain aspect of our relations with others and an aspect that reveals itself in certain modes of behaviour that we adopt towards society.*

Man, Marx said, is an object for mankind. That is true. But it is also true that I am a subject for myself to the very extent that my fellow man is an object in my eyes: this is what divides us; he and I are not *homogeneous*, we cannot be part of a single whole except in the eyes of a third party who perceives both of us as a single object. If all of us, in perfect simultaneity and perfect reciprocity,

---

* Physical isolation is not solitude. A colonial stuck out in the bush may long for home, and miss his family, friends and wife. But since he is still part of society, and his relatives and his fellow-men have not ceased to approve of him and love him, he remains integrated with *all*; his relation to others has just moved from concrete to abstract, without changing in kind.

and understood ideas conceal something that is incommunicable: I can have them thought as I think them, but not lived as I live them. We find it in the depth of mutual love: when you cannot make your wife share a taste that you have in common with thousands of unknown strangers, when you remain separated from her at the heart of pleasure. In these examples, subjectivity is unable to break down objectivities. But we are *also* alone when we cannot make ourselves *objects enough*: surrounded, supported, fed and restored by your party, you would like to be nothing more than a cell in this great organism, yet you feel your solitude for the simple reason that the possibility is always there of leaving it, and your very loyalty is intentional, or else out of fear of one day being led to criticize the leaders and to refuse obedience, in short by the anguish that you feel when confronted by your own freedom – and to the precise extent that you are *not* the stick or the corpse that you are trying to make yourself. The victor is alone because he cannot identify entirely with the fine object that is being paraded in triumph; so, by his hidden defeat. This vague sense of a mismatch between subjective and objective would still be nothing, since we spend our time concealing it from ourselves; but our professional mistakes, our blunders, our slip-ups and our mishaps suddenly exasperate it: error, shortcoming and misconduct create a void around us; at once, others *see* us, we emerge from our primitive indistinctness, we become objects; at the same time we *feel ourselves being looked at*, we feel ourselves go pale or blush: now we are subjects. In short, our solitude is the way we feel our objectivity for the Other, in our subjectivity and in the event of a failure. At the extreme, the criminal and the madman are pure objects and solitary subjects; their frenzied subjectivity is taken to the point of solipsism at the moment when they are reduced for all others to the state of pure manipulated *thing*, of pure *being-there* with no future, prisoners who have to be dressed and undressed, and fed by hand. On one side is dream, autism and absence; on the other, the concentration camp; on one side, the impotent shame and hatred that turns against itself and vainly defies the heavens; on the other, the opaque being of the pebble, mere 'human material'. Whoever becomes conscious in himself of this explosive contradiction knows true solitude, that of the monster, a failure of both Nature and Society; this latent, hidden solitude which is our lot and which we try not to mention – he lives it to the extreme, to the limits of the possible. One is not alone if one is in the right, because the Truth must out; nor if one is in the wrong, because one has only to confess one's sins for them to be wiped away. One is alone when one is in the right and in the wrong *at the same time*: when one feels oneself to be right as subject – because one is conscious and alive, and one cannot and will not deny what one has willed – and when one feels oneself to be wrong as object, because one cannot reject the objective condemnation of Society as a whole. There is only one road to go down into the solitude of the unique being: that of error and failure, which leads through impotence and despair. You will be alone if you know that, in the eyes of everybody, you are no more than a guilty object, while your conscience, despite itself, continues to accord you its approval. You will be alone if Society abolishes you and you cannot annihilate yourself: Genet's 'impossible nullity' is solitude. But it is not enough to know it; one must live it, and hence do it: from that point, two attitudes become possible.

Bukharin[1] conspires; that does not mean that he is opposed *as a subject* to the policy of the government: he does what the objective situation demands. Everything is conducted between objects: objective deviations demand an objective correction of course, nothing more. Had he seized the levers of command in time, the Revolution would have continued without a hitch: who in the USSR would have dared criticize a change in the ruling group? If Bukharin had won, he would have remained a stick and a corpse, an instrument wielded by history, and it would not have been he who changed things, but things that were changed by him. And since, as Merleau-Ponty says:[*] 'The paradox of history ... consists in the fact that a contingent future appears once it has come into the present as real,

---

1. *Bukharin*: Nikolai Bukharin (1888–1938), a Bolshevik political leader, associate of Lenin. He was executed by Stalin on false charges of counter-revolutionary activity.
* Merleau-Ponty, *Humanisme et terreur*.

not to say necessary'; so the manifest necessity of his victory would have completed his dissolution into the historical process. But he failed; and now, on the contrary, the necessity of his defeat shows him that his venture was impossible, and that it was rejected *a priori* by objective reality: it had only the consistency of a shadow and could only derive from a shadow, that nothingness: a Communist turning against history.* Bukharin learns what he is not and what he will not do: he *is not* the historical process, he *will not* accomplish the prescribed correction of course. Now that history has rejected him, he doesn't define himself in his own eyes except as *non-being*: he is the one who has *not* succeeded, who *could not have* succeeded; he is error, he is powerlessness. Does he preserve the hope that others will one day succeed? Perhaps, but these will be other men, with other means, in other circumstances. Their victory will demonstrate that his venture was useless and premature; it will make him more guilty than ever; whatever happens, history can only put him in the wrong: it did not choose him, he chose himself; wrong, error, presumption, failure, powerlessness: these negations define him in his own eyes as a *subject*. A subject by default and not because of excess: through everything that he did not understand, everything that he did not do. Subject because of the nothingness within him – an impossible nullity. So does he think that he was mistaken even in his assessment of the historical circumstances? Probably not, but it was not the moment to correct these deviations; history was taking a different course, slower but surer, the only possible and the only necessary one; it was not for *him* to reason and to reflect; he *was wrong to be right*. And since his plan was to lead to catastrophe, it was flawed from the start. 'Here we have a hard concept of responsibility, which is not to do with what men intended, but what

---

* The Christian who has turned away from God is afflicted by a similar nothingness. For him the Worst is not certain. In Marxist terms: a single traitor is not enough to deflect the course of history. Jouhandeau's[2] abasement, which revealed to him his *person* in and through the radical inadequacy of his being, is the religious equivalent of Bukharin's treachery.

2. *Jouhandeau*: Marcel Jouhandeau (1888–1979), an unorthodox, tormented Catholic novelist.

they discover they have done, in the light of events.' An opposition that takes power can save a country in danger; an opposition that fails can only weaken it. 'In the light of events,' Bukharin discovers at one and the same time his subjectivity and his treason. Of course, he did not mean to betray, but that is not enough; he should have meant not to betray, and so kept quiet; once again, he is reproached with a nothingness, an absence in intention; in the same way, the car driver is found guilty of manslaughter *through negligence*, that is for *not having thought* to slow down: for what was not in his mind, not for what was there. Thus he is a traitor. A traitor for having taken the risk, in the event of failure, of serving the enemies of the Revolution; a traitor for having let go of objectivity, for having judged as a subject and having accepted the possibility that his attempted move would remain subjective, that is to say would be a failure and damage the building of socialism; a traitor not for having departed from revolutionary principles, but on the contrary because he still accepted them at the moment when he put the Revolution at risk. Since he cannot appeal to his former comrades, who are condemning him, nor to the enemies whom he continues to hate, nor to posterity which may perhaps not accuse him of treachery but which will classify him among the unfortunates and blunderers of history, he is alone. All he can find in himself is nothingness and failure. And since he is nothingness, he turns violently against this subjectivity which isolates him; his last action – alas, still subjective – is to annihilate himself; he refuses to listen to his own evidence and to see anything else in himself but an object. He will no longer be anything other than the traitor that everyone takes him for, a stick still, if a broken one: he confesses his treason. This is the first attitude: the solitary man escapes his solitude by a moral suicide; rejected by mankind, he becomes a pebble among pebbles.

Here is the second attitude (for Genet is the Bukharin of bourgeois society). The chosen victim of a compact and militant community, he has been cast into a ditch while it continues on its way. He, too, has discovered his solitude through failure and powerlessness, and he knows that bourgeois history will eternally judge him to be in the wrong. Alone because he continues to assert the principles by which he is condemned, as Bukharin right to the end maintained the revolutionary principles in the name of which he was executed. 'Since the accused Marxists . . . are in agreement with the accusation on the principle of historical responsibility, they become their own accusers and, to discover their subjective honesty, we have to go through their own statements as well as the indictment against them.' This sentence, by Merleau-Ponty, can be applied word for word to Genet: agreeing as he does with the court on the sacred value of private property, he becomes his own prosecutor in the name of the fundamental principle of the bourgeoisie that rejects him. In short, like Bukharin, he discovers his subjectivity by judging himself according to the objective criteria of his society. Both of them confessed; once the deposition has been signed, one will be a traitor for ever and the other a rogue in the eyes of eternity.

The difference is that Bukharin humbly confesses his treachery, while Genet is proud of his. Of course, Bukharin cannot entirely destroy that subjectivity which he has discovered in defeat, and which he condemns with his judges: 'Though he does not accept the idea of personal honour . . . he does defend his revolutionary honour and rejects the accusation of spying and sabotage.' On the eve of death, he was still revising his defeat; this pure nothingness that was unable to annihilate itself tried to the end to make liveable the impossibility of living. But Genet belongs to another society, which has other myths and other manners: and since bourgeois society recognizes each person's right to exist, this is the right that he asserts. As the corrupt member of a revolutionary society, Bukharin persists in calling himself revolutionary; while Genet, the black sheep of a 'liberal' society, demands in the name of liberalism the right to life for the monster he has become. In other words, he stubbornly persists in his failure, clings to his peculiarities, raises the cost of exiling him and, since he is now nothing more than nothingness, makes himself a consciousness proud of not being; powerless, wicked, unreasoned, and wishing to be so to the point of annihilation, he will be no more than the narrow limit that separates negativity from nothingness, non-being from the consciousness of being nothing. The negation of everything, including the negation of negation, he chooses in the light of his failure to be pure, incommunicable, non-recoverable subjectivity, wavering between the Nothingness that can annihilate him and the Nothing that makes itself exist through the sole consciousness of not being. He is bound to the pillory; the Righteous come and spit in his face and list his wrongdoings; but, unlike Bukharin, he proclaims to all that *he is right to be wrong*. He justifies himself *alone*, knows that his testimony will not be enough and persists in it *because of* its inadequacy: his boast is to have been *impossibly* right and to bear witness to all of the impossibility of everything. Do you finally understand who Genet is? Remember Merleau-Ponty's remark about Bukharin which caused such a fuss: 'Every opponent is a traitor, but every traitor is only an opponent.' Not sharing the principles of Soviet society, you describe Bukharin as a defeated opponent and you are indignant at the idea that he can be called a traitor. So, then, admit that this Genet, who appals you, may, in the eyes of those who do not share your principles, be merely a defeated opponent of bourgeois society. I know that he inspires sincere disgust in you. But do you think that Bukharin does not inspire disgust in the faithful Communist and the Stakhanovite? In any given society, the guilty person is solitary and the solitary person is guilty; there is no other way of fully accepting solitude than to admit the sin and, consequently, to inspire horror; because solitude is the social relationship itself when lived in despair, it is the negative relation of each person to all persons. The origin of Genet is *clumsiness* – a contraceptive would have been enough to ensure no Genet – then *rejection* – someone rejected this hated outcome of a mistake – then *failure* – the child was unable to integrate in the milieu that took him in. Clumsiness, rejection, failure: all add up to a *No*. And since the objective essence of the kid is No, Genet gave himself a personality by giving himself the subjectivity of No. He is the absolute opponent because he is opposed to Being and to any integration. As a taboo object for all, he makes himself a sacred subject for himself and the subjectivity that he demands is a proud integration of pure being-there-in-the-eyes of the object, of the tube of vaseline,[3] for example. A pure thing – which Bukharin will only become through confession and the death that immediately follows it – and unassimilable (*because it is a thing*) into a society of subjects-objects: here is Genet, first and foremost; and his subjectivity is only the interiorization of his 'thingness' as a separating inertia. The insolence with which the tube of vaseline despises the indignant cops, is merely its *inertia*, an inertia lived out and acted as bravado by the guilty man, a consciousness, fearfully active and restless, which *becomes passivity*: this is the *person* of Genet as a singularity. But also as a universal: theft, pederasty and betrayal, as the contents of this singular essence, come afterwards: 'first, one must be guilty', that is, *an object for everyone*. By demanding absolute objectivity, Genet ceases to be a particular opponent of *one* historical society: he embodies for everyone the pure form of opposition reduced to powerlessness. For everyone: for you, for me, for each reader. Because we are all *simultaneously* victorious conformists and defeated opponents. All of us, in the depths of ourselves, hide a scandalous schism which, were it to be revealed, would suddenly change us into 'an object of reproach'; isolated, blamed for our failures, above all in minor matters, we all know the agony of being in the wrong and not being able to consider ourselves wrong, of being right and not being able to justify ourselves. We all swing between the temptation of preferring ourselves to everything because our consciousness is for us the centre of the world, and the temptation of preferring everything to our consciousness; defeated in debate, we have all built 'tourniquets', moulded sophistries, in order to delay the moment of objective defeat, when we already knew ourselves to be beaten in our hearts, so that we can sustain our mistake, that nothingness, even longer against the dazzling fullness of the evidence, thus becoming kings of shadows and masks: so hard is it for consciousness – which is, in principle, self-approval – to conceive its errors and its death. In his latest article for *La Table ronde*, Thierry

---

3. *the tube of vaseline*: a reference to the opening pages of Genet's autobiographical *Thief's Journal*. The tube of vaseline, evidence of his passive homosexuality, exposes him to the scorn of the police who have arrested him.

Maulnier talks about: 'one of the strangest, most debased inventions of our age, which are those Chinese meetings of accusation at which the crowd in a town or village gathers and enjoys the agony and repentance, the pale and sweating faces of the accused, then itself condemns them by a show of hands, with anonymity, irresponsibility and supreme cowardice, before once more enjoying the sight of the verdict on the faces of the condemned prisoners and following them to the place of execution, to watch them die amid cries of joy, derision and insults'.* This is certainly base; but why 'Chinese'? Or else we are all Chinese without knowing it, Chinese victims and Chinese executioners, because these accusation meetings seem to me the image of our condition: accusers with everyone, we are also, at the same time, alone and accused by all. Since the social relationship is ambiguous and always involves a measure of failure; since we are simultaneously the Chinese crowd laughing and the terrified Chinese person being dragged to execution; since every thought divides as much as it unites; since every word draws us together through what it expresses and isolates us by what it does not; since an impassable abyss separates the subjective certainty we have of ourselves and the objective truth that we are for others; since we do not cease to consider ourselves guilty even when we are innocent; since events transform our best intentions into criminal desires, not only in history but in the heart of family life; since we can never be sure of not retrospectively becoming traitors; since we constantly fail to communicate, to love, to make ourselves loved – and every failure forces us to an awareness of our loneliness; since at one moment we dream of effacing our criminal singularity by humbly confessing it, and at another of asserting it defiantly in the vain hope of taking it entirely upon ourselves; since we are conformists in daylight, but defeated and wicked in the privacy of our souls; since the guilty person's only recourse and only dignity is stubborn obstinacy, sulking, 'bad faith' and resentment; since we cannot either tear ourselves away from the objectivity that is crushing us, nor divest ourselves of the subjectivity that is exiling us; since it

---

* Thierry Maulnier, 'Mort courageusement', *La Table ronde*, January 1952.

is not permitted us either to raise ourselves to the state of being nor to plunge ourselves into nothingness; since we are, when all's said and done, *impossible nonentities*, we must listen to the voice of Genet, our neighbour, our brother. He pushes to the extreme that latent, concealed solitude that is our own; he blows up our sophistries until they burst; he enlarges our failures to the point of catastrophe; he exaggerates our bad faith until it becomes intolerable for us; and he exposes our guilt in the full light of day. It is true: whatever society succeeds this one, its readers will continue to put him in the wrong because he is opposed to *all society*; but this is the very reason why we are his brothers, because our age has a guilty conscience with regard to history. There have been more criminal periods, but they cared nothing for posterity; while others made history with a quiet conscience: men did not feel cut off from the future, they felt that they were creating it and that their children would agree with them: the succession of generations was only an environment in which they felt at ease. Nowadays, revolutions are impossible and we are threatened by the most bloody and idiotic war; the property-owning classes are no longer very sure of their rights and the working class is in retreat; we can perceive injustice more clearly than ever, yet we have neither the means nor the will to redress it; however the dramatic progress of science gives an obsessive presence to the centuries to come: the future is here, more present than the present. Perhaps we will go to the moon, perhaps we will create life. Those men, their features hidden, who are to succeed us and who will have an understanding of everything that we cannot even imagine, seem to be judging us; our age will be an object to those future eyes whose look haunts us. And a guilty object. They unveil to us our failure and our guilt. Already dead, already *thing* – even though we have yet to live it – our age is *alone* in history and this historical solitude determines our very perceptions: what we see *will no longer be*; people will laugh at our ignorance and become indignant at our sins. What resource remains to us? There is one, which I can see and which I shall describe elsewhere; but the general line for the time being is to settle into this moment in history and to want it, against all and with the stubbornness of the defeated; we invent sophistries to uphold principles which we know will vanish and truths which we know will becomes errors. This is why Genet the sophist is one of the heroes of our time. He is pinned to the pillory before our eyes – as we are in the eyes of the centuries – and the Righteous will not cease blaming him any more than History will cease to blame our age. Genet is us; that is why we should read him. Of course, he wants to charge us with crimes that we have not committed, or even dreamed of committing. What matter? Just wait to be accused: the technique has been perfected, you will make a full confession; and *that means* you will be guilty. From that point on, you have only to choose: either to be Bukharin or Genet. Bukharin, or our desire to *be together*, taken to the extreme of martyrdom; Genet, or our solitude taken to the extreme of Crucifixion.

If we preserve hope and a strong will to escape from these alternatives, if there is still time to do so and, by a final effort, to reconcile object and subject, we must – if only once and in the realm of the imaginary – make real the latent solitude that gnaws away our action and our thoughts. We spend our time fleeing from the objective into the subjective and from subjectivity to objectivity: this game of hide-and-seek will only end the day when we have the courage to go to the end of ourselves in both directions at once. For the time being, we must conjure up the subject, the guilty party, that monstrous and miserable beast that we are in danger at any minute of becoming. Genet holds the mirror up to us: we must look at ourselves in it.

Tintoretto: The Prisoner of Venice

First published in *Les Temps modernes* in November 1957 and reprinted in *Situations IV* (1964), this was part of a book about Tintoretto, abandoned when almost completed.

THE WILES OF JACOPO

Nothing. A life swallowed up. A few dates, a few facts and the prattling of old writers. But we should not be put off: *Venice speaks to us*; its voice, that of a lying witness, sometimes high-pitched, sometimes whispering, interspersed with silence, is his voice. The story of Tintoretto, a portrait of the artist painted in his lifetime by his native city, betrays an unfailing animosity. The City of the Doges tells us that she has taken a strong dislike to the most famous of her sons. Nothing is said openly: it is intimated, suggested, then the subject is dropped. This unyielding hatred is as shifting as sand: more than open aversion, it is a coldness, a sullen mood, the insidiousness of an ungraspable rejection. But that is all we need to know. Jacopo fought an uncertain battle against this uncountable enemy, wearied, was defeated and died; that, in broad outline, is his life. We shall see all of it, in its sombre nakedness, if we push aside for a moment the undergrowth of slander that bars our way.

Jacopo was born in 1518. His father was a dyer. Straight away, Venice murmurs in our ear that this was a very bad beginning: *in around 1530, the boy joined Titian's studio as an apprentice, but after a few days, the famous painter, then in his fifties, realized his genius and kicked him out.* Just like that. This anecdote is relayed by everyone and eventually impresses us through constant repetition.

Titian doesn't come out of it well, you might say. And he doesn't, at least, not *today*, not in our eyes. But when Vasari recorded it, in 1567, Titian had reigned for half a century: nothing is more respectable than a long period of impunity. And then, according to the rules of the day, he was master after God in his own studio: no one would deny him the right to dismiss one of his employees. On the contrary, it is the victims who are assumed to be guilty: branded by misfortune, perhaps contagious, they carry the evil eye. In short, this is the first time that an unhappy childhood has appeared in the gilded annals of Italian painting. I feel sure that there is something to be made of that – but later. The Voice of Venice never lies, provided we are able to hear it, and we shall listen to it when we are better informed. For the time being, whatever may be the deeper truth, we must merely emphasize the improbability of the facts.

Titian was a notoriously difficult man. But Jacopo was twelve years old. At twelve, a gift is nothing, a trifle can wipe it out; it takes patience and time to harden a delicate facility and transform it into talent; even the most touchy artist is not, at the height of his fame, going to take offence at a mere boy. But suppose that we accept that the Master did jealously dismiss his apprentice: this is equivalent to killing him. A curse from someone so universally famous is a heavy, very heavy burden, especially since Titian was not honest enough to reveal his true motives. He was the king, he frowned; and all doors closed to the black sheep. He was denied access to the profession itself.

It is not every day that you see a child put on a blacklist. Our interest is aroused: we want to know how he escaped from this dreadful situation. We want in vain: immediately, in all the books, the thread of the narrative is broken and we come up against a conspiracy of silence: nobody will tell us what became of him between the ages of twelve and twenty. Some have tried to fill the gap by suggesting that he must have trained himself. But this, at least, we do know must be impossible, and writers in the past knew it even better than we: in the early sixteenth century, the art of painting was still a technically complicated, faintly ceremonial business, involving a whole mass of recipes and rituals: it meant acquiring skills rather than understanding, a set of procedures rather than a method, while professional rules, traditions and trade secrets all helped to make an apprenticeship a social obligation and a necessity. The silence of the biographers shows that they are embarrassed. Unable to explain the contradiction of young Robusti's early fame and his excommunication, they cast a veil over the eight years separating one from the other. This amounts to an admission: no one expelled Jacopo. Since he did not wither away or die of resentment at his father's dye-shop, he must have been working regularly and normally in the studio of a painter about whom we know nothing, except that *he was not* Titian. In mistrustful and close-knit social groups, hatred is retroactive: if the mysterious beginning of this life seems like a premonition of its mysterious end, if the curtain, which has risen on a miraculously interrupted shipwreck, then falls on one where there is no miracle, it is because Venice arranged everything after the event, so that the child would be marked by his future old age. Nothing happens, nothing lasts; birth is the mirror image of death; between the two is scorched earth, eaten away by misfortune.

Let us pass right through these mirages; on the far side, the air is clear and one can see to the horizon: what rises before us is an adolescent setting off at full speed and racing for glory. As early as 1539, Jacopo left his master to set up on his own: he was a *past master*. This young employer had acquired independence, a name and a clientele; he took on workers and apprentices of his own. Make no mistake: in a city bursting with painters, where an economic crisis was threatening to stifle the market, becoming a master at twenty was the exception. To achieve it, it was not enough to be deserving, hard-working and good with people; you needed good luck. Robusti had everything going for him: Paolo Caliari was ten years old, Titian was sixty-two. Between this unknown child and an old man who would surely not be around for much longer, one might find a lot of good painters, but only Tintoretto gave signs of excellence: in his own generation, at least, he had no equal, so the road was clear ahead. And indeed for a few years more he did continue his upward career: commissions flowed in, and he was popular with the public, with the patricians and with connoisseurs.

Aretino himself deigned to congratulate him. Here is a young man enjoying the supernatural gifts that Fate bestows on young men who are about to die.

He didn't die, and his troubles began. Titian went on living for an appallingly long time and was assiduous in the malicious attention he paid to his young rival; the old monarch was unkind enough to appoint his own official successor and, as one might have guessed, it was Veronese. Aretino's condescension turned to rancour: criticism was starting to pinch, bite, scratch and howl; in short, it was entering the modern era. This would still have been nothing if Jacopo had retained the favour of the public; but, suddenly, the wheel turned. At thirty, confident in his talent, he asserted himself, painting *Saint Mark Saving the Slave* and putting everything of himself into it. It was just like him to hit hard, evoke a gasp of astonishment and triumph by surprise. But, for once, he was the first to be surprised: the work astonished his contemporaries, but it also outraged them. He met with relentless critics, but no equally passionate defenders. One suspects that, behind the scenes, there was a conspiracy: everything came to a halt.* Face to face, united and divided by the same feeling of unease, Venice and her painter looked at one another with incomprehension. 'Jacopo has not kept the promise of his youth,' said the City. And the artist replied: 'To disappoint them I had only to show myself; so it was not *me* that they loved.' The misunderstanding degenerated into a mutual exchange of abuse: a stitch had come undone in the weave of Venice.

This turning-point came in the year 1548: before that, the gods were for him, afterwards, against. There were no major disasters, just small pieces of bad luck, but they would mount up until he choked: they had only smiled on the child, the better to destroy the man. Overnight, Jacopo changed into himself, becoming that frenzied, hunted outlaw, Tintoretto. *Before*, we know nothing about him, except that he worked himself nearly to death: one cannot make a name for oneself at the age of twenty without relentless

---

* Ridolfi even claims that the Scuola San Marco rejected the painting and Tintoretto had to take it home.

hard work. *Afterwards*, the perseverence became furious anger: he wanted to produce, constantly to produce, to sell, to crush his rivals by the sheer number and size of his pictures. There is something desperate in the way he piles on the pressure: until his death, Robusti was to be in a race against time, and it is impossible to decide whether he is trying to find himself in work or to escape from himself in overwork. Tintoretto-the-thunderbolt sailed under the skull-and-crossbones, a swift pirate to whom all means were fair – but with a marked preference for foul ones. Disinterested whenever there was something to gain by disinterest, he would lower his eyes and refuse to name a price, like a luggage porter: 'It shall be as you wish . . .' But porters know better than anyone that there is a scale of charges for carrying baggage, and they count on the customer to fleece himself, out of generosity.

At other times, in order to secure an order, he would offer the goods at cost price, a ruinous deal that would bring better ones in its wake. He learns that the *Crociferi* are on the point of commissioning Paolo Caliari and, pretending to know nothing about it, goes and offers them his own services. They try to send him away politely: 'We would be delighted, but we want a Veronese.' 'Very well, a Veronese,' he says. 'And who is going to do it for you?' They are somewhat nonplussed at this, and answer: 'But we thought that Paolo Caliari was just the person . . .' Now it is Tintoretto who is amazed: 'Caliari? What an odd notion. I'll do a better Veronese for you than he can, and cheaper into the bargain.' Everything is signed and sealed. The same thing happened twenty times: he also 'did' Pordenones and Titians, always at cut price.

The question that tormented him was how to cut costs. One day, he found his answer, at once mean and inspired; it would overturn a whole tradition. The masters habitually had their paintings copied; the studio would make these copies and be sure to set a good price for them, which meant that there was a second market in works of art. In order to win over the customers for this kind of work, Jacopo offered them *something better* for *less*: he cut out copying. Instead, his assistants would be inspired by his works, but forbidden to copy them. All they had to do was to reverse the composition, putting what was on the right, to the left, and vice versa, or to take an old man from another picture and substitute him for a woman, who was thus freed to serve elsewhere. The procedure required some training, but took no longer than simple copying; and Tintoretto could say quite openly: 'Here you can get an original for the price of a copy.'

When no one wanted to buy his pictures, he gave them away. On 31 May 1564, the Presidency of the Confraternity at the Scuola San Rocco decided it would decorate the chamber where it used to meet, putting a painted canvas in the oval in the centre of the ceiling. Paolo Caliari, Jacopo Robusti, Sciavone, Salviati and Zuccaro were invited to submit their sketches. Tintoretto bribed some servants and got the precise measurements. He had already worked for the Confraternity and it is not impossible that he had accomplices in its governing body, the Banca e Zonta. On the appointed day, each artist was to show his drawing. When Robusti's turn came, lo and behold: the artist climbed up a ladder, took away a board and unveiled above them a dazzling picture, already in place, completely finished. There was an uproar. So he explained: 'A drawing may be misunderstood and while I was about it, I preferred to carry on to the end. But, gentlemen, if my work does not please you, I shall give it away. Not to you: to your patron, San Rocco, who has shown me such favour.' This was the trump card, and he knew it, the rogue: the statutes of the Confraternity forbade them to refuse any pious donation. There was nothing for it but to record the event in the records of the Scuola: 'On this day, the undersigned Jacopo Tintoretto, painter, donated a picture to us; he demands no remuneration, agrees to complete the work if required and proclaims himself satisfied.' And the undersigned, in his turn, wrote: '*Io Jachomo Tentoretto pitor contento et prometo ut supra.*'

Contento? I should think he was! His gift caused a panic among his rivals: it opened every door in the Scuola to him, delivered vast areas of unpainted wall space over to his brush and eventually brought him an annual pension of 100 ducats. Indeed, he was so *contento* that he played the same trick again in 1571, this time at the Doges' Palace. The Signoria wanted to commemorate the Battle of Lepanto, so it organized a competition, asking artists to submit sketches. Tintoretto brought a painting and donated it. It was gratefully accepted. Shortly afterwards, he sent in his bill.

One might be tempted to see the base cunning of this charming rogue as a characteristic of the times rather than the man. The trickster was not Tintoretto, but his century, you might say; and up to a point you would be right. If he were to be arraigned on the strength of these stories, I know just what the defence might say. First of all this, the most serious argument: in those days no one could *work for himself*. In our times, painting is a picture sale, but then the market was in painters. They offered themselves in the town square like *braccianti* in small towns in the South. Purchasers came, examined all of them, then chose one whom they took back to their church, their *scuola* or their *palazzo*. So you had to make yourself available and have yourself seen, like a film director today, accepting any work just as a director will take on any script, in the wild hope of being able to prove himself. Everything was laid down in the contract: the subject; the number, status and sometimes even the pose to be adopted by the characters; and the size of the painting. Further constraints came from religious tradition and the demands of good taste. Customers would have the same kind of moods and whims as a film producer today – and (God help us!) the same sudden flashes of inspiration: they would nod and everything had to be done over again. In the Medici Palace, Benozzo Gozzoli suffered extended, exquisite torture at the hands of half-witted patrons; as for Tintoretto, one has only to compare the *Paradise* in the Louvre with that in the Doges' Palace to guess the pressures he must have been under. Intransigence, a refusal to compromise, a haughty preference for poverty were not an option: the family had to be fed and the studio kept in working order, just like a modern machine. In a word, one had either to give up painting, or paint to order. No one can blame Tintoretto for wanting to make money. Certainly, around the mid-point in his life, he was never without work and did not lack cash; he was a utilitarian who went on the principle that one should do nothing for nothing: painting would only be a hobby if it was not a money-making concern. Eventually, we shall see him buying a comfortable, plebeian home in a working-class quarter: he was set up and this was the high point in his career. But it cost him all his savings, and the Robusti children would have only a paltry inheritance between them: the studio equipment, a declining clientele and, of course, the house itself, which went to the eldest son and then to the son-in-law. Twelve years after her husband's death, Faustina bitterly recalled that he had left his family in financial difficulties; and she was right to complain: the deceased had always done just as he pleased. He undoubtedly loved money, but as Americans do: he saw it purely as the outward sign of his success. Basically, all this contract-chaser wanted was one thing: the means to exercise his profession. And besides, his dishonesties were not entirely inexcusable: they would not even have been conceivable if he had not carried them off thanks to his professional skill, his capacity for work and his speed. He owed his advantage over his rivals to the final sprint: it took him the same time to paint a good picture as the others took to do a poor sketch.

In any case, if he plagiarized Veronese, Veronese did no less to him. One must consider their mutual borrowings with the eyes of their contemporaries. For many people at the time, the greatest painters were trade names, persons only in the legal and collective sense. What we want, nowadays, is *that* particular picture, first and foremost; and then, through it, a whole man: we hang Matisse on the wall. But consider the *Crociferi*: they didn't give a hoot for Caliari; what they wanted was a particular style which spoke directly to their souls – blissful stupidity, pleasing magnificence, with nothing disturbing about it. They recognized a trademark and a slogan: a 'Veronese' painting is one that you feel at home with, which is what they wanted, nothing more. Caliari could do better and proved as much: he painted a terrific *Crucifixion*;* but he was too good a businessman to squander his genius. Given this, we should be quite unfair in blaming Tintoretto if he were sometimes to appropriate a style that, in reality, belonged to no one. After all, he was making

---

* It is in the Louvre. The irony is that it was inspired by the *real* Robusti.

a perfectly honest proposition: 'You want something bright and meaningless? Well, that's what I'll give you.'

I am quite prepared to accept all this. It is not a matter of judging him, but of deciding whether his age was content to see itself reflected in him. And, on this score, the evidence is clear: his behaviour shocked his contemporaries, who reproached him with it. They might perhaps have put up with a certain degree of disloyalty, but Tintoretto overdid it; all Venice was agreed: 'He goes too far!' Even in this merchant city, this merchant was so smart as to appear eccentric. At the Scuola San Rocco, when he stole the order from them, his colleagues complained so loudly that he felt obliged to appease them in some way: the building had other ceilings and walls, the work was just beginning; and, as far as he was concerned, once his offering had been accepted, he would vanish and leave the field free to others, more worthy than himself. It was not long before the poor men learned that he had been lying through his teeth: the Scuola would become his private preserve and as long as he lived, no other painter would set foot in it. In any case, they certainly didn't need this excuse to hate him. But one may note that the scandal occurred in 1561 and that the first *Life* of Tintoretto appeared in 1567: the closeness of the two dates throws some further light on the meaning of the malevolent rumours gathered by Vasari. Were the calumnies inspired by jealousy? But they all envied one another frantically; why should these slanders have been directed at Robusti alone, were it not that he served as the 'bad odour' of these artists, representing for each of them the failings of their neighbours, concentrated in one man and taken to the extreme? Moreover, even his customers seemed shocked by his methods – admittedly, not all; but he had made many confirmed enemies. Messire Zammaria de Zigninoni, a member of the Confraternity of San Rocco, promised fifteen ducats for the costs of decoration, provided Jacopo was not given the work. And the records of the Confraternity give us to understand that, after his coup, the Banca e Zonta held some sensitive and quite stormy meetings at the Scuola itself, in the wake of the embarrassing donation; agreement was reached, but Messire de Zigninoni kept his ducats. Nor did the authorities appear any better disposed towards him. In 1571, Tintoretto made a gift of his *Battle of Lepanto*; in 1577, the painting was destroyed by fire, so when it came to replacing it, the original painter might have appeared justified in thinking that the Signoria would turn to him. Not at all: he was deliberately set aside in favour of the mediocre Vicentino. Was this because the original picture had displeased them? This hardly seems likely: Jacopo toed the line when working for the authorities; he 'did a Titian' and effaced himself. In any case, the government had commissioned several canvases from him since 1571. No, the Venetian authorities did not mean to deprive themselves of his services, but to punish him for his unacceptable tactics. In short, there is general agreement: he is a disloyal colleague, a quack, a crooked painter; there must be something wrong with him, since he has no known friends. So, you fine, troubled souls, who make the dead serve to instruct the living – and especially yourselves – see, if you like, whether you can find the shining proof of his passion in his excesses. The fact remains that passions are as varied as people: some are consuming, others reflective; some dreamy, others anxious, practical, abstract, dawdling, precipitate and a hundred more. I would call Tintoretto's practical, anxiously recriminating and consumingly precipitous. The more I think about these ridiculous combinations, the more convinced I am that they derive from a bruised heart. What a nest of vipers! Everything is there: the delirium of pride and the madness of humility, thwarted ambitions and limitless confusion, repression and bad luck, a desire to achieve and the giddying sense of failure. His life is the story of a careerist driven by fear; it began merrily and joyfully enough, with a well-conducted campaign; then, after the terrible blow of 1548, the pace quickened crazily, faster and faster, until it became hell. Jacopo would fight on until he died, but he knew that he could not win. Opportunism and anguish: these are the two largest vipers in the nest. If we really want to know him, we must come closer and examine them.

THE PURITANS OF THE RIALTO

No one is a cynic. Heaping coals on one's own head without giving in to despondency is a pastime for saints – and then only up to a certain point: the chaste chasten their lusts, the generous condemn their avarice; but if they discover the gangrene that is really eating into them, which is sanctity, then like all guilty men they seek to justify themselves. Tintoretto is not a saint. He knows that the whole city condemns his methods and if he refuses to change, then it is because he feels he is in the right despite what they think. And don't go saying that he is aware of his own genius: genius, a silly gamble, knows what it dares, but not what it is worth. Nothing is more wretched than that sullen temerity that grasps at the moon and dies without reaching it: pride comes first, without proof or papers; when it gives way to panic, one can call it genius if one likes, but I don't actually see what is gained by that. No: Tintoretto doesn't justify his raiding tactics either by the brief achievement of his talents or by the infinite void of his aspirations: he is defending his rights. Every time that a commission goes to one of his rivals, he feels wronged. Just give him the chance and he will cover every wall in the city with his paintings. No *campo* will be so vast, no *sotto portico* so obscure that he will refuse to decorate them. He will smother the ceilings with paint, passers-by will walk over his finest pictures, and his brush will spare neither the façades of the palaces on the Grand Canal, nor the gondolas – nor, perhaps, the gondoliers. This man believes that he has been born with the privilege of transforming the city into himself; and, to some extent, one might argue that he is right.

When he began his apprenticeship, painting was in dire straits. In Florence, the crisis was openly admitted. Venice, as usual, remained silent, or lied; but we have proof positive that the sources of inspiration around the Rialto had dried up. At the end of the fifteenth century, the city was deeply affected when Antonello da Messina stayed there: this was a decisive turning-point; from then on, it imported its painters. This is not to say that it went very far for them, but the fact remains that the most renowned of its artists came from *terra firma*: Giorgione, from Castelfranco; Titian, from Pieve di Colori; Paolo Caliari and Bonifazio dei Pitati, from Verona; Palma Vecchio, from Bergamo; Girolamo the Elder and Paris Bordone, from Treviso; and Andrea Schiavone, from Zara; and there are more. In truth, this aristocratic republic was first of all a technocracy: it had always had the audacity to recruit its specialists from all sides and the sense to treat them as its own sons. Moreover, this was a time when La Serenissima, thwarted at sea and threatened by coalitions on land, was starting to turn towards its hinterland and trying to ensure its power by conquest there: the new immigrants were, on the whole, natives of territories it had annexed. No matter: through this huge import of talent, Venice reveals its unease: when you think that most of the artists of the Quattrocento were born within the walls or at Murano, one cannot help thinking that the line could not have been carried on after the Vivarini and Bellini families became extinct, without an injection of new blood.

Painting is like other trades: it was the patrician element that encouraged the immigation of good craftsmen and – showing evidence of what one might call cosmopolitan chauvinism – considered the Republic of the Doges as a sort of melting pot. In the minds of this suspicious, jealous aristocracy, foreigners make the best Venetians: if they were prepared to adopt Venice as their home, it was because they had fallen in love with the place, so they would prove flexible if they wanted it to take them in. But one can be sure that local craftsmen did not see the newcomers in the same light; why should they? This was foreign competition. They did not risk protesting, they greeted them with smiles, but there were conflicts even so, constant tensions and a host of recriminations. Forced to bow to the technical superiority of the interlopers, the native would disguise his humiliation from himself by enhancing his own prerogatives; he might agree to give way to someone more expert and more skilled, but this was a sacrifice to his homeland; his rights remained unchanged. A Rialtan was *at home* in Venice; German workers might be more skilled in blowing glass, but they could never acquire this God-given birthright. Before they died, the great painters of the

Quattrocento had the bitter experience of seeing the public abandon them, preferring young intruders who despised them. Titian, for example, that foreigner, when he left Gentile, one of the Bellini brothers, for the other, Giovanni, did so in pursuit of another foreigner, Antonello, a meteor who had streaked across the sky and the waters of the lagoon twenty years earlier. As for Giovanni himself, Tiziano Vecellio was not concerned with him: what he was looking for was a reflection – as he proved by rapidly abandoning the master for his disciple and joining the school of Giorgione: this third incomer appeared to the second the true heir of the first. Yet Tiziano and Giorgione belong to the same generation; the pupil might in fact have been older than the teacher. Did the two Bellinis not realize, then, that their time was up? What about the true disciples of Giovanni? What did they say? And what did those others think, the last representatives of the school of Murano? Many of them were young people – or men who were not yet old. They all felt the influence of Antonello, but through Bellini: their colour and light had come from the first, but it was Giovanni Bellini who had acclimatized them, making them Venetian. These men made it a point of honour to remain loyal, but their loyalty was stifling them. They did their best to adapt to the new methods without giving up the rather crude techniques that they had been taught. This meant condemning themselves to mediocrity: what bitterness they must have felt when they saw two newcomers joining forces and breaking with local tradition to uncover the secrets of a Sicilian and effortlessly raise painting to its highest degree of perfection. Yet Giovanni was still the acknowledged leader, an admirable artist whose fame extended throughout Northern Italy: the barbarian invasion started during his final years and, after his death in 1516, became a devastating flood.

And then, at the height of the invasion, it so happened that the greatest painter of the century saw the light of day at the heart of this occupied city, in a small street on the Rialto. Dark plebeian pride, ever on its guard, constantly humiliated and repressed, entered into the heart of the only Rialtan who still had some talent and set it on fire. Remember: he was not directly a son of the people, nor entirely one of the bourgeoisie: his father belonged to the well-off artisan class. These petit-bourgeois made it a point of honour not to work for anyone else. Had he been a worker's son, Jacopo might have remained the obscure assistant to an artist; as the son of a master, he must become one himself, or fail. He will come up through the ranks, but the honour of his family and his class will not allow him to remain in them. One can understand if he did not leave a good impression behind him in the studio where he did his apprenticeship: he only went there to get out as soon as possible and take up the place reserved for him in the social hierarchy. And what if he did? No doubt Schiavone (or Bordone or Bonifazio dei Pitati – it's all the same) thought of him as an intruder, but then Jacopo, for his part, considered his master a foreigner, in other words, a thief. He was a *native*, this little dyer: Venice belonged to him by right of birth. Had he been untalented, he would have contained himself, shown humility and felt resentment. But he was brilliant, he knew it, so he wanted to surpass everyone. In the eyes of a Rialtan, these outsiders had no protection except their professional worth, so if Jacopo did better than they, they would have to go, even if it meant killing them. No one can paint or write without a mandate to do so: would anyone dare if '*I* was not Another'? Jacopo does have a mandate, granted to him by an entire people of workers, for him to recover through his art the privileges of the native-born Venetian. This is the explanation for his clear conscience: in his heart, popular recrimination becomes a self-denying passion for compensation. He has been given a duty to have his rights recognized, and to someone upholding such a just cause any means of achieving it are good: no pardon, no quarter. Unfortunately, his struggle against the undesirables, in the name of native craftsmen, brings him into conflict with the Venetian authorities and their policy of assimilation. It is the government he is criticizing when he proclaims: 'Veronese to Verona!' As soon as he realizes this, he takes a step back, then straight away resumes his obstinate forward march. Hence the curious mixture of rigidity and flexibility: as a cautious subject in a police state, he always gives in, or pretends to; as the *native-born* citizen of the most beautiful city of all, he finds his arrogance bursting out despite himself: he can become servile without losing his stiff-necked pride. It is no use. His impatience or his irreparable clumsiness in carrying them out spoil the plots that he hatches against the protégés of the aristocracy; or else they turn against him of their own accord. Here is something that throws a new light on the grudge that the Serenissima held against him. Perhaps this one among its subjects is only, when it comes down to it, demanding what might be granted him, but his belligerent submission irritates the authorities: they see him as a rebel, or at least a potential one; and taking all in all they are right. See where his first outburst was to lead him.

It led, first of all, to that diligent and almost sadistic violence that I might call: making full use of oneself. Coming from those humble folk who bore the full weight of a heavily hierarchical society, he shared their fears and their tastes: even in his presumption one can see something of their caution. His family, shrewd, brave, somewhat wary of strangers, taught him the price of things and the dangers of life, which hopes are legitimate and which not. Having precise and limited opportunities, a fate set out in advance, clearly inscribed, a half-open future; being the prisoner of this transparency, like a little bunch of flowers too clearly visible in the glass of a paperweight – all this kills dreams: one wants only what one can have. Such moderation creates madmen and arouses the most unbridled ambitions, but short-term ones: Jacopo's ambition sprang into birth like the goddess Athena, girt for battle; and, with its virulence and its varied forms, was identical with that slim shaft of light, the possible. Or, rather, nothing was possible: there was the end and the means, the set task. One would rise above the heaviest and lowest clouds, and reach up to touch a taut, luminous skin – the ceiling. There are other ceilings, other membranes, each more transparent than the last, each slighter; and perhaps, at the very summit, the blue of the sky. But Tintoretto didn't give a damn for that; each man has his own upward drive and his own natural resting-place. This one knew that he had a gift and had been told that it was an asset. If he exploited his abilities, his business would become profitable and he would find the money to fit himself out.

Now he was mobilized for the whole of a long life and otherwise unavailable: he had this seam to quarry until the mine and the miner were exhausted. At about the same moment, that other glutton for work, Michelangelo, adopted a different pose: the work sickened him, he would start a job, turn away, leave it unfinished. Tintoretto *always* finished what he had started, with the awful persistence of someone who insists on completing every sentence whatever happens. Even death waited for him, at San Giorgio, allowing him to put his last brush-stroke on his last picture (or at least to give his final instructions to his assistants). Through his whole life, he never permitted himself a whim, a feeling of distaste, a preference, or even space to dream. On the days when he was exhausted, he must have told himself repeatedly: if you turn down a commission, you make a present of it to your rivals.

He had to produce at any cost. Here the will of one man and that of the city met. A century earlier, Donatello had accused Uccello of sacrificing creation to refinement and taking his love of painting to the extent of not producing pictures; but that was in Florence. Florentine artists had just embarked on the dangerous adventure of *perspective* and were trying to construct a new plastic space by applying the laws of geometrical optics to painted objects. *Autres temps, autres mœurs*. In Venice, when Titian reigned, everyone thought that painting had just reached its highest point of perfection and that there was nothing more to be achieved by experiment: art is dead, long live life. The great barbarism began with the simple-minded remarks of Aretino: 'How lifelike it is! How true! *You'd never guess it was painted!*' In short, it was time for painting to give way to *positive achievement*: inspired dealers wanted beauty with utility. A work of art must give pleasure to connoisseurs, express the glory of Venice to the rest of Europe and strike awe into the hearts of the people. The awe is what has endured: nowadays we humble tourists murmur, when confronted by the Cinemascope of Venice: Titian directed it, it's a Paolo Caliari production, it's a performance by Pordenone with sets by Vicentino. Jacopo Robusti shared the prejudices of his time and today those in the know hold it against him. How many times have I heard people say: 'Huh!

TINTORETTO: THE PRISONER OF VENICE

Tintoretto is just cinema!' Yet no one, either before or since, has taken further his passion for experimental refinements. With Titian, painting is stifled by flowers and repudiates itself by its own perfection; Jacopo sees its demise as the necessary condition for its resurrection: everything is beginning again, everything still needs to be done (something we shall discuss later). But (and here is the central contradiction) he will never allow his experiments to get in the way of productivity. Even if there were in Venice only a single wall left unpainted, the painter's task would be to cover it: it would be immoral to transform the studio into a laboratory. Art is at one and the same time a serious profession and a hand-to-hand struggle against the invaders. Like Titian, like Veronese, Jacopo would deliver exquisite corpses; the only difference is that these bodies are racked by a fever, and it is impossible to tell at first whether it is a resurgence of life or the start of decay. And if one really must compare him to present-day film-makers, *this* is where the comparison lies: he is ready to take on idiotic scripts so that he can quietly load them with his obsessions. The buyer has to be duped, given his money's worth: he will have his Saint Catherine, Teresa or Sebastian; for the same fee, the painter will put him on the canvas, with his wife or his brothers, if that's what he wants. But, underneath, behind the sumptuous and clichéd façade of this *production*, he goes on with his experiments: all his great works have a double meaning; his narrow utilitarianism disguises an endless questioning. By carrying on his investigations in the context of paid commissions, he had to change the nature of painting while respecting his customer's requirements. This is the underlying reason for his overworking and this will eventually be the cause of his downfall.

He still had to capture the market: as we have seen, he was doing his best. But let us once again consider his methods, which can now be seen in a new light. Tintoretto's rebellion became more radical: having originally revolted against the melting-pot policy, he was now obliged to infringe the rules and customs of the guilds. Since they were unable to repress competition (and, in any case, recognized its advantages), the authorities were forced to channel it through contests: if their taste was to be, in the last resort, decisive, then the rich and powerful could save the established order and set up that more pliable form of protectionism, managed competition. Were they sincere? No doubt, and all would be well if we had proof of their abilities; but we have to take them at their word. Sometimes, they hit it right and at others they chose Vicentino. As for Tintoretto, he always managed to avoid being tested. Was it because he considered them utterly incompetent? No, not at all! But he did consider that they had no right to judge a native on the same basis as an outsider. The fact remains that the competitions took place and that in bypassing them the rebel was striking a deliberate blow at protectionism. He is cornered: since the authorities claimed to base their judgements solely on value and since he rejected their claim, he must either give up painting or impose himself by the sole quality of his work. Don't worry: he would find other means, overtaking his competitors by sheer speed, presenting the jury with a *fait accompli*, and dedicating his skill, his promptness and the diligence of his assistants to a form of mass production that broke all records and allowed him to sell his pictures at rock-bottom prices, or even to give them away. There are two second-hand clothes shops which stand on opposite sides of a particular street in Rome; and I feel sure that the owners have agreed that they will pretend to wage a pitiless war against one another – unless, of course, these two boutiques belong to one and the same person, a tragi-comic actor who enjoys pitching the two sides of his nature against each other in an everlasting duel of cut-and-thrust. On one side we have the window smothered in funereal warnings of impending death: *Prezzi disastrosi!* On the other, the glass is covered with multicoloured stickers: *Prezzi da ridere! da ridere! da ridere!* This has been going on for years, and I can never see the shops without the two of them together reminding me of Tintoretto. Did he opt for laughter or tears? Both, in my opinion, according to the customer. One may even guess that, on his own, he would have a quiet laugh about it, while lamenting to the family that they were cutting his throat. No matter, in the studio it was sale time all year round, from New Year's Day to New Year's Eve, and the clients succumbed to the lure of these well-judged bargain prices. They would start by ordering a medallion from him and end up by giving him every wall in the house. He was the first to shatter the already crumbling bonds of the brotherhood of the guild: to this premature Darwinist, a colleague was an intimate enemy; before Hobbes, he had discovered the slogan of absolute competition: *Homo homini lupus*. Venice was in turmoil. If it did not find a vaccine against the Tintoretto virus, he would destroy the fine order of the Corporation and leave behind only a rubble of antagonisms and particles of solitude. The Republic condemned these new tactics, calling them felony and speaking of botched work, undercutting and monopolization. Later – much later – other cities, in other languages, would dignify these tactics with such names as *struggle for life*, *mass production*, *dumping*, *trust* and so on. For the time being, this notorious fellow would lose on the swings what he gained on the roundabout: he carried off commissions at swordpoint, but was boycotted meanwhile. By a strange irony, it was he, the *native*, the Rialtan one hundred per cent, who seemed the intruder, and almost an undesirable one, in his own city. The inevitable result would be that, if he did not found a family, he would die. He had to do so first of all to stifle competition within his own studio: this champion of liberalism was to reverse the biblical precept and make sure that others could never do unto him what he did unto them. In any case, he needed total approval: if he had strangers as his assistants, they might take fright or be discouraged by the vague sense of scandal surrounding him. What a lot of time might be lost in winning them over. From now on, the mighty thunderbolt would only release a muffled roar. Why did he need disciples, anyway? What he needed were other hands and other arms, nothing more. Through absolute competition to family exploitation: that was the way. In 1550, he married Faustina dei Vescovi and immediately started to make children with her – as he made pictures, in tireless bursts of energy. She was a fine layer, with only one defect: she overdid the daughters a little. Too bad! He would put them all in convents, except two: Marietta, whom he would keep with him, and Ottavia, whom he married to a painter. The lightning struck Faustina often enough to get two sons out of her: Domenico and Marco. As it happens, he did not wait for them before starting to teach the craft to his eldest daughter, Marietta. A woman painter in Venice was something quite out of the ordinary: he must have been in a hurry! Finally, around 1575, the operation appears to have been complete: the new studio staff consisted of Sebastian Casser, his son-in-law; plus Marietta, Domenico and Marco. The symbol of a domestic association is the *domus* which houses and imprisons its members. At about the same date, Jacopo bought a house. He would never have another. In this little isolation ward, the leper would live in a state of semi-quarantine, surrounded by his family, loving them all the more, the more *others* there were to hate him. If we look at him *at home*, in his work, in his relations with his wife and children, we see a quite different face: what a harsh moralist he was! Was he, perhaps, a trifle Calvinist underneath? He has all the qualifications: pessimism and hard work, an urge to make money and devotion to the family. Human nature is flawed by an original sin: men are divided by self-interest. The Christian will be saved by his works: let him fight against the whole world, be as hard on himself as he is on others, toil without ceasing to embellish the Earth that God has confided to his care; he will find the marks of divine favour in the material success of his undertakings. As for the stirrings of his heart, let him keep those for the flesh of his flesh, for his sons. Was Venice affected by the Reformation? Indeed, it was. In the second half of the century, we come across a peculiar character there, Fra Paolo Sarpi, who had considerable influence among the Patricians: he was a friend of Galileo, an enemy of Rome, and openly maintained close relations with foreign Protestant circles. But while one may discern in some intellectual milieux ideas which are vaguely sympathetic to the Reformation, it is more than probable that the petit-bourgeoisie was unaware of them. It would be truer to say that the Serenissima had been reforming herself, and for some time already: the merchants lived on credit and could not accept the Church's interdict on those which she persisted in calling 'usurers'; they favoured science – as long as it was applied science – and despised Roman obscurantism; and the Venetian State had always affirmed the pre-eminence of the civil authority: that was its doctrine, and it would not abandon it. In practice, it ruled over its clergy and when Pius V attempted to remove ecclesiastics from the jurisdiction of lay courts, the Senate simply refused. In any case, there were many reasons why the government considered the Holy See to be a temporal and military power rather than a spiritual one – though this did not prevent it, when the interests of the Republic were at stake, from siding with the Pope, hunting down heretics and, in order to please the most Christian monarch, organizing a magnificent celebration in honour of Saint Bartholomew. Tintoretto's pseudo-Calvinism came from his native city: without knowing it, the painter absorbed the latent Protestantism which was to be found at the time in all the great capitalist cities.* The status of artists in those days was very ambiguous, especially in Venice. But let's take a chance on it: perhaps this very ambiguity will allow us to understand Jacopo's dark, puritanical passions.

Vuillemin wrote that the Renaissance 'attributed to the artist the characteristics reserved in Antiquity for the man of action and in the Middle Ages for saints'. This is not untrue. But it seems to me that the contrary is at least equally true: '[In the sixteenth century] painting and sculpture were still considered manual arts; all honour was reserved for poetry; hence the effort made by the plastic arts to rival literature.'† Indeed, there is no doubt that Aretino, the poor man's Petronius, the rich man's Malaparte, was the arbiter of style and taste for the dandies of the Venetian patriciate, and that Titian was proud to associate with him: for all his fame, the artist never felt equal to the poet. And Michelangelo? He suffered from the weakness of thinking that he was a *born* aristocrat and the illusion ruined his life. When he was quite young, he would like to have studied the Humanities and write: a nobleman deprived of his sword could take up the pen without loss of status. He took up a chisel out of necessity and never reconciled himself to it: Michelangelo

---

* This is what protected the Italian cities against the spread of Lutheranism and led Italy to have its own religious revolution, known as the Counter-Reformation.
† Eugenio Battista, in a fine article on Michelangelo published in *Epoca* (25 August 1957).

looked down on sculpture and painting from the height of his shame, and had the empty, gnawing satisfaction of feeling superior to what he was doing. Forced into silence, he tried to give a language to the silent arts, piling on allegories and symbols, and writing a book across the ceiling of the Sistine Chapel and torturing marble to make it speak.

What conclusion can we draw? Are the painters of the Renaissance demi-gods, or manual workers? Well, it all depends: it depends on the customer, and the method of remuneration. Or, rather, they are manual workers *first of all*; afterwards, they become court employees or remain local masters. It is up to them to choose – or to be chosen. Raphael and Michelangelo are employees: they live in a state of luxury and dependence; but if they fall out of favour, even temporarily, they are back on the streets; on the other hand, the sovereign takes charge of their advertising. This sacred figure endows his elected followers with a portion of his supernatural powers: the glory of the throne descends on them like a ray of sunlight, which they reflect on to the people; the divine right of kings makes painters with divine rights. Our daubers are transformed into supermen. So what are they, if not men lifted above the common run of mankind, these petit-bourgeois whom a giant hand has plucked out of the crowd to raise them between heaven and earth, these satellites shining with borrowed light? Heroes, certainly, that is to say intercessors, intermediaries. Even today nostalgic republicans worship in them, under the name of genius, the light of that dead star, monarchy.

Tintoretto belonged to the other kind. He worked for merchants, for civil servants, for parish churches. I am not saying that he was uneducated: he went to school for seven years and must have come out at the age of twelve, knowing how to write and add up; and, more than that, how could we deny the name of education to that patient cultivation of the sense, the hand and the mind, to that traditionalist empiricism which studio painting still represented, around 1530? But he would never have the cultural baggage of the court painters. Michelangelo wrote sonnets, Raphael is claimed nowadays to have known Latin, and Titian himself eventually acquired some polish by rubbing shoulders with the intelligentsia.

Beside these society men, Tintoretto seemed an ignoramus: he would never have enough time or leisure to indulge in word games and mind games. He didn't give a fig for the humanism of scholars. Venice had few poets and still fewer philosophers: even they were more than enough for Tintoretto, who associated with none of them. Not that he avoided them: he was unaware of their existence. He granted their social superiority: Aretino had the right to congratulate him with protective condescension; this prominent personality was *received*, he belonged to the cream of Venetian society and patricians who would not dream of greeting a painter in the street invited him to dine with them. But need one also envy him? Should one envy him *because he was a writer*? Jacopo considered that the disinterested air adopted by the works of the mind was highly immoral. God put us on earth to earn our bread by the sweat of our brow; but writers didn't sweat. Did they even work? Jacopo never opened a book, apart from his missal; he was not the sort of man to have the weird idea of distorting his gifts so that he could compete with literature. Everything was in his paintings, but they were not *trying* to say anything: they were as dumb as the world itself. In the end, this craft worker's son only respected physical effort and the work of the hands. What delighted him in the craft of painting was that it pushed professional skill to the point where it became magic and took the delicacy of the product to its quintessence. The artist was the supreme worker: he exhausted himself and matter itself, in order to produce and sell his visions.

This would not stop him from working for princes if he had liked them; but he didn't like them, that's what it came down to: they inspired fear in him and nothing else. He never tried to go near them nor to make himself known: it was as though he were trying to contain his fame within the walls of Venice. Did you know that he never left the city, except once, in his sixties, to go to Mantua, just nearby? Even then, he had to be begged: they wanted him to hang some of his paintings himself and he said bluntly that he would not go unless his wife came with him. The requirement is evidence of his conjugal feelings, but it also tells us a lot about his deep dislike of travel. And don't imagine that other Venetian painters were the same. They would go gallivanting around in all directions: a century earlier, Gentile Bellini was sailing the seas. What an adventurous bunch they were! But he was a mole, only at home in the narrow tunnels of his molehill. If he imagined the world, he was struck down with agoraphobia; and yet, if the choice had to be made, he would rather risk his skin than his paintings. He did accept commissions from abroad – 'abroad' for Tintoretto began in Padua – but he did not ask for them. What a contrast between this indifference and his frenzied search for work at the Palace of the Doges, at the Scuola San Rocco and from the *Crociferi*! He passed the actual painting to his assistants, supervised these mass-production foreign commissions from a distance and was careful not to turn his own hand to them, as though he were afraid to let the merest hint of his talent go outside his homeland: Europe was entitled only to the B pictures. You can find Raphael, Titian and a hundred others in the Uffizi, the Prado, the National Gallery, the Louvre, in Munich, in Vienna ... everyone, or almost: the exception is Tintoretto. He kept himself strictly for his fellow-citizens and you will know nothing of him unless you go and search in his native city, for the good reason that he *wanted* not to go anywhere else.

We must clarify: in Venice, he had two quite distinct kinds of customer. He besieged public officials and, of course, if the Senate gave him work the whole studio got down to it, including the head of the family. One can still see at the Palace of the Doges, in lighting that shows them off to advantage, the works of a strong collective personality bearing the name of 'Tintoretto'. But if it is Jacopo Robusti who interests you, leave the Piazzetta, cross the Piazza San Marco, go over the humpbacked bridges that span the canals, turn off into a maze of dark little streets and slip inside some still darker churches: that's where he is. You've got him in the Scuola San Rocco, himself, without Marietta or Domenica or Sebastiano Casser; he worked there alone. A dirty mist has clouded these canvases, or else the artificial light has corroded them. Wait patiently until your eyes grow accustomed to the gloom and, in the end, you will see a rose in the darkness, a genius in the half-light. And who paid for these pictures? Either the faithful of the parish, or the members of the Guild: bourgeois all, upper or petty: they were his audience, the only one that he loved.

There was nothing of the demi-god in this shopkeeper. With a little luck he would be notorious, famous, but never crowned with glory: his secular clientele was not in a position to elevate him. Of course, the renown of his noble colleagues honoured the whole profession; he, too, might shine a little. Did he envy them their fame? Perhaps. But he did none of the things necessary to share it: to hell with the favours of princes – they offered only slavery. Jacopo Robusti took pride in remaining a small employer, a speculator in Fine Arts, paid piecework, but master in his own house. He made no distinction between the economic independence of the producer and the freedom of the artist; his efforts in that direction prove that he had a vague desire to reverse the conditions of the market, to stimulate demand by supply: did he not slowly and patiently create the need for art – for a particular kind of art – in the Confraternity of San Rocco, a need that only he could satisfy? His autonomy was all the better protected in that he worked for collectives – *consorterie*, parishes – and that these large bodies made decisions on a majority vote.

Michelangelo, that false aristocrat, and Titian, the peasants' son, experienced directly the appeal of the monarchy. But Tintoretto was born into a family of self-employed workers. The artisan is an amphibian: as a manual worker, he is proud of his handiwork; as a petit-bourgeois, he feels attracted to the higher bourgeoisie: it is they who, simply by encouraging competition, ensure that some air penetrates into the stifling world of protectionism. At that time there were *bourgeois aspirations* in Venice. They were very slight: the aristocracy had long since taken its precautions. In this hierarchical universe, one could be allowed to *become* rich, but you had to be *born* a patrician. And even wealth was limited: not only did the businessman and the industrialist remain confined to their class, but they had long ago been forbidden to exercise the most lucrative professions. The State granted the *appalto* – the hiring of galleys – to the nobility alone. Sombre and wistful bourgeoisie! Everywhere else in Europe, its members were repudiating it and, as soon as they could, buying titles and castles. But in Venice, it was denied everything, even the modest happiness of betrayal. So it would deny itself in imagination. Giovita Fontana, arriving from Piacenza, launched herself in business, made a pile of gold and spent it building a palace on the Grand Canal. A whole life is in those few words: a raging need, satisfied, turns belatedly into a wistful form of snobbery; a businesswoman dies and is reborn as an imaginary noblewoman. Rich commoners thrash about, harbouring their nocturnal fantasies. Grouped into guilds, they put their efforts into charitable works, and their melancholy austerity contrasts with the melancholy orgies of a disenchanted aristocracy.

The reason is that the Republic had lost its domination of the seas. Bit by bit the aristocracy lapsed into decay, bankruptcies piled up, and there was an increase in the number of the impoverished gentry while those who were not yet impoverished had lost their spirit of enterprise: these shipbuilders' sons bought property and set up as landowners. Already mere 'citizens' were replacing them in certain official posts, and even galleys might fall under the command of bourgeois. The bourgeoisie was still far from considering itself a rising class, it didn't even consider that it might one day replace the declining nobility; but one might say that a vague sense of agitation had overtaken it, making its condition less bearable and resignation harder.

Tintoretto doesn't dream. Never. If a person's ambition is calculated on the openness of his social horizon, the most ambitious among the commoners of Venice are the petit-bourgeois, they do still have a chance of rising above their class. But the painter feels a deep affinity with his customers: he understands their love of hard work, their morality and their common sense; he likes their nostalgia and, above all, he shares their deep aspiration: each of them, whether in order to produce, to buy or to sell, needs freedom. This is the key to his opportunism: he yearns for the clean air of the heights. A troubled sky, an invisible, distant ascent, open up a vertical future for him: this bubble rises, lifted by a current; the new spirit fills him: he has been thinking like a bourgeois since childhood. But his ambitions will be limited by the contradictions of the class from which he comes: as a speculator, he would like to cross the line; as a worker, he works with his hands, which is enough to show where he stands. There are in Venice roughly 7,600 patricians, 13,600 citizens, 127,000 craftsmen, workers and small tradesmen, 1,500 Jews, 12,900 domestic servants and 550 beggars. Leaving aside the Jews and the noblemen, the beggars and the servants, Tintoretto is concerned only with that imaginary line separating the commoners into two groups, with 13,600 on one side and 127,000 on the other. He wants to be first among the latter and last among the former: in other words, the most modest of the rich and the most distinguished of those who supply their needs – which makes this craftsman, at the heart of restless Venice, a false bourgeois who is more genuine than the real ones. In him and in his paintings, the confraternity of San Rocco will adore the embellished image of a bourgeoisie which is not disloyal.

Even when working for the Supreme Pontiff, Michelangelo feels he is demeaning himself. This contempt at times gives him a certain objectivity: he is a gentleman who has an offhand view of art. Tintoretto is quite the opposite: he surpasses himself. Without art, what would he be? A dyer. Art is the force that raises him above his origins and the milieu that supports him; it is his dignity. One must work or fall back into the depths. A point of view? Objectivity? Where would he find such things? He has no time to wonder about painting: perhaps he doesn't even see it. Michelangelo thinks too much: he is a Marquis de Carabas, an intellectual. Tintoretto has no idea about what he's doing, he just paints.

So much for his opportunism. This artist's destiny is to be the incarnation of bourgeois puritanism in an aristocratic republic in decline. In other places, this sombre humanism would triumph, but in Venice it will vanish without even becoming aware of its own existence – but not before it has aroused the suspicions of an ever-alert aristocracy. The morose attitude of the official, bureaucratic leaders of Venetian society towards Tintoretto is the very same that the patricians show towards the Venetian bourgeoisie. These unruly tradesmen and their painter are a danger to the Serenissima; we must keep an eye on them.

PORTRAITS

A HUNTED MAN

One might feel there is a touch of magnificence in this stubborn refusal to compete: 'I know no rival, I acknowledge no judge.' Michelangelo might perhaps have said that. Unfortunately, this is not what Tintoretto is saying. On the contrary: when invited to submit a sketch, he is only too eager to comply. After that, we know that he flings his thunderbolt: yes, rather like a squid squirts its ink. Lightning blinds, the spectators cannot even see the picture; and, indeed, everything has been arranged so that they will never need to consider it, and especially not to assess it. When the first shock has past, the picture is already in place, the gift has been made and all that was seen was a flash. Either I am very mistaken, or this is a sort of evasion: one would think he was afraid of confronting his rivals. Would he expend all that ingenuity if he was certain that his talent would triumph? Would he deign to dazzle his contemporaries by the quantity of his output, if the quality elicited their unreserved admiration?

And then, his urge to assert himself by absenting himself is at its most striking in work done for competitions. But that was his style, his trademark. The slightest comparison he found offensive, any juxtaposition made him nervous. In 1559, the Church of San Rocco commissioned him to do *The Healing of the Paralysed Man* to complement a Pordenone. No one asked him to imitate the style of his predecessor and there could be no competition* between the two men: Antonio Di Sacchis (Pordenone) had been dead for twenty years; and if, at one time, he might have influenced the younger painter, the time for influence had passed: Jacopo was fully master of his art. Yet, he couldn't help it, he had to 'do a Pordenone', and it has been clearly demonstrated how he 'exaggerates the baroque violence of the gesture ... through the clash between monumental figures and the architecture in which they are so tightly pressed',

---

* Ridolfi, deceived by the similarity of the styles, said that the painting was done *in concurrenza con il Pordenone*.

and how he 'achieved this effect by lowering the ceiling of the hall
... and (using) even the columns ... to halt the gestures and freeze
their violence'.* In short, he is scared by the idea of being forever
imprisoned in a motionless confrontation: 'Compare Pordenone to
Pordenone, if you want; I, Jacopo Robusti, am on my way.' Of
course, he made sure that the false Di Sacchis would crush the real
one. His retreat is not a rout: he leaves with a challenge: 'Old masters
and new, I take them all on and beat them on their own ground.'
But this is precisely what seems suspect: why does he need to play
their game, by their rules, when he has only to be himself to defeat
them? How much resentment there is in this insolence: he is a Cain
killing every Abel who is preferred to him: 'You like Veronese?
Well, I can do better when I deign to imitate him; you think he is a
man when in fact he is only a method.' How much humility there
is, too: from time to time, this outcast slips into another man's skin
so that he can experience for himself the sweetness of being loved.
And, then, sometimes, one might feel that he lacks the daring to
exhibit his scandalous genius. War-weary, he remains in the half-
light and tries to prove his genius by the absurd: 'since I do the best
Veroneses and the best Pordenones, just think *what I could do* if I
were to be myself for once!' In truth, he hardly ever does allow
himself to be himself, unless they trust him from the start and leave
him alone in an empty room. All this derives, of course, from the
hostility that people show him. But the painter's timidity and the
prejudices of his fellow-citizens have their source in a single feeling
of unease: in 1548, in Venice, in Tintoretto's hands, before patricians,
art lovers and aesthetes, *painting inspired fear in itself.*

This is the start of a long development, which will everywhere
substitute the secular for the sacred: cold, sparkling, icy, the different
branches of human activity would emerge one after another from
the warm promiscuity of the divine. Art is affected, too: from a
bank of mist surges that wonderful disenchantment: painting. It still
recalls the time when Duccio or Giotto would show God His

---

* Vuillemin, op.cit. See also Lietze, p. 372 and Newton, p. 72.

Creation, as it had come from His hands; as soon as He recognized His work, the deal was in the bag, the world in a frame, for ever and ever. Between the picture, the Realm of Light, and the Supreme Eye, the transparent forms of monks and priests would sometimes glide, coming on tiptoe to see what God could see; then they bowed themselves out. But now it was over: the Eye was shut, Heaven was blind. What had happened? First of all, a change of clientele: when the employers were the clergy, then all was well, but as soon as the biggest of the Florentine bankers had the crazy idea of decorating his house with frescoes, the Almighty decided in disgust that he would confine Himself to being a connoisseur of souls. And then there was that Florentine adventure, the discovery of perspective. Perspective is secular, profane, sometimes even a profanation: just look at Mantegna: that Christ stretched out, feet foremost, his head way back in the distance. Do you think that the Father is pleased to have a foreshortened Son? God is the absolute proximity and universal envelopment of Love: can one show Him the Universe *from a distance*, the universe He made, which He saves from annihilation at every moment? Is it for Being to conceive and create Non-Being? For the Absolute to engender the Relative? For Light to contemplate Shadow? For Reality to confuse itself with illusion? No; the old story was beginning again: Innocence, the Tree of Knowledge, Original Sin, Expulsion. This time the apple was called 'perspective'. But the Florentine Adamites nibbled at it instead of eating it, and thus failed to learn immediately of their Fall: in the midst of the Quattrocento, Uccello thought he was still in Paradise and poor Alberti, theoretician of the 'perspectivists', was still presenting geometrical optics as an Ontology of Visibility. However, he did retain enough innocence to ask that the Divine Gaze should sanction the lines as they converged towards the vanishing point.

Heaven did not respond favourably to this absurd request: the creature was swiftly returned to the void which was its proper home and which it had just rediscovered once more: distance, exile, separation: these negatives define our limits; only man has a horizon. Alberti's window opens on a measurable universe, but this precise miniature entirely depends on the point that defines our anchorage and our dispersal: our eyes. In his *Annunciation*, between the Angel and the Virgin Mary, Piero della Francesca places a vanishing line of columns: their disappearance is an illusion; in themselves and for their Creator, all identical and each comparable, these inert masses of white still slumber: perspective is a violence that human weakness perpetrates on God's little world. A hundred years later, in the Low Countries, they will rediscover being in the depths of appearance and appearance will once more assume its dignity as an apparition: painting will set itself other goals and find a new meaning. But before Vermeer can give us the sky and the stars, day and night, the moon and the earth in the form of a little brick wall, the bourgeois of the North will have to achieve their greatest triumph and forge their humanism.

In the sixteenth century, in Italy, faith still burns the artist's heart, struggling against the atheism of eye and hand. In their attempt to get closer to the Absolute, they have perfected techniques that plunge them into a relativism they abhor. These mystified dogmatists cannot carry on or go back. If God is no longer looking at the images that they paint, then who will bear witness for them? They reflect man's own impotence back to him: where will he find the power to make them secure? And then, if painting has no other aim except to take the measure of our short-sightedness, then it is not worth an hour of anyone's effort. To show mankind to the Almighty who dragged him out of the mire was an act of grace, a sacrifice. But why bother to show mankind to itself? And why show it *as it is not*? The artists at the end of the century, those born around 1480 – Titian, Giorgione, Raphael – reached an accommodation with Heaven; we shall have more to say about it. And then the richness and efficiency of the means still disguised the sinister indeterminacy of the ends. Even so, one may think that Raphael had a presentiment of it: he didn't give a damn for anything, went whoring, sold poor quality prints and, out of *Schadenfreude*, encouraged his assistants to do obscene engravings: this was a suicide of over-facility. In any case, the joy of painting vanishes with these sacred monsters. In the second quarter of the century, painting went overboard, misled by its own perfection. One senses an unease in the barbarous taste shown by people at the time for big projects: the public demands the deployment of all the splendours of realism to prevent it seeing its own subjectivity. Let the author of the work disappear, let life take over, let him be forgotten. Ideally one should encounter a painting by surprise, at the edge of a wood, and the characters in it should burst out of the canvas in a shower of broken fragments of picture frame and grab the spectator by the throat. Let the object reabsorb its visibility, contain it in itself and distract attention from it by a constant assault on all the senses, most of all touch. Let every means be employed to replace *representation* by a mute participation of the spectator in the spectacle, let horror and pity bring men face to face with their own likenesses and, if possible, in the midst of these, let desire, blazing with all the lights of perspective, discover that *ersatz* version of divine ubiquity: the immediate presence of flesh. Let the Reason of the eye be respected, but countered by the reasons of the heart. They wanted the *thing itself*, in its immensity, larger than nature, more actual and more beautiful: this is Terror. But Terror is a sickness of Rhetoric; Art, ashamed, goes into hiding once it has lost its letters of credit. Tied down, closely guarded, subject to the constraints of the State, the Church and good taste, the artist, given more support and honour perhaps than ever before, for the first time in history becomes aware of his solitude. Who has licenced him? Whence does he obtain the rights that he asserts? It is Night, God is dying. How can one paint in the dark? For *whom*? About *what*? And *why*? The object of art remains the world, that absolute, but reality is in flight and the relation of the finite to the infinite has been reversed. An immense fullness used to support the wretchedness and fragility of the body; now, fragility is the only fullness, the only security. The Infinite is the void, blackness, inside the creature and outside it. The Absolute is absence, God who has taken refuge in souls – the desert. It is too late to *show*, too early to *create*. Painting is in hell; something is being born, a new damnation: genius, that uncertainty, that mad longing to go through the Night of the world, to contemplate it from outside, and to crush it against the walls, on canvases, sifting unknown splendours from it. Genius is a new word in Europe, the conflict of relative and absolute, of limited presence and infinite absence. For the painter knows quite well that he will not escape from the world, and even if he were to do so, he would take with him everywhere that nothingness on which he is impaled: perspective cannot be transcended until one has granted oneself the right to create other plastic spaces.

Michelangelo died a haunted man, summing up his despair and contempt in two words: original sin. Tintoretto said nothing; he cheated: if he were to confess his solitude, he would not be able to bear it. But for this very reason we can understand that he suffered from it more than anyone did: this fake bourgeois working for the bourgeoisie did not even have the excuse of fame. This is the nest of vipers: the little dyer shivers, a characteristic case of that neurosis that Henri Jeanson rightly called 'the terrifying moral health of the ambitious man'. He sets himself quite modest goals: to rise above his father by the judicious use of his gifts and to capture the market by flattering public taste. Light-hearted opportunism, resource, speed and talent: he had all of these and all eaten away by that dizzying gulf: Art without God. This Art is ugly, wicked and nocturnal, a half-witted passion of the part for the whole, a wind of ice and darkness that howls through pierced hearts. Sucked into the void, Jacopo was caught up in a motionless journey from which he would never return.

Genius does not exist: it is the shameful audacity of nothingness. But the little dyer does exist and knows his own limitations: this sensible boy wanted to darn the tear. All he asked for was modest fulfilment: what does he have to do with infinity? And how would he admit to himself that the slightest brush stroke was enough to challenge his judges? His sullen, petty ambition would fray in the Night of Unknowing. It is not his fault, after all, that painting is a stray dog: later, there will come madmen crazy enough to rejoice at having been deserted; in the mid-sixteenth century, the first victim of monocular perspective tried to conceal it. To work alone and for nothing meant being frightened to death. One must have judges, at any cost: a jury. God was silent; that left Venice, Venice which filled gaps, blocked outlets, stopped bleeding and leaks. In the Doges' Republic, a good subject owed the State an account of his every activity; if he happened to paint, it would be to decorate the city. Jacopo trusted himself to the hands of his fellow-citizens: they had a particular, highly academic idea of art and he hastened to espouse it – all the more so, since it was the one he had always had. He had been told this from his earliest childhood, and believed it: the value of craftsmen may be measured by the number and size of the commissions they are given and the honours paid to them. He was to disguise his genius behind his ambition and to consider social success the only clear sign of the mystical victory. He is patently insincere, in bad faith: on earth, he loads the dice; then there is the throw that he launches at heaven with perfectly clean ones: so, if he can win here below with all the aces up his sleeve, he dares to claim that he has won up there as well; if he sells his paintings, it is because he fooled people. But who could hold the trick against him? It was the nineteenth century that proclaimed the separation of the artist from his public; in the sixteenth century, while it is *true* that painting was going mad, having ceased to be a religious sacrifice, it is *no less true* that it was becoming more rationalized: it remained a social service. Who then, in Venice, would dare to say: 'I paint for myself, I am my own judge'? Can one be sure that those who say it today are not lying? Everyone is judge, no one is judge: try to sort that one out. Tintoretto seems to have been more unfortunate than guilty: his art traverses his age like a ball of fire, but he can only see it through the eyes of his own time. The fact remains that he chose his own hell: at a single stroke, the finite closes upon the infinite and ambition on genius and Venice on its painter, who will never leave it. But captive infinity erodes everything: Jacopo's reasonable opportunism becomes a frenzy: there was nothing left but to succeed; now he had *to prove* something. Having voluntarily given himself up for judgement, the unfortunate man is involved in an unending trial, and he would conduct his own defence, calling each picture to witness in his case, pleading his cause endlessly. There is a whole city to convince, with its magistrates and its burghers who alone and without the possibility of an appeal will pronounce on his mortal future and his subsequent immortality. Yet it was he, and he alone, who had brought about this odd combination. He had to choose: either to have recourse to himself alone and legislate without appeal to anyone, or else to transform the Most Serene Republic into an absolute seat of judgement. Having said that, he made the only choice he could – to his own detriment. How well I understand the indifference that he showed towards the rest of the universe! What need had he for approval from Germany, or even from Florence? Venice was the finest and richest, she had the best painters, the best critics and the most enlightened connoisseurs: it was *here* that the game had to be played, without taking a single move back, *here*, in a brick passage, between a thin strip of sky and dead water, in the blazing absence of sun, Eternity would be won or lost, in a single life, for ever.

Very well, you may say; but why cheat? Why borrow the plumage of Veronese? If he wanted to dazzle everyone by his genius, why did he so often smother it? And why elect judges for himself, only to corrupt and deceive them?

Why? Because the court is prejudiced, the case lost and the sentence passed – and he knows it. In 1548, he asked Venice to sanction the infinite, but she took fright and refused. What a destiny! Abandoned by God, he had to cheat to choose judges for himself and when he had done so, cheat again to obtain an adjournment of the trial. Throughout his life, he would keep them in suspense, sometimes fleeing, sometimes turning round and blinding them. It is all there: the pain and the aggression, the arrogance, the pliability, the frantic hard work, the rancour, the unbending pride and the modest wish to be loved. Tintoretto's painting is first and foremost a passionate affair between a man and a city.

A MOLE IN THE SUN

In this tale told by an idiot, the city appears to be even crazier than the man. She managed to honour all her painters. Why should she exhibit this narrow-minded distrust, this sullen dislike towards the greatest of them all? Well, the answer is quite simply that she was in love with someone else.

La Serenissma was hungry for prestige. For a long time, her ships had been her glory; but now, weary, past her prime, she gloried in an artist. By himself, Titian was worth a whole fleet: he had stolen the sparks from tiaras and crowns to make his halo. *More than anything* what his adopted country admired was the respect that he inspired in the Emperor, and she claimed to recognize her own glory in the light that played around his brow, sacred, still awesome, but entirely harmless. The painter of kings can only be the king of painters: the Queen of the Seas considers him to be her son and, thanks to him, recovers a little of her former majesty. She had previously given him a profession and a reputation; now, when he is at work, divine right streams through the wall and shines as far as the Piazza San Marco; and she knows then that he is paying her back a hundredfold what she has given him: he is a National Treasure. Moreover, this man is as long-lived as a tree: he would last a century and gradually be transformed into an institution. The young were discouraged by the presence of this one-member academy, born before their time and fully intending to outlive them, exasperating them and damping down their ambition: they imagined that their city had the power to immortalize the living and that it had reserved the exercise of it for Titian alone. A victim of this misunderstanding, Tintoretto – behind the fallacious excuse of 'I deserve it' – demanded that she should make him the equal of his illustrious predecessor. But merit is not the issue: one does not demand from a Republic what belongs by right to hereditary monarchies. Jacopo is wrong when he blames the City of the Doges for concentrating all its spotlights on the baobab of the Rialto. The contrary is in fact the case: a shaft of light, with its source in Rome or in Madrid, in any case, outside the city walls, has struck the old trunk, reflected back on Venice and brought it out of the half-darkness; it was a matter of indirect light, in a sense. And I was wrong, too, when I thought at first of calling this chapter *In the Shadow of Titian* – because Titian casts no shadow. Consider this: when Jacopo was born, the Old Man was forty-one; he was seventy-two when the younger one was making his first attempts to establish himself. This was the moment to give way: it would have been a nice gesture had he chosen to die. Not a hope! The monarch was impossible to put down; he reigned another twenty-seven years and when he died, at the age of a hundred, he had the supreme happiness of leaving an unfinished *Pietà*, like a promising young artist cut off in his prime. For more than half a century, Tintoretto-the-Mole burrowed away in a labyrinth, the walls of which were spattered with reflected glory; until the age of fifty-eight, he was a nocturnal animal, hunted by artificial daylight, dazzled by the pitiless fame of Another. When that light finally died, Jacopo Robusti was quite old enough to be a corpse himself. He was determined to survive the tyrant, but it would profit him nothing: Titian was crafty enough to combine two contradictory functions, becoming an employee of the court while retaining the independence of a small businessman; it is not often in history that one finds this fortunate combination. We are far from it, in any event, in the case of Tintoretto who put all his eggs in the same basket. Go and look at their two tombs, then you will grasp the price that he still has to pay for having prepared his country for every eventuality. The Old Man's radioactive corpse was buried under a mountain of lard in Santa Maria dei Frari, a veritable cemetery of Doges, while Tintoretto's body lies beneath a slab in the murky darkness of a plain parish church. Personally, I find this quite fitting. Titian gets lard, sugar and nougat – poetic justice indeed. I should think it even better had he been buried in Rome, beneath the monument to Victor Emmanuel, the most hideous in all Italy after the central station in Milan. For Jacopo, the honour of naked stone: his name is enough. But since this is strictly a personal opinion, I would understand if an indignant traveller were to ask Venice to explain herself: 'Is this all you could do, ungrateful town, for the finest of your sons? Why, you petty-minded city, should you put a battery of lights around that Titianesque opera, *The Assumption*, and so wickedly begrudge electricity for Robusti's paintings?' I know what Venice would say in reply, because it is to be found as early as 1549 in the correspondence of Aretino: 'If Robusti wants to be honoured, why doesn't he paint like Vecellio?' This was a refrain that Jacopo was to hear every day of his life; it would be repeated in front of each of his paintings, before his death and after it, as it is still repeated today: 'Where has he gone wrong? Why does he stray from the royal road when he was lucky enough to have it already marked out for him? Our great Vecellio raised painting to such a level of perfection that it ought not to be interfered with: newcomers must follow in the Master's footsteps, otherwise Art will revert to barbarism.' Capricious Venetians! Inconsistent bourgeois! Tintoretto is *their* painter; he shows them what they see and feel, yet they cannot abide him; while Titian makes fun of them – and they adore him. Titian spends most of his time settling the minds of princes, assuring them through his paintings that everything is for the best in the best of possible worlds. Discord is merely an illusion and the worst of enemies are reconciled by the colour of their coats. Violence? A ballet danced, without too much conviction, by pseudo toughies with woollen beards: so war is justified. The painter's art is almost an apology, it becomes theodicy: suffering, injustice and evil do not exist, nor does mortal sin: Adam and Eve only transgressed so that they could know, and let us know, that they were naked. In a great, four-branched gesture, at once noble and limp, God leaning forward from the heights of heaven, and Mankind leaning backwards, reach out to one another. Order reigns: perspective, tamed, enslaved, is a respecter of hierarchies, and a discreet seating plan ensures that the kings and saints get the best places. If someone is wandering in the distance, in the mists of some plot of waste land, under the smoky torches of a place of ill repute, it is never by accident: the half-light corresponds to the obscurity of his condition and, moreover, is necessary to bring out the highlights in the foreground. The brush pretends that it is describing an event and following a ceremony; sacrificing movement to order and relief to unity, it caresses the figures rather than shaping them. Out of all the bearded men who are applauding the Assumption, not one exists in himself. First of all, it is a group with legs and raised arms; a bush burns. After that the substance assumes a measure of diversity by producing those figures that emerge briefly, if at all, from the collective mass, but may at any moment be reabsorbed by it: such is the condition of the ordinary people. Individuality, in Titian, is reserved for the

Great. And even then he is careful to smooth off their outlines; relief isolates and distances, it is a form of pessimism; while the courtier, a professional optimist, shows as much, mists things over and uses every colour together to sing the glory of God. After that, he starts to polish up his picture, scraping and rubbing, with lacquer and varnishes. He will spare no effort to conceal his work and ends by conjuring himself out of it. We go into a deserted picture, walk amid flowers, under a perfect sun, but the landowner is dead. The person who walks here is so alone that he forgets himself and vanishes, leaving the greatest treachery of all: Beauty.

For once, the traitor has the excuse that he believes in what he is doing. He is not a townsman, but an upstart peasant. When he arrived in Venice, he came straight from the countryside and from childhood, from the depths of the Middle Ages. For a long time this yokel had felt the people's reverential love for the nobility. He went right through the bourgeoisie without seeing it, to the heaven where he joined his true masters, all the more certain that he would please them because of the sincerity of his love. It is frequently said that he secretly considered himself their equal; I don't believe it. Where would he have got that idea from? He was a vassal: ennobled by the glory that only kings can dispense, he owed them everything, even his pride; why should he wish to turn it against them? His outrageous good fortune, the hierarchy of powers and the beauty of the world are, in his view, only a matter of corresponding reflections; with the best will in the world, he puts the bourgeois techniques of the Renaissance in the service of feudalism; but the tools are stolen.

Despite that, bourgeois and patricians both admire him: he gave an excuse to the technocrats of Venice: he spoke of happiness, glory and pre-existing harmony just when they were making the most laudable efforts to disguise their decline. Every merchant, whether of noble or common birth, was enchanted by these vacuous canvases which hold a mirror to the serenity of kings. If everything is for the best, if evil is only a beautiful illusion, and if everybody will keep his place in the divine and social order for ever, this is because nothing has happened in the past century: the Turks have not taken Constantinople, Columbus has not discovered America and the

Portuguese have not even dreamed of dumping spices on the market or the continental powers of forming a coalition against La Serenissima. It had been believed that the seas were packed with Barbary pirates, that the source of precious metals in Africa had dried up and that the scarcity of currency in the first half of the century had slowed down commerce; then, suddenly, Peruvian gold, pouring out of the Spanish reservoirs, had reversed the trend and caused a rise in prices, flooding the market: it was only a dream. Venice still reigns over the Mediterranean, she is at the summit of her powers, of riches, of grandeur. In other words, these anxious men want Beauty because it reassures them. I sympathize. I have taken a plane two hundred times, but I am still not used to it and have been too long a crawler on the earth to consider flight normal. From time to time, my fear is awakened, especially when my fellow-travellers are as ugly as I am; but all it needs is for a lovely young woman to be on the flight, or a handsome youth, or a delightful couple of lovers, and my fear vanishes. Ugliness is a prophecy: there is a sort of extremism in it that tries to take negation to the point of horror. Beauty, on the other hand, is indestructible; we are protected by its sacred image: as long as it remains among us, the catastrophe will not happen. It is the same with Venice: the city starts to fear that she will sink into the mire of the lagoons, so she imagines she can save herself by Beauty, that supremely light quality: she aims to make buoys and floats of her palaces and paintings. The ones who ensure Titian's success are the same who desert the sea, flee from disappointment in orgies and prefer the security of rents from property to the profits of commerce.

Tintoretto was born into a city in turmoil. He breathed in the anxiety of Venice, it gnawed away at him and it was the only thing that he could paint. Had they been in his place, his harshest critics would have acted in just the same way. But they were not in his place, of course: they could not help feeling the anxiety but they didn't want anyone to show it to them: they attack the pictures that *represent* it. It was Jacopo's misfortune to become unwittingly witness to an age that did not want to know itself. Here we can see both the meaning of his destiny and the hidden reason for Venice's dislike of him. Tintoretto displeased everyone: the patricians, because he showed them the puritanism of the bourgeoisie and their nervous, wistful agitation; the artisan class because he was destroying the guild system and uncovering, beneath the appearance of professional solidarity, the rumbling of hatred and rivalries; patriots, because the disturbing quality of painting and the absence of God disclosed to them, through his brush, an absurd and dangerous world where anything could happen, including even the death of Venice. At least, you might think, this socially mobile painter would appeal to his adoptive class. Not at all: the bourgeoisie did not accept him without reservations: it always found him fascinating, but often frightening, too. This is because it was not yet conscious of itself. Messire Zigninoni doubtless dreamed of treachery; he sought vaguely how he might rise to the patrician class and, in short, escape from the bourgeois reality which, despite himself, he was contributing to create: what most disgusted him in the paintings of Robusti were their radicalism and their qualities of demystification. In short, this evidence had at all cost to be denied, Tintoretto's attempts to be presented as a failure, denying the originality of his experiments and *getting rid of him*.

Just consider what he was charged with: firstly, of working too fast and letting his hand and its work show everywhere: what they wanted was something smoothed off, finished and above all *impersonal*. If the painter shows himself, he questions himself; and if he questions himself, he puts the public in question. Venice imposes on its artists the puritan maxim *no personal remarks*, and deliberately confuses Jacopo's lyricism with the haste of an overworked supplier who does a shoddy job. Then there is Ridolfi's story, that Tintoretto wrote on the walls of his studio: 'Titian's colour, Michelangelo's figure painting.' This is idiotic: the formula is found for the first time much later in the writings of a Venetian art critic, and with no reference to Robusti. In reality, he could not have known the work of Michelangelo, except through the reproductions of Daniele de Volterra – and, consequently, in 1557 *at the earliest*. And who do they think he is? Do they really think that he would *seriously* devote himself to carrying out such an absurd formula? In fact, this is a piece of wishful thinking of the age: to counter the threat from Spain, the cities of northern and central Italy considered an alliance; but it was too late. However, the awakening of national consciousness, though it was soon to return to its slumbers, was to have a temporary influence in the Fine Arts. 'Michelangelo and Titian' signified Florence and Venice: how lovely it would be, this unified painting!

Nothing wrong with that: the dream was quite innocuous as long as it remained the dream of everybody. But those who claimed to see it as an obsession of Robusti *alone* must have wanted to destroy the artist by planting an explosive nightmare at the heart of his work. Colour is laughter, draughtmanship tears: on the one hand, unity, on the other a constant threat of anarchy; on one side, the harmony of the spheres, on the other, abandonment. The two Titans of the century hurled themselves at one another, grappled together, tried to strangle each other, and Jacopo was the battleground. Now Titian has won a round, but by a narrow margin; now Michelangelo struggles to gain it back. In any event, the loser retains enough strength to ruin the winner's triumph: the result of this Pyrrhic victory is a spoiled painting – spoiled by excess: Tintoretto appears to his contemporaries as a Titian gone mad, devoured by the dark passion of Buonarroti, racked with St Vitus' dance. A case of possession, a peculiarly split personality. In one sense, Jacopo does not exist, except as a battlefield; in another, he is a monster, a freak. Vasari's story now appears in a peculiar light: Adam Robusti wanted to taste the fruits of the tree of knowledge and the archangel Tiziano, with pointed finger and beating wings, drove him out of paradise.

To have bad luck or to be a bearer of it is all the same in Italy, even today. If you have recently had money troubles, a car crash or a broken leg, if your wife has just left you, don't expect to be invited out to dinner: a hostess would not be happy to expose her other guests to premature baldness, a head cold or, should the worst come to the worst, to breaking their necks on her staircase. I know a Milanese who has the evil eye. It was discovered last year; now he has no friends and cooks for himself, at home. Jacopo was the same: a bringer of bad luck because he had been cursed himself; or perhaps his mother while she was carrying him. In fact, the *jettatura* came not from him, but from Venice, anxious, accursed: she it was that produced this anxious creature, then cursed her own unease in him. The poor man loves desperately a city in despair that will not admit the fact: his love appals its object. People draw aside when Tintoretto goes by: he smells of death. Quite true. But is there not the same smell in those patrician feasts, the charity of the bourgeois, the docility of the people? In the pink houses with their flooded cellars and their walls crisscrossed by the rats that pass between them? What is the smell that rises from the stagnant canals with their piss-scented watercress and grey mussels which some foul slime fastens beneath the quays? In the depths of a canal there is a bubble stuck to the clay which is loosened by the wash of the gondolas; it rises through the muddy water, skims the surface, turns, shimmers and bursts, unleashing a fart – and everything bursts with it: bourgeois nostalgia, the grandeur of the Republic, God and Italian painting.

Tintoretto led the mourning for Venice and a whole world. But, when he died, no one wore mourning for him. Silence fell and hypocritically pious hands draped his canvases with crepe. If we tear aside this black veil, we find a portrait, started over and over, a hundred times. Is it Jacopo's? Is it the Queen of the Seas? As you wish: the city and her painter wear one and the same face.